ALSO BY GEORGE PACKER

THE
UNWINDING

THE UNWINDING

AN INNER HISTORY OF THE NEW AMERICA

———

GEORGE PACKER

FARRAR, STRAUS AND GIROUX   NEW YORK

Farrar, Straus and Giroux
18 West 18th Street, New York 10011

Portions of this work originally appeared, in different form, in *The New Yorker*.

Library of Congress Cataloging-in-Publication Data
Packer, George, 1960–
    The unwinding : an inner history of the new America / George Packer. —
First edition.
        pages   cm
    ISBN 978-0-374-10241-8 (hardcover)
    1. United States—History—1969–   2. United States—Social
conditions—1980–   3. United States—Biography.   4. Social problems—
United States.   5. Crises—United States.   6. United States—Politics
and government—1989–   7. Politicians—United States—Biography.
8. Celebrities—United States—Biography.   I. Title.

E839 .P28 2013
973.924—dc23

                                                        2013004431

Designed by Jonathan D. Lippincott

www.fsgbooks.com
www.twitter.com/fsgbooks • www.facebook.com/fsgbooks

1   3   5   7   9   10   8   6   4   2

FOR LAURA, CHARLIE, AND JULIA

CONTENTS

THE
UNWINDING

PROLOGUE

No one can say when the unwinding began—when the coil that held Americans together in its secure and sometimes stifling grip first gave way. Like any great change, the unwinding began at countless times, in countless ways—and at some moment the country, always the same country, crossed a line of history and became irretrievably different.

If you were born around 1960 or afterward, you have spent your adult life in the vertigo of that unwinding. You watched structures that had been in place before your birth collapse like pillars of salt across the vast visible landscape—the farms of the Carolina Piedmont, the factories of the Mahoning Valley, Florida subdivisions, California schools. And other things, harder to see but no less vital in supporting the order of everyday life, changed beyond recognition—ways and means in Washington caucus rooms, taboos on New York trading desks, manners and morals everywhere. When the norms that made the old institutions useful began to unwind, and the leaders abandoned their posts, the Roosevelt Republic that had reigned for almost half a century came undone. The void was filled by the default force in American life, organized money.

The unwinding is nothing new. There have been unwindings every generation or two: the fall to earth of the Founders' heavenly Republic in a noisy marketplace of quarrelsome factions; the war that tore the United States apart and turned them from plural to singular; the crash that laid waste to the business of America, making way for a democracy of bureaucrats and everymen. Each decline brought renewal, each implosion released energy, out of each unwinding came a new cohesion.

The unwinding brings freedom, more than the world has ever granted, and to more kinds of people than ever before—freedom to go away, freedom to return, freedom to change your story, get your facts, get hired, get fired, get high, marry, divorce, go broke, begin again, start a business, have it both ways, take it to the limit, walk away from the ruins, succeed beyond your dreams and boast about it, fail abjectly and try again. And with freedom the unwinding brings its illusions, for all these pursuits are as fragile as thought balloons popping against circumstances. Winning and losing are all-American games, and in the unwinding winners win bigger than ever, floating away like bloated dirigibles, and losers have a long way to fall before they hit bottom, and sometimes they never do.

This much freedom leaves you on your own. More Americans than ever before live alone, but even a family can exist in isolation, just managing to survive in the shadow of a huge military base without a soul to lend a hand. A shiny new community can spring up overnight miles from anywhere, then fade away just as fast. An old city can lose its industrial foundation and two-thirds of its people, while all its mainstays—churches, government, businesses, charities, unions—fall like building flats in a strong wind, hardly making a sound.

Alone on a landscape without solid structures, Americans have to improvise their own destinies, plot their own stories of success and salvation. A North Carolina boy clutching a Bible in the sunlight grows up to receive a new vision of how the countryside could be resurrected. A young man goes to Washington and spends the rest of his career trying to recall the idea that drew him there in the first place. An Ohio girl has to hold her life together as everything around her falls apart, until, in middle age, she finally seizes the chance to do more than survive.

As these obscure Americans find their way in the unwinding, they pass alongside new monuments where the old institutions once stood—the outsized lives of their most famous countrymen, celebrities who only grow more exalted as other things recede. These icons sometimes occupy the personal place of household gods, and they offer themselves as answers to the riddle of how to live a good or better life.

In the unwinding, everything changes and nothing lasts, except for the voices, American voices, open, sentimental, angry, matter-of-fact; inflected with borrowed ideas, God, TV, and the dimly remembered past—telling a joke above the noise of the assembly line, complaining behind window shades drawn against the world, thundering justice to a crowded park or an empty chamber, closing a deal on the phone, dreaming aloud late at night on a front porch as trucks rush by in the darkness.

PART I

1978

I want to have a frank talk with you tonight about our most serious domestic problem. That problem is inflation. . . . *twenty-twenty-twenty-four hours to go / I wanna be sedated* . . . We must face a time of national austerity. Hard choices are necessary if we want to avoid consequences that are even worse. I intend to make those hard choices. . . . *nothin to do nowhere to go-o-o / I wanna be sedated* . . . Seven years of college down the drain. Might as well join the fucking Peace Corps. . . . **CARTER DEALT MAJOR DEFEAT ON CONSUMER BILLS** . . . I don't know if the people of Mahoning Valley realize that the closing of the Youngstown Sheet and Tube Campbell Works not only affects the steelworkers and their families, but the community . . . **THE LURE OF OUR MANY CULTS** . . . The communards, most of them over the age of fifty, subsisted on a meager diet of rice and beans. They worked the fields from dawn to dusk while Jones harangued them with lectures and sermons over a public address system. . . . What man could afford to pay for all the things a wife does, when she's a cook, a mistress, a chauffeur, a nurse, a babysitter? But because of all this, I feel women ought to have equal rights. . . . **Unfortunately, most low tar cigarettes tasted like nothing. Then I tried Vantage. Vantage gives me the taste I enjoy. And the low tar I've been looking for.** . . . **FILIBUSTER DEFEATS UNION ORGANIZING BILL** . . . The leaders of industry, commerce and finance in the United States have broken and discarded the fragile, unwritten compact previously existing during a past period of growth and progress. . . . **ELVIS LOVE LETTERS Fans pour out their hearts; Plus Super Color Special: The day Elvis's home became a shrine** . . . Noise pollution in a New York slum! People are being mugged right and left, children are being bitten by rats, junkies are ripping out the plumbing of decaying tenements—and the EPA is worried about noise pollution! These same EPA officials, of course, go home at night and tranquilly observe their children doing homework to the accompaniment of thumping, blaring . . . **CALIFORNIA VOTERS APPROVE A PLAN TO CUT PROPERTY TAX $7 BILLION** "The hell with county employees," said one man as he left a precinct polling place in a Los Angeles suburb.

DEAN PRICE

At the turn of the millennium, when he was in his late thirties, Dean Price had a dream. He was walking to his minister's house on a hard-surface road, and it veered off and became a dirt road, and that road veered off again and became another dirt road, with tracks where wagon wheels had worn it bare, but the grass between the tracks grew chest high, as if it had been a long time since anybody had gone down the road. Dean walked along one of the wagon tracks holding his arms out spread-eagle and felt the grass on either side hitting the underneath of his arms. Then he heard a voice—it came from within, like a thought: "I want you to go back home, and I want you to get your tractor, and I want you to come back here and bush-hog this road, so that others can follow where it's been traveled down before. You will show others the way. But it needs to be cleared again." Dean woke up in tears. All his life he had wondered what he was put on earth for, while going in circles like a rudderless ship. He didn't know what the dream meant, but he believed that it contained his calling, his destiny.

At the time, Dean had just gotten into the convenience store business, which was no calling at all. It would be another five years before he would find one. He had pale freckled skin and black hair, with dark eyes that crinkled up when he smiled or laughed his high-pitched giggle. He got the coloring from his father and the good looks from his mother. He'd been chewing Levi Garrett tobacco since age twelve, and he spoke with the soft intensity of a crusader who never stopped being a country boy. His manner was gentle, respectful, with a quality of refinement that made the men drinking vodka out of plastic cups down at the local Moose Lodge question whether Dean could properly be called a redneck. From childhood on, his favorite Bible verse was Matthew 7:7: "Ask, and it shall be given you; seek, and ye shall find; knock, and it shall be opened unto you." What he sought his whole life was independence—especially financial independence. His greatest fears, which haunted him all his life, were poverty and failure. He came by them naturally.

His grandparents on both sides had been tobacco farmers, and so had their grandparents, and their grandparents, back to the eighteenth century, all of them on the same few square miles of Rockingham County, North Carolina. They all had Scotch-Irish names that fit neatly on a tombstone: Price, Neal, Hall. And they were all poor. "It's like if I were to walk down to the creek, I'm going to wear a path," Dean said. "And every day I'm going to go the same way. That's how the roads in this country were built, basically. The people that built the roads followed the animals' paths. And once that path is set, it takes a tremendous amount of effort and energy to take another path. Because you get in that set pattern of thinking, and it's passed down generation to generation to generation."

When Dean was a boy, tobacco grew fencepost to fencepost. From April till October you could smell it all over Rockingham County. He was raised in Madison, forty minutes' drive up Route 220 from Greensboro, and though the Prices lived in town, Dean's real life was spent out on the tobacco farm of his grandfather Norfleet Price. Norfleet got his name when his daddy, Dean's great-grandfather, brought a load of tobacco on a two-horse wagon to Winston-Salem, where a man by that last name gave him a very good price. Dean's father was born on the family land, in a clapboard shack with a front porch, at the edge of a clearing in the hardwood trees. A few feet away was the tobacco barn, a cabin of oak logs cross-stacked with dovetail joints, which Norfleet built with an ax. When Dean was a boy, during the late-summer days when the bright leaf tobacco was primed and hung in the barn for flue curing, he would beg to be allowed to stay there overnight with his grandfather and wake up every hour or two to check that none of the tobacco leaves had fallen into the flames of the oil fire. Priming was backbreaking work, but he loved the smell of tobacco, the big yellowing leaves that grew heavy as leather on stalks four feet high, the way his hands were stained black with sticky tar during the priming, the rhythm of looping the leaves through the stringer and hanging them in bundles like dried flounder from tobacco sticks across the rafters in the barn, the family togetherness. The Prices raised their own meat and grew their own vegetables and got their buttermilk from a lady with a milk cow down the road. School was delayed if the crop came in late, and in the early fall the auction warehouses in Madison burst into life with the harvest jubilee and the brass band parades, a celebration for families that now had their cash for the year, leading up to the holiday feasts. Dean thought that he would grow up to be a tobacco farmer and raise his kids the same way.

Dean's best friend was his grandfather. Norfleet Price cut wood until the fall before he died, at age eighty-nine, in 2001. Near the end Dean visited him in the rest home and found him strapped to a wheelchair. "Hoss, you got your pocketknife?" his grandfather said.

"Pa, I can't do that."

Norfleet wanted to be cut out of the wheelchair. He lasted just a month and a half in the rest home. He was buried in the Price family plot, on a gentle rise in the red clay fields. Norfleet had always worked two or three jobs to get away from his wife, but the name Ruth was carved right next to his on the same headstone, waiting for the body and date of death.

Dean's father had a chance to break the spell of the family's poverty thinking. Harold Dean Price, called Pete, was bright and liked to read. Three blank pages at the back of his copy of Merriam-Webster's dictionary were filled with handwritten definitions of words like "obtuse," "obviate," "transpontine," "miscegenation," "simulacrum," "pejorative." He was a good talker, a fervent hard-shell Baptist, and a bitter racist. Once, Dean visited the civil rights museum in the old Woolworth's building in downtown Greensboro, where the first sit-ins took place at the lunch counter in 1960. There was a blown-up picture of the four black students from North Carolina A&T walking out onto the street past a mob of white youths who stared them down—hot rods with their hands in their pockets, T-shirts and rolled-up jeans, slicked-back hair, cigarettes hanging from angry mouths. That was Dean's father. He hated the defiance of the civil rights people, though he never felt that way about Charlie and Adele Smith, the black tenant farmers on the Price land who took care of him when Dean's grandmother was working at the mill. They were kindhearted and full of humor and understood their place in the scheme of things.

Pete Price met Barbara Neal at a local dance hall and married her in 1961, the year he graduated from Western Carolina College—the first person in his family to get that far. Harold Dean Price II was born in 1963, followed by three sisters. The family moved into a small brick house in Madison, around the corner from the Sharp and Smith tobacco warehouse. Madison and its neighbor Mayodan were textile towns, and in the sixties and seventies the mills had jobs for any young man coming out of high school who wanted one, and if you had a college degree you could take your pick. The brick storefronts on Main Street—pharmacies and haberdasheries and furniture stores and luncheonettes—were full of shoppers, especially on days when the textile warehouses held their sales. "Our country probably prospered as much as it's ever going to prosper, right there in that era," Dean said. "They had cheap energy, they had oil in the ground, they had working farms in the surrounding countryside, they had a people that didn't mind working, they knew what work was about. There was money to be made."

Dean's father went to work for the big DuPont plant that manufactured nylon up in Martinsville, just across the Virginia state line. In the late sixties, he fell for the era's version of a snake oil salesman in the person of Glenn W. Turner, the semiliterate son of a South Carolina sharecropper, who wore shiny three-piece suits and calfskin boots and spoke with the bad lisp of a harelip. In 1967, Turner started a company, Koscot Interplanetary, that sold cosmetics distributorships for five thousand dollars apiece, with the promise of a finder's fee for every new subfranchisee that the distributor signed up. His followers were also lured into purchasing a black briefcase full of Glenn W. Turner motivational cassette tapes, called "Dare to Be Great," that went for up to five thousand dollars, with a similar view to getting rich off selling the rights to sell the program. The Prices paid for a distributorship and hosted rousing "Dare to Be Great" parties at their house in Madison: a movie projector showed a film on Turner's rags-to-riches life story, then the prospects shouted Turner lines about standing on your tiptoes and reaching for the stars. By 1971, "Dare to Be Great" had swept through blue-collar neighborhoods across the country, and Turner was profiled in *Life* magazine. Then he was investigated for running a pyramid scheme and ultimately served five years in prison, and the Prices lost their money.

In the early seventies, Pete Price got a job as a supervisor at the Duke Energy power station in Belews Creek. After that, he became a vice president at Gem-Dandy in Madison, which made men's accessories like suspenders for socks. Later still, he was a shift supervisor at the Pine Hall brickyard, on the Dan River near Mayodan. But every time, he got fired by a boss he considered less intelligent than himself, or, more likely, he quit. Quitting became a habit, "just like a crease in your britches," Dean said. "Once that crease is there it's virtually impossible to get it out. That's the way it was with failure to him, and you could not get it out of him. He thought it, he breathed it, he lived it." The crease started on the Price tobacco farm, where Dean's father received a disadvantaged piece of land that had no road frontage. Dean's uncles ended up doing much better in farming. He also suffered from little man's disease—he stood five seven and a half—and it didn't help that he lost his hair early. But the biggest failure came in the work that meant the most to Pete Price.

Decades later, Dean kept a black-and-white picture in a frame on his fireplace mantel. A boy with a bowl of shiny black hair cut straight above his eyes, wearing a dark suit with narrow pants that were too short for him, was squinting in the sunlight and hugging a Bible against his chest with both arms, as if for protection. Next to him stood a little girl in a lace-collared dress. It was April 6, 1971. Dean was a few weeks shy of eight, and he was about to give his life to Jesus and be saved. During the seventies, Dean's father had a series of small churches in little towns, and in each church his dogmatism and rigidity created a rift in the congregation. Each time, the church members voted on whether to keep him as their preacher, and sometimes they went for him and sometimes against him, but he always ended up leaving (for he would get restless, he wanted to be a Jerry Falwell, leading a church that had thousands of members) with hard feelings on all sides. Eventually he had trouble getting another church. He would visit a new town and try out for the job by preaching a sermon, always fire and brimstone, only to be voted down. There was one church in particular, Davidson Memorial Baptist Church, down in Cleveland County, which he'd had his heart set on, and after failing to get that pulpit he never really recovered.

From his father Dean acquired ambition and a love of reading. He went straight through the family's set of World Book encyclopedias from beginning to end. One night at dinner, when he was around nine or ten, the subject of his ambitions for the future came up. "Well, what do you want to do?" Dean's father said with a sneer.

"I'd like to be a brain surgeon, a neurologist," Dean said. It was a word he'd learned in the encyclopedia. "That's really what I think I'd like to do."

His father laughed in his face. "You got as much chance of being a neurologist as I've got to flying to the moon."

Dean's father could be funny and kindhearted, but not with Dean, and Dean hated him for being a quitter and for being cruel. He heard his father preach many sermons, even a few on street corners in Madison, but on some level he didn't believe them because the meanness and the beatings at home made his father a hypocrite in the pulpit. As a boy, Dean loved baseball more than anything else. In seventh grade he was intimidated by girls, and at ninety pounds soaking wet he was too skinny to play football, but he was a pretty good shortstop at Madison-Mayodan Middle School. In 1976 there were black and white boys on the team, and his father didn't want him around the black boys. To get Dean away from them, and to win points with his congregation of the moment, Dean's father pulled him out of public school (Dean begged him not to) and sent him to Gospel Light Christian, a strict, all-white Independent Fundamental Baptist school in Walkertown, a two-hour bus ride from the parsonage on Mayodan Mountain where the Prices then lived. That was the end of Dean's baseball career, and of his black friends. When Dean was in tenth grade, his father started teaching American and Bible history at Gospel Light, and it would have been easy enough for him to let Dean play baseball after school and then drive the boy home at the end of the day, but his father insisted on leaving school at three o'clock so he could go home and read in his study. It was as if Dean was the competition in the family, and his father had the upper hand and wouldn't give an inch.

When Dean was seventeen, his father quit the church on Mayodan Mountain and moved the family out to the eastern part of the state, near Greenville, where he took the pulpit of a small church in the town of Ayden. It was his last one. After four months there, Minister Price was sent packing, and the family went back to Rockingham County. They had very little money and moved into Dean's mother's family house on Route 220, outside the little town of Stokesdale, a few miles south of Madison. Dean's grandmother Ollie Neal lived in an apartment they had built in back, and behind the house was the tobacco farm that his grandfather, Birch Neal, had won in a card game in 1932, when Route 220 was a dirt road.

By then, Dean wanted only to escape his father's dominion. When he turned eighteen, he drove to Winston-Salem and met with a Marine recruiter. He was supposed to return the next morning to enlist, but overnight he changed his mind. He wanted to see the world and live life to its fullest, but he would do it on his own.

At the time Dean graduated from high school, in 1981, the best job around was making cigarettes at the huge R.J. Reynolds factories in Winston-Salem. If you got a job there you were set for life, with good pay

and benefits plus two cartons of cigarettes a week. That's where the
B students ended up. The C and D students went to work at the textile
mills, where the pay was lower—DuPont and Tultex in Martinsville, Dan
River in Danville, Cone in Greensboro, or one of the smaller mills around
Madison—or in the furniture factories down in High Point and up in
Martinsville and Bassett, Virginia. The A students—three in his class—
went to college. (Thirty years later, at his high school reunion, Dean found
that his classmates had grown fat and were working in pest control or
peddling T-shirts at carnivals. One guy, a career employee at R.J. Reynolds, had lost a job he'd believed to be secure and never got over it.)

Dean never applied himself in school, and the summer after graduating he got a job in the shipping department of a copper tube factory in
Madison. He made damn good money for 1981, but it was the kind of job
he'd always feared ending up in—the lifers around him with no ambition,
spending their days talking about drinking, racing, and fucking. Dean
hated it so much that he decided to go to college.

The only one his father would help pay for was Bob Jones University,
a Bible school in South Carolina. Bob Jones barred interracial dating and
marriage, and in early 1982, a few months after Dean enrolled, the school
became national news when the Reagan administration challenged an
IRS decision that had denied Bob Jones tax-exempt status. After a storm
of criticism, Reagan reversed himself. According to Dean, Bob Jones was
the only college in the world where the barbed wire around the campus
was turned inward, not outward, like at a prison. The boys had to keep
their hair above their ears, and the only way to communicate with the
girls on the other side of campus was to write a note and put it in a box
that a runner would take from dorm to dorm. The only thing Dean liked
about Bob Jones was singing old hymns in morning chapel, like "Praise
God, from Whom All Blessings Flow." He stopped going to class and failed
every course his first semester.

At Christmas, he came home and told his father that he was quitting
school and moving out of the house. His father slapped him silly, knocked
him to the floor. Dean got up and said, "If you ever touch me again I will
kill you, I promise you that." It was the last time he ever lived under his
father's roof.

After Dean moved out, his father went into a downward spiral. He
took oxycodone pills by the handful, for back pain, headaches, and other
real or invented ailments, prescribed by a dozen different doctors who

didn't know about the others. Dean's mother found pills hidden in his suit pockets, stashed away in garbage bags. They gave his father a vacant look and wore away his stomach lining. He would retreat into his study as if to read one of his religious books, but that was where he'd pop some oxycodone and zone out. He was admitted into rehab several times.

Out in the world, Dean went hog wild. He quickly discovered the pleasures of alcohol, gambling, marijuana, fighting, and women. His first girl was a minister's daughter, and he lost his virginity right under the church piano. He was full of rebellion and wanted no part of his father's God. "I was a shit-ass," Dean said. "I had no respect for anybody." He moved to Greensboro and shared a house with a pothead. For a while he had a job as the assistant golf pro at the Greensboro Country Club for a hundred twenty dollars a week. In 1983, when he was twenty, he decided to go back to college and enrolled at the state university in Greensboro. It took Dean six years of bartending to graduate—at one stage his education was interrupted by a five-month trip with his best friend, Chris, to California, where they lived in a VW bus and pursued girls and good times— but in 1989 he finally earned his degree, in political science.

Dean was a registered Republican, and Reagan was his idol. To Dean, Reagan was like a soothing grandfather: he had that ability to communicate and inspire people, like when he spoke about "a city upon a hill." It was something Dean thought he could do as well, since he was a good speaker and came from a family of preachers. When Reagan talked, you trusted him, and he gave you hope that America could be great again. He was the only politician who ever made Dean want to become one himself— an idea that ended the week he was busted for smoking pot on the steps of a campus building and arrested a few days later for driving under the influence.

He had told himself that he would see the world, and after graduating, Dean bummed around Europe for a few months, sleeping in hostels and sometimes even on park benches. But he was still ambitious—"insanely ambitious," he liked to say. When he came home, he decided to look for the best job with the best company that he could find.

In his mind, that had always been Johnson & Johnson, up in New Jersey. The employees at Johnson & Johnson wore blue suits, they were clean, articulate, well paid, they drove company cars and had health benefits. Dean moved to Philadelphia with a girlfriend and set out to meet anyone who worked at the company. His first contact was a fellow with perfectly combed blond hair, in a blue seersucker suit, white shoes, and a bow tie—the sharpest dresser Dean had ever seen. He called the corporate offices almost every day of the week, he went in for seven or eight interviews, he spent a year trying to will himself into a job, and in 1991 Johnson & Johnson finally submitted and made him a pharmaceutical rep in Harrisburg. Dean bought a blue suit and cut his hair short and tried to lose the southern accent, which he thought would be taken for backwardness. He was given a pager and a computer, and he drove around in a company car from one doctor's office to another, sometimes eight a day, with samples of drugs, explaining the benefits and side effects.

It didn't take him long to realize that he hated the job. At the end of every day, he had to report back to the office about every stop he'd made. He was a robot, a number, and the company was Big Brother watching. Any personal initiative was frowned on if it didn't fit the Johnson & Johnson mold. After eight months, less time than he'd spent trying to get the position, Dean quit.

He had bought into a lie: go to college, get a good education, get a job with a Fortune 500 company, and you'd be happy. He had done all that and he was miserable. He'd gotten out of his father's house only to find another kind of servitude. He decided to start over and do things his own way. He would become an entrepreneur.

TOTAL WAR:
NEWT GINGRICH

Big Newt McPherson was a bar brawler in Harrisburg, Pennsylvania, during World War II. On the third morning after he married Kit Daugherty, a sixteen-year-old housecleaner, Big Newt's young bride tried to wake him up from a hangover, and he punched her. That was the end of the marriage, but it had lasted just long enough for Kit to get pregnant. In 1943 she gave birth to a boy and, in spite of everything, named him after her soon-to-be-ex-husband. Three years later, Kit married an army officer named Robert Gingrich, and Big Newt allowed him to adopt Little Newtie to get out of paying child support. "Isn't it awful," Kit said years later, "a man willing to sell off his own son?"

Long after Little Newtie became a politician, when he was nearly seventy and grasping for his life's ambition, he would say, "I grew up in kind of an idyllic children's background," but that was on a presidential campaign video. The Gingriches lived above a gas station on the main square in lower-middle-class Hummelstown, and life was narrow and harsh and unforgiving. Little Newtie's male relatives—farmers, industrial laborers, highway workers—were hard, physical men. His stepfather (also adopted, like Little Newtie, like Big Newt) was a tyrant around the house, silent and intimidating. Little Newtie absorbed his stepfather's code of toughness, but the pudgy, garrulous boy could never talk his way into the affections of Lieutenant Colonel Bob Gingrich, so they fought constantly. Kit was a manic depressive, spending most of her life tranquilized. Little Newtie was a weird, myopic kid with no close friends. He sought out the older women around him, who fed him sugar cookies and encouraged him to read. The boy who would seem like a nine-year-old at fifty seemed fifty years old at nine. He escaped from life into books and movies. He passionately loved animals, dinosaurs, ancient history, and John Wayne heroes.

On a bright summer's afternoon when Newt was ten, while his stepfather was stationed in Korea, his mother let him ride the bus by himself into Harrisburg, where he watched a double feature of African safari films. Newt came out into the sunlight at four in the afternoon under the spell of crocodiles and rhinos and adventure, looked up, and noticed a sign pointing down an alley: CITY HALL. Being mature beyond his years, he knew about the importance of citizenship. He was directed to the Parks Department and tried to persuade an official that Harrisburg should set aside money to build a zoo. The story made it onto the front page of the local paper. That was the moment when Newt knew he was destined for leadership.

It took another five years before his mission became clear. At Easter in 1958, while Newt's stepfather was serving in France, the Gingriches visited Verdun—*l'enfer de Verdun*, total war. Forty years after World War I, the city still bore artillery wounds. Newt wandered around the scarred battlefield and picked up a couple of rusted helmets he found lying on the ground, which eventually made it onto his bedroom wall along with a grenade fragment. He peered through a window into the Ossuary, where the bones of more than a hundred thousand French and German soldiers lay in huge piles. He saw that life was real. He saw that civilizations could die. He saw what could happen when bad leaders failed to keep their countries safe. He realized that some people had to be willing to give up their lives in order to protect their way of life.

He read Toynbee and Asimov, and his mind filled with visions of civilization in decay. It could happen to America. He decided that he would not be a zoo director or paleontologist after all. His future was in politics. Not as county administrator, or chairman of the transportation committee, or secretary of defense, or even just as president. He was going to be a Great Leader of his people. The models were Lincoln, Roosevelt, and Churchill. (There would be a fourth, but he was still an ex-actor hosting *General Electric Theater* when Newt walked around Verdun.) He resolved to spend his life figuring out three things: what America needed to survive, how he would persuade the American people to let him provide it, and how he would keep his country free.

Decades later, Gingrich scrawled his destiny in notes on a classroom easel, like ancient hieroglyphs in praise of a conquering warrior:

Gingrich—primary mission
Advocate of civilization
Definer of civilization

Teacher of the Rules of Civilization
Arouser of those who Fan Civilization
Organizer of the pro-civilization activists
Leader (Possibly) of the civilizing forces
A universal rather than an optimal Mission

But first, he had to get through the sixties.

When Bob Gingrich was sent home in 1960, Kit and her son joined him at Fort Benning, Georgia, where Newt campaigned for Nixon against Kennedy. Nixon was his first political interest, and Gingrich read everything he could find on him—another son of the lower middle class, after all, another brooding loner with a hard father and more resentments than friends, nurturing dreams of greatness. In November, Gingrich spent one of the longest nights of his life by the radio listening to Nixon lose to Kennedy.

In high school he secretly dated his geometry teacher, Jackie Battley—seven years his senior, another doting older woman. When Gingrich was nineteen, they married (Bob Gingrich refused to attend), then had two daughters.

As a family man he wasn't drafted, didn't enlist, and never set foot in Vietnam. His stepfather despised him for it: "He couldn't see across the room. Flattest feet I've ever seen. He's physically incapable of doing military service."

While Jackie worked, Gingrich studied history at Emory, went to Tulane for his Ph.D., became a campus activist. When the Tulane administration banned two pictures it considered obscene from the school paper, Gingrich organized protests against the decision and joined a sit-in. He was still a Republican, but he had reformist views on civil rights, the environment, ethics in government. He read the Tofflers and became a futurist nerd, a cheerleader for the information revolution. Most of all, he liked throwing verbal rocks at established institutions. He had a favorite phrase, "corrupt elite," that could be hurled in any direction, and for the rest of his life he kept it in his pocket. He would reach power denouncing the cesspool of the sixties and the liberals who swam there, but the decade made him, too.

In 1970 he went back to Georgia and started teaching history at West Georgia College, outside Atlanta. Immediately offered himself for the college presidency—was turned down. In 1974 challenged the conservative Democrat in a district that had never sent a Republican to Congress—

lost in the Watergate wipeout. Ran again in 1976—lost again, while a peanut farmer from Plains was elected president. "Gerald Ford personally cost me a congressional seat," he fumed. But Gingrich wasn't about to run low on ambition. And he was getting closer. When the incumbent announced his retirement, 1978 began to look like Gingrich's year. Gingrich and 1978 were made for each other.

He was something new in politics—a man of the New South (not really a southerner at all), the modern, middle-class South of the space program and the gated community. He didn't make racial appeals, didn't seem very religious. The suburbs north of Atlanta were a mix of Norman Rockwell and fiber optics, the incarnation of a trend forecast a decade earlier in Nixon's 1968 campaign: an emerging Republican majority concentrated in the Sunbelt. Gingrich, who loved aircraft carriers, moon launches, and personal computers, understood these people.

In 1978, with vandalism in the cities, stagflation across the country, and a humorless moralizer in the White House preaching sacrifice, the public's mood was sour, frustrated, suspicious of bureaucracies and special interests, antigovernment, antitax—populist and conservative. Gingrich's Democratic opponent was made to order, a wealthy liberal female state senator originally from New York. Gingrich knew exactly what to do. He moved to the right and went after her on welfare and taxes. He had a new rock in his pocket, "the corrupt liberal welfare state," and he nailed her between the eyes with it. The Moral Majority was about to take Washington by storm, and Gingrich talked about family values, said that his opponent would break her family up if she went to Washington, and featured Jackie and the girls in his ads.

But Jackie looked fat and unattractive, and it was an open secret in political circles that Newt was cheating on her. Like most Arousers of those who Fan Civilization, he had powerful appetites, but he had not grown up to be the most desirable of men—big head under big graying helmet, cold clever grin, belly pushing against his sky-blue waistline—and his successes were limited. He tried to keep it to oral sex so he could claim literal fidelity if anyone asked, but within two years the marriage was over, another adoring woman about to become the next Mrs. Gingrich, the Advocate of civilization standing at Jackie's hospital bed as she lay recovering from uterine cancer, a yellow legal pad with divorce terms in his hand. Years later, Gingrich would attribute his indiscretions to hard work brought on by patriotic zeal.

Gingrich won easily in 1978, and his party picked up fifteen seats in the House (the freshman class included Dick Cheney). It was a sign of what was coming in 1980.

The Organizer of the pro-civilization activists arrived in Washington with a plan. He would kick over the old order, put fear in the ruling Democrats, call them a "corrupt left-wing machine" (another rock—his pocket was bottomless), go after committee chairmen, bait Speakers of the House until they were red-faced with rage. He would shake up the timid Republicans, too, shame their leaders, create a cadre of young fighters, teach them the ways of politics (he liked to quote Mao: "war without blood"), give them a new language, an ecstatic vision, until the party would turn to its terrible child for deliverance. Then he would save the country— Speaker—President—Leader (Possibly) of the civilizing forces.

And Gingrich did most of it.

He saw all the available weapons on the battlefield, some never used before. Two months after his arrival, C-SPAN switched on its cameras in the House of Representatives, broadcasting Congress to the public for the first time. Gingrich immediately knew what to do—take the floor after regular order was over and give incendiary speeches to an empty chamber that would bring media attention and slowly build a devoted TV following. (Regardless of the rock labeled "elite liberal media," he knew they loved a fight more than anything else.) In 1984, a speech calling the Democrats appeasers brought down the wrath of Tip O'Neill—"It's the lowest thing that I've ever seen in my thirty-two years here!" But the Speaker's remarks, being personal, were stricken from the record, and the incident landed Gingrich on the nightly news. "I am now a famous person," he crowed, understanding the new rules of celebrity—that it would not be a bad thing to say, for example, "I have an enormous personal ambition. I want to shift the entire planet. And I'm doing it."

The old party system had become obsolete, snuffed out by high-minded reformers who wanted to end patronage and political bosses in smoke-filled rooms. Gingrich saw this happening, too—how politicians were turning into entrepreneurs who depended on special-interest PACs, think tanks, media, and lobbyists more than on the party hierarchy. So he gave speeches around Washington, wrote a book (financed by supporters), and created his own power base, with a fundraising apparatus and a political action committee. He recruited Republican candidates around the country and trained them with his own words and ideas on videotapes and cassettes, like a motivational speaker, understanding that language was the key to power. His memos included vocabulary lessons: if you discussed your opponent with words like *betray bizarre bosses bureaucracy cheat corrupt crisis cynicism decay destroy disgrace impose incompetent liberal lie limit(s) obsolete pathetic radical shame sick stagnation status quo steal taxes they/them threaten traitors unionized waste welfare*, you had him on the defensive, and if you described your side with *change children choice/choose common sense courage crusade dream duty empower(ment) family freedom hard work lead liberty light moral opportunity pro-(issue) proud/pride reform strength success tough truth vision we/us/our*, you had already won the argument. The Gingrich lexicon could be arranged into potent sentences regardless of context, or even meaning: *"We can empower our children and families to dream by leading a moral crusade for liberty and truth if only we are tough and have common sense." "Corrupt liberal bosses cheat, lie, and steal to impose their sick pathetic cynicism and bizarre radical stagnation in order to destroy America."* Thus a whole generation of politicians learned to sound like Newt Gingrich.

And he saw that the voters no longer felt much connection to the local parties or national institutions. They got their politics on TV, and they were not persuaded by policy descriptions or rational arguments. They responded to symbols and emotions. They were growing more partisan, too, living in districts that were increasingly Democratic or Republican, liberal or conservative. Donors were more likely to send money if they could be frightened or angered, if the issues were framed as simple choices between good and evil—which was easy for a man whose America stood forever at a historic crossroads, its civilization in perpetual peril.

By the end of the eighties, Gingrich was radically changing Washington and the Republican Party. Maybe more than Reagan—maybe more than anyone else. Then history went into high gear.

In 1989 he bagged his biggest prey when Jim Wright, the Democratic Speaker, resigned because of ethics charges that had been relentlessly pressed by backbencher Gingrich. Seeing what total war could achieve, the Republicans made him one of their leaders, and the Teacher of the Rules of Civilization did not fail them. In 1994 he nationalized the midterms by getting nearly every Republican candidate to sign his Contract with America in front of the Capitol, pronouncing it "a first step towards renewing American civilization." In November his party took both houses of Congress, for the first time since that African safari double feature. It

was the Gingrich revolution, and he became its Robespierre—Speaker of
the House, media obsession, equal ruler with the red-cheeked Arkansas
boy in the White House, whose origins and desires bore such a striking
resemblance to his own.

Gingrich called Clinton a "counterculture McGovernik" and "the enemy of normal Americans." He thought he could bend the president to
his will: Clinton wanted to be loved, Gingrich wanted to be feared. They
spent 1995 circling around the budget. When they met in the White
House, Gingrich dictated terms, while Clinton studied Gingrich. He saw
the nine-year-old's insecurities writhing beneath the fiery words. He understood why none of Gingrich's colleagues could stand him. He saw how to
exploit the grandiosity. Clinton's need for love gave him insight, and he
used it to seduce his adversary while setting traps for him, and when at
the end of the year the United States of America was forced to close for
business, it was Gingrich who got the blame.

And that was the end of the primary mission.

Gingrich remained Speaker for three more years. He achieved things
that the media would never give him credit for—credit went to the boy from
Arkansas (he always got the hottest women, they wanted him even before he
came to power). Then the logic of total war caught up with both men. In
1997, Gingrich was reprimanded by the House and fined a record three
hundred thousand dollars for laundering political contributions through his
various nonprofits (some of his allies wanted to escort him to the guillotine).
In 1998 there was only one thing, and that was Monica. When oral sex and
lying failed to destroy Clinton, and the Democrats defied history by picking
up seats in the midterms, the Gingrich revolutionaries turned on their
leader. He resigned the Speakership and his seat, saying, "I'm not willing to
preside over people who are cannibals." The last vote he ever cast was to
impeach his rival. Later, he admitted to carrying on an affair throughout
his time as Speaker with a woman twenty-three years his junior. He left
Congress after two decades but stayed on in Washington.

By then it was Newt Gingrich's city as much as anyone's. Whether he
ever truly believed his own rhetoric, the generation he brought to power
fervently did. He gave them mustard gas and they used it on every con-
ceivable enemy, including him. At the millennium the two sides were dug
deep in opposing trenches, the positions forever fixed, bodies piling up in
the mud, last year's corpses this year's bones, a war whose causes no one
could quite explain, with no end in sight: *l'enfer de Washington*.

Perhaps he had wanted it this way all along. Politics without war could be rather boring.

The young Tiffany-wearing congressional aide with whom he had been cheating on the second Mrs. Gingrich became the third. Washington's think tanks and partisan media made a place for him, because he had helped make theirs. Like his rival, he spent his time out of office with rich people. Never having had money (he was in debt throughout most of his career), he set out to make a lot of it, selling his connections and influence—for shifting the entire planet required him to grab every opportunity in the bipartisan lobbying industry. And his books came out in frantic conveyor-belt fashion, seventeen in eight years—for America's decay kept growing deeper, its elite liberal media more destructive, its secular-socialist machine more radical, the Democrat in the White House more alien, and the desire to save America was undimmed, and the need to be heard was unquenchable.

He finally ran for president when it was much too late, but the old man in the white helmet with the cold clever boyish grin still found what he wanted whenever he reached into his pocket.

JEFF CONNAUGHTON

Jeff Connaughton first saw Joe Biden in 1979. Biden was thirty-six, the sixth-youngest person ever elected to the United States Senate. Connaughton was nineteen, a business major at the University of Alabama. His parents lived up in Huntsville, where his father worked for thirty years as a chemical engineer with the Army Missile Command, a job he'd landed after flying forty-seven missions over Europe, China, and Japan with the Army Air Corps, then attending Tuscaloosa on the GI Bill, then going from a dollar an hour in a Birmingham steel mill to an Arkansas furniture factory to National Gypsum in Mobile to the booming postwar defense industry. Working on small-rocket propulsion was a good middle-class job, topping out at fifty-five thousand a year, underwritten by the federal government and the Cold War, but Mr. and Mrs. Connaughton had both grown up in poverty. Jeff's father had watched his father march through Washington, D.C., with the Bonus Army in 1932. Jeff's mother was from Town Creek, Alabama, and as a little girl she and her sisters had helped out during the hard times by picking cotton on her grandmother's farm. When she was five, she saved a nickel to buy her mother a birthday present. One day, the little girl fell ill with a 104-degree fever, and when the ice truck passed outside and her mother wanted to buy a block of ice to cool her fever, she refused, because her five cents was the only money in the house. It was a story Jeff always thought he'd tell if he ever ran for office.

The Connaughtons split their vote. Jeff's mother could remember the day FDR came to Town Creek to open the Wheeler Dam, and all the children ran down to the station and watched in a solemn hush as the president was lifted from the train into a car. She would vote Democrat all her life. The first time Jeff's father went to vote, in Alabama after the war, and asked how to do it, the poll worker said, "Just vote for the names beneath the rooster," which was the symbol of the Alabama Democratic Party, the only one that mattered back then. On the spot Mr. Connaughton became a Republican, and he remained one over the following decades as the rest of the white South caught up with him. But years later, after Jeff went to Washington to work for Biden and became what he would call a Professional Democrat, his dad voted for Clinton—even for Obama. By then, most everyone in their suburb was staunchly Republican, and someone stole the Obama-Biden signs right out of the Connaughtons' front yard. Mr. Connaughton was voting for his son.

Jeff Connaughton was short and sandy-haired, smart and hardworking, with the lifelong inferiority complex that's bred into boys from Alabama. Growing up, he had no clear political views. In 1976 he was inspired when Ronald Reagan spoke at the Republican convention about "the erosion of freedom that has taken place under Democratic rule in this country"; in 1979, when Jimmy Carter diagnosed a "crisis of confidence" in America, warning that "too many of us now tend to worship self-indulgence and consumption," Connaughton defended what came to be called the "malaise" speech in an opinion piece for *The Tuscaloosa News*. He was a swing voter until he moved to Washington; he also revered the Kennedys. Once, in 1994, he attended a fundraiser at Hickory Hill for Kathleen Kennedy Townsend, with Ethel and other Kennedys graciously welcoming every guest on the front lawn of the manor. Connaughton slipped off into the study, where he wasn't supposed to go, and took from the shelf a bound volume of Robert F. Kennedy's speeches—the original manuscripts, with handwritten notes. Connaughton's eyes fell on a sentence that read, "We should do better." Kennedy had crossed out "should" and replaced it with "must." Connaughton was holding holy scripture. That was his first idea of politics: great speeches, historic events (the assassinations), black-and-white portraits of JFK in the Oval Office and the Rose Garden. He was that overlooked and necessary thing in the annals of Washington, not Hamlet but Rosencrantz, not a principal but a follower—years later he would say, "I am the perfect number two guy"—drawn to the romance of public service and to power, which eventually became inextricable.

In early 1979, when Connaughton was a sophomore, a friend at the University of Pennsylvania asked him to be Alabama's delegate to the annual meeting of the National Student Congress, in Philadelphia. The plane ticket would cost a hundred fifty dollars. Connaughton was granted twenty-five bucks from the student government's budget, and *The Tuscaloosa News* offered to give him seventy-five dollars for a story based on the experience. The last fifty dollars came out of the cash register at a Wendy's where Connaughton ate a couple of meals a week—the manager was touched by the story of a college student trying to pay his way to a national assembly whose purpose was to combat apathy on campus and restore faith in politics a few years after Watergate and Vietnam.

The first speaker at the meeting in Philadelphia was an ultraconservative Republican congressman from Illinois named Dan Crane, one of the many thousands of men and women who go to Washington as the elected representatives of the American people and serve out their time in the halls of Congress without leaving a trace. The second was Joe Biden. He began by saying, "If Representative Crane had just given you the liberal point of view, this would be the conservative view: You're all under arrest." The line brought down the house. The rest of the speech didn't leave a mark on Connaughton's memory, but the speaker did. Biden was youthful, he was witty, he knew how to talk to college students. Connaughton never forgot the moment.

Back in Tuscaloosa, he started the Alabama Political Union, and for its first event in the fall he invited Biden and Senator Jake Garn, a Republican from Utah, to debate the SALT II arms control treaty. Both senators accepted (in 1979 there was no ban on accepting the five-hundred-dollar honorarium the university was offering—just a restriction limiting outside income to 15 percent of a senator's $57,500 salary, which had taken effect on January 1), but then Garn backed out. The debate threatened to be reduced to a mere speech.

Connaughton got in his Chevy Nova with a friend who was visiting from Brigham Young University and who, like Garn, was a Mormon. They drove fourteen hours to the nation's capital to change Senator Garn's mind. Connaughton had never been to Washington, and the Beltway offered no obvious exits into the city—it was more of a moat than a conduit—and the Capitol dome kept appearing in the distance and then disappearing. Finally they found their way onto backstreets that led toward Capitol Hill. This was poor, black Washington, blighted Washington, the Washington of the district's 80 percent, neighborhoods that Connaughton would rarely see again in the two decades he would live and work in the city.

In the morning, they found Garn's office in the Russell Senate Office Building, along one of the lofty and immensely long corridors, behind one of the high, forbidding mahogany doors. Because he had brought a Utah

Mormon with him, Connaughton was granted an unscheduled audience right there in the waiting room with the senator himself, but he was unable to change Garn's mind—he had another commitment the day of the debate. So Connaughton and the Mormon friend left and wandered around Russell—two young out-of-towners dwarfed by the white Vermont marble and Concord granite and dark mahogany and the clubby, bipartisan institutional dignity that was still intact, though it would soon begin to crack and then crumble—looking for a Republican senator to sign up. But the halls were nearly empty, in an undemocratic hush, and Connaughton barely knew what any senators looked like. He might have glimpsed Howard Baker, Jacob Javits, Chuck Percy, or Barry Goldwater. Among the Democrats, Hubert Humphrey had died recently, but Edmund Muskie was still there, and Frank Church, Birch Bayh, Gaylord Nelson, George McGovern. All of them soon to be swept away.

Suddenly a buzzer went off, and out of nowhere the corridor filled with tall, gray-haired, distinguished-looking men. Connaughton and his friend followed them into an elevator (wasn't that little Japanese man in the tam-o'-shanter S. I. Hayakawa?), down to the basement and the subterranean electric cars that shuttled back and forth along a thirty-second track between Russell and the Capitol. Among the senators striding toward the next car was Ted Kennedy, who smiled at being recognized and shook hands with the friend, who had stepped forward. As for Connaughton, he was too awestruck to move. (The public didn't know it, but Kennedy was preparing to challenge President Carter for the 1980 Democratic nomination: it was Biden who had first alerted Carter, in early 1978, that Kennedy was coming after him.)

Connaughton returned to Tuscaloosa without a Republican to debate SALT II. It didn't matter. Biden arrived that September wearing one of his tailored suits and power ties, trim and flashing his white-toothed smile, and he charmed the hell out of the lovely coeds over dinner at Phi Mu on Sorority Row (Connaughton's girlfriend was a member), with Jeff attached to the senator's elbow as his adjutant for the evening and now seriously considering a political career. Two hundred people filled the student center for Biden's speech. Connaughton made the introduction, then took his seat in the front row as Biden came to the lectern.

"I know you're all here tonight because you've heard what a great man I am," Biden began. "Yep, I'm widely known as what they call 'presidential timber.'" The crowd laughed nervously, thrown by his sense of humor.

"Why, just earlier tonight I spoke to a group of students who had put up a great big sign, 'Welcome Senator Biden.' And then when I walked under the sign I heard someone say, 'That must be Senator Bidden.'" The laughter rose. Now Biden had the crowd, and he turned to his subject and spent ninety minutes arguing lucidly and without notes for the importance of reducing the American and Soviet nuclear arsenals, while he dismantled the arguments of SALT II's opponents in the Senate. The day before, the treaty had suffered a blow with the supposed revelation of a brigade of Soviet troops in Cuba. "Folks, I'm going to let you in on a little secret," Biden whispered, and he took the microphone and walked toward his audience, gesturing for the crowd to lean in and listen. "Those troops have been in Cuba all along!" he shouted. "And everyone knows it!" At the end of the lecture, the applause was loud and long. When Connaughton got up to approach Biden and thank him, he accidentally started a standing ovation.

A campus security guard drove Biden back to the Birmingham airport, and Connaughton went along. Biden looked tired from his speech, but he answered every beginner's question from the guard ("What's the difference between a Democrat and a Republican?") as thoughtfully as if it had come from David Brinkley. When Connaughton asked Biden why he rode the train from Wilmington to Washington every day, the senator calmly told the story of the car accident that had nearly wiped out his young family in December 1972, just a month after his election to the Senate. "My wife and baby girl were killed," Biden said, "and my sons were badly injured. So I stayed with my sons at the hospital. I really didn't want to be a senator. But eventually I was sworn in at my son's bedside. And I served, but I went home every night to be with my sons. And over the years, Delaware just got used to having me home every day. And so I really can't ever move to Washington."

That was the moment Jeff Connaughton was hooked by Joe Biden. Here was tragedy, here was energy, here was oratory—just like the Kennedys. Biden turned his charisma on everyone who crossed his path and didn't move on until he had made a connection—the sorority girls, the audience at the speech (many of the students attending for course credit), the security guard, the junior business major who had invited him to Tuscaloosa in the first place. This was the need and drive of a man who wanted to be president, and as they got out at the airport, Connaughton produced a spiral notebook that Biden signed, "To Jeff and the APU,

Please stay involved in politics. We need you all," and he knew that he would end up following this man to the White House. What he would do once he got there wasn't clear, and didn't really matter. The point was to be in the room, at the summit of American life.

Before graduating from Alabama, Connaughton brought Biden (along with dozens of other elected officials) down twice more on paid speaking gigs, and Biden told the same jokes each time before giving his speech, which, by the third visit, was worth a thousand dollars. The last time he dropped Biden off at the Birmingham airport, Connaughton told the senator, "If you ever run for president, I'm going to be there."

He didn't immediately head to Washington. First he went to the University of Chicago Business School, with a letter of recommendation from Biden himself. It was 1981, and *Time* ran a cover story called "The Money Chase," about the vogue for MBAs; the cover image showed a graduating student whose mortarboard had a tassel made of dollars. Connaughton had never had any money, and Wall Street's magnetic pull was almost as strong as the allure of the White House. The whole point of an MBA was Wall Street. Just as it would be absurd to go to Washington and end up at the Interior Department, there was no appeal in getting a prestigious business degree only to work for a company like Procter & Gamble or IBM. Among his classmates, a job with a company that actually made things meant you were being left behind. Toward the end of his second year, Connaughton flew to Miami to interview with Ryder Truck, and the whole time he was thinking that if it weren't Miami and a day at the beach he wouldn't know why he was bothering. He'd had a summer job at Conoco Oil in Houston between his first and second years, and they wanted him to come back and make a career there, but the thought of starting out at thirty-two grand and moving laterally every six months from Lake Charles, Louisiana, to Ponca City, Oklahoma, was at least as dismal as working for a trucking company. Connaughton *came* from flyover country—he didn't want to work there. If he didn't get a position at an investment bank like Salomon Brothers or Goldman Sachs, or else a management consulting firm like McKinsey, he would feel like a failure.

Connaughton didn't forget about Joe Biden. Working till midnight in the university library, he would put aside his finance books and dig up old issues of *Time* from the sixties and read again about the assassinations, Jack's presidency, Bobby's rise. He still wanted to find himself in those black-and-white photos. Even as he applied to Wall Street, he followed Biden's career closely and wrote several letters asking for a job—not to the senator's office, or to the staff guy there whom he'd gotten to know a little, who might have actually written back, but to Biden himself: "Dear Senator Biden, I'm coming up on graduating from Chicago and . . ." He didn't understand that the office answered mail only from Delaware— that his letters went straight into a wastebasket.

Connaughton was hired by Smith Barney's public finance department, beginning at forty-eight thousand dollars, and he moved to New York in the summer of 1983. It was just the right moment to start out on Wall Street, and if Connaughton had stayed, like some of his Chicago classmates, he might have made a small fortune. Public finance meant tax-exempt bonds for state and local governments, which was not the place to make a pile, but it suited Connaughton, who had written in his business school application that he wanted to understand the intersection between business and government and have a career in which he moved back and forth between them. Smith Barney was underwriting water and sewer bonds in Florida, where the cities and towns were doubling their populations every few years and needed help raising fifty or a hundred million dollars for infrastructure projects.

The firm would throw lavish thirty-thousand-dollar closing dinners at Lutèce in Manhattan, with limos provided, and assure clients that it wouldn't cost their home state a thing: they could recoup the underwriting fees (including the dinner) by investing funds that they'd raised in the tax-exempt market and make 3 percent more on interest rates than they were paying on their public bonds. Connaughton would tell officials, "I can give you front-row seats to *Cats*, just let me know, it won't cost your taxpayers a dime." They would hesitate, but almost every time he'd have a message on his answering machine the next morning: "We changed our mind— we *would* like to go to *Cats*." Once, another banker went down to Jackson County, Tennessee, and explained to the board of commissioners that the higher the bank's fees, the more money the county would eventually save. From the back of the room a man drawled out a reply: "Bullll-shit . . ." As a southerner, Connaughton believed that whenever an investment banker from New York came down saying "We can save you money," there needed to be someone in the room saying "Bullll-shit."

Connaughton shared an apartment (rented by the firm) on the Upper East Side. He would roll into Smith Barney's midtown headquarters around 9:30 in the morning, work all day, step out with colleagues for dinner, and go back to the office till midnight. He wasn't as smart as some of the geeks running numbers on bond scenarios at the computers around him, but as a southerner he was more fun, and he had connections to Alabama women in Manhattan. He never did drugs, not once (years later, when he was hired to work at the Clinton White House and was asked about drug use as part of his security clearance, Connaughton said, "I've been waiting my entire life to answer that question"). But he drank plenty of bourbon and once danced all night at Studio 54. From November on, the only topic among his coworkers was the size of their year-end bonus.

After a year, he was transferred to Chicago. Hating the cold and missing the South, he passed up a twenty-thousand-dollar bonus and, at the start of 1985, jumped over to E. F. Hutton's office in Atlanta. Several months after his arrival, the firm pleaded guilty to two thousand counts of wire and mail fraud in a massive check-kiting scandal. Throughout the eighties E. F. Hutton had been writing checks for sums it couldn't cover and transferring the money between accounts, using the funds for a day or two as interest-free loans and making millions of dollars on the float. Up in Washington, Joe Biden of the Senate Judiciary Committee was on the case. He began going on TV talking about the growing epidemic of white-collar crime on Wall Street and the failure of the Reagan Justice Department to police it. In a speech at NYU he said, "People believe that our system of law and those who manage it have failed, and may not even have tried, to deal effectively with unethical and possibly illegal misconduct in high places." Reagan was in his senescent second term, his administration riddled with corruption, and Biden was setting himself up to go after the big prize.

The guilty plea cost E. F. Hutton clients and began to hollow out the firm, but Connaughton survived. As he learned the business, he would fly down to Florida by himself and meet with city treasurers. He even came up with a marketable idea: The towns and counties had huge pension liabilities—why not arbitrage them? Issue a hundred-million-dollar pension bond tax-free at 4 percent, then invest the money for a few years at 6 or 7 percent? It was a kind of scam on the U.S. taxpayer. But a bond firm gave a favorable opinion (it was legal if you could get a law firm to tell you it was legal—lawyers were becoming more creative as the action got exponentially more profitable), and his boss, a former bond lawyer himself, was pleased. Connaughton was figuring out how to do investment banking in the 1980s. Playing the tax rules was a racket.

He was a twenty-seven-year-old assistant vice president making more than a hundred grand, and yet he went home in the evenings thinking this was not what he wanted to do with his life. By the end of 1986 it was clear that Biden would run for president. Connaughton had never forgotten him. He pulled a string with an E. F. Hutton lobbyist who had connections to the campaign. It worked.

"Biden was like a cult figure to me," Connaughton said much later. "He was the guy I was going to follow because he was my horse. I was going to ride that horse into the White House. That was going to be my next stop in life. I had done Wall Street, and I was going to do the White House next."

1984

On January 24, Apple Computer will introduce Macintosh. And you'll see why 1984 won't be like *1984*. . . . **BANK SECURITIES UNITS MAY UNDERWRITE BONDS** . . . It's morning again in America, and under the leadership of President Reagan, our country is prouder and stronger and better. Why would we ever want to return to where we were less than four short years ago? . . . *I had a job, I had a girl / I had something going mister in this world / I got laid off down at the lumberyard / Our love went bad, times got hard* . . . **TAMPA SEES GAINS FOR ITS HARD WORK** "But those kinds of things can't do for us, long-term, what a Super Bowl can do. This is a real opportunity for us to show people what a great place this is, that they can come here and not expect to get taken advantage of." . . . **MISS AMERICA IS ORDERED TO QUIT FOR POS-ING NUDE** . . . You're judged by performance. Why drive a car that lives by a lesser code? . . . At Bank of New England, Vice President David E. Hersee, Jr., went apartment hunting for the daughter of a California customer who was moving to Boston. Of course, apartment hunting is reserved for the very best clients. . . . **LINDA GRAY'S SECRET LOVE Just Like "Dallas" Role—She Falls for Younger Man** . . . In the four years before we took office, country after country fell under the Soviet yoke. Since January 20, 1981, not one inch of soil has fallen to the Communists. . . . *U.S.A.! U.S.A.! U.S.A.!* . . . **BEEPERS SAID TO LINK LEGIONS OF AREA'S WORKAHOLICS Devices Now Perceived As Lifelines; No Longer a High-Tech Oddity** . . . The housing finance industry needs a national mortgage exchange that does for mortgages and mortgage-backed securi-ties trading "what the New York Stock Exchange does for corporate stock trading," Fannie Mae Chairman David O. Maxwell told . . . **NEW U.S. REPORT NAMES VIRUS THAT MAY CAUSE AIDS** . . . There are times in everyone's life when something constructive is born out of adversity. There are times when things seem so bad that you've got to grab your fate by the shoulders and shake it. I'm convinced it was that morning at the warehouse that pushed me to take on the presidency of Chrysler. . . . **REAGAN WINS RE-ELECTION IN LANDSLIDE Victory Shows Broad Appeal of President** . . . *And I feel like I'm a rider on a downbound train.*

TAMMY THOMAS

Tammy Thomas grew up on the east side of Youngstown, Ohio. Years after she left when things got bad there and moved down to the south side, and after she left the south side when things got bad there and moved up to the north side, in certain moods she would drive her metal-gray 2002 Pontiac Sunfire over the expressway, which broke up the city when it came through in the late sixties, and return to look around her old neighborhood.

When Tammy was coming up in the sixties and seventies, the east side was still a mixed area. Next door to her house on Charlotte Avenue there had been an Italian family. Hungarians lived across the street, the blue house was Puerto Rican, and there were a few black homeowners, too. The wide-open field at the corner of Charlotte and Bruce had once been her elementary school. Down Bruce Street there had been a church that was later hit by a storm and torn down. A few streets away on Shehy, where three wooden crosses now rose from the earth and the sidewalk was spray-painted BLOOD and FROM PHILLY TO YOUNGSTOWN NIGGA, there had been a neighborhood store, next to the house where Tammy's mother lived before it was firebombed. A depression that cut through the grass of two lots had been an alley lined with peach and apple trees. Back then, everyone raised flowers and vegetables in their yard—around her house on Charlotte there had been rose of Sharon, forsythia, tulips, hyacinth. As a girl she used to sit on her front porch and look down the street and see the tops of the smokestacks, and if the wind blew right she could smell the sulfur. The men on the east side had good jobs, most of them in the mills. Families kept up their property and were proud to own three-story houses with gable roofs and front porches and yards, all of them big compared to a working-class home in the Northeast (the first time Tammy saw row houses in Philly she thought, "Where are their yards, where are their driveways?"). Back then the mob kept things in order, so there weren't a whole lot of shenanigans going on.

Tammy had a friend, Sybil West, whom she called Miss Sybil because she was Tammy's mother's age. Miss Sybil once wrote down in a little spiral memo book all the things that she could remember from when she was coming up on the east side in the fifties and sixties.

pool halls
confectionery w/music for teens
Isaly dairy
first mall
buses that hook up to live wires
Lincoln Park w/pool
knife sharpeners w/monkeys to entertain kids
farmers selling fruits + vegetables in neighborhood trucks
City at that time was so safe people slept w/doors unlocked. People
    very neighborly + much interaction occurred in schools as well
    as neighborhoods.

As Tammy drove over the crumbling asphalt of the streets, she was still amazed by the gaps and silence where there had once been so much life. It was as if she still expected to see the old families, and the east side had just disappeared. Where had it all gone? The things that had made it a community—stores, schools, churches, playgrounds, fruit trees—were gone, along with half the houses and two-thirds of the people, and if you didn't know the history, you wouldn't know what was missing. The east side had never been the best part of Youngstown, but it had the most black homeowners, and to Tammy it had always been the greenest, the least dense, the most beautiful—you could pick peaches around Lincoln Park—and now parts of it were almost returning to nature, with deer wandering across overgrown lots where people came to dump their garbage.

It made her damn mad to see how McGuffey Plaza was abandoned— a model shopping mall that was built in the fifties by the Cafaro family, with a bowling alley, an A&P, a bunch of other stores, and a huge parking lot in front—now just a concrete desert, with nothing but one black hair-care shop left open. It frustrated her that everyone had forgotten about the east side. Not sad, not sentimental, she was frustrated, because she hadn't given up and wouldn't slip into the resignation that had settled over

Youngstown, because this city was where she had lived her whole life, and her past was still real to her, and there was still something to be done.

It frustrated her to see the house on Charlotte, with the gable off to the right side and the brick chimney in back, where she had lived for twenty years. The house had been vacant since the mid-2000s, and the yellow paint on the clapboards was weathering bare. It would have been easy to push open her old front door or climb in through a hollow window and walk upstairs to the second-floor front bedroom that had been hers when she was little, but she sat idling the Pontiac and stared through the windshield. "Oh my God," she muttered. She was afraid she would feel a little emotional if she went in. She knew the wiring and woodwork had been stripped, and her granny had worked so hard for that house.

Granny was Tammy's great-grandmother, her mother's father's mother. It was Granny who had raised Tammy from a girl. There was a lot Tammy didn't know for certain about Granny. She had two birth dates, one in 1904 (according to Social Security) and one in 1900 (according to herself). Granny's mother, Big Mama, might have been born near Raleigh, North Carolina, and sold off by her family to a white man in Richmond, Virginia, where Granny was born (unless she was born in Winston-Salem, North Carolina), and Granny very well could have been a mulatto—she was very fair, with long straight hair. Granny's name was Virginia Miller, but when she had a son he was given the last name Thomas because by then Big Mama had married Henry Thomas, Granny's stepfather, and Papa Thomas and Big Mama raised the boy.

Tammy tried to research the family history at the Freedom Center in Cincinnati, but a lot of it had vanished. Granny didn't appear in the 1920 census, and in 1930 she was listed as a "niece" in the Thomas household, age seventeen, with a son, age five—so the census had her age wrong, and also her place in the family. The farther Tammy went, the more mysteries she ran into. There were other names in the 1930 census, great-aunts and great-uncles listed as Big Mama's children who were not hers, which was normal in black families. "You took care of the kids," Tammy said later, "and the kids would be raised alongside cousins and brothers and sisters. But it creates a lot of confusion because you really don't know whose is whose, and they didn't talk about it." Granny never talked about these things, either, and now she was gone.

One thing Tammy knew almost for sure was that Granny had had to drop out of school near Winston-Salem in the eighth grade and go to work in the tobacco fields. In the twenties she left the South and came up to Ohio, where she found day work cleaning houses, and later a job in the arc engraving department of the Youngstown *Vindicator*. During the Depression the rest of the Thomas household—Papa Thomas, Big Mama, various great-aunts and great-uncles, and Granny's son—followed her north and settled in Struthers, across the Mahoning River on the southeastern edge of Youngstown, where there was a coking plant with a smokestack that shot out blue flames. Some of Tammy's relatives got jobs in the steel mills, and the family owned several houses in Struthers. Papa Thomas brought his farming skills north and cultivated the yards. They had plum trees, an apple tree, a peach tree, a chestnut tree, and five cherry trees. Two of the neighbor women made jelly and swapped it with Tammy's great-aunt for plum wine. When Tammy was a girl, she and Granny would visit their Struthers family on weekends. "To me this was living in the country," she said, "and as I grew older I realized our family who lived up here kind of had it going on."

Tammy's line of the family did not have it going on. Her grandfather came back from World War II with a heroin addiction. His wife became an alcoholic. In 1966, their daughter Vickie, a pretty, fine-boned seventeen-year-old, gave birth to a girl and named her Tammy. The father was a street-smart fifteen-year-old from the projects named Gary Sharp, nicknamed Razor. He and Vickie had no use for each other. She dropped out of high school, and soon after becoming a mother she started using. Vickie and Tammy went to live with Granny, who was approaching seventy and working as a maid, cleaning, cooking, and providing companionship for a rich widow on the north side for around fifty dollars a week. The care of the baby fell to Granny.

They lived on Lane Avenue after the I-680 expressway came through Granny's old apartment—Tammy, Granny, Vickie, and Tammy's grandfather and his wife and children, while whoever else came in and out. When Granny was off at work, pretty much everyone in the household was using. Vickie also smoked, and sometimes she fell asleep with a cigarette still burning. As a little girl Tammy would try to stay awake until after her mother went to sleep, then take the cigarette out of her hand. From the age of three she was taking care of her mother.

She loved sleeping in her granny's bed, but sometimes—less often—she would climb in with her mother, and maybe because she never got enough of that when she was little, she kept doing it as an adult, especially when she wasn't feeling good and needed comfort, just crawled into her mom's bed, even at the hospital with the nurses telling her to get out.

It was Granny who took Tammy to church on Sunday with the Thomas relatives in Struthers, and shopping in Youngstown on Saturday. They would put on their gloves and hats, and Tammy would wear her little lace tops and patent leather shoes, and they would ride the bus downtown to West Federal Street, stop by the shoe store where Granny's sister Jesse worked, then have lunch at Woolworth's, shop for household things at McCrory's Five and Dime and meat at Huges's, look at clothes at Strouss's without spending, and buy a dress at Higbee's. Granny kept her money at Home Savings and Loan, but she didn't have a checking account, so they would also go downtown to pay the bills, stopping by the electric company, the gas company, the water company, the phone company.

At home in the kitchen Tammy would be under Granny's feet watching her cook collard greens fresh from the Thomas garden in Struthers. She loved being around older women and doing them little favors and listening to them. She realized from early on that they had wisdom to pass on to her. She wanted to grow up to be a nurse and take care of people.

Granny performed day work in a lot of white homes in Youngstown, but the family she was with longest was the Purnells, and by the end she was spending weeknights there. Sometimes Tammy went with Granny to work and cleaned the glass doorknobs with something Granny put on a rag, or squirted the clean laundry in a basket under Granny's ironing board. Once, when Vickie disappeared for a few days, Tammy stayed with Granny in the Purnell house, in her quarters up on the third floor. She watched Mrs. Purnell feed the squirrels out of her hand from the back porch, and Mrs. Purnell gave her a Mickey Mouse phone, and later a bedroom set.

Tammy was too young to know it, but the Purnells were one of the wealthiest and most prominent families in Youngstown. Anne Tod Purnell was a direct descendant of David Tod, founder of the first coal mine on Brier Hill, which in 1844 initiated iron manufacturing in the Mahoning Valley just in time for the Civil War, when Tod was elected governor of Ohio. Her husband, Frank Purnell, was chairman of the board of Dollar Savings Bank and, from 1930 to 1950, president of the Youngstown Sheet and Tube Company, the fifth-largest steelmaker in the country and the largest employer in the Valley. The Purnells lived in the upper-class district around Crandall Park on the north side, in a brick mansion at

280 Tod Lane, with seven bedrooms, four bathrooms, several fireplaces, a library, a ballroom, a conservatory, and a carriage house. They belonged to Youngstown's industrial Protestant elite in the middle of the twentieth century, when the city was at its zenith, an elite that had controlled Youngstown since the Civil War—controlled it to an extent that was unusual even for a small, landlocked, parochial steel town—and that was already fading by the time a black girl with roots in North Carolina was born on the east side in 1966. And yet Tammy had a living memory of it, in the Purnell mansion.

From the 1920s until 1977, twenty-five uninterrupted miles of steel mills ran northwest to southeast along the Mahoning River: from the Republic Steel plants around Warren and Niles, through the U.S. Steel plant in McDonald and the Youngstown Sheet and Tube blast furnaces on Brier Hill, to U.S. Steel's Ohio Works right in the middle of Youngstown, and on down to the sprawling Sheet and Tube plants in Campbell and Struthers. The blast furnaces ran twenty-four hours a day, and the wall of heat, the clang of metal and hiss of steam, the pervasive smell of sulfur dioxide, the smudged charcoal sky by day and hellish red glare by night, the soot-covered houses, the dead river, the packed taverns, the prayers to Saint Joseph the Provider, patron saint of workers, the rumble of train cars carrying iron ore and limestone and coal over dense networks of tracks through the city—all of it said that Youngstown was steel, nothing but steel, that everyone here owed life to the molten pour of iron shaped to human ends, that without it there was no life.

The city's industrial families—the Tods, Butlers, Stambaughs, Campbells, Wicks—made sure things stayed that way. They were the only elite that Youngstown produced, and they prevented other industries from taking hold and competing for its large immigrant workforce. Youngstown had two symphony orchestras, one made up entirely of steelworkers and their families. The city was prosperous and inward, isolated in a valley halfway between Cleveland and Pittsburgh. And, neighborhood by neighborhood, it was cut off from itself—Italians from Slovaks and Hungarians, native-born workers from foreigners, laborers from managers, blacks from everyone else.

Youngstown Sheet and Tube was the city's largest steelmaker to remain independent and locally owned, with four blast furnaces at the

Campbell Works and two at the Brier Hill Works just north of downtown. Sheet and Tube embodied the ferocity of industrial work in Youngstown—rapacious growth, brutal conditions, segregation of mill jobs by ethnicity and race, unalterable hostility to unions, constant strife. Frank Purnell started working at Sheet and Tube as a fifteen-year-old hall boy in the city office in 1902, two years after the company was founded. In 1911 he married Anne Tod, considerably improving his social position in Youngstown, and in the early twenties they built a grand house on Tod Lane. He rose through the ranks of Sheet and Tube to become president in 1930. In official portraits he wore the starched collar of his time, with a watch chain hanging from his suit vest—a hatchet-nosed man with a double chin, a tousle of silver hair, and the faint smile of imperturbable confidence that belonged to a secure capitalist class.

In the thirties, the old order began to give way. In 1936, John L. Lewis, the volcanic head of the mine workers' union and of the Committee for Industrial Organization, announced the formation of the Steel Workers Organizing Committee in a Pittsburgh skyscraper where the steel barons also had their offices; he placed his deputy, a mild Scotsman named Philip Murray, at its head. Lewis and Murray's aim was to achieve what no one had ever succeeded in doing: finally bring the workers of this giant industry under a union. Soon, organizers were driving into steel cities like Youngstown and talking with workers in ethnic clubs, churches, and meeting halls. But the thinking of the new industrial organizers was the opposite of parochial: they preached class consciousness above ethnicity, religion, race, and sex—not in the name of overthrowing capitalism, but in order to bring workers into the middle class, making them full-fledged members of an egalitarian democracy. Lewis's tactics were radical, but his goals were entirely within the American system.

In the spring of 1937, twenty-five thousand workers in the Mahoning Valley joined a national steel strike. Banned from the airwaves, they mounted loudspeakers on trucks and went neighborhood to neighborhood to announce the next meeting or picket. They also stockpiled baseball bats. Almost none of the strikers were black. In the past, black workers had been brought up from the South as strikebreakers, and for decades they were consigned to the dirtiest, most menial jobs in the mills, like scarfer—taking the defects out of the steel with a blowtorch. They shared a deep mutual wariness with their white coworkers, one that even the idealistic rhetoric of SWOC couldn't overcome.

It became known as the Little Steel strike. The organizers didn't target the behemoth U.S. Steel, which had already yielded to labor's economic power and recognized the union in March, having just the month before been given the object lesson of a successful sit-down strike by auto workers at General Motors plants in Flint, Michigan. Instead, SWOC went after a group of smaller companies, including Republic Steel, headquartered in Chicago, and Sheet and Tube. Unlike U.S. Steel, which was a national company with a larger sense of its role in a modern industrial society, the Little Steel companies were narrow in outlook and regarded unions with undiluted hatred. They kept the mills open by forming groups of "loyal employees," and they set up heavily armed private forces that were resupplied by air on landing strips built inside the gates.

Violence was inevitable. It came first in South Chicago, on Memorial Day, when police opened fire into the backs of a crowd of union sympathizers, killing ten men and wounding women and children. The following month it was Youngstown's turn, and on June 19, two strikers were killed outside the gate of a Republic Steel plant. Frances Perkins, President Roosevelt's secretary of labor, called for arbitration, but instead the owners asked for the mills to be protected by state troops. The governor of Ohio sent in the National Guard, the strike was broken, and the workers returned to their jobs. Altogether, seventeen people were killed in the Little Steel strike of 1937. The public began to turn against labor's new militancy, and in the short run the companies won.

But the defeat of 1937 led to victory in 1942, when the National Labor Relations Board ruled that Republic and Sheet and Tube had used illegal tactics to crush the strike. The companies were forced to recognize SWOC and enter collective bargaining. Youngstown became a solidly union city, just as World War II was beginning, bringing with it the economic security that workers had always craved—even, as the years went by, for black workers. The mill was hot, filthy, body- and soul-crushing, but its wages and pensions came to represent the golden age of American economic life.

Frank Purnell continued to run Youngstown Sheet and Tube after the war, speaking the new institutional language of labor-management relations, while the old class conflicts remained alive. In 1950, he stepped down as president and became chairman of the board, and in 1953 he died of a cerebral hemorrhage. His widow, Anne, lived on for almost two more decades in the mansion at 280 Tod Lane—years when most of the

other elite families sold their mills and left Youngstown for more cosmo-
politan, better-smelling locales. The steel companies continued to keep
out other industries that might have competed for Youngstown's labor
force. In the fifties, when Henry Ford II was exploring the possibility of
opening an auto plant on a railroad scrap yard north of the city, local industrialists and absentee-owned corporations threw up enough obstacles
to kill the idea. In 1950, Edward DeBartolo built one of the country's
first strip malls out in Boardman, and the growth of shopping plazas
began to sap the commercial heart of town. White workers moved to the
suburbs for work in lighter industry, opening up good jobs in the steel
mills for the first time to the black workers who stayed behind. As transportation costs rose, the geography of American steelmaking moved
to deepwater ports like Cleveland, Gary, Baltimore, and Chicago, and
Youngstown's steel industry stagnated while foreign competition began to
catch up.

Finally, in 1969, Youngstown Sheet and Tube—by then the country's
eighth-largest steelmaker, and the last one in the city to remain locally
owned—was sold to Lykes Corporation, a New Orleans–based shipbuild-
ing conglomerate, which planned to pull money out of its new acquisition,
using the company's cash flow to pay down debt and expand other operations, eventually cutting its dividend and dropping "Youngstown" from its
name. So by the early 1970s, though no one knew it yet, the city was already in a state of decline.

The Purnells had no children, and the widow lived alone, except for
her sister, Lena, and also an aging colored maid named Virginia. After the
sister died, and Mrs. Purnell fell and broke her hip on her way to tend the
furnace in the carriage house, the maid began staying overnight Mondays
through Fridays and became Mrs. Purnell's companion. Anne Tod Purnell died in 1971. During the months when the disposition of the estate
remained uncertain, the maid was brought to live in the mansion as a care-
taker, along with her granddaughter and five-year-old great-granddaughter.

Tammy couldn't remember how long they lived in the Purnell mansion,
but at the time it felt like forever. When they moved there, the tulips and
rose garden were in bloom, and Tammy started kindergarten there, and
they celebrated Christmas there. When they arrived, some of the furniture
was being taken out of the house, and all the beautiful rugs were gone

from the great foyer. Soon after that, the living room furniture disappeared, and at Christmas the dining room table was gone, and then someone tore out the chandelier that had hung in the dining room, leaving exposed wires, which outraged Granny. Piece by piece the estate was dismantled before the sale of the house. Mrs. Purnell's driver was given her car, and the gardener and household staff, Granny included, received five thousand dollars each. Tammy's mother kept Mrs. Purnell's silver-framed mirror and silver hairbrush. At Christmas Tammy got a bicycle, and she learned to ride it in the empty living room.

The house was bigger and fancier than anything she could imagine. There were so many places to hide, and flowers she'd never seen before in the garden, and a front-loading washing machine in one of the seven rooms in the basement, nickel-plated counters in the kitchen, and a buzzer on the dining room floor to call servants. Tammy, who wasn't supposed to play in that part of the house, once stepped on it and scared herself when the thing went off. Her favorite room was Miss Lena's old bedroom on the second floor, with a back porch. It was painted green, like the rest of the house, except for Miss Lena's long bathroom, which had gold-colored tiles and a stand-up shower that was amber. They shared the bathroom with Tammy's mother when she was there, but Vickie didn't like being in the big empty house—she believed that it was haunted. Tammy found a hoop slip in an old trunk, with wire rings and ruffles, and she would put it on and twirl around the third-floor ballroom the way she imagined people dancing in an earlier time. She descended the grand stairway like a princess, and she performed shows on the circular patio for an audience of bushes. Granny kept her close to the house, forbidding her to leave the yard or climb the big tree, which she did anyway. On weekends they walked down to Crandall Park and fed the swans.

The adventure ended in early 1972, around Tammy's sixth birthday, when a family bought the mansion. Granny was allowed to take some surviving furniture and dishes, including Mrs. Purnell's handmade bed and dressing table, white with gold trim. She and Tammy returned to the east side, and with her bequest Granny made a down payment on a wood-frame house at 1319 Charlotte Avenue, which she bought for ten thousand dollars. And it was there that Tammy lived, almost continuously, until she was twenty-six.

She attended a series of schools named after presidents—Lincoln, Madison, Grant, Wilson; not one of them would escape the wrecking ball. In class pictures she was the thin, light-skinned girl in pigtails, with soft, expectant eyes, as if something good was about to happen. She loved going to the old amusement park at Idora and riding the Wildcat roller coaster, but her favorite place in the city was Mill Creek Park, eight hundred acres of woods and ponds and gardens on the border of the south and west sides. From the northern end of the park you could see the steel mills and train tracks, but you could also scramble over rocks, lose yourself on the trails, and talk to yourself and God. Granny sometimes took her there, or she would go with the Pearl Street Mission, where she was sent after school. At the mission, which was near her house on the east side, the kids would scoop out the insides of oranges, fill them with peanut butter, poke a hole in the rind, thread a piece of yarn through it, then hang the oranges from trees in Mill Creek Park for the birds—though Tammy never saw a bird eating peanut butter out of an orange. If she could live anywhere in the city, it would have been near the park.

The first time Vickie was locked up, Tammy was in second grade. She was taken to visit her mother in the county jail and told that she was on vacation there. A year or two later, her mother went away to the penitentiary for a longer stay. This time no one told Tammy where her mother was, and she didn't ask, but one day on the school bus an older girl from the neighborhood taunted Tammy, saying her mother was in jail. "No she's not," Tammy said, "she's on vacation," but the girl kept it up, until they started fighting and were thrown off the bus. When Granny got home from work, she told Tammy where her mother was, and Tammy became upset. But the day her mother came home from the penitentiary, Tammy was so happy that it didn't matter. Vickie had gained a little weight in jail, and she had pretty hair and pretty legs and a beautiful smile, and Tammy thought she was the most beautiful black woman she'd ever seen.

During Tammy's childhood her mother was in and out of jail for drugs, check fraud, even aggravated robbery. When Vickie was trying to get off heroin, she would take Tammy with her to a brick building called Buddha, on the south side, where she would drink methadone from a little cup, and Tammy wanted to taste it but her mother would never allow it. She often ran out of food, so that Tammy had to learn to shop with coupons and bag up food in individual meals for the week. More than once Vickie left her alone somewhere and didn't come back, and the time Tammy saw her overdose she wondered why her mommy didn't love her enough to stop using. She thought that if she could just make her mommy love her a little more, then she would stop. "My mother put me in some really jacked-up situations as a kid," she said later. "There were times she would just leave me, and I went through some things that I really repressed, but at the end of the day none of that mattered because she was my mom. And I loved her to pieces. I loved the ground she walked on. She was my mother."

But it was her great-grandmother who shaped Tammy. Granny, with her crappy maid's job, cooking and cleaning past retirement age, had bought a house—not the best house, but it was hers. Tammy's father's mother was the same way—she was a nurse's aide at St. Elizabeth's Hospital and always came home worn out in her starched white uniform, worked until she almost died of cancer, but she saved enough money to buy a house and get out of the projects. Those women did what they were supposed to do. Tammy was that kind of person—it was programmed into her. Maybe it came from Papa Thomas, who had owned all that land in Struthers and given a piece of it to the church.

After Granny stopped working they lived on her Social Security and Vickie's welfare checks, and there was so little money that sometimes the gas was shut off. When her father and grandmother were still living in the West Lake projects, north of downtown, Tammy sometimes visited them, and when she was a little older she had friends living in the east side projects, generation after generation on welfare who never got out. They could buy things only at the start of the month, when stores raised prices to take advantage of the checks. Even if they got on a program to pay their gas bill they would always owe, they'd die owing that money. Tammy vowed to herself that she would not go on welfare and live in the projects. She didn't want to have just enough to barely get by but not enough to actually be able to do anything. She didn't want to get stuck.

When Tammy was in fifth grade, her mother got together with a man named Wilkins, whom Tammy thought of as her stepfather. Tammy had to leave her granny's house and go live with her mother and stepfather on the lower south side, which was the black part of the south side, in a house with several apartments where her stepfather's cousin lived. Their apartment was on the attic floor, and it had only one bedroom; Tammy's room was actually a closet, with hardly enough room to stand, and they shared a bathroom on the floor below with several other apartments. On Charlotte she had had her own large bedroom, with twin beds from

Mrs. Purnell. But she was okay with it—she was fine. During this period Tammy's mother was clean. Her stepfather had a good job at the mill, but he never had money and they were as poor as ever. Tammy played flute in the orchestra throughout elementary school, but when her new school started charging rent for musical instruments, she had to quit. She went back to Granny's every weekend.

It was while she was living on the south side that Youngstown entered its death spiral.

On Monday, September 19, 1977, Lykes Corporation of New Orleans announced that it would close Sheet and Tube's Campbell Works, the largest mill in the Mahoning Valley, by the end of the week. There had been no advance word—the decision had been made the day before, at the Pittsburgh airport, where corporate board members flew in, voted, and then flew back home to New Orleans or Chicago. Five thousand people would lose their jobs, including Tammy's godmother, who had only nine or ten years in, not enough for retirement, and had bought a house and was raising her kids by herself. In Youngstown, that day became known as Black Monday.

No one saw it coming. In the recollections she jotted down in a notebook years later, Tammy's friend Miss Sybil wrote:

Mills closed
City started to decline as though a cancer was slowly killing it.
Decline started slowly at first as though people were in state of shock.

There had been warning signs but they were ignored. Profits had been declining, though not sharply, and the absentee steel corporations had not reinvested in the mills. Instead, they cannibalized machines and parts, moving them from one mill to another—World War I technology, not a single new blast furnace in Youngstown since 1921. Youngstown steel became the weak man in the industry, first to close and last to reopen during slowdowns. The United Steel Workers union was focused on contract disputes—cost of living allowances, pensions—not the overall health of the companies. The union system in the mills made room for everyone and took care of everyone, as long as you showed up and acted responsible.

If a worker lost his hand in a crane accident, he got a job as a bell ringer on the hot-metal cart. Their hard-won security had the workers lulled to sleep, even when they went on strike. A month before Black Monday, the United Steel Workers district manager in Youngstown called local union leaders into his mahogany-paneled office near the Campbell Works to assure them that everything was going to be all right.

One of those leaders was Gerald Dickey. The son of a steelworker, in 1968 he got a job at Sheet and Tube straight out of the air force. Some workers showed up with stainless steel lunch buckets and Stanley thermoses, meaning they were in till retirement, but Dickey was a brown-paper-bag guy, eight hours at a time. "I didn't go there saying, 'I want to do this for thirty years.' I wanted to make some money." He started at $3.25 an hour, and within a year he had a car, and the desire to leave started to fade. "Something happens when you've been there two years—your health insurance goes up. Three years, your vacation goes up. This great big security blanket wraps around you. That's the way they trapped you into those industrial jobs." A black guy in Dickey's local named Granison Trimiar said, "Once you had that Sheet and Tube pay stub, you could go downtown, get you a refrigerator, get you anything—your credit was good. And you could get into the nightclubs."

Throughout the seventies, smaller factories in the Valley—joist plants, structural steel manufacturers, industrial bakeries, Isaly's dairy—kept closing, like tremors preceding a massive quake. But no one imagined that Sheet and Tube would go down overnight. When it happened, there was no local industrialist, no member of the Youngstown elite, no powerful institution or organization, to step in and try to stop it. The steel barons were long gone, local businesses had no clout, city politicians were fractious and corrupt, the Youngstown *Vindicator* resorted to shallow optimism. The city had no civic core to rally around. The one glimmer of hope came a few days after Black Monday, at a meeting of local clergymen and militant steelworkers. Gerald Dickey, by then the secretary of Local 1462, got up and said, "Let's buy the damned thing and run it ourselves." He saw that food stamps and unemployment benefits weren't going to get the workers through the crisis, that without those jobs the community would never be the same. The city's Episcopal and Catholic bishops agreed, and the Ecumenical Coalition of the Mahoning Valley was born.

The crusade was named Save Our Valley, and the idea was to pool enough money from local savings accounts and federal grants and loan guarantees to bring the Campbell Works under community ownership. This was something new in the industrial heartland, and for a few months it caught people's imaginations. The Mahoning Valley became a cause célèbre among liberals and radicals. Famous activists came to Youngstown to help and the national media came to watch. Five busloads of steelworkers went to Washington to protest outside the White House, and the Carter administration accepted their petition and formed a task force to study the issue. But the local response was halfhearted—meetings were poorly attended, with no more than a hundred people showing up. Save Our Valley bank accounts raised just a few million dollars, while making the mills viable would have cost at least half a billion. The steel companies actively lobbied against local ownership, and the United Steel Workers never got behind an idea that was highly risky and sounded too much like socialism. Even some workers who had lost their jobs were tepid. If they were fifty-five and had their years, they could retire on a full pension, while the younger guys started leaving the area. Finally, a study at Harvard found that even a billion dollars in subsidies wouldn't be enough to renovate the mills and make them competitive. The federal government—the essential institution for keeping the industry alive— bowed out, and the fate of the mills was sealed.

If the institutions and the people who led them had understood what was about to happen to Youngstown, and then to the wider region, they might have worked out a policy to manage deindustrialization instead of simply allowing it to happen. Over the next five years, every major steel plant in Youngstown shut down: Sheet and Tube's Brier Hill Works in 1980, U.S. Steel's Ohio Works in 1980, its McDonald Mills in 1981, Republic Steel in 1982. And not just the mills. Higbee's and Strouss's, two of the shopping mainstays downtown, soon closed. Idora, the amusement park on the south side that dated back to 1899, went into a swift decline, before the Wildcat roller coaster caught fire in 1984, which closed Idora down; its spectacular carousel was auctioned off and ended up on the Brooklyn waterfront. Between 1979 and 1980, bankruptcies in Youngstown doubled, and in 1982, unemployment in the Mahoning Valley reached almost 22 percent—the highest anywhere in the country. Black workers, who had only recently entered the better mill jobs, were hit especially

hard. Houses on the east side, parts of the south side, and even Smokey
Hollow on the edge of downtown emptied out with foreclosures and
white flight. The vacancies began an epidemic of house burnings, two or
more incidents a day throughout the eighties. On the wall by the pay phone
at Cyrak's, a well-known mob bar, there was a number you could call to
have a house torched at less than half the cost of having it demolished by
the city. But during a decade of hundreds of arson fires, only two people
were convicted of anything—a black woman who killed her two children
in an insurance fire, and the city official in charge of demolitions, who
used the mob to get the job done. Between 1970 and 1990, the city's population fell from 140,000 to 95,000, with no end in sight.

John Russo, a former auto worker from Michigan and professor of
labor studies, started teaching at Youngstown State University in 1980.
When he arrived, he could look down almost every city street straight into
a mill and the fire of a blast furnace. He came just in time to watch the
steel industry vanish before his eyes. Russo calculated that during the decade between 1975 and 1985, fifty thousand jobs were lost in the Mahoning Valley—an economic catastrophe on an unheard-of scale. Yet, Russo
said, "The idea that this was systemic didn't occur." As a resident expert,
he would get a call from *Time* or *Newsweek* every six months, with a reporter on the line asking if Youngstown had turned the corner yet. Apparently it was impossible to imagine that so much machinery and so many
men were no longer needed.

It was happening in Cleveland, Toledo, Akron, Buffalo, Syracuse, Pittsburgh, Bethlehem, Detroit, Flint, Milwaukee, Chicago, Gary, St. Louis,
and other cities across a region that in 1983 was given a new name: the Rust
Belt. But it happened in Youngstown first, fastest, and most completely,
and because Youngstown had nothing else, no major-league baseball team
or world-class symphony, the city became an icon of deindustrialization, a
song title, a cliché. "It was one of the quietest revolutions we've ever had,"
Russo said. "If a plague had taken away this many people in the Midwest,
it would be considered a huge historical event." But because it was caused
by the loss of blue-collar jobs, not a bacterial infection, Youngstown's demise was regarded as almost normal.

Tammy was eleven when the mills started closing. She was too young to
know or care about Steeltown, the historic strikes, deindustrialization, or

the specter of a whole city's ruin. She had her hands full surviving her own life. The year after Black Monday, she moved back with her mother and stepfather to the east side. Officially, she lived with them in a house on Bruce Street, but in fact she was staying with Granny again on Charlotte. The summer after she returned, their front door was stolen—it was a solid oak antique, with a glass oval—along with the ornamental cut-glass windows that surrounded it. A few of their neighbors' houses got hit by the same thieves. Granny couldn't afford to replace it, so they boarded up the front door and for several years they went in and out the back door. There were times when Tammy was too embarrassed to have friends visit.

The theft of the door marked a turning point that she would often refer to in later years, a sign that the family's struggles were becoming part of something larger. The mob no longer had control of the streets (even though Cyrak's wasn't far from Charlotte Avenue), and the neighborhood was getting bad. By the midseventies most of the white families had moved out of the east side, and Black Monday finished the exit. When Miss Sybil had graduated from East High School in 1964, the majority of the student body was white, and after her class elected a black girl as homecoming queen, a white teacher overruled the vote, saying "It's not time yet." But with every year of the seventies, Tammy's class photo had one or two fewer white kids, until, by the time she entered high school in 1980, East was almost all black and Puerto Rican. The high school was within walking distance of Charlotte Avenue, but in ninth grade Tammy was bused to Wilson High on the south side for racial balance. Her best friend, Gwen, was the only other black kid in math class, and the teacher would totally ignore them when they had their hands up. She missed being at a predominantly black school, so in tenth grade she transferred to East.

She took on bigger responsibilities at home, learning to do simple repairs, taking the bus to shop for groceries and pay the bills. Eventually, Granny turned over ownership of the house to her with a quitclaim deed. The roles were reversed: now she was taking care of Granny.

And then, when she was fifteen, she got pregnant.

She wrote a letter to her mother and mailed it, even though her mother lived three blocks away, because she was too frightened to tell her face-to-face. When the conversation came, her mother got angry and demanded, "Do you want to get rid of it? How are you going to take care of it?" Tammy said that she would take care of her baby, period. The father was a debonair-looking boy, a year older, named Barry. His mother had been Vickie's probation officer, and she thought the Thomas girl so unsuitable for her son that she called up Tammy's father's mother and told her that Barry couldn't be the one. But Tammy was in love with him, and she told her mother so.

"It's just puppy love," Vickie said.

Tammy insisted, "No, Mommy, I love him."

"It'll change."

She and her mother had never talked about sex, even though Vickie was about to conceive her third son in four years by Tammy's stepfather (Tammy would be due five months sooner). When Vickie was in sixth or seventh grade, Big Mama had told her that babies came from under rocks and she had believed it, which was the sum of her education on the subject. Granny wasn't about to offer any information, either.

The worst moment came when Tammy had to tell Granny. Tammy couldn't remember her great-grandmother crying when Big Mama died, but she cried when she heard Tammy's news, and that hurt Tammy to her core. Years later, she understood: no one in the family had ever graduated from high school, and Tammy was supposed to be the first. "Here's another one that is not going to graduate," Tammy said. "Granny was saying that she's worked, scrubbed floors, cooked people's food, spent time away from her family, and what mattered most for her is that I was educated and had a home, and that hadn't happened yet. We had a home but nobody was getting educated." Tammy's father stormed into the house on Charlotte and told her, "You're never going to be anything but a welfare bitch."

A resolve formed in Tammy then. She wouldn't end up like those girls in the projects, and she wouldn't end up like her mother. She would stay in school and start taking it seriously—she had been a mediocre student, but now she was going to work at it—and then she was going to find a good job (nursing wasn't realistic anymore, not with her grades in chemistry), because her child was going to have a much better life than she did, better than her baby brothers, with a mother who took care of her. She had something to prove now, not just to her father and them, but to herself.

The baby girl was born on May 9, 1982. Barry didn't show up when he was supposed to sign the birth certificate, and Tammy learned that he was fooling around with other girls. They quarreled, and she refused to see him anymore. She went back to school in time to take her finals. A few months later, she ran into Barry at the West Lake projects, where she had a summer job as a day camp counselor. He was standing in line at the community center for some sort of giveaway with one of his girlfriends, who was pregnant. That broke Tammy's heart—but it was okay, it was all right, she knew she'd rebound. She stopped going to church because her situation was considered shameful. When Barry tried to get back together with her, she turned him away. "This is not your job," she told him. "She's not yours. You didn't sign the birth certificate." She didn't want her daughter to grow up like her, having a tumultuous relationship with a man who never seemed to care about her. She wanted her daughter to be loved and wanted by everyone around her. She and the baby were on their own, while everything on the east side went to hell.

Tammy got off her mother's check and signed up for her own. She hated being on welfare—the agency workers were nasty—but she needed it to pay for food and child care. She finished high school on time, in 1984, and became the first person in her family to get a diploma. The feminine style of her senior year recalled the forties, with the girls in their yearbook pictures arranging their hair and dress and lipstick like Billie Holiday. Tammy posed in a gray felt hat with a black ribbon and a mesh veil, but the look in her eyes told of the life that had intervened since she was a girl in pigtails.

She got an associate's degree at a technical college and worked for two years as a supermarket cashier in the hope that she'd get a management job, but none opened up. She had two more children, both by a man named Jordan: a boy in 1985 and another girl in 1987. She was always careful with money—now that she could drive, she shopped in the suburbs, where prices were lower, and she bought the kids' Christmas presents on layaway, securing the gifts at the store with a deposit until she could pay in full. But with three kids, Granny, and the house on Charlotte to take care of, she had to find more secure work.

By the late eighties, Youngstown was building a museum to its industrial history, designed by the architect Michael Graves in the shape of a steel mill, with stylized smokestacks. But up in Warren, the Packard Electric plants were still operating, with eight thousand workers making wiring harnesses and electrical components for General Motors cars. It was lighter, cleaner work than steelmaking, and two-thirds of the employees were women, a lot of them single mothers like Tammy. She went in to interview and was hired for the assembly line at $7.30 an hour. So in 1988 she got off welfare and became a factory worker.

HER OWN:
OPRAH WINFREY

She was so big that she owned the letter O. She was the richest black woman in the world—*in the world*—but she remained Everywoman and made that her theme song. Five afternoons a week, forty million Americans in at least 138 markets (and millions more viewers in 145 countries) laughed and wept and gasped and gossiped and wished and celebrated with her. Being a billionaire only made her more beloved. She was still just like them, she knew them, came from them, from below them, and she made millions of women feel they were not alone. What they felt she felt, and what she felt they felt (and how you felt about yourself was the most important thing). When she learned to go with her heart, they learned to go with theirs, and when she learned to say no and not feel guilty about it even though it meant people wouldn't like her (which was her greatest achievement), they learned to do the same thing. She wanted to get the whole country reading again. She wanted to destroy the welfare mentality and lift a hundred families out of the Chicago projects. She wanted to lead a national conversation about race and heal the wounds of slavery with a movie, because, she said, "Everything is about imagery." She wanted to help people live their best lives. She wanted her studio audiences to get their favorite things every Christmas (Sony 52-inch 3-D HDTVs, Pontiac G6s, Royal Caribbean cruises). She wanted to open a door so that her viewers could see themselves more clearly, to be the light to get them to God, or whatever else they called it. She wanted them to have it all, like her.

She exalted openness and authenticity, but she could afford them on her own terms. Anyone allowed into her presence had to sign away freedom of speech for life. She bought the rights to every photograph of herself and threatened to sue anyone who infringed the inviolability of her image. She withdrew her autobiography just weeks before publication after friends warned that it revealed too much about some parts of her life even as it falsified others. Her face underwent drastic alterations year by year.

"According to the laws of the Universe, I am not likely to get mugged, because I am helping people be all that they can be," she said. "A black person has to ask herself, 'If Oprah Winfrey can make it, what does it say about me?' They no longer have any excuse," she said. "Harriet Tubman, Sojourner Truth, Fannie Lou Hamer are all a part of me. I've always felt that my life is their life fulfilled. They never dreamed it could be this good. I still feel they're all with me, going, 'Go, girl. Go for it,'" she said. "I feel tremendously powerful because I do believe I have reached a point in life where my personality is aligned with what my soul came to do," she said. "I'm the kind of person who can get along with anyone. I have a fear of being disliked, even by people I dislike," she said. "Doing talk shows is like breathing to me," she said. "I stopped wanting to be white when I was ten years old and saw Diana Ross and the Supremes perform on *The Ed Sullivan Show*," she said. "Nobody had any clue that my life could be anything but working in some factory or a cotton field in Mississippi," she said. "I was just a poor little ole nappy-headed colored chile."

The yellow brick road of blessings that led to the purple fields of her vast empire (Harpo Productions, Harpo Studios, Harpo Films, *The Oprah Winfrey Show*, Oprah Winfrey Network, *O: The Oprah Magazine*—her picture on every cover—*O at Home*, The Oprah Radio Network, Oprah and Friends, Oprah's Studio Merchandise, The Oprah Store, Oprah Winfrey's Boutique, Oprah's Book Club, Oprah's Favorite Things, Oprah's Big Give, the Oprah Winfrey Leadership Academy for Girls, Oprah's Angel Network, oprah.com) began on a farm in the middle of Mississippi in 1954. Her name was a misspelling of the biblical Orpah. For the first six years she was raised by her grandmother, Hattie Mae Lee, a cook and housekeeper who was the granddaughter of slaves, and her grandfather, Earlist, who scared her to death. They were so poor that she never wore a store-bought dress, and her only pets were a pair of cockroaches in a jar. At least, that was what she would tell interviewers. Her family would say that she was stretching it to make a better story, that she was provided for and doted on, that her self-confidence came from those years.

When Oprah was six, her grandmother could no longer care for her, so she was sent to Milwaukee to live in a rooming house with her mother. Vernita Lee worked as a maid, bore two more children by two more fathers, and went on welfare. Mother and daughter didn't get along, and

Oprah grew up a wild child to the sounds of Motown, stealing her mother's cash, promiscuous at thirteen, doing "the Horse" with young men for money, her sister would later say, while Vernita was at work. But she also attracted the attention of white authority figures who admired her bookishness, her theatrical voice, and her drive and wanted to promote her. At fourteen she was sent to Nashville to live under the Christian discipline of her father, Vernon Winfrey, a barber (it turned out that Vernon couldn't have been her father—she never learned who was). In Nashville, as in Milwaukee, she had better relations with white people than with her own family, and later she would say that she never felt oppressed except by black people who disliked her very dark skin or envied her success.

She quit Tennessee State before graduating and went to work at a local TV station. When she got a job on an evening newscast in Baltimore in 1976, she was going to be the black Barbara Walters, or Mary Tyler Moore. But she couldn't write copy, and she was too breezy and uninformed for news, so they moved her over to the morning talk show. It was a comedown in her own eyes, but she became a local star. She was so likable, so funny, wearing her heart on her sleeve, asking the juicy, borderline-rude questions that the audience wanted asked (Did it bother Frank Perdue when people said he looked like a chicken?). At the end of 1983, WLS in Chicago offered her a two-hundred-thousand-dollar job on its morning show.

She was a figure of the eighties and Chicago, the center of a new black elite. When she arrived, Harold Washington had just been elected mayor, Jesse Jackson was beginning his first presidential campaign, Michael Jordan was about to be drafted by the Bulls. There was a quote taped to Oprah's mirror that she attributed to Jackson: "If my mind can conceive it, and my heart can believe it, I know I can achieve it." Empowerment, entrepreneurship, the self-made celeb, wealth as the ultimate and inevitable emblem of worth—that was her ethos (she had hated Black Power at Tennessee State in the early seventies, didn't care about politics at all). They said an overweight black talk show host would never make it in racist Chicago, but it took exactly a week for her to kick Phil Donahue's butt in the ratings, and within a year he moved his show to New York. She knew what the mostly white, suburban, stay-at-home moms in her viewing audience wanted, and she wasn't afraid to get down and dirty—"Men Who Rape and Treatment for Rapists," "Housewife Prostitutes," "Man-Stealing Relatives," "I Want My Abused Kids Back." She wasn't afraid of racists or baby killers or the profoundly handicapped. She could dish, she could empathize, she could mock herself, she could say *penis* on the air (*vajayjay* would take two more decades).

And on the morning of December 5, 1985, during a show about incest, she stood by with the microphone as a white, late-middle-aged, conservatively dressed, nearly inaudible woman in the audience confessed that her son was her father's child, and the young, dark, heavy, puff-haired host with the giant bronze earrings suddenly asked for a commercial break, hid her own crumpling face with her hand, cried into the woman's shoulder, wrapped her arms around the woman for comfort, and said, "The same thing happened to me." She had been molested by various male relatives almost continuously from ages nine to fourteen. (Five years later, the world learned that at fourteen Oprah had borne a son who died after five weeks. Her drug-addicted sister sold the story to a tabloid for nineteen thousand dollars.)

Letters poured in, the switchboard was overloaded, ratings soared. She had broken the silence for millions of women, and in that moment Oprah Winfrey became Oprah—Everywoman battling and overcoming victimhood, girlfriend of everyone watching the show. Fame and money were not enough: to be Oprah, she had to find the secret path to the hidden wound inside every member of her vast and isolated audience. Then her greatness could be theirs, too. Her material and spiritual success were not a privilege that set her apart but the mark of triumph over suffering that connected her to every one of them. She invited them into her life through her public struggles with the pounds, which she kept taking off and putting on again, like so many women (she ate the way she spent and gave, impulsively and lavishly), and the wedding to Stedman Graham, postponed year after year (but he was perfect for her: tall, handsome, light-skinned, boring, a corporate marketing executive, author of *You Can Make It Happen* and *Build Your Own Life Brand*).

Her bond with her viewers was unbreakable. Many of them had never had a black person in their living room before, except on a sitcom, and she made them less lonely, more tolerant and open, more curious about books and ideas, while they made her unimaginably rich. As she got bigger and bigger, from $100 million a year to $260 million, from $725 million net worth to $1.5 billion, from "Unforgivable Acts Between Couples" and "Women Who Are Allergic to Their Husbands" to "Change Your Life" and "The Seat of the Soul," from Laurie the abuse victim to Maya Angelou the abuse victim, she never lost the love of her audience. As she spent more and more of her on-camera time with her friends Tom and Julia and Diane and Toni and Maria and Arnold and Barack and Michelle, celebrities celebrating celebrity, her most loyal friends were still her seven million day-in-day-out viewers. As the end of a typical day had her flying back from Rancho La Puerta to Chicago on her private jet ("It's great to have a private jet. Anyone that tells you that having your own private jet isn't great is lying") to attend Stedman's book party on the top floor of Michael Jordan's restaurant, arriving in a state of rage because the *National Enquirer* had just published unauthorized photos of the ornate marble, satin, velvet, and silk furnishings in her lakefront condo, her most ardent supporters remained the aging lower-middle-class women from Rockford and Eau Claire who lined up for hours outside Harpo Studios on the Near West Side.

They had things that she didn't—children, debts, spare time. They consumed the products that she advertised but would never buy—Maybelline, Jenny Craig, Little Caesar's, IKEA. As their financial troubles grew, she would thrill them by selecting one of them and wiping out her debts on the air or buying her a house, or ramping up Oprah's Favorite Things at Christmas to give away luxury items like diamond watches and Tory Burch gray flannel totes. But being instructed in Oprah's magical thinking (vaccinations cause autism; positive thoughts lead to wealth, love, and success), and watching Oprah always doing more, owning more, not all her viewers began to live their best life. They didn't have nine houses, or maybe any house; they couldn't call John Travolta their friend; the laws of the universe left them vulnerable to mugging; they were not always attuned to their divine self; they were never all that they could be. And since there was no random suffering in life, Oprah left them with no excuse.

JEFF CONNAUGHTON

In 1987 the revolving door that was supposed to send Wall Street bankers into high-level positions at Treasury landed Connaughton a junior staff job on the Biden for President campaign, at twenty-four thousand dollars a year. He traded his brand-new Peugeot for his parents' 1976 Chevy Malibu because he could no longer afford the lease payments. That was all right with him.

His first assignment, before he'd even left Atlanta, was to find twenty people in Georgia to write the campaign a two-hundred-fifty-dollar check. Do that in twenty states, and the candidate qualified for federal matching funds. It was one of the hardest things Connaughton had ever done, but the fear of failing spurred him, and he begged everyone he knew in Georgia to write a check. He succeeded, and in the process he learned how fundraising worked: you didn't have to convince anyone that Biden was going to win, or even that he was right on the issues—only that *you* needed this, as a favor. "Do it for me." What mattered was who did the calling. But when he asked the ex-girlfriend who'd been a member of Phi Mu and now lived in Georgia, she refused: she'd heard, thirdhand, that Biden "would sell his own grandmother to be president."

It was the first post-Reagan election. Like every campaign, Biden's was chaotic and sleepless, fueled by improvisation and junk food: we don't know what you'll be doing, just show up in three days. In March, Connaughton rented a room outside Washington in Alexandria, Virginia, in the house of an official with the potato chip trade association, only to learn upon arrival that he would not be working in the campaign's Washington offices, but out of Wilmington, Delaware. Biden for President occupied a huge empty store in a downscale office complex on the edge of town, with dozens of desks stretching out across a blue carpet. The path to the White House had been climbed from less glamorous base camps.

Connaughton's success at dialing up checks in Georgia meant that he would be a fundraiser. It sure as hell wasn't politics as he'd imagined it the night of Biden's speech in Tuscaloosa, but he was determined to be a good soldier. "Just tell me where to go," he said. He was given a desk and began working twelve-hour days, commuting two hours each way from Virginia, eventually spending Tuesday through Thursday nights at a Days Inn near the office.

Connaughton worked under Ted Kaufman, Biden's veteran chief of staff, an El Greco beanpole with an elongated jaw and a dome of curly hair. Kaufman stood in the innermost Biden circle, and when the senator's sister, Valerie, introduced Kaufman to Jeff, she said, "You're lucky to be working for Ted, he's so close to Joe he doesn't have to worry." Connaughton wished he'd had the presence of mind to ask, "Do people worry? Could you please elaborate on that in a couple of paragraphs?" The implication was pretty clear: "You, on the other hand, ought to be really worried because you don't have any kind of relationship with Biden, and Bidenland is strewn with mines, some marked, others not."

Kaufman and Connaughton hit it off. They were both MBAs and decided to run the fundraising operation like a company. Connaughton helped draft the strategic plan, constructing an organizational pyramid of captains and subcaptains. The more money the subcaptains raised, the more access to Biden their captain received. Connaughton kept track of the contest and decided who got a lapel pin, who got dinner with the candidate. He also set up a system for contributors. If one of them wanted to see Biden, he needed to donate at least a thousand dollars. Connaughton would tell big-time donors, "For fifty thousand dollars I can get you dinner with the senator at his house. For twenty-five thousand I can get you dinner with the senator, but not at his house." And some of the check writers would cough up the extra twenty-five just to be able to tell their friends, "I had dinner with Joe at his house in Wilmington."

After Gary Hart was caught fooling around with Donna Rice on board the *Monkey Business* and became the year's first victim of scandal and media frenzy, Biden became a strong contender for the nomination. Connaughton worked all day at his desk in the giant blue-carpeted room, took no breaks, drove back to Alexandria at midnight, fell into bed exhausted, then woke up in the morning and headed back to Wilmington to do it again, thinking: "I am living my purpose right now."

One day that spring, Biden showed up at the Wilmington office, looking great in a turtleneck and aviator sunglasses. He greeted the campaign workers—many of whom had been with him since he was first elected to the Senate at the age of twenty-nine, in 1972—and gave them a brief pep talk about the progress of the campaign. It was six years since Connaughton had last seen Biden in Alabama, all those unanswered letters ago. If Biden recognized him, he gave no indication. As the senator turned to go, Connaughton imagined running to catch up, standing in his path, declaring: "I invited you down to the University of Alabama three times. The last time, I promised you I'd help you become president. Here I am." Instead, he went back to his desk.

Connaughton rose in the ranks, putting together fifty-thousand-dollar fundraisers with trial lawyers and the Jewish community in southern cities. He started traveling with the candidate, and if the plane was delayed, or if on arrival Biden talked too long or not long enough, Connaughton caught the flak from donors. He and Biden never spoke.

One day, on a flight to a fundraiser in Houston, Connaughton was told to brief Biden about the event. He carried the briefing book up the aisle to the first-class cabin where Biden was sitting with his wife, Jill.

"Senator, can I speak with you for a minute?" Connaughton asked.

"Just gimme what you got," Biden said, hardly looking up.

Biden apparently didn't remember Alabama. Long after Connaughton went to work for him, his boss would butcher the original connection, saying, "I'm glad I met you when you were in law school all those years ago." Biden always had time for strangers, especially if they bore any relation to Delaware. If you were family, or part of a small circle of long-serving aides, like Kaufman, and you "bled Biden blue," as the senator liked to say, then he was intensely loyal. But if you just worked your ass off for him for a few years, he ignored you, intimidated you, sometimes humiliated you, took no interest in your advancement, and never learned your name. "Hey, Chief," he'd say, or "How's it going, Cap'n," unless he was ticked off at you, in which case he'd employ one of his favorite terms for male underlings: "dumb fuck." "Dumb fuck over here didn't get me the briefing materials I needed." It was both noun and adjective: "Is the event leader a Democrat or a Republican? Or are you too dumb fuck to know?"

Connaughton was doing the hard, thankless, essential work of soliciting money, and for this he was forever stigmatized, because Biden hated fundraising, the drudgery and compromises it entailed. Some of his colleagues seemed to spend half their lives dialing for dollars—Alan Cranston, the California senator, made call after call soliciting five hundred bucks while pedaling an Exercycle at the gym—but Biden hardly ever called anyone. As a senator from a state the size of some counties, he'd never had to raise much money, and he didn't adjust well to the financial pressures of a presidential campaign. He resented any demands placed on him by the people who helped him raise money and the people who wrote checks, as if he couldn't stand owing them. He didn't hang out with the permanent class in Washington, but left his Capitol office every evening, walked across Massachusetts Avenue to Union Station, and took Amtrak home to his family in Wilmington. Remaining Ordinary Joe became a point of aggressive pride. He was as incorruptible as he was ungrateful.

In Washington, elected officials considered themselves a higher breed. They were "principals," had shown the moxie and endured the humiliation of standing before the public, and in their eyes, staff were a lower form of human beings—parasites that attached themselves to the front man for the ride. Connaughton knew that he had nothing to teach Joe Biden, a political natural who had been doing this for almost two decades, with a fingertip feel for what the American people wanted. Connaughton was thoroughly expendable, unless he could prove himself a workhorse.

"He saw the uncertainty in my eyes," Connaughton later said. "I was so new to it. I had been trained on Wall Street and I was coming into a completely different world. I had an outsized view of our relationship because I'd waited so long to join him. From his perspective, I was just one more guy who'd shown up to work on his campaign. I was attracted to power. There were not a whole lot of issues in the forefront of my mind. I wanted to be part of a small group of people that moves into the West Wing on Inauguration Day to run the country. That's the ultimate game in Washington. And after his campaign failed, I was lost."

In early September, Connaughton took a break from the campaign to attend the Alabama–Penn State game. He was driving through the Pennsylvania countryside when a news bulletin came on the radio station: Biden, at a debate in Iowa, had plagiarized a speech by a British Labour politician named Neil Kinnock, even stealing Kinnock's identity as a descendant of coal miners.

As an isolated case it would have been a story without legs. But having already brought down Hart, the media—Maureen Dowd and E. J. Dionne in the *Times*, Eleanor Clift in *Newsweek*—smelled another scandal and they competed to dig up other Biden faults: lines lifted from Hubert

Humphrey and RFK; a badly footnoted law school essay that resulted in a failing grade; exaggerated claims about his past. Then an incident recorded by C-SPAN in a New Hampshire resident's kitchen surfaced. Biden had agreed to wear a mike for an entire, unedited campaign event—a first in political history. He was brilliant for eighty-nine of the ninety minutes, but he had spent his whole career saying too much, and just before the end, a voter asked him about his law school grades. Biden snapped, "I think I probably have a much higher IQ than you do," then made at least three false statements about his education while taking the guy's head off.

Connaughton hadn't heard of the Kinnock speech or how Biden was using it. Honestly, he didn't care much for Biden's stump speech, which always brought the house down with the line, "Just because our political heroes were murdered does not mean that the dream does not still live, buried deep in our broken hearts." Connaughton revered the Kennedys as much as anyone, but that line left him flat—it was overwrought, and pitched at Americans a decade or more older. Why couldn't Biden give substantive speeches, with issues and facts and solutions, like the one on SALT II in Tuscaloosa? He seemed to be running for president on his ability to move people—to make the young Jeff Connaughtons wait six years to join his campaign. Move them to do what? He was trying to sound like the murdered heroes themselves. The Kennedys quoted the Greeks, pundits said, and Biden quoted the Kennedys. Sometimes without attribution.

The rules of the ultimate game had been changing. In 1968, George Romney said on TV that he'd been brainwashed by the generals in Vietnam, and his presidential campaign was finished. In 1972, Ed Muskie stood on a flatbed truck in the falling snow outside William Loeb's *Union Leader* in Manchester, New Hampshire, as the cameras rolled and wept tears of rage at the editor who had slandered his wife, Jane—and that was the end of Ed Muskie. In 1980, Ronald Reagan cocked his head and chuckled, "There you go again," and Jimmy Carter shrank into a one-term president. In 1984, Walter Mondale asked, "Where's the beef?" and Gary Hart suddenly looked like a slick young man with a full head of hair. Ten seconds on TV could frame a character forever, could crown or end a campaign. Presidents and contenders could commit assisted suicide with the eager help of the media.

But the new rules of the ultimate game only came into focus the year

Jeff Connaughton attached his aspirations to Joe Biden's. In 1987, what had once been the dramatic sideshows of politics became the main event: the candidate and his humiliated wife under the hot lights, the nominee at the televised hearing table talking through and around and against his own past, the ideologues and interest groups on each side of every question large and small mobilizing for total war, the daily excavation of old and recent sins in the life of a politician, the momentum building to a crescendo, the reporters a pack of wild dogs outracing one another on the blood scent of some powerful but wounded quarry. In 1987, there was Gary Hart, there was Robert Bork, and there was Joe Biden—the last two happening at the same moment.

Inside the campaign, the two weeks after the Kinnock story were a frantic nightmare, every day a new shock. But in retrospect, the dénouement looked as mechanical and inevitable as an ancient sacrificial rite at the center of a tribal culture. The candidate vows to carry on and tries to ignore the baying of the hounds. The media keep drawing more blood. The candidate receives expressions of support from his colleagues. But the stories are creating an overwhelming and awful impression, one that may never be lifted. The candidate gathers his family and inner circle around him and, one by one, asks their advice. They want him to stay in so he can defend his honor; they want him to get out so he can defend his honor. Amid tears, the candidate decides to stand down. He faces the cameras chin up, in a contained rage.

On the morning of September 23, Kaufman told Connaughton to notify the fundraising captains across the country that Biden would announce his withdrawal at noon. Two minutes before the press conference, Connaughton called his parents in Alabama, and all he could say was "Turn on the TV." He wept in the bathroom while the rest of the staff listened to Biden's statement in the Russell Building. "I'm angry with myself for having been put in this position—for having put *myself* in this position," Biden announced to the firing squad of cameras. "And, lest I say something that might be somewhat sarcastic, I should go to the Bork hearings." With that, Biden went to the Senate Caucus Room on the third floor and took his seat as chairman of the Judiciary Committee hearings that would lead to the defeat of Judge Robert Bork's nomination to the Supreme Court and begin Biden's political rehabilitation.

Connaughton was shell-shocked. His hero had been exposed as a phony, reduced from White House material to national joke in two weeks.

"His strength, he claimed, was his ability to speak and move people," Connaughton said. "Then, when it appeared he was borrowing other people's words, that completely undermined it." Now Connaughton didn't know what to do: his life was suddenly directionless. When Kaufman asked him to stick around Wilmington for a couple of months and help close down the campaign, he said yes. It made him seem like a good soldier, but the truth was that he was too paralyzed to look for a better option. He now had the worst job in politics—spending hours on the phone with angry supporters who wanted their money back, or with furious staffers in Iowa and New Hampshire who had taken campaign computers hostage until they got their last paycheck. Everyone who'd ever given the campaign a ham sandwich sent a bill. And it fell on Connaughton to help archive every step of Biden's disgrace, every anti-Biden news story and op-ed that might be used against him in his next Senate race, in 1990. There were hundreds of them, and by the end of the ordeal they left no aspect of Biden unexamined—even his hair plugs. It was like cleaning up body parts after a grisly accident and preserving bits and pieces as evidence in case of a lawsuit.

At the end of 1987, Connaughton was offered a job as a fundraiser for the Democratic Senatorial Campaign Committee. He said no—he didn't want to spend his career keeping track of checks and lapel pins. He still wanted to be involved in the substance of politics, the issues. Then Kaufman told him of an opening on the staff of the Judiciary Committee; the salary, forty-eight thousand a year, was that of a first-year Wall Street associate. But there would be interesting work on antitrust law, intellectual property, civil justice reform. Connaughton felt a strong bond with Kaufman, and he hadn't given up on Biden. In any case, Wall Street wasn't likely to hire him: the stock market had crashed on October 19, the biggest one-day drop in history, and the 1986 tax reform act had shut down many of the arbitrage tricks that had kept public finance departments thriving. He decided to stay in Washington.

Everyone in D.C. was someone's guy. Connaughton was a Biden guy.

1987

The shouts, the imprecations, the gesticulations, the fucking fear and greed, enveloped him, and he loved it. He was the number one bond salesman, "the biggest producer," as the phrase went, in the bond trading room . . . **PROSECUTOR IN BOESKY SCANDAL PREDICTS A CHANGE IN WALL STREET'S ETHICS** . . . **DONNA RICE—WHAT REALLY HAPPENED** Gary Hart Asked Me to Marry Him; Exclusive Photos of Fun-Filled Weekend in the Bahamas . . . I believe that the demise of the liberal perspective on the ghetto underclass has made the intellectual discourse on this topic too one-sided. It has made it more difficult to achieve . . . **SHOCKING NEW TREND—AMERICANS AFRAID TO LEAVE THEIR HOMES** . . . Well, you're fucked up, you look like shit, but hey no problem, all you need is a better cut of cocaine. . . . Relativism succeeds in destroying the West's universal or intellectually imperialistic claims, leaving it to just be another culture . . . Gravity Will Never Be the Same. The Air Revolution from Nike. . . . **GREENSPAN CALLS WIDENING OF TRADE GAP "AN ABERRATION," PREDICTS IMPROVEMENT** . . . Over the next 14 months, bidders seeking to build Florida's visionary bullet train will get serious. They will start negotiating big land deals with developers interested in building stations from Tampa to . . . General Secretary Gorbachev, if you seek peace, if you seek prosperity for the Soviet Union and Eastern Europe, if you seek liberalization: Come here to this gate! . . . **PRESIDENT ASSUMES RESPONSIBILITY FOR IRAN-CONTRA AFFAIR** . . . Many employees share Gates's young-techie vocabulary. "Randomness" applies to any confused or haphazard situation. "Bandwidth" means the amount of information one can absorb. Things that go right are "radical," "cool," or, Gates's favorite, "super." . . . Biden, fighting to salvage his presidential campaign, today acknowledged "a mistake" in his youth, when he plagiarized . . . **PANIC! DOW PLUNGES THROUGH FLOOR—508 PTS**

CRAFTSMAN: RAYMOND CARVER

Ray was a drinker. He picked it up from C.R., his father. C.R. was a saw filer at a lumber mill in the Yakima Valley and a good storyteller. Ray picked that up, too. C.R. could go for months without sipping a beer, then he would disappear from home for a while, and Ray and his mother and younger brother would sit down to dinner with a sense of doom. That was how Ray drank: once he started, he couldn't stop.

Ray grew up in the 1940s and '50s. He was a tall, fat boy. He stood hunched over, with an arm or leg bent at a bad angle, and his eyes had a fat boy's hooded squint even after he lost the weight. His pants and shirts looked like gabardine, what an unemployed forty-year-old would wear. He spoke in a faint mumble so you had to listen close, but it often turned out that he had said something funny or sharp.

The Carvers lived in four rooms in a seven-hundred-square-foot box of a house on a concrete slab. There was nowhere to be alone and they lived together like strangers.

Ray loved to shoot geese and fish for trout along the Columbia River. He liked to read the pulps and outdoor magazines. One day, he told the man who took him along hunting that he had sent a story to one of the magazines and it had come back. That was why Ray had looked nervous all morning.

"Well, what did you write?" the man said.

"I wrote a story about this wild country," Ray said, "the flight of the wild geese and hunting the geese and everything in this remote country down here. It's not what appeals to the public, they said."

But he didn't give up.

Ray saw an ad in *Writer's Digest* for the Palmer Institute of Authorship in Hollywood. It was a correspondence course. C.R. paid the twenty-five-dollar enrollment fee and Ray started doing the sixteen installments, but he ran out of money for the monthly payments. After he received his high school diploma, his parents expected him to go to work in the sawmill. That wasn't how things went.

Ray got a pretty girl named Maryann pregnant. She was going to study at the University of Washington, but Ray and Maryann were crazy about each other, so they got married instead. In 1957 their daughter was born in a hospital two floors below the psychiatric ward where C.R. was being treated for a nervous breakdown. A year later a baby boy arrived. Ray was twenty and Maryann was eighteen, and that was their youth.

They began to wander. They had great dreams and believed that hard work would make those dreams come true. Ray was going to be a writer. Everything else would come after that.

They moved around the West and they never stopped. They lived in Chico and Paradise and Eureka and Arcata and Sacramento and Palo Alto and Missoula and Santa Cruz and Cupertino. Every time they started to settle in, Ray would get restless and they would move on to somewhere else. The family's main support was Maryann. She packed fruit, waited tables, sold encyclopedias door-to-door. Ray worked at a drugstore, a sawmill, a service station, and a stockroom, and as a night janitor at a hospital. The work was not ennobling. He would come home too wiped out to do anything.

Ray wanted to write a novel. But a man who was trying to wash six loads of clothes in a Laundromat while his wife was serving food somewhere and the kids were waiting for him to come pick them up somewhere else and it was getting late and the woman ahead of him kept putting more dimes in her dryer—that man could never write a novel. To do that, he would need to be living in a world that made sense, a world that stayed fixed in one place so that he could describe it accurately. That wasn't Ray's world.

In Ray's world the rules changed every day, and he couldn't see past the first of next month, when he would have to find money for rent and school clothes. The most important fact of his life was that he had two children, and he would never get out from under the baleful responsibility of having them. Hard work, good intentions, doing the right things— these would not be enough, things would not get better. He and Maryann would never get their reward. That was the other thing he understood in the Laundromat. And somewhere along the way, his dreams started to go bust.

Without the heart to write anything long, which might have brought in real money, and with the deep frustration of seeing no way out, Ray could write only poems, and very short stories. Then he rewrote them, again and again, sometimes over many years.

The stories were about people who did not succeed. That had been Ray's experience, and those were his people. His characters were unemployed salesmen, waitresses, mill hands. They lived nowhere in particular, in bedrooms and living rooms and front yards where they couldn't get away from one another or themselves and everyone was alone and adrift. Their names weren't fancy—Earl, Arlene, L.D., Rae—and they seldom had more than one, if that. Nothing like religion or politics or community surrounded them, except the Safeway and the bingo hall. Nothing was happening anywhere in the world, there was only a boy fighting a fish, a wife selling a used car, two couples talking themselves into paralysis. Ray left almost everything out.

In one story, a wife learns that her husband, just back from a fishing trip with his buddies, left the brutalized corpse of a girl lying in the river for three days before reporting it.

My husband eats with good appetite but he seems tired, edgy. He chews slowly, arms on the table, and stares at something across the room. He looks at me and looks away again. He wipes his mouth on the napkin. He shrugs and goes on eating. Something has come between us though he would like me to believe otherwise.

"What are you staring at me for?" he asks. "What is it?" he says and puts his fork down.

"Was I staring?" I say and shake my head stupidly, stupidly.

His characters spoke a language that sounded ordinary, except that every word echoed with the strange, and in the silences between words a kind of panic rose. These lives were trembling over a void.

"Most of my characters would like their actions to count for something," Ray once said. "But at the same time they've reached the point—as many people do—that they know it isn't so. It doesn't add up any longer. The things you once thought important or even worth dying for aren't worth a nickel now. It's their lives they've become uncomfortable with, lives they see breaking down. They'd like to set things right, but they can't."

Ray was doing things the long, hard way, going against every trend of the period. In those years, the short story was a minor literary form. Realism seemed played out. The writer Ray brought most quickly to mind, Hemingway, was at the start of a posthumous eclipse. In the sixties and seventies, the most discussed writers—Mailer, Bellow, Roth, Updike, Barth, Wolfe, Pynchon—reached for overstatement, not restraint, writing sprawling novels of intellectual, linguistic, or erotic excess, and high-octane journalism. There was a kind of competition to swallow American life whole—to mirror and distort in prose the social facts of a country that had a limitless capacity for flux and shock.

Ray, whose hero was Chekhov, moved in the opposite direction from literary trends and kept faith with a quieter task, following Ezra Pound's maxim that "fundamental accuracy of statement is the one sole morality of writing." By paying close attention to the lives of marginal, lost people, people who scarcely figured and were rarely taken seriously in contemporary American fiction (if they appeared anywhere, it was in the paintings of Edward Hopper), Ray had his fingers on the pulse of a deeper loneliness. He seemed to know, in the unintentional way of a fiction writer, that the country's future would be most unnerving in its very ordinariness, in the late-night trip to the supermarket, the yard sale at the end of the line. He sensed that beneath the surface of life there was nothing to stand on.

In the early seventies, Maryann got her degree and began to teach high school English. That freed Ray to put his effort into writing and finding a college teaching job. He began publishing stories in big East Coast magazines. The Carvers bought their first house, in the future Silicon Valley. There was a nonstop party scene with other working-class writers and their wives in the area. Things were looking up for the Carvers. That was when everything went to pieces.

The children became teenagers, and Ray felt that they now held the reins. Ray and Maryann each had an affair. They went into bankruptcy twice. He was convicted of lying to the state of California on his unemployment claim and almost sent to prison. Instead, he went in and out of detox. His drinking turned poisonous, with long blackouts. Maryann tried to keep up in order not to lose him. Ray was a quiet, spooked-looking man, but with the scotch he grew menacing, and one night, after Maryann flirted with a friend, Ray hit her with a wine bottle. She lost 60 percent of her blood from the severed artery by her ear and was taken to the emergency room while Ray hid in the kitchen.

A few months later, in 1976, his first book of stories, *Will You Please*

Be Quiet, Please?—written over nearly two decades—was published in New York. The dedication page said: THIS BOOK IS FOR MARYANN.

Ray was a drinker and a writer. The two had always gone along separate tracks. What the first self fled or wrecked or rued or resented, the second stared into high art. But now his writing dwindled to nothing.

"The time came and went when everything my wife and I held sacred or considered worthy of respect, every spiritual value, crumbled away," he later wrote. "Something terrible had happened to us." He never intended to become an alcoholic, a bankrupt, a cheat, a thief, and a liar. But he was all those. It was the 1970s, and a lot of people were having a good time, but Ray knew ahead of the years that the life of partying and drinking poor was a road into darkness.

In the middle of 1977 he went to live by himself on the remote California coast near Oregon. It was fear for his writing, not for his own life or the life of his family, that made him take his last drink there. Sober, he began to write again. In 1978 he and Maryann split.

That was the end of Bad Ray and the beginning of Good Raymond. He had ten more years before a lifetime of smoking finally caught up with him and he died at fifty, in 1988. During that decade he found happiness with a poet. He wrote some of his best stories and escaped the trap of self-parody that had begun to be called minimalism, turning to more fullness of expression in the service of a more generous vision. He became famous and entered the middle class. He received prestigious appointments and won major prizes, a literary hero redeemed from hell. He walked with the happy carefulness of someone pardoned on the verge of execution.

The turn to flash and glitz in the eighties worked in his favor. During the Reagan years he was named the chronicler of blue-collar despair. The less articulate his characters, the more his many new readers loved the creator. If the sinking working class fascinated and frightened them, they could imagine that they knew its spirit through his stories, and so they fetishized him. The New York literary scene, hot and flush again, took him to its heart. He became a Vintage Contemporary alongside writers in their twenties who had learned to mimic the austere prose without having first forged it in personal fires. He posed for jacket portraits with some of the old menace, like a man who had wandered into a book party from the scary part of town.

"They sold his stories of inadequate, failed, embarrassed and embarrassing men, many of them drunkards, all of them losers, to yuppies," one of his old friends said. "His people confirmed the yuppies in their sense of superiority."

But every morning, Good Raymond got up, made coffee, sat at his desk, and did exactly what Bad Ray had always done. After all, they were the same craftsman. The distractions were different now, but he was still trying to set down what he saw and felt with utmost accuracy, and in the American din, that small thing was everything.

DEAN PRICE

Dean spent seven years in Pennsylvania. He married a girl who also worked for Johnson & Johnson, and they lived in Harrisburg and had two boys—Chase in 1993, Ryan in 1995. After leaving the company, Dean went to work as an independent contractor selling Johnson & Johnson orthopedic knees and hips. He made good money, but within a few years the marriage fell apart, and Dean turned to drinking. It got harder and harder to walk out the front door in the morning, and eventually he stopped making his sales quotas. He quit before the company could terminate his contract.

He decided to return to Rockingham County. He couldn't live in the North, couldn't stand the winters, the unfriendliness, the fact that drivers didn't lift their fingers from the wheel and wave when they passed you on the road. He was afraid that his boys would grow up not knowing the land or farming or fishing, not knowing their kin who all lived within ten miles of one another. The court gave primary custody to the boys' mother, with Dean getting them the first ten days of every month until they started school, then every other weekend. Dean felt that if he went back home, he would eventually be able to lure them and their mother down there. Until then, he would drive north to pick up and return his sons as often as necessary, even six times a month, even crying at the wheel.

Dean always said, "I'm a great father, a pretty good businessman, and a shitty husband."

When he moved back to Stokesdale in 1997, he was thirty-four. He vowed that the divorce would not make him bitter. He resolved to change his life and become a better father, a more honest human being. He loved the fact that so much about his part of the country was old. The backbone of America was right here, the self-sufficiency and loyalty. Jefferson had written, "Cultivators of the earth are the most valuable citizens. They are the most vigorous, the most independent, the most virtuous, and they are tied to their country and wedded to its liberty and interests by the most lasting bands." It was still true. If the United States was invaded, how many people in California or New York would pick up a pistol and fight? "The thing about the farmers is it's in their blood to be entrepreneurs," Dean said. "That's why they came here two hundred years ago. They didn't want to have to punch the clock, they didn't want to have to work for the Man. They could have a hundred fifty acres of land and be their own boss. If you had a Petri dish and you were trying to grow an entrepreneur, the environment in this country is perfect, because there is reward with the risk."

He joined the Sardis Primitive Baptist Church, a simple redbrick building under a giant old oak that had been around since 1801, next to the little graveyard where his grandparents Birch and Ollie Neal lay buried. By the time Dean joined, the congregation at Sardis had dwindled to no more than eight or nine people, most of them twice his age. He loved the smell of old wood in the church, the a cappella singing of old hymns. The Primitive Baptists put a lot of store in dreams, and the preacher, Elder Mintor, often spoke of them from the pulpit. How else would God talk to you if not through your dreams, your imagination? The theology was called sacred hope. Dean was no longer a Christian in the way of his parents. He hoped to goodness he was saved, but he didn't know anything for sure—didn't know if he would make it home at the end of the day. You did the best you could. He was baptized in the Dan River, his third time—the first two hadn't taken—and came out of the water rejoicing, feeling that he could have a fresh start.

The plateau of hardwood hills and red clay fields between the Appalachian range and the Atlantic coastal plain is called the Piedmont. Along the border between Virginia and North Carolina, from Danville and Martinsville down to Greensboro and Winston-Salem, the mainstays of Piedmont life in the twentieth century were tobacco, textiles, and furniture. In the last years of the century they all started to die, more or less simultaneously, as if a mysterious and highly communicable plague swept through the region. Dean Price returned home just as the first bad signs were showing up across the landscape.

Most of the tobacco grown in the area was bought, warehoused, aged, processed, blended, rolled, and cut into cigarettes by the R.J. Reynolds Tobacco Company in Winston-Salem. Dean liked to drive up the Jeb Stuart Highway across the Virginia line and visit the Reynolds homestead, within view of No Business Mountain, which got its name from moonshining. He admired Richard Joshua Reynolds—born in 1850, rode into Winston on a horse in 1874, started manufacturing tobacco there the next year, and became the richest man in North Carolina by inventing the packaged cigarette. That was a good time to be an entrepreneur, Dean thought—virgin territory in business, with the best ideas rising to the top. Reynolds was an innovator, a modern industrialist at a time when the South was still rural and dirt poor. There was a stone marker at the homestead with a quotation from his grandson saying how Reynolds had given a decent life to thousands of people "who otherwise would have been doomed to the backwardness of a region that had no future and was burdened with a past that had failed." R.J. Reynolds Tobacco made the city of Winston-Salem, took care of its workers with (segregated) company housing and free day care, gave them Class A stock that paid a handsome yearly dividend, and built a local bank, called Wachovia, to house its stock and deposits.

By the early 1980s, the company had slipped out of Reynolds family control and was coming under heavy pressure from competitors. Reynolds sales peaked in 1983 and fell every year after that. In the same period, the federal government applied a different kind of pressure—banning cigarette advertisements and doubling the excise tax on cigarettes in 1983, while antismoking crusaders carried out a huge public awareness campaign. To stay on top, Reynolds merged with Nabisco Foods in 1985, and the headquarters was moved to Atlanta, which made a lot of people in Winston-Salem unhappy. In 1988, RJR Nabisco became the target of the biggest leveraged buyout in history until that point, acquired for twenty-five billion dollars by the Wall Street firm of Kohlberg Kravis Roberts. The factory workers had little understanding of the deal, but almost immediately Reynolds started cutting its workforce in Winston-Salem to pay off the pile of debt in New York. The writing was on the wall for tobacco.

In 1990 a tobacco farmer Dean Price knew, James Lee Albert, was interviewed and photographed by the Greensboro *News & Record*. When he was twenty-five, in 1964, Albert had bought a hundred-seventy-five-acre farm in Rockingham County for a hundred dollars an acre, when top tobacco brought forty-seven cents a pound. As he raised his family and added on to his house, the price went up ten or fifteen cents a year after that, almost every year, until it hit its peak at $2.25 around 1990. That was when Albert told the paper that the government was going to put the tobacco farmers who had built this country out of business.

In the years that followed, congressional hearings and litigation against the companies drove the price of tobacco steadily downward as demand declined. In 1998, to end the lawsuits, Big Tobacco agreed to pay the states more than two hundred billion dollars to cover the health costs incurred by smoking. In 2004 the federal government ended the tobacco subsidy. Under the buyout, tobacco company money would pay farmers around seven dollars for every pound of tobacco they didn't grow for the next decade.

Most of the farmers in Dean's area took the buyout. James Lee Albert received his and almost immediately underwent open-heart surgery at age sixty-seven, and that was the end of his working life. One of his sons started boarding horses on the land. Dean's cousin Terry Neal, who had two hundred prime acres right across Route 220 from Dean's house, quit farming in 2005 and used most of his buyout money to pay off his taxes and debts. It was too expensive for most tobacco farmers to convert to strawberries or soy, so they just grew hay or let the land sit fallow, and the strange sight of denuded fields at the height of the growing season was seen in Rockingham County.

The fall of textiles had different causes. The mills came to the Piedmont in the late nineteenth century, mostly dispersed in small towns. Dan River opened in Danville in 1882; the Cone brothers brought Proximity to Greensboro in 1895. The social code in the mill towns was paternalistic and insular—the company took care of its employees and fiercely opposed any union drives. In a place like Martinsville there was never a real middle class, just managers and workers, and when the collapse began in the 1990s, the mill towns had nothing to fall back on. Some workers and local officials blamed it on NAFTA, which took effect on the first day of 1994, ushered into being by Democrats and Republicans alike. Others said it was the selfishness and greed of the owners, who had prevented other industries from getting a foothold, then sold out to conglomerates and Wall Street firms that had no loyalty to Danville or Greensboro. Pro-business locals blamed high labor costs. Analysts in Washington and New York said that it was all inevitable—technology and globalization. After years of cutbacks and other warning signs, the end came with breathtaking speed, as companies that had been the most important institutional pillars of their communities for over a century and looked set to continue forever disappeared in rapid order: Tultex of Martinsville filed for bankruptcy in 1999, Proximity of Greensboro in 2003, Dan River of Danville in 2005; Hanes of Winston-Salem started closing plants in 2006, and by 2010 only one skeletal factory was left. Hundreds of smaller businesses went away with them. A single rural county in North Carolina— Surry, population seventy-three thousand—lost ten thousand jobs in one decade.

Furniture making in the Piedmont was even older than textiles. In 2002, Bassett Furniture celebrated its hundredth anniversary by constructing out of solid ash a chair more than twenty feet high and weighing three tons. The chair toured the country for seven years, going wherever Bassett Furniture stores were opened, before returning to Martinsville and being installed in a parking lot on Main Street. But by then, low-cost Chinese competition had wiped out most of the local furniture industry. Companies that couldn't convert to smaller, high-end domestic markets were doomed. The giant chair became a memorial.

In 1997, the Piedmont was still in the early stages of the plague. Brick factories stretching block after block were still alive, though starting to weaken. Miles of acreage didn't yet lie fallow, though some tobacco farmers were already getting out. Most people still worked—it was rare to find employable locals on disability—and the crack and meth scourge hadn't yet made it to Rockingham County. In the center of Madison, McFall Drug was still open with its lunch counter, alongside a men's clothing store, two furniture shops, a shoe store, and a couple of banks. Kmart had brought the first big-box store to the area back in the 1980s, but there was not yet a single Wal-Mart in Rockingham County. Still, most people knew that large forces were bearing down and the area might be left behind. Dean always said that ambition wasn't in the DNA down here, but those who had a little and were still young didn't stay around. The return of a native with a college degree who had started a family and career up north was rare enough to be noted. To people who didn't know Dean Price well, it might have looked like defeat.

He saw it as just the opposite. He came home to free himself from the grip of the past, the poverty thinking. His father had tried to get away from it but he'd been pulled back down, for those chains were strong. But Dean thought he could break them.

His mother was living alone in the house on Route 220, having finally kicked his father out and divorced him. Dean's father had moved to Burlington and married a woman there and was living on a disability check from the government. Dean's mother worked as a nurse and worshipped at an ultraconservative Pentecostal church that was too much for Dean. He moved into his late grandmother's apartment at the back of the house.

In the early nineties, Route 220 had been widened into a four-lane highway starting less than a mile south of the house and going all the way north to Roanoke, Virginia. That was the family's one saving grace, because land values multiplied as the road became a long-haul trucking route. It also gave Dean a plan. From Greensboro to Roanoke there were only one or two truck stops. Dean's house stood on the roadside with nothing much for several miles in either direction except a church with talking murals. He decided to build a convenience store, fast-food restaurant, and gas station right next to the house, on a couple of acres of land that he'd inherited from his grandmother. And he came up with a marketing plan that reflected the sum total of his life experience to that point.

In Pennsylvania he had learned about guerrilla marketing from a local chain of gas stations and convenience stores called Sheetz. Dean had never seen anything like Sheetz. In the South, you opened up a business and hoped people came in. But in Pennsylvania, Sheetz grabbed the customers and brought them in, by lowballing the price of gas by a few pennies. When Sheetz came into your area, you knew they were coming after your business. Dean admired its success and decided to introduce discount fuel to the Southeast. He bought a Tastee Freez franchise, which charged a low fee because the profit margins on ice cream were also low. And to reach out and pull more local people in, he styled his convenience store after a country market, with a front porch and old farm vehicles parked outside. He drove around antique shops and flea markets looking for vintage cola signs and ads for bread and grain painted on wood. His dream was to grow produce on the Price tobacco farm—melons, strawberries, tomatoes, corn—and sell it fresh at the store and teach his boys about farming. He came up with a name that caught on fast: Red Birch Country Market. Birch for his maternal grandfather, red for the Redeemer's sacrifice. The company's slogan was "A family business covered in the blood of Christ." His minority partners were his oldest sister and her husband. He imagined a chain of Red Birch truck stops across the Southeast.

Dean opened for business on October 2, 1997. The price of gas was eighty-nine cents a gallon.

The house stood just fifty feet from the store—too close, with the floodlights and noise of trucks at all hours. His mother wanted to tear the house down and build a new one farther from the road. Dean had a different idea. The house contained three generations of family history, good and bad, and he didn't want to lose that. So, three days after opening the store, he undertook the monumental task of moving the house away from the road down the grassy slope toward the tobacco fields and fishpond on the Neal family land. First, he removed every brick from the outside walls and chimney. He chainsawed the apartment off from the main house. Then he bolted six-by-sixes underneath the house, jacked it up, laid other six-by-sixes on the ground, placed six-inch metal poles between the two sets of six-by-sixes, and attached the house to his front-end loader. It was something that he'd seen the Amish do in Pennsylvania. Dean began rolling the house downhill on the metal pipes a few feet at a time. El Niño slowed things down—there were four straight months of rain and mud—but by Thanksgiving 1998 the house was standing on a new foundation several hundred feet from Route 220, now with white clapboard siding and a stone chimney, like a nineteenth-century farmhouse. That whole year, Dean ran like a madman between the house and the store, keeping both projects going. There had been plenty of skeptics, but when it was over, he knew that he could do just about whatever he set his mind to.

The truck stop did well enough that in the summer of 2000, Dean opened another, forty-five minutes' drive north on 220 in Virginia, near the NASCAR speedway outside Martinsville. Along with the store and gas station he opened a Bojangles' franchise—the fried chicken, biscuits, and pinto beans appealed to southern taste, and the margins were higher than with Tastee Freez. His profits came from the Bojangles'—gas paid him just pennies on the gallon. As for the country market, people loved the idea, but there was little interest in fresh melons and vegetables. His customers wanted the convenience and taste of fast food. Anyway, Food Lion could sell packaged produce trucked halfway across the country for cheaper than what Dean grew on his grandpa Norfleet's farm. "Something changed in our country where quality doesn't matter like it used to," Dean said. "I got to the point where I would lose money on the produce

just to give it that country image so people would come in for other
things, such as Bojangles'. Cantaloupes were a loss leader."

Soon after opening the store in Virginia, Dean learned that Sheetz
was coming to Martinsville—one mile south of him on 220, all the way
from Pennsylvania. He never thought there was a chance in the world
he'd have to compete with Sheetz, and for months after getting the news
he was worried sick, as if he were the prey and Sheetz the predator stalk-
ing him. One day, while driving back from an antiquing trip to Mount
Airy with the woman who had become his second, and shortest-lived,
wife, Dean had an epiphany: the only thing Sheetz had on him was the
price of fuel. But that was everything, since there was no loyalty in this
business and customers would leave you over two cents. Somehow he
hadn't understood the importance of gas prices until that moment. The
next week he got on the phone with his jobber, the middleman who sold
him his fuel. "We've got 'em on the food, we've got 'em on the location.
When they open up they're going to drop the price of their fuel and try to
take our business. Why don't we try to be the aggressor and drop our
price now and gain volume when they open six months from now?"

Instead of pumping a hundred thousand gallons a month and making
fifteen cents a gallon, he would pump two hundred fifty thousand gallons
and make five cents a gallon. The jobber would get half of that, and most
of Dean's half would go to the credit card companies—with the new business model Dean would barely break even on gas. But it was the only way
to survive. After Sheetz opened, his margins went down, but he kept his
price right at theirs and stayed in business. What he learned later was
that Exxon Mobil was selling gas to Sheetz for three or four cents a gallon
less than he had to pay. That was the difference between two hundred
fifty Sheetz stores and two Red Birches. That was life as an entrepreneur.

Dean continued to pursue his goal of owning a chain of stores across
the region, because it was the closest he had ever come to freedom. He
opened a third truck stop, with a Bojangles' and a Red Birch Country
Market, a few miles north up 220 from the second one, in a little furniture town called Bassett, and then a stand-alone Bojangles' restaurant on
the 220 Business strip heading out of Martinsville. So Route 220 became
his chain, linked all along that thirty-five-mile stretch of highway between two states, the chain that he lived on. But the epiphany on the road
from Mount Airy stayed with him. Dean had a word for it: the oil companies had him hog-tied.

•

One day in the late nineties, shortly before he opened his second truck stop, Dean was at an antiques store in Reidsville, a town between Stokesdale and Danville, and he found himself reading a self-help book. Its message was: decide what you want to do, believe beyond a shadow of a doubt that you can do it, then act on it. With one part of his mind he was thinking, "I've got to be doing something else," because he was always antsy about wasting time, and he knew he was in that antiques store to avoid going to his truck stop, which was already losing its appeal—the monotony of day-to-day operations. But another part of him thought: "This is an investment in you and your mind. You can't be doing anything better than improving yourself." So he sat in the store all day and finished the book. He was aware of something stirring within, a hunger to learn awakened—or reawakened, since he'd had it as a boy before losing it out in the world of work.

Soon afterward, Dean made a discovery that changed his life. An electrician who had done some work for him when he was moving the house asked what plans he had for his business. Dean said, "I'd really like to go to Martinsville and build another convenience store up there on the corner at the race track. But I'll need about a million dollars. Do you know anybody who's got a million dollars?"

"I sure do," the electrician said. "Rocky Carter."

"You got his telephone number?"

"I'll call him." And the electrician called Rocky Carter on the spot.

Carter was a commercial builder in Kernersville, a little tobacco auction town between Greensboro and Winston-Salem. After meeting Dean, he agreed to build the truck stop in Martinsville. But Carter was also one of the most spiritual people Dean had ever met, always seeking after the things that you couldn't see. He gave Dean a book called *Think and Grow Rich*, written by a man named Napoleon Hill and published in 1937. Dean must have read it twenty-five times without putting it down.

Napoleon Hill was born in 1883, in a one-room cabin in the Appalachians of southwestern Virginia. As a young man he became a reporter, and in 1908 he went to Pittsburgh to interview Andrew Carnegie on assignment for *Success* magazine. The interview was supposed to last three hours, but Carnegie kept Hill at his house for three days, talking about the principles of life that had made him the richest man in the world and about the need for a new economic philosophy that would allow other men to become successful. On the third day, Carnegie said, "If I commission you to become the author of this philosophy, give you letters of introduction to men whose experiences you will need"—he mentioned titans of industry such as Henry Ford, Thomas Edison, and John D. Rockefeller— "are you willing to put in twenty years of research, because that's how long it will take, and pay your own way as you go along, without any subsidy from me? Yes or no?" Hill thought about it for twenty-nine seconds and said yes. Carnegie was timing him with a pocket watch under his desk, and if Hill's answer had taken more than a minute, Carnegie would have withdrawn the offer.

For the next two decades, drawing on Carnegie's contacts, Napoleon Hill interviewed more than five hundred of the most successful men of his age—not just industrialists like Ford and Rockefeller, but politicians like Theodore Roosevelt and Woodrow Wilson, the inventor Wilbur Wright, the department store magnate F. W. Woolworth, the trial lawyer Clarence Darrow. "He went from one adversity to the next," Dean said. "His son was born with no ears, and Napoleon refused to believe that his son would not be able to hear. Every night, he would go in before his son went to bed, he would talk to him like for an hour, and he would tell him, 'You will hear, one day in your life you're going to hear, you've got to believe you're going to hear.' When his son was older, he came to hear. He willed it."

In 1928, Hill published his findings in several volumes under the title *The Law of Success*. A decade later, after a stint advising President Franklin D. Roosevelt, he gathered its sixteen lessons in the single volume *Think and Grow Rich*. What Hill called the Philosophy of Achievement began and ended with the mind. Getting rich was a matter of wanting to be rich, wanting it with "a white heat of desire," teaching yourself to imagine wealth as specifically as possible, learning to concentrate your mind on the desired goal and the means, and to eliminate besetting fears and other negative thoughts. These were lessons that Americans, living under a system of capitalism and democracy, were uniquely equipped to apply in their lives. More than half a century later, Napoleon Hill's message reached Dean Price and became an invisible but powerful force in his life, like gravity or love.

"When I was growing up and there was ever a problem," Dean said, "Mom and Dad would say, 'Well, just pray about it.' I couldn't buy into that. There had to be something more. What Napoleon Hill taught me was there's magical power in your mind that probably one in a million even fathom that they have. Napoleon's famous quote is 'If you can conceive it and believe it, you can achieve it.' If your imagination can come up with it, then that means it's possible. That's the way nature works. Whether you have the persistence, determination, dedication to see it through—that's a different story."

Dean absorbed *Think and Grow Rich* so completely that he began referring to it as often and as naturally as a minister quotes the Bible. For every situation he encountered, the book articulated a truth. "Napoleon once said the best thing that a leader can give the people is hope." "Napoleon Hill talks about men wanting to prey on other men financially. If they can't do it physically, then they prey on each other financially, and it's innate, it's in our genes—instead of being our brother's keeper." "Napoleon Hill, he has a saying—for every adversity that comes into your life, there is a seed of equal benefit to it." "Napoleon Hill wrote that sometimes your subconscious is a few years ahead."

Hill explained to his readers how to train the subconscious mind with "auto-suggestion" by concentrating their thoughts before they went to sleep. Every night they should repeat aloud, like an incantation, a written statement of the amount of money they wanted to make, the date by which they wanted to have it, and the work they intended to do to make it. Night after night, Dean lay in bed and faithfully followed Hill's instructions before falling asleep.

Hill also warned against the six basic fears. First and strongest of them was the fear of poverty, which had most of the country in its grip during the years leading up to the publication of *Think and Grow Rich*. "The people of America began to think of poverty, following the Wall Street crash of 1929," Hill wrote. "Slowly but surely that mass thought was crystallized into its physical equivalent, which was known as a 'depression.' This had to happen, it is in conformity with the laws of Nature." Some people attributed to Hill one of the most famous lines in American history, from FDR's inaugural address in 1933: "The only thing we have to fear is fear itself." Dean knew all about that first fear. He searched himself and recognized the power of his father's poverty thinking. But here was an author who could explain how to master it: "You either control your mind or it controls you."

Anyone peddling the secrets of success might turn out to be a snake oil salesman. Glenn W. Turner, the cosmetics emperor, claimed to have read

Napoleon Hill in 1966 and taken him as an inspiration, but all Turner had done was con Dean's parents by perverting Hill's message into "Dare to Be Great." Spiritual and material thirsting were always mingled in Americans, leaving them easy prey to hucksters of the cloth, the book, the screen. What Hill did was to take the limitless native belief in the powers of the self and organize it into a system that sounded like a practical philosophy. He taught Dean to believe that he was the author of his own destiny.

It was around the time Dean found Napoleon Hill that he had the dream about walking down an old wagon road.

TAMMY THOMAS

The job wasn't that hard once she got used to it, but starting out on the assembly line she had to remember where all the freaking wires went and all the parts, and the line was moving, that thing was rotating at eye level, and if you weren't paying attention it would get away from you. They were making wiring harnesses for GM electrical components, and the assembly table was oblong, fifty feet or so, eight or ten stations per aisle, the women standing at their stations in safety glasses and gloves. The wiring harness started out blank, and then the first station would put on connectors and a couple of wires, and then the next station would have eight or ten wires to plug in, and it would get built as it went around, and the last person would take it off the line, grease it if it needed greasing, and pack it. They pulled a harness off every two or three minutes, which might seem like plenty of time unless you fell behind.

More experienced workers figured out shortcuts, like draping wires over their shoulders or hanging a connector with plug-in wires around their neck instead of walking back to the rack to pull out new wires each time, or plugging their wires into the connector ahead of time so when the harness came down they could just stick the connector in instead of doing everything then. As long as you made rate, that left time to read a book, or talk to the next person, or listen to your music. When she had been at it for a few months and was good enough to have her own system, Tammy could actually work two stations. At the Austintown plant they took their lunch break at the bars, and some of them came back drunk, and there was one guy who paid her twenty dollars to work his station for an hour while he sobered up. All you needed to succeed on the line was discipline and a little creativity, and she had those. But at first she did it exactly the way Methods told her, and sometimes she'd end up trying to finish in someone else's station. A few people put down a piece of red tape, telling you, "I don't want nobody in my station, don't cross this tape."

Her first year, she was laid off before she had her ninety days, which was when health benefits kicked in—then they brought her line back. For a while after that she was laid off every year, usually around February or March, five months at the longest, and during those stretches she made as much as 80 percent of her pay for doing nothing. The 1984 agreement between Packard and Local 717 of the Electrical Workers started her out at 55 percent of the base rate for everything, wages and benefits and vacation, and then she had to work ten years to get up to maximum rate. Once she had seniority she could bump someone with less time out of a better job, like running the high lift at the distribution center, or a better shift, like day turn so she could be home when the kids got out of school. But in her first ten years she got bumped around a lot by older workers. Most of Packard's plants were in Warren, but there were others scattered all over the Valley, and Tammy worked in just about every one of them. In Warren, the main factory on North River Road was a quarter-mile stretch of numbered buildings all joined together—Plant 10, the cable-making area, Plant 11, where the high-speed presses ran—and you could walk straight from one end of the factory to the other, like a street. They called it Route 66.

The worst was Plant 8. Tammy hated working there. The job was bad—a harness with two wires, a couple of clips, and a grommet, and you assembled a bazillion of them for eight hours. Plus, the work rules—you couldn't clock out and leave the plant, you had to work straight eight and bring your lunch with you. The Jobs Bank was at Plant 8, where they put the newer hires, the third-tier people who didn't have the same benefits. On the other hand, the Hubbard plant was her favorite. You didn't have to go through turnstiles if you wanted to eat your lunch outside. Hubbard was like a close-knit family, until they closed it in 1999 and she had to go to Plant 8 despite having seniority, since there were no other openings.

At first Tammy was kind of excited about being in a union. Youngstown was a union town and she understood that power, even if the steelworkers had taken a beating. One year Local 717 went on strike. She had heard all the stories about the mills and imagined being Rosie the Riveter, a rebel walking the picket line. But she was on second shift, and by the time it was her turn to walk the line, they had settled. Over time, she got pretty jaded about the union. She went to a meeting and spent it watching a couple of white guys argue. She wasn't paying a babysitter and driving half an hour to Warren so she could watch two white guys argue. Some of the union reps were just about themselves, trying to move up to the international so they could draw down two pensions. At one plant, Thomas Road, which was like a freaking dungeon, everything dingy and dirty, there was a foreman who would turn on the machines to shorten people's breaks and once locked up the phones so the new hires couldn't receive calls, and the union rep just sat in his office and didn't do anything. As Packard cut more jobs and sent more work off to the maquiladoras in Juarez, the union got weaker, and you knew in the end it wasn't going to save you.

The work didn't destroy your body like in the steel mills, but it beat you down. Tammy developed asthma after she worked the solder pot at Thomas Road, dipping copper wires into melted lead—it felt like her chest and back were trying to touch, and it got so bad that sometimes she had to be hospitalized. Like a lot of workers, she also got carpal tunnel syndrome—they called it "Packard hands," treated with splints and medication—and years after she had stopped working in the factory the pain still sometimes woke her up at night.

She found out that she could be a little rebellious. Once, a temp came to work in her area, a white woman in her thirties, divorced with children. This girl was too scared to take breaks, she was scared to go to the bathroom or talk to anyone, because she thought she would lose her job. She was one of those people who would come to work early, when everyone else clocked in five minutes before their shift. She looked worn and stressed out. One day, Tammy saw the girl down on her hands and knees scrubbing up oil on the cement floor. That oil had been there for twenty years—she wasn't going to get it off, and anyway you were supposed to suck up spilled oil with a vacuum—but she thought this was something she had to do. The labor gang was getting paid twenty-two dollars an hour to keep the plant clean, but there she was on her hands and knees, and the labor gang person sat on his fat behind with his feet up and watched this girl trying to clean the floor. Tammy hated to see that—how scared the girl was. "You don't need to be down there," she told the girl. She was pissed off enough to speak to their foreman. "Bob, you know that ain't right." But what could she do? Some of the guys in the skilled trades made life hard for the temps who were coming in and doing twice the work for half the money. Later, Tammy said, "I felt like this girl had a family. She needed a job, period. She needed to make money just like you did twenty, twenty-five, thirty years ago, to take care of your family, and she was willing to dehumanize herself because she needed that job and she could get fired for any reason. I don't think our department had ever been that clean before she came."

Mainly, working on the line was about finding ways to make the hours go by so she could get home to her kids. Sometimes she would change up and work her board front to back, sometimes back to front. She played her music (mostly seventies R&B and funk—she wasn't that into hip-hop, she liked music made by instruments, not computers), which she had to hear over an industrial fan and four or five other radios on the line. Once, a white girl complained that Tammy's radio was too loud, which actually meant that Tammy's music was too loud, which meant that it was too black. That was one of the few run-ins she had on the line.

Most of all, she talked.

She spent more time with some people in the plant than she did with her family. She went out for lunch with them—Eli's Famous Bar-B-Que on Thomas Road, Cabaret on North River Road where they cashed their checks on payday—and to bars like the Triangle Inn and Café 83. Tammy didn't drink like some of the others and go back to work and get on that damn line that was going around and around—she didn't know how they did it. They had fun at work, too. There was this one old lady on the line who was the nastiest, most ignorant person Tammy had ever met, but she was *funny*—she would come to work with a pig nose on her face and go around startling people, groping the men. They celebrated everybody's birthday in the department with a cake, and they played football pools. Once, when she was out for a few months with Packard hands, she and a coworker won the Super Bowl pool, and she had no idea until he brought her half of the eight hundred dollars over to her house—he didn't even have to tell her.

A few of them became her close friends, like Karen, a black girl from the north side, who got bumped off day turn and put on Tammy's line in the afternoons, and Tammy trained her. She called Karen her little big sister because Karen was ten years older and a lot shorter. Karen had three kids, too, and they became best friends over that. Or Judy, who shared a table with her at her final job at Packard, Judy's machine on one side, hers on the other, for three years. "That is how you build relationships," Tammy said, "and it's not like we were just running all over the place like it is in an office. We were stuck with each other. What else do you talk about? The tool and die guy—'How is your wife doing? How are your kids? How is your son doing in football?'" When you worked with people that long, you watched their children grow up in the pictures they showed. Later, after she had left the factory, what she would miss was the camaraderie.

Miss Sybil, Tammy's friend from the east side, worked at a General Electric lightbulb factory for thirty-eight years, from 1971 until she retired at age sixty-three, hauling fifty-pound bags of cement. "Anybody who thinks factory jobs were good jobs needs to go visit somebody on a line," she said. "Most people wouldn't survive in a factory. Mitt Romney would die in a week."

Tammy survived for nineteen years. She never thought of that as anything special, and when anyone asked how she got through the work of doing the same thing a bazillion times, she hardly knew what to say. She did what she was supposed to do. It was a paycheck, a decent paycheck, and that saved her so she could save her kids.

Tammy didn't know Flip Williams very well, he was ten years older, though she knew his brother. Flip controlled the drug trade in the KimmelBrooks projects on the east side. He went to California and became a Crip and did prison time for cocaine trafficking in the late eighties. When he got out, he came back to Youngstown and tried to take over again at the Brooks. On the night of Labor Day in 1991, Flip went with three teenagers to a house in the Brooks where a dealer who had taken control of the local crack trade lived, and they handcuffed him and duct-taped his mouth. (He had planned everything, drawn maps of the house, used walkie-talkies he bought at RadioShack.) Flip told one of the teenagers, his girlfriend, to phone the guy's two friends who ran the trade with him, and she lured them to the house. While all this was happening, a fourth man, Teddy Wynn—he was a cousin of Barry, the father of Tammy's first child, and had just gotten out of the air force—happened to stop by the house for a visit. Wrong place, wrong time. Flip tied them all up, then he strangled Teddy and one of the others, had his girlfriend turn up the stereo to muffle the noise, went room to room, and shot all four in the head.

By the time Flip was finally executed for the Labor Day Massacre by lethal injection in 2005, the KimmelBrooks projects had been torn down, rebuilt, and renamed Rockford Village. Tammy felt the execution was long overdue. Flip had committed a lot of other murders on the east side that they didn't even catch him for. How do you hold someone in jail who caused so much devastation in one community?

In the late eighties and nineties, Youngstown always made the top ten cities for homicides, and it led the country in the murder of black women under sixty-five. The media put the focus on Mafia killings, because during those years Youngstown was the scene of a border war between the Genovese and Lucchese families, with a lot of high-profile mob hits—in 1996 a Mahoning County prosecutor, just about the only county official not in the pay of organized crime, was shot in his kitchen and lived. By the end of the nineties there was no money left in Youngstown to fight over, and the Mafia wars died out. But Youngstown went on being Murdertown, because most of the killings were happening in neighborhoods like Tammy's, over drugs and dis.

Tammy knew too many people who'd been killed to count. When she looked over the smiling faces in her yearbooks, she could point to the kids who'd ended up dead, or in jail or on drugs, and it was at least half. A girl at her high school was shot in a drive-by at the Brooks. One of her best friends from childhood, Geneva, dropped out of high school and had two daughters, and right around the time Tammy graduated from East, a guy got out of a car and started arguing with Geneva, threw her down to the ground, and shot her in the head. No one was ever arrested. Tammy's uncle Anthony, a junkie like his older sister Vickie, was killed and his body dumped on the east side. "The late eighties through the nineties, Youngstown just got crazy, really crazy," Tammy said. "When you think about it, there weren't jobs."

When Tammy's brothers were coming up, she assumed they identified as Crips because they were always wearing the blue. They lived with their mother on Shehy Street, two blocks from Charlotte, and sold outside the house and ruled the street. Tammy never saw their father give them any discipline. Their mother tried—she wanted more for them, it hurt her that they were always getting into trouble—but they talked back to her in a way Tammy never would have. Vickie was using again, though Tammy didn't know it at the time—for years she believed that her mother had stayed clean since Tammy was in sixth or seventh grade. Vickie would

have Tammy drive her to pick up something from a friend, or bring money
to someone she owed, and only later Tammy understood that it was drugs,
and she was enabling her mother. She found out the truth when her mother
got addicted to the Oxycontin they were giving her for pain because she
had degenerative osteoarthritis, where her joints just disintegrated and her
bones got so brittle they would crack if she moved the wrong way, and the
doctor at the nursing home where Vickie was a patient let Tammy know
that her mother was on heroin.

Around the corner from Vickie's house there was another gang, the
Ayers Street Playas, who identified as Bloods. In the late nineties, Tammy's
brothers were on the front line of a gang turf war over the crack trade,
though Tammy didn't realize that until later, either—"I wasn't really en-
trenched in the stuff that was going on, because I had kids and I was
trying to keep them out of it." One day, the oldest brother, James, was
shot and wounded in broad daylight on the front porch of the house on
Shehy Street. The youngest brother, Edwin, was sitting in a car with a
friend in the vacant lot next to the house one night—a guy with a gun
walked up to the window and reached past Edwin and shot his friend. A
few years later, a different car, sitting with a different friend and the
middle brother, Dwayne, Edwin was shot three times in the back by a
gunman in a ski mask. He survived. Both Dwayne and Edwin ended up
doing serious prison time.

Vickie's house on Shehy Street was right next door to a store, F&N
Food Market, that was notorious for trouble outside, including a craps
game that drew violent gamblers. One day, Edwin and Dwayne—they were
in their late teens—were shooting dice behind the store with two Puerto
Rican guys. Dwayne had his gun under a chair cushion in case of trouble.
A friend of the Thomas boys, John Perdue, drove up and joined the game.
Within minutes Perdue and one of the Puerto Ricans, Raymond Ortiz,
were arguing about a five-dollar bet. Ortiz grabbed Dwayne's gun and
demanded the money. Perdue refused to pay. Dwayne calmed Ortiz down,
and Ortiz and his friend walked away to their car, but then they came
back—Ortiz was still in a rage—and the argument continued. It ended
when Ortiz threatened or hit Perdue with the gun, and Perdue grabbed
the gun and shot Ortiz in the head.

Vickie knew the dead man's mother, and because it was the Thomas
boys' friend who'd killed him, with Dwayne's gun, over a craps game next

to Vickie's house, there was a lot of bad blood between the two families. Not long after the killing, Vickie's house was shot up—bullet holes in her refrigerator and oven—and Tammy moved her mother out. Then someone threw a Molotov cocktail into the house and the first floor was gutted. The mayor of Youngstown ordered his staff "to immediately tear down the fire-damaged, drug-ridden, violence-prone home at 1343 Shehy St.," *The Vindicator* reported, under the headline NUISANCE HOUSE DESTROYED. A city backhoe rolled onto the lawn and began to claw down the front porch while neighbors watched in approval. "The East Side eyesore was gone by early afternoon." The house had been worth around four thousand dollars. Its loss devastated Vickie.

By then, Tammy had left the east side.

Several times in the early nineties, kids broke into the house on Charlotte. Granny was around ninety and legally blind, and Tammy had moved her to the first floor. Tammy was stuck working afternoon turn, which meant that she didn't get home until midnight, but she couldn't afford to pay someone to stay at the house. Her children had to be babysat after school at her friend's mother's house on the south side, where Tammy picked them up on her way home. Until then, Granny was alone, and Tammy was afraid that someone would break in again and do something to hurt her because she couldn't see. After twenty years at 1319 Charlotte Avenue she moved the family out in May 1992. Granny had lived on the east side for more than half a century, and she lasted just three months on the south side before she died.

Tammy rented out the house on Charlotte for three years. In 1995 she decided to sell it. All she could get was five thousand dollars, half of what Granny had paid in 1972, from a lady who then moved back to Puerto Rico and rented it out. After that the house started to decline, until it went vacant in the 2000s.

Tammy paid twenty-three thousand dollars for her house on the south side. It was painted orange, with four thick columns across the front porch, and beautiful on the inside. The neighborhood was above Indianola, an area that had been all white when Tammy lived on the south side as a girl, but now it was changing fast, with whites hurrying out and Section 8 renters moving in, including a lot of people she knew from the east side. Tammy had a fiancé on the south side. His name was Brian, and she had known him in high school, though he was two years older (most of her friends were older). They started dating in 1990, and Brian became like a father to all three of her kids, especially her younger daughter. He didn't have a steady job—he worked on and off as an aide for the schools—but he helped Tammy deal with losing Granny, and he loved her kids. In 1995, around the time of her twenty-ninth birthday, Brian asked Tammy to marry him. She didn't answer right away. She went to Cleveland with three of her girlfriends on a birthday trip, and they checked into a hotel, and Tammy discussed it with her girlfriends and decided to say yes, and it was right around the time they checked out of the hotel to go shopping that Brian was killed.

She never found out exactly what happened—an argument with someone whose family Tammy had known since he was four or five. "Brian was such a good guy," she said, "but I don't know what affiliations he had. I didn't know anything wrong or bad about him. He had the biggest heart that I've ever found in a guy, and my kids loved him." A friend told Tammy that her younger daughter, who was seven, needed to go see a counselor, but Tammy shrugged it off—"She's okay"—because that was how Tammy had made it through three decades of life, telling herself, "It's okay, it's all right, I'll rebound." Ten years later, Tammy went away on a church retreat, and when she returned she was livid to find that her daughter had gotten a tattoo. But she softened when she saw that it was the years of Brian's birth and death and his initials. That's when she understood: her daughter had never grieved for the only man she called Dad.

In the year after Brian got killed, Tammy started going to Mill Creek Park three days a week, sometimes every day, after taking the kids to school if she was working afternoon turn, or when she got off work if she was doing day turn. She would walk the trails and sit by the old wooden flour mill along the river, with the sound of a waterfall rushing over the dam, and be alone with God, and think and rejuvenate.

The blight was spreading, gathering speed, and it followed Tammy after she moved. What had crept through the east side over a decade or two took just a few years on the south side. Tammy's neighborhood got really bad—a gang called the Dale Boys, because they lived on Avondale and Auburndale, took over. In 1997 she moved with the kids to a house right next door to Brian's mom, but she couldn't sell the house they had left—it turned out to have a lot of things wrong—and she ended up cutting a deal with the bank, giving the house back in exchange for having the mortgage written off.

She considered getting out of Youngstown. Crime was terrible just about everywhere, and there was no opportunity beyond the job she had. Most of the people who had something going on were leaving or had left. The whole city was on a downward slide. But within a couple of years she would have her ten years in at Packard, which meant full pay and benefits, including her pension when she retired. She was thankful to have a good job, and Youngstown was affordable. Over time, she started a side business on her closed-in porch, helping people plan weddings, designing invitations and printing them on her laser printer, then she got into Valentine's Day baskets, graduation cards, even funeral programs. She called her business "A Perfect Cup of T." One night she and her younger daughter sat in front of a movie and hand-tied 350 bows and glued 350 pearls onto the bows for bridal bookmarks. And she sold Avon at the factory—you could make a lot of money in a plant full of women. She wasn't going anywhere.

It was harder to get to Packard from the south side than the east, and Tammy was constantly juggling babysitters and after-school programs and work schedules. She used her vacation days to see her older daughter's performances and her son's football games. On weekends she kept her kids entertained without spending much money, going for country drives to pick strawberries and apples. She made them go to church on Sunday and Bible study after school. If she couldn't get to the parent-teacher conference, she talked to the teacher in the morning before class, and once cell phones came along, the teachers always had her number so they could reach her at the factory. She didn't work overtime until the kids were older. They would congregate with their friends at her house because she wanted to know who their friends were and what they were doing. The girls were not allowed to wear makeup until they were sixteen, and when her son was thirteen and came back from a visit to his father's with his ear pierced, Tammy made him take it out because she had told him no piercing until high school, and by then he no longer wanted it. Even as high school seniors they were never out later than midnight, or 1:00 a.m. on special occasions. She didn't abuse them, she bent sometimes, but they needed discipline and Tammy didn't play. It was crazy out there. And her daughters did not get pregnant, her son stayed out of the gangs, they all graduated from high school and went on to college. God blessed her with three good kids.

Once, someone she knew expressed amazement that she raised three children in Youngstown and they were all doing okay. Tammy got what the person was saying, but she had only done what she was supposed to do. "I had no choice, because my kids were going to have it better than I did. They were going to have it better than my brothers. I did what I needed to do, and that is what my great-grandmother did."

MR. SAM:
SAM WALTON

Sam was born in 1918 in Kingfisher, Oklahoma, right in the middle of the country. He grew up in a pretty hardscrabble time. After the Depression hit, his father, Thomas Walton, got a job repossessing farms around Missouri on behalf of Metropolitan Life Insurance Co. Sam sometimes traveled with his dad and saw how he tried to leave a little dignity to the farmers who had defaulted on their loans and were about to lose their land. No question, that was where Sam got his cautious attitude toward money. He was just plain cheap. It was the way he was brought up. Even after he became the richest man in America—and he hated it when *Forbes* put that spotlight on him in 1985, the attention caused his family a lot of extra trouble—he'd still stop to pick up a nickel off the ground. He never liked showy lifestyles. Honesty, neighborliness, hard work, and thrift—those were the bedrock values. Everyone put on their trousers one leg at a time.

"Money never has meant that much to me," he wrote near the end of his life. "If we had enough groceries, and a nice place to live, plenty of room to keep and feed my bird dogs, a place to hunt, a place to play tennis, and the means to get the kids good educations—that's rich. No question about it."

His father was never much of a success, but his mother had ambitions for their two boys, and the couple quarreled all the time. Maybe that was why Sam always needed to stay busy. He was a joiner and a competitor— Eagle Scout, quarterback and student body president at Hickman High in Columbia, Beta Theta Pi at the University of Missouri. He learned to speak to people coming down the sidewalk before they spoke to him. He was small and wiry with a face like a good-natured bird of prey, and he always wanted to win.

Sam found out pretty young that he could sell things. He worked his way through high school and college delivering newspapers, and he won a contest selling subscriptions door-to-door. After college he went to work at a J. C. Penney store in Des Moines for seventy-five dollars a week. That was his first job in retail, and it lasted long enough for Sam to learn that if employees were called "associates," they gained a sense of pride in the company. Then came the war. He spent three years in the army, stateside because of a heart irregularity. When he got out, he was determined to get back into retail, this time for himself.

Sam wanted to buy a Federated department store franchise in St. Louis, but his new wife, a wealthy Oklahoma lawyer's daughter named Helen, refused to live in a town with more than ten thousand people. So they ended up in Newport, Arkansas, population five thousand, where Sam bought a Ben Franklin variety store with help from his father-in-law. There was another store right across the street, and he would wander over and spend hours studying how the competition did things. That turned into a lifelong habit. It was in Newport that Sam got to thinking in ways that became the foundation of his success.

He was buying ladies' satin panties from the Ben Franklin supplier at $2.50 for a dozen, and selling them at three pairs for a dollar. But when he found a manufacturer's agent in New York who would sell him a dozen for two dollars, he put them out at four pairs for a dollar and had a great promotion. His profit per panty dropped by a third, but he sold three times as many. Buy low, sell cheap, high volume, fast turn. That became Sam's whole philosophy, and in five years he tripled his sales, making his the number one Ben Franklin in the six-state region.

People were cheap. They'd never pass up a rock-bottom price. It was true in the little all-white towns around Arkansas and Oklahoma and Missouri after the war. It was true everywhere all the time.

It was true in Bentonville, Arkansas, where Sam and Helen moved with their four kids in 1950 after a clever landlord took away the store in Newport. Sam opened Walton's 5&10 on the main square in Bentonville, population three thousand, and it did so well that over the next decade he and his brother Bud opened another fifteen stores. They were in the tiny backwaters that Kmart and Sears didn't bother with—Siloam Springs, Arkansas, and Coffeyville, Kansas, and St. Robert, Missouri. People were cheap, but there was higher volume in those places than the smart money in Chicago and New York knew. Sam spotted the locations in his two-seater Air Coupe, flying low over a town, scouting the roads and building patterns, then finding the right piece of empty land.

In the grip of his retail fever dream, he left his family on vacations to go check out stores in the area where they were staying. He scoured the competition and hired away their best men with offers of an investment stake in his franchises. He thought up stunts to bring in business and mislead his competitors into thinking he was a cornball. He squeezed every penny out of his suppliers. He never stopped working. He had to keep growing and growing. Nothing could get in his way.

On July 2, 1962, Sam opened his first independent discount store, in Rogers, Arkansas. Huge discounters, selling everything from name brand clothes to auto parts, were the wave of the future. He would ride it or be swept away. He was so cheap that he kept the sign to as few letters as possible: the new store was called "Wal-Mart." It promised "everyday low prices."

By 1969 he had 32 stores in four states. The next year, Sam took the company public. The Walton family owned 69 percent of the shares, and Sam was worth around $15 million. Entrepreneurship, free enterprise, risk—the only ways to improve other people's quality of life.

Throughout the 1970s, Wal-Mart doubled its sales every two years. By 1973 there were 55 stores in five states. By 1976 there were 125 stores, with sales of $340 million. Wal-Mart was spreading outward through the forgotten towns of middle America in a great circle whose center was Bentonville, laying waste to local hardware stores and pharmacies, saturating the regions it conquered so that no one else could compete, each new Wal-Mart built cookie-cutter fashion within a day's drive of company headquarters, where the distribution center was located. The stores were as big as airplane hangars, no windows, with giant parking lots paved over fields and trees, situated away from the center of town to attract sprawl. Sophisticated computers kept minute-by-minute track of every item of stock that was ordered, shipped, and sold.

By 1980 there were 276 stores, and sales passed $1 billion. Throughout the eighties Wal-Mart grew explosively, to all corners of the country and then overseas. Sam even built stores in big cities like Dallas and Houston, where there was more stealing and it was harder to come up with people of the right moral character who were willing to work there. Hillary Clinton became the first woman to join Wal-Mart's board. Her husband—the governor—and other politicians came to Bentonville to pay homage. In the middle of the decade, Sam officially became the richest man in America, worth $2.8 billion. He was as cheap as ever—he still got a five-dollar haircut in downtown Bentonville and didn't leave a tip. He and his company gave almost nothing to charity. But every year each Wal-Mart store would hand out a thousand-dollar college scholarship to a local high school senior, and somehow that bought better publicity than generous corporate philanthropy.

Sam still flew around in a twin-engine plane and visited hundreds of stores a year. He would lead the crowd of assembled associates in a bois-terous chant (the idea had come to him on a trip to South Korea in the seventies):

"Give me a W!"

"W!"

"Give me an A!"

"Give me an L!"

"Give me a squiggly!" (Everyone including Sam performed a little twist.)

"Give me an M!"

"Give me an A!"

"Give me an R!"

"Give me a T!"

"What's that spell?"

"WAL-MART!"

"Who's number one?"

"The customer!"

Sam always showed up with his first name on a plastic tag, just like all his store clerks. He made a point of collecting suggestions, listening to complaints, and promising to act on them, and hourly workers felt more attended to by this friendly man than they ever did by their managers. The associates were given moral instruction and needed permission from the district manager to date one another. They would hold up their hands and repeat a pledge: "From this day forward, I solemnly promise and de-clare that every customer that comes within ten feet of me, I will smile, look them in the eye, and greet them, so help me Sam."

The boss became Mr. Sam, the object of a folksy personality cult. An-nual meetings drew thousands of people to Arkansas and were staged as pep rallies, lit with evangelical fervor. From his spartan office in Bentonville, the chairman wrote a monthly letter that went out to his tens of thousands of employees, thanking and exhorting them. After he was diagnosed with leukemia in 1982, he assured them, "I'll be coming around—maybe more infrequently—but I'll be trying and wanting to see you. You know how much I love to visit with you all on how you're doing."

When a town in Louisiana tried to keep Wal-Mart out, fearing that it would leave the main street deserted, the story stayed local. When reports surfaced that Wal-Mart workers were so badly paid, in part-time jobs without benefits, that they often depended on public assistance, Mr. Sam would talk about the hourly associate who retired with two hundred thousand dollars in her stock ownership plan, and he would claim that he was raising standards of living by lowering the cost of living. When clerks and truck drivers tried to join unions and Wal-Mart ruthlessly crushed them, firing anyone foolish enough to speak out, Mr. Sam would come around afterward and apologize to any associates who felt ill-treated, vowing to do better, and some of them said that if only Mr. Sam knew what was going on, things wouldn't be so bad. When the departure of factory jobs for overseas turned into a flood, Mr. Sam launched a Buy American campaign, winning praise from politicians and newspapers around the country, and Wal-Mart stores put up MADE IN THE U.S.A. signs over racks of clothing imported from Bangladesh, and consumers didn't stop to consider that Wal-Mart was driving American manufacturers overseas or out of business by demanding killingly low prices.

The face like a good-natured bird of prey under a blue-and-white Wal-Mart baseball cap smiled more as it aged. As long as Mr. Sam was alive, Wal-Mart was a great American story out of Bentonville.

In 1989 the cancer came back in his bones, incurable multiple myeloma. Mr. Sam tried not to slow down. At the next annual meeting, he predicted more than $100 billion in sales by the millennium. "Can we do it?" he shouted to nine thousand people in an arena at the University of Arkansas, and they shouted back, "Yes we can!" He wrote his memoirs, asking himself whether he should have spent more time with his family in his later years, or devoted himself to good works, and concluded that he would do the same exact things all over again. Partnerships had kept the money in the family, and Helen and the four children (they had all received your everyday heartland upbringing) were worth $23 billion, and eventually six of the surviving Waltons would have as much money as the bottom 30 percent of Americans.

By early 1992, Mr. Sam was fading. In March, President and Mrs.

Bush came to Bentonville, and Mr. Sam rose unsteadily from his wheel-chair to receive the Presidential Medal of Freedom. In his final days, nothing cheered him more than a hospital visit from a local store manager who wanted to talk about sales figures. In April, just after turning seventy-four, Mr. Sam died.

And it was only after his death, after Wal-Mart's downhome founder was no longer its public face, that the country began to understand what his company had done. Over the years, America had become more like Wal-Mart. It had gotten cheap. Prices were lower, and wages were lower. There were fewer union factory jobs, and more part-time jobs as store greeters. The small towns where Mr. Sam had seen his opportunity were getting poorer, which meant that consumers there depended more and more on everyday low prices, and made every last purchase at Wal-Mart, and maybe had to work there, too. The hollowing out of the heartland was good for the company's bottom line. And in parts of the country that were getting richer, on the coasts and in some big cities, many consumers regarded Wal-Mart and its vast aisles full of crappy, if not dangerous, Chinese-made goods with horror, and instead purchased their shoes and meat in expensive boutiques as if overpaying might inoculate them against the spread of cheapness, while stores like Macy's, the bastions of a former middle-class economy, faded out, and America began to look once more like the country Mr. Sam had grown up in.

1994

WITH NEW YEAR COMES NEW FREE-TRADE ZONE, NEW UNCERTAIN-TIES . . . "I don't feel threatened," says the 35-year-old weaver, who has worked at Cone Mills, the world's largest producer of denim fabric, since she was 18. "It will be good for textiles. It will help save the future of our jobs." . . . **MTV'S "REAL WORLD" HOUSEMATE GRAVELY ILL** . . . *Fuck the world, fuck my moms and my girl / My life is played out like a Jheri curl / I'm ready to die* . . . **KURT COBAIN, 1967–1994 In Seattle, a Mood of Teen Dispirit** . . . a result of heightened concerns among parents. "Increasingly," Lieberman said, "you hear from constituents who say, 'We're worried about values, we're worried about moral decline in our society.'" . . . Alison Quigg, 14, for one, spent $500 on her orange sags and huge T-shirts. "We see these clothes on MTV," she says. "I thought they looked good." . . . If the United States did as much to encourage high-IQ women to have babies as it now does to encourage low-IQ women, it would rightly be described as engaging in aggressive manipulation of fertility. . . . **AS CITIES REACH RECORD NUMBERS OF KILL-INGS, YOUTHS PLAY GRIM ROLE** . . . **SHAMEFUL DAWDLING ON RWANDA** . . . Television viewers nationwide watched last night as a white Ford Bronco carrying O. J. Simpson was chased across the freeways of . . . While the Democratic leaders in Congress are struggling to write health legislation that follows President Clinton's principles, Newt Gingrich, the Republican whip, has united his party . . . Call toll free. Know the facts. If we let the government choose, we lose. . . . **OPRAH OVERCOMES She Lost 67 Pounds, Then Gained 90. Now, After a Five-Year War with Her Weight, She Is Once Again Queen of Lean** . . . **A HISTORIC REPUBLICAN TRIUMPH** . . . The freshman class, which included not a single "femi-Nazi," one of Mr. Limbaugh's favorite epithets for supporters of women's rights, whooped and applauded, proving itself one big fan club of the man it believes was primarily responsible for . . . *I switched my motto—instead of sayin fuck tomorrow / That buck that bought a bottle could've struck the lotto*

JEFF CONNAUGHTON

Connaughton lived in a basement apartment on Sixth Street, on Capitol Hill, beneath Mitch McConnell and next door to Daniel Patrick Moynihan. A few blocks east, north, and south were the kind of run-down streets he'd seen back in 1979 when he got lost on his way from Alabama to find a Republican senator to debate Biden. But Connaughton never went into those neighborhoods. While he was on Biden's staff, Capitol Hill was where he worked, slept, and socialized. The hours at the office were long; then he spent weekday evenings with other young staffers at the Tune Inn, the Hawk 'n' Dove, and other Hill meeting places.

For the next two decades he remained a Biden guy, yet he actually worked for the senator only four years. During that time Biden learned Connaughton's name, if not his value. He could do the kind of staff work—research, writing, bringing in experts, and sounding out interest groups—that would make the senator look substantive. That was the purpose of the postdisgrace Biden operation, after the senator recovered from an aneurysm that nearly ended his life and brain surgery that put him out of action the first half of 1988: to prove that he wasn't just a flashy talker who'd been caught out, that he had the gravitas and legislative prowess to deserve a second chance at the presidency. Connaughton worked with the Association of Trial Lawyers and blocked a change on a law regarding international airline liability. He proposed setting up several hearings on drug policy, which would give Biden a reputation for being tough on crime. He put together a dossier of the senator's achievements—a counterpoint to the scandal archive—that was used for Biden's 1990 reelection campaign. And he endured the muttered rebuke at a hearing, the silence that answered every joke he tried. Eventually, Connaughton sat at a desk right outside Biden's office, but he never dared to ask to see the boss. "I just didn't have the foundation under me to deal with Biden, who is like a political genius," he said. "If you went in there and he could sense any confusion, doubt, or uncertainty in your mind, he'd pounce on it." Just like the journalists who had pounced on Biden when they smelled his blood.

Then, in 1991, Connaughton decided that he needed to go to law school. A law degree would allow him to move in and out of politics, to know the substance of government, to make money in the course of a career, and—perhaps—to move back to Alabama. He spent his Wall Street savings on three years at Stanford. When he graduated in 1994, he went to clerk for Chief Judge Abner Mikva, of the D.C. Court of Appeals (a Biden aide helped him get the job). Mikva was a former congressman from Chicago, widely respected and liked. Almost immediately, there were rumors that Mikva would be named President Clinton's counsel. Suddenly Connaughton's dream of a path to the White House took a shortcut that had nothing to do with Joe Biden. He called Ted Kaufman. "I need Biden to call Mikva and tell him I'm great and that he should definitely take me with him." Connaughton had worked for Mikva only a month, and a word from the chairman of the Senate Judiciary Committee would be worth a lot.

A few days later, Kaufman called Connaughton back. "Biden doesn't want to call Mikva."

"What?"

"He doesn't want to call Mikva. It has nothing to do with you. He doesn't like Mikva."

For once, Connaughton was too angry to bite his tongue. "Who cares whether he likes Mikva! This is about me."

Kaufman sighed. It was one of his duties to defend the principal to his underlings, to protect Biden from the consequences of the slights and indignities he dealt out. Usually this meant the tactical silences, feigned ignorance, or euphemisms with which the wife of a tyrannical father mollifies the children. But Kaufman cared about Connaughton, and he spoke candidly. "Jeff, don't take this personally," Kaufman said. "Biden disappoints everyone. He's an equal opportunity disappointer."

Connaughton never really forgave Biden, and would never be truly surprised or disappointed by him again. For many years to come he would continue to associate himself with Biden, raise money for him, campaign for him, *be a Biden guy*, but the romance of that pursuit died with the phone call Biden refused to make. There had always been a transactional aspect to Connaughton's obsession, and now it was the central aspect. Biden had used him, and he had used Biden, and they would go on using each other, but that would be all. It was a Washington relationship.

Mikva took Connaughton to the White House anyway, because Connaughton did what he always did as a number two, which was to make himself indispensable. Before being offered a job, he wrote a detailed transition plan for Mikva's move to the counsel's office, with a media strategy and a summary of the issues that he would face. Mikva named Connaughton special assistant to the counsel, at thirty-two thousand a year (his clerkship salary). Neither of them had any idea what the job meant.

Connaughton first set foot in the West Wing on October 1, 1994. It was a Saturday, and he was wearing what he thought would be appropriate attire for a weekend in the White House: blue blazer, white shirt, khakis, and loafers, as if dressing for dinner at the country club. The first person he recognized was George Stephanopoulos—slouching down a hallway in sweatpants and stubble. Offices in the West Wing were surprisingly small and antiquated, like rooms in a shabby-elegant museum from the Federal period. The counsel's office was up the staircase to the right of the lobby, in a corner of the second floor. There were four desks in the reception area, and Connaughton was given the one used by a volunteer named Kathleen Willey, whom everyone understood to have a "special relationship" with the president, and whom Mikva's deputy, Joel Klein, wanted to get out of the West Wing. Another desk had recently been vacated by Linda Tripp, an executive assistant to the late deputy counsel and close Clinton friend Vince Foster, dead the year before of a self-inflicted pistol shot in the mouth.

To Connaughton, the whole building was sacred real estate, and the awe never really wore off. He started giving after-hours tours to everyone he knew who wanted one. By the time he left, sixteen months later, he must have given three hundred fifty.

On that October Saturday, the president used his morning radio address to urge Congress to pass a bill that would prohibit gifts from lobbyists and require full disclosure of their business. The U.S. military intervention in Haiti was a week old. The siege of Sarajevo was in its third year. The First Lady's health care initiative had recently been euthanized in the Senate. Some of the Clintons' top aides and best friends—Webster Hubbell, Bruce Lindsey—were under investigation by Kenneth Starr, the newly appointed special prosecutor in the Whitewater matter. The president was being sued for sexual harassment by Paula Jones, an Arkansas state employee. Within a month, Congress would fall to the Gingrich Republicans, blowing a massive hole in the middle of Clinton's first term.

Whitewater, Travelgate, the daily pounding of the press corps, the relentless attacks of the Republicans, the independent counsel's drilling: a fog of siege and paranoia spread through both wings of the White House, but the worst start to any presidency in living memory always led back to the corner office on the second floor. That was why Clinton was burning through counsels at a record clip—Mikva was the third, after less than two years. Colleagues joked that Connaughton was the only lawyer in the White House who didn't have a lawyer of his own.

Not long after starting work, Mikva and Connaughton met with an official from the communications team named David Dreyer. Mikva was speaking the next morning at *The Christian Science Monitor's* monthly breakfast, and Dreyer came with instructions: Mikva was to announce that he had looked into Whitewater and found nothing.

Judge Mikva, in his late sixties, white-haired and sage, was silent.

"Why would he say that?" Connaughton said. "He's only been here two weeks."

"I'll tell you why," Dreyer snapped. "It's his job to say that."

"It's not his job to throw away a lifetime's worth of credibility in a single morning. No one would believe him."

Dreyer insisted: Mikva was the president's lawyer and had an obligation to defend him. That was what working in the White House meant—everyone worked for the president, personal loyalty was the highest imperative.

"Let me think about it," Mikva finally said.

At the breakfast, Mikva avoided committing himself to a position on Whitewater. He was asked about Clinton's legal defense fund, which had been started by the president's supporters after Jones filed her lawsuit accusing Clinton of having her escorted to his Little Rock hotel room in May 1991, dropping his pants, and asking her to fellate him. (The charges were eventually settled in November 1998 when the president's defense fund and insurance companies paid the sum of the plaintiff's claim, $850,000, without a presidential apology—one month before his impeachment by a narrowly partisan vote of the House on charges of perjury resulting from his testimony in the Jones lawsuit; three months before his acquittal by the Senate; two years before Jones posed nude in *Penthouse* to pay off a large tax bill on the house she'd bought with her settlement money; twenty-six months before Clinton was stripped of his Arkansas law license for five years on his penultimate day in the White House; and four years before Jones lost a match on Fox TV's *Celebrity Boxing* to the former figure skater turned felon Tonya Harding while filling in for the former teen shooter Amy Fisher.) "I'm uncomfortable," Judge Mikva replied. "I expect the president is uncomfortable." He added that he saw no alternative to a legal defense fund other than limiting the presidency to the very rich.

Every paper in the country ran with the story, and Mikva learned that Hillary Clinton wasn't happy that he had sounded off about the First Family's controversies without permission. Mikva, who was as naïve about politics in the age of the war room and the Drudge Report as he was wise about constitutional law, stopped talking to the media. It would be months before he understood that Hillary Clinton, not he, was in charge of Whitewater and related matters, through a back-channel team of lawyers that she had installed under Mikva's nose while the Clintons benefited from his reputation in Congress for cover.

At first, as the Clintons and their staff fumed and schemed and battled for their lives, Connaughton had almost nothing to do. He had finally made it to the top of Everest, and he was bored out of his mind because Mikva had never defined his role. There was only one wall between him and the high-stakes meetings in Mikva's office, but in Washington that wall made all the difference. The odd jobs given to him took an hour or two out of the day. He was so worried about looking superfluous that he'd leave the West Wing with a handful of papers and head next door to the Old Executive Office Building, where he walked the halls and shuffled through the papers as if he were on important business.

This was a different kind of humiliation from working for Joe Biden. Connaughton called Ted Kaufman and said that he was thinking about leaving. Kaufman urged patience.

One day, Connaughton and another aide went with Mikva to Biden's office in the Russell Building. Mikva wanted to have a good relationship with the chairman of the Senate Judiciary Committee. They ran into Biden in the hall, and Biden draped an arm over Connaughton's shoulder. "Jeff, how you doing, buddy?" he said. "Great to have you here. You know from all your years with me where to take these fine people. Go make yourselves at home in my office, and I'll be right down."

As they continued toward Biden's office, Mikva quietly asked, "Did Joe know you were with me before today?"

"Oh, yes. He knew."

"I always thought he'd call me."

Now Connaughton understood why Mikva was keeping him at a distance. But just as a twenty-seven-year-old campaign aide couldn't tell a presidential candidate, "I waited six years and left Wall Street to work for you, but you can't give me five minutes," a thirty-five-year-old White House special assistant couldn't tell his boss, "Biden didn't call you about me because he thinks you're a fool." So Connaughton smiled and said nothing. A whole life in politics could pass with such omissions.

At the meeting, Biden dropped Connaughton's name a dozen times, as if he'd been part of his inner circle. "Jeff would be the first to tell you that when he was here . . ." Connaughton played along.

Over time, he found his place on the counsel's staff. He helped write Mikva's speeches. After the Republican landslide in the midterms, he prepared a memo on legal reform issues that the White House would face with the next Congress. And he began to understand how power worked in the White House. People didn't have it—they made it. If you wanted to be included in a meeting, you didn't wait for an invitation; you just showed up. He told Mikva, "If you don't use your power, you won't have any power." It was like fundraising, where you *wanted* to ask people for favors, just as a cow had to be milked in order to keep the milk coming.

Connaughton soon realized that he was working in the treetops, above the forest, dealing only with other people at the top, only the heads of organizations that had business with the administration, only American elites. A key indicator of status in Washington was whether you could get your phone calls returned, and for the first time, Connaughton's were returned instantly—especially by reporters, who found him a reliable source.

Once a week, Janet Reno, the attorney general, would come to the White House to discuss legal matters with Mikva. One day, as she left their meeting, Vernon Jordan, the president's consigliere, happened to be standing by the outer door of the office.

"Hi, Vernon, how are you?" Reno said.

"Hi, General Reno. You haven't returned my call."

"Oh, I'm sorry," she said, "I've been so busy."

Jordan, from his imposing height, in his super-elegant suit, glared at her. "That's no excuse."

Connaughton, sitting fifteen feet away, drew an instant lesson: if Vernon Jordan couldn't get Janet Reno to return his calls, he wasn't going to be able to make shit happen for his clients. He *had* to face her down. And he wondered how Reno would handle this naked power move. Was she thinking, "I know you're the president's best friend, but I'm the attorney general of the United States?" In a couple of years, Reno would authorize Kenneth Starr to widen his investigation of Whitewater and the Paula Jones case to include an intern named Monica Lewinsky, whose story would place Vernon Jordan under suspicion (though never more than that) of obstructing justice. But this time, she yielded.

"Let's have lunch next week."

Connaughton came to believe that there were two kinds of people in Washington: those who crossed the room at a party to greet someone they knew, and those who waited for the other person to cross the room. Several years later, he and Jack Quinn, a Democratic Party insider who succeeded Mikva in the counsel's office, ran into Jordan.

"Let's have lunch someday," Quinn said. "Give me a call."

"*You* call *me*," Jordan replied. "You're the junior partner in this friendship."

An obscure item in Newt Gingrich's Contract with America became the highlight of Connaughton's tenure in the White House. The Private Securities Litigation Reform Act of 1995 was drafted by Republicans to weaken the antifraud provisions of the Securities Exchange Act of 1934 and to make it harder for companies whose executives talked up their stock prices with misleading forecasts of performance to be sued. Corporations considered these suits frivolous and extortionate, and they were determined to keep them out of court. The bill had the most powerful axis of support in American business—Wall Street and Silicon Valley. One of its authors was Christopher Cox, who would go on to preside over the gutting of the Securities and Exchange Commission in the administration of George W. Bush and whose performance during the financial crisis of 2008 was so passive that he would earn the contempt, once they needed him, of the very bankers who had profited from his negligent approach to regulation. By the time the bill got the full attention of the Clinton White House, in the early summer of 1995, it had passed the House of Representatives and was under consideration in the Senate.

Connaughton thought it was a corporate power play and a gift to Wall Street. He saw the world of civil law through the eyes of plaintiffs rather than corporations, and he knew the importance of trial lawyers to the Democratic Party. He also saw a chance to raise his stature in the White House and create a small power base. He talked daily to lobbyists for trial lawyers and leaked information to a few reporters. He forged a bond with regulators at the SEC, and even with its chairman, Arthur Levitt, who wanted modifications to the Republican bill. Against the view of others on the president's staff, who didn't want to offend a hair on the head of the technology companies that wrote some of the Democrats' biggest checks and gave them cover as friendly to business, Connaughton urged Mikva to push Clinton to demand changes that would make the bill less onerous to plaintiffs.

One night in June, Connaughton was working late when the presidential scheduler called the counsel's office with a summons: the president was ready to discuss the issue. Mikva, Connaughton, and Clinton's old friend Bruce Lindsey, who was Mikva's deputy, crossed over to the East Wing, where they were told to wait for Clinton in his private study on the second floor. The Clintons had covered its walls in vermilion simulated leather, which at this hour looked closer to dark burgundy. On one wall, Connaughton noticed the famous oil painting *The Peacemakers*, which depicted Lincoln and his generals planning the last phase of the Civil War on board a steamship in Virginia, a rainbow shining in the sky outside their window. Few members of the White House staff ever got to see the president's private study, but it was too late for an official White House photographer to be on hand—so, for the purposes of impressing friends and clients with a photo behind the desk where he would work in his post–White House career, the peak moment of Connaughton's political life might as well not have happened.

At a little after nine, Clinton walked in. Despite his suit and tie and graying hair, he still looked like the ebullient, red-cheeked, slightly overweight high school sax player Connaughton had seen in photographs. The president and Lindsey exchanged banter about an old acquaintance from Arkansas who had refused to sleep in the Lincoln Bedroom the night before out of loyalty to the Lost Cause. Then Clinton said tersely, "So what have we got?"

Lindsey and Connaughton described the burdens the bill would place on plaintiffs in fraud lawsuits.

"Well, that's just too high," Clinton drawled. "I've stood out there in Silicon Valley, and I've heard them go on and on about how bad some of these class action suits are, but I can't be in a position where it looks like I'm protecting securities fraud." He mimicked the voice of a radio attack ad that could use the issue against him.

When the briefing was over, Mikva and Lindsey walked over to the dining area, where Hillary Clinton was having dinner with Ann Landers, an old friend of hers and Mikva's. Connaughton waited, alone, in the hall outside the study. After a few minutes, Clinton came out and looked him in the eye. "You think I'm doing the right thing, don't you?"

Connaughton would never forget this moment. He would always feel an emotional connection with Bill Clinton and believe that Clinton was in politics for all the right reasons. When someone on the White House staff would get up at a function and say, "Why are we here? We're here for America's children," Connaughton would think: "Are we? Or are we really here to climb the greasy pole of Washington power?" But Clinton and his wife were in the White House because they wanted to do good for people. Years later, Connaughton still got choked up thinking about a speech the president gave to his staff on the South Lawn—no press, no cameras—after the crushing defeat in the 1994 midterms. "I don't know how much time we've got left," Clinton had said. "But whether it's one day, one week, one month, two years or six years, we have a responsibility to come to work every day and do the right thing for the American people." During another dark hour, the Lewinsky scandal and impeachment, Connaughton—by then two years out of the administration—went on television at least thirty times as a B-list talking head on *Crossfire* and *Meet the Press* and *Geraldo Live!* to defend Clinton against overzealous prosecutors and a partisan Congress. He never felt that way about any other president.

"Absolutely, Mr. President," Connaughton said in the hallway. "You can't undercut the chairman of the Securities and Exchange Commission on a question of securities fraud." Chairman Levitt, a former Wall Street broker, was getting angry phone calls from the bill's supporters in the Senate, especially Christopher Dodd, the Connecticut Democrat, who was one of the finance industry's biggest champions in Washington.

"Yeah, that's right," Clinton said. "And Levitt is an establishment figure, right?"

Levitt had been the chairman of the American Stock Exchange for a decade. Before that, he had been a Wall Street partner of Sanford Weill, the future head of Citigroup. He had owned a Capitol Hill newspaper, *Roll Call*. During his eight years at the SEC, he allowed Enron and other companies to loosen their accounting controls. After leaving the commission, he would work as an adviser to the Carlyle Group, Goldman Sachs, and AIG. Without question, Levitt was an establishment figure.

"Yes, Mr. President," Connaughton said. "That's right." And it was remarkable that the president of the United States needed Jeff Connaughton to assure him of it—to say, in essence, "Yes, Mr. President, you'll have some cover when the financial and political elite come after you," because the establishment was much bigger than any president. In his second term, Clinton would prove it by moving in the opposite direction, supporting the deregulation of banks, including the repeal of the Glass-Steagall Act, and preventing financial derivatives from being regulated. For now, though, he stood fast.

The Senate passed the securities litigation bill in spite of the president's objections. Clinton vetoed it, and Congress overrode the veto, one of only two times that happened to Clinton. Even Ted Kennedy changed his mind and joined Dodd in voting with the corporations. Biden, a former trial lawyer, stuck with the president.

At the end of the year, Mikva quit, and Connaughton left as well. After almost a decade in politics, he was thirty-six and broke, renting a modest apartment in Virginia. In December 1995, he took a job as a junior associate with Covington & Burling, a top Washington law firm. If he made partner, he'd become a millionaire.

He hated the work. A minute ago he'd been briefing the president and battling Congress, and now he was literally on his knees, sifting through fifty boxes of documents one page at a time doing an attorney-client privilege review, or stuck at his desk, writing memos on behalf of a silver mine that was polluting groundwater in Idaho. As far as Connaughton was concerned, the firm was just churning the client for billable hours. He did research on another case in which the plaintiff had been moving bottles of acid with a forklift, accidentally broke some bottles, and burned most of his body as he repeatedly slipped into the acid. Covington was representing the company.

"I hope you're asking me to research whether there's enough money in the world to compensate this man," Connaughton told the partner who gave him the assignment. "No, I'm not," the partner replied.

So much in the world of power came down to chance. One day, Jack

Quinn, Mikva's replacement, needed someone to write a speech for him about executive privilege. A staffer in the White House counsel's office recommended Connaughton. As so often before, he worked his ass off for no pay or immediate advantage and wrote the speech nights and weekends. When Quinn needed another speech, on the separation of powers, Connaughton wrote that one, too.

At the end of 1996, Quinn left the White House to restart his lobbying practice at Arnold & Porter, a Washington law firm with venerable ties to the Democratic Party. To get things running, he looked around for a number two—someone who knew how to make his boss look good. His eye fell on Connaughton.

Clinton had banned top officials who left the administration from contacting the federal government for five years. The rule applied to Quinn but not to Connaughton, who wasn't senior enough. So, at the age of thirty-seven, he joined Arnold & Porter and launched a new career: as a lobbyist.

SILICON VALLEY

Peter Thiel was three years old when he found out that he was going to die. It was in 1971, and he was sitting on a rug in his family's apartment in Cleveland. Peter asked his father, "Where did the rug come from?"

"It came from a cow," his father said.

They were speaking German, Peter's first language—the Thiels were from Germany, Peter had been born in Frankfurt.

"What happened to the cow?"

"The cow died."

"What does that mean?"

"It means that the cow is no longer alive. Death happens to all animals. All people. It will happen to me one day. It will happen to you one day."

As he said these things, Peter's father seemed sad. Peter became sad as well. That day was a very disturbing day, and Peter never got over it. Well after he became a Silicon Valley billionaire he would remain radically disturbed by the prospect of dying. The initial shock was still alive in him forty years later. He never made his peace with death, the way most people learned to do, by ignoring it. Theirs was the acquiescence of an unthinking and doomed herd. The boy on the cowskin rug would grow up to view the inevitability of death as an ideology, not a fact—one that had already claimed a hundred billion human lives.

Peter's father was a chemical engineer who worked in management for various mining companies. The Thiels moved around a lot when Peter was young—he attended seven different elementary schools. Although he had a younger brother, he was a lonely boy, almost without friends until he approached his teens, lonely and inward in the way of the extremely gifted. By the age of five he knew the names of all the countries and could draw the world map from memory. When he was six, his father got a job with a uranium mining company—it was just after the 1973 oil shock, when America seemed to be headed toward nuclear energy—and the Thiels spent two and a half years in South Africa and South-West Africa, under apartheid. Peter began to play chess with his parents and quickly mastered it. In Swakopmund, a little German town on the coast of South-West Africa, he spent hours making up adventures for himself in the dried-up riverbed facing the desert sand dunes behind their house, or reading atlases, nature books, and French comics in the local bookstore. He attended schools where the boys had to wear a blazer and tie, and the teacher rapped their hands with a ruler for every misspelled word on the weekly test. When he got home, he would tear off the uniform as fast as he could, hating the regimentation. He almost always got perfect scores and avoided the beatings.

When Peter was nine, the Thiels returned to Cleveland, and when he was ten, in 1977, they moved to Foster City, California, a planned town on the San Francisco Bay, just twenty minutes' drive north of Stanford.

In 1977 hardly anyone used the term "Silicon Valley" to describe the peninsula stretching from San Francisco to San Jose. The technology firms in the area—Hewlett-Packard, Varian, Fairchild Semiconductor, Intel—were postwar companies built with the boom in military research and federal grant money that made Stanford one of the country's leading universities. The silicon transistor chip and the integrated circuit were the concern of electrical engineers and tech hobbyists, not average consumers; the personal computer was in its infancy. In 1977 the Apple Computer Company was incorporated, with a dozen employees, and the Apple II was introduced at the West Coast Computer Faire, but the head office had only just been moved out of the Jobs family garage in Los Altos to rental space in Cupertino.

The Valley was egalitarian, educated, and comfortable—one of the finest examples of postwar middle-class life in America. More than almost anywhere else, ethnicity and religion and even class tended to bleach out in the golden sunlight. Residential streets around the Valley were lined with modest two-thousand-square-foot midcentury Eichlers built on quarter-acre lots. The average house in Palo Alto cost $125,000. Commerce in downtown Palo Alto consisted of variety stores, sports shops, several movie theaters, and a pizza parlor. Across El Camino Real, the Stanford Shopping Center was dominated by Macy's, Emporium, and Woolworth's; in 1977 Victoria's Secret opened a shop, but there was no

Williams-Sonoma or Burberry, no upscale boutiques at all. The parking lot was full of Pintos and Datsuns.

Almost all the children in the Valley, even ones from the few wealthy families, went to local public schools, and they were good schools—California was ranked number one in the country. The best students went on to Berkeley, Davis, or UCLA (a few made it to Stanford or the Ivies), the average ones went to San Francisco State or Chico State, and the burnouts and heads could always get a two-year degree at Foothill or De Anza. The tax revolt—Proposition 13, a referendum that would limit property taxes in California to 1 percent of assessed value, sending the state's public schools into a long decline—was still a year away.

Peter Thiel moved to the Valley in the last year of its middle-class heyday. Everything was about to change, including the name.

After Swakopmund, Foster City in the school year of *Saturday Night Fever* seemed riotous and decadent. A lot of the kids had divorced parents. In Peter's fifth-grade classroom, the teacher was a long-term substitute who lost all control. Kids stood on their desks and yelled at one another and the teacher. "I hate you!" one boy screamed. "Why don't you go home?" The teacher managed a weak smile. Peter withdrew into his mind and became fiercely devoted to getting perfect scores, every test a matter of life and death, as if to stave off the chaos of his classmates—the California equivalent of a ruler to the hand. He was lousy at PE but exceptional at math, and as a chess player he was ranked seventh nationally in the under-thirteen bracket. He was as insanely competitive at chess as at school—later, he put a sticker on his chess kit that said BORN TO WIN—and on the rare occasions when he lost he would sweep the pieces off the board in total disgust at himself. In high school he ran the math team, which was competing for the district championship. At one point the team's faculty adviser said offhandedly, "Well, someone is going to win," and Peter thought, "This is why you are still a high school teacher."

He preferred *Star Wars* to *Star Trek* but loved them both. He read the novels of Asimov, Heinlein, and Arthur C. Clarke—the sci-fi of the fifties and sixties that dreamed of interplanetary travel, visitors from Mars, underwater cities, flying cars. A generation later, Peter lived in that mental world with the belief that miracles of technology would make the future wondrous. No TV was allowed in the Thiel house until he was twelve, but by then he was more interested in playing computer games on the family's Tandy TRS-80—such as Zork, a text-based, nongraphic adventure game set in the ruins of an ancient underground empire—as well as endless hours of Dungeons & Dragons with his nerdy friends. He also discovered J.R.R. Tolkien and read the *Lord of the Rings* trilogy at least ten straight times, almost memorized it—he loved the quality of its fantasy, the value placed on the individual against mechanistic and collective forces, the theme of power corrupting.

The Thiels were conservative evangelical Christians. Communism was the worst thing imaginable, and it was taking over the world country by country during the Carter era, and the process was irreversible. The U.S. government was bad at everything it tried, from reducing inflation to keeping cities safe. In his eighth-grade social studies class during the 1980 election, Peter supported Reagan and collected newspaper clippings on the conservative hero. Tolkien, sci-fi, chess, math, computers: in the 1970s and '80s, especially among high-achieving boys in places like the San Francisco Bay Area, these attributes were often correlated with one another and with a worldview, which was libertarianism. It had the prestige of abstract logic behind it. Peter became a libertarian in his teens, at first infused with Reagan-era conservatism, eventually taken to the purified limit. He didn't read Ayn Rand until his early twenties, and then he found the heroes of *Atlas Shrugged* and *The Fountainhead* to be implausibly righteous, the villains excessively evil, the outlook too Manichean and pessimistic after Tolkien—maybe having something to do with Rand's early years under Soviet totalitarianism, which made her see America in a similarly sinister light. Still, she was prescient in ways that no one could have imagined when *Atlas Shrugged* was published in 1957—so when the two main characters go on vacation, they end up in the worst place in America, a place no one visits because everything has fallen apart, everyone is angry, nobody works, and there they discover traces of a revolutionary engine model in the ruined factory of the Twentieth Century Motor Company, which has gone bankrupt due to the socialism of its feckless heirs. Rand foresaw that outcome at a time when General Motors had the largest market capitalization of any company in the world, and the average income in Detroit was 40 percent higher than in New York. As the years went by, Peter was more and more impressed by Ayn Rand.

In high school he never drank or did drugs. He earned straight A's at San Mateo High and was class valedictorian in 1985. He got in everywhere he applied, including Harvard, but he was afraid that Harvard might be too competitive, that he might get beaten there, and after all the uprootings of his childhood he wanted to stay near home. So he went to Stanford, the epicenter of what was beginning to be known as Silicon Valley.

"I remember 1985 as just very optimistic," he later said. He didn't have a clear plan—he could go into biotech, law, finance, even politics. "My default view was that you could do everything. You could make lots of money, and you could have a respectable job, and you could do something intellectually stimulating, and somehow one could combine everything. It was part of the eighties optimism that I didn't feel I needed to be too concrete about it. The ambition was to somehow have an impact on the world."

Well into middle age, Thiel could be fairly easily imagined as a college freshman. He walked bent slightly forward at the waist, as if he found it awkward to have a body. He had copper-colored hair, pale blue eyes, a long fleshy nose, and fantastically white teeth, but his most striking feature was his voice: something metallic seemed to be caught in his throat, deepening and flattening the timbre into an authoritative drone. During intense moments of cerebration, he could get stuck on a thought and fall silent, or else stutter for a full forty seconds.

In a philosophy class his sophomore year, Mind, Matter, and Meaning, Thiel met another brilliant student, named Reid Hoffman, who was far to the left of him. They stayed up late arguing about things like the nature of property rights (that was how Thiel made friends, at Stanford and all his life). Hoffman said that property was a social construct, it didn't exist without society, while Thiel quoted Margaret Thatcher: "There is no such thing as society. There are individual men and women." Hoffman became one of Thiel's closest friends, and their undergraduate debates would have a long afterlife when they both went into business. Most of his friends, though, were fellow conservatives. They were an isolated and besieged group, and they relished it. Stanford in the late eighties became the scene of a furious fight over the core curriculum—Western Culture, as it was called—a fight that amounted to the last campus battle of the sixties. One side, led by minority and liberal student groups, argued that Stanford's required freshman humanities courses were biased toward "dead white males" while shutting out the experience of other cultures. On the other side were traditionalists who believed that the anti–Western Civ students were using the curriculum to push a left-wing political agenda on Stanford. The quarrel over reading lists seemed every bit as meaningful to undergraduates at the time as demonstrations over civil rights and Vietnam. A group of students even took over the Stanford president's office.

At the end of his sophomore year, in June 1987, Thiel and a friend leaped into the ring by founding a conservative publication called *The Stanford Review*. They had funding and intellectual guidance from a national organization that had been started in 1978 by Irving Kristol, the father of neoconservatism, to help just such right-wing student efforts. Though Thiel rarely wrote for the *Review*, every issue carried its editor's stamp—a mix of high-minded, rational-sounding attacks on leftist ideology and mischievous ridicule of political correctness among students, faculty, and administrators.

Because it was Stanford, and because it was the latest setting of a decades-long culture war, the fight went national. In early 1987, Jesse Jackson, preparing a second run for president, came to Stanford and led students in a march with the chant, "Hey hey, ho ho, Western Culture's got to go!" A year later, William Bennett, Reagan's education secretary, was invited by Thiel's publication to speak on campus about the revisions Stanford was making to its core curriculum, which included new courses on non-Western cultures and books by nonwhite or nonmale writers. "A great university was brought low," Bennett said, "by the very forces which modern universities came into being to oppose—ignorance, irrationality and intimidation."

In his last piece as editor in chief, just before graduation in 1989, Thiel wrote, "I've learned a great deal as editor, but I still don't know how one convinces people to listen . . . To those committed leftists who would like to politicize and wreck Stanford (if you're reading this, then you probably don't belong in this category), we'll continue to fight you at every turn." Unsure what else to do, he entered Stanford Law School.

The culture war continued into its fourth decade. Under its new editor, Thiel's friend David Sacks, the *Review* moved on to speech codes, gay rights, and sex (in 1992 an entire issue was devoted to rape and the university's widening of its definition of unlawful coercion to include "belittlement" and "verbal pressure without threat"). In 1992, Thiel's friend and fellow law student Keith Rabois decided to test the limits of free speech on campus by standing outside the residence of an instructor and shouting,

"Faggot! Faggot   ⟶ you die of AIDS!" The furious reaction to this provocation even   drove Rabois out of Stanford. Not long afterward, Thiel and Sacks decided to write a book exposing the dangers of PC and multiculturalism on campus, with Thiel handling the heavy analytical lifting and Sacks doing the journalistic legwork. *The Diversity Myth* was published in 1995, with praise from well-known conservatives. The book included an account of the Rabois incident, championed as a case of individual courage in the face of a collective witch hunt. "His demonstration directly challenged one of the most fundamental taboos," Thiel and Sacks wrote: "To suggest a correlation between homosexual acts and AIDS implies that one of the multiculturalists' favorite lifestyles is more prone to contracting disease and that not all lifestyles are equally desirable."

Sacks and other friends didn't consider the deeper personal implications behind Thiel's taking a hostile view of homosexuality, because they didn't know that he was gay. No one knew. He wouldn't come out until 2003, when he was in his midthirties, and only then to his closest friends, explaining to one that his identity would have gotten in the way of his work. And anyway, he never thought of being gay as the core of who he was. Perhaps it helped make him a contrarian, but perhaps it didn't. "Maybe I'm more of an outsider because I was a gifted and introverted child," he said—not because he was gay. "And maybe I'm not even an outsider." It was a subject that he never liked to discuss, even with those closest to him.

The Diversity Myth remained Thiel's only book, which chagrined him a little, since, after all, it was of its moment, and over the years the urgency of its polemics faded considerably, and Thiel's views of identity broadened as he got older, until he began to wonder if the target had been worth the effort. Even as the book was published, Stanford was undergoing an immense cultural change that would soon leave the humanities courses that had been the object of so much contention forgotten, rendering the era of curriculum wars quaint, if not ridiculous.

Thiel always harbored the ambition to be a public intellectual, while doubting that such a career was even viable in an age of academic specialization. He wanted to dedicate his life to the spirit of capitalism, but he wasn't sure if that meant defending it intellectually, or getting rich, or both. If he defended capitalism without making money, his commitment might be questionable; if he just made money (and not a little—he wanted enormous sums of it), he would merely be one more capitalist. Sacks believed that Thiel could be the next William F. Buckley *and* a billionaire, though perhaps not in that sequence.

Just before graduating from Stanford Law School, Thiel wrote a final editorial for the *Review* that mocked the liberal aversion to lucrative careers, the preference for "'public interest law,' which, as far as can be discerned, is neither for the good of the public nor very interesting nor particularly law-related." He diagnosed the causes: "The PC alternative to greed is not personal fulfillment or happiness, but anger at and envy of the people who are doing something more worthwhile"—such as a career in management consulting, investment banking, options trading, or real estate development, with an emphasis on golf courses. (He also mentioned joining a start-up—still unusual at Stanford in 1992, though not for long.) Thiel concluded that "greed is far preferable to envy: It is less destructive (I'd rather live in a society where people don't share than in one where they try to take what belongs to everybody else) and it is more honest."

After seven years at Stanford, Thiel left for a clerkship in Atlanta (he had interviews at the Supreme Court with Justices Antonin Scalia and Anthony Kennedy but wasn't hired—the first setback of his life, and a traumatic one). Then he went to New York to practice securities law at the white-shoe firm of Sullivan & Cromwell. That was when things began to get away from him a bit. He later called his time in New York "a rolling quarter-life crisis."

The job was boring. If he were a Marxist, he would have called it alienated labor—working eighty hours a week at something he didn't believe in so that eight years on he might make partner, with the next forty years of his life laid out before him. His chief rivals were under the same roof, working right next to him, competing like crazy for stakes that were all internally assigned, with no transcendent value. And that was the deeper problem: Thiel was beginning to question the competitive life. In law school he hadn't worked quite as hard as usual and hadn't quite made his usual superior grades, because he didn't know precisely what they were for anymore. In high school he had known—good grades were for good colleges—but now he was no longer so quick to think, "This is why you are still a high school teacher." His last editorial for the *Review* had struck a posture of contemptuous certainty that masked unease.

After seven months at the law firm, he quit and went to work as a derivatives trader—currency options—at Credit Suisse. It was mathematically challenging, and he lasted longer on Wall Street than at the law firm, but not much. There was the same problem as at Sullivan & Cromwell: he was competing feverishly with his coworkers, and with little conviction in the socially designated stakes. The economic value of the work wasn't at all evident—financial innovation seemed to have reached diminishing returns—and he harbored doubts that he could ever master the game enough to win at it. He lacked the political skills, which included schmoozing and backstabbing. And the older generation in both institutions, law and finance—men who had come on in the midsixties and gotten their big reward in the seventies—was totally oblivious to the fact that it had become much harder for young people to move up.

There was a philosophical dimension to his rolling quarter-life crisis, too. At Stanford he had attended a lecture given by a French professor named René Girard, which had led him to Girard's books, and he became a devotee. Girard had developed a theory of mimetic desire, of people learning to want and compete for the same things, which attempted to explain the origins of violence. The theory had a sacred and mythic aspect—Girard, a conservative Catholic, explained the role of sacrifice and the scapegoat in resolving social conflict—which appealed to Thiel, offering a basis for Christian belief without the fundamentalism of his parents. Mimetic theory was also a challenge to Thiel's worldview, because its explanation of human behavior by group attraction ran counter to his libertarianism. He was both intensely competitive and averse to conflict—he never gossiped, avoided the infighting that was part of working with other people, and presented such a rational demeanor that it became a barrier to intimacy. He also had a horror of violence. In the end, he recognized himself in Girard's ideas: "People compete hard for things," he said, "and once you get them you are sort of disappointed, because the intensity is driven by the fact that all these people want it, but it is not necessarily a good thing. I was very open to the Girard theory because I was more guilty of it than most."

There was a contemporary word for what Girard described: status. In New York the struggle for it was ubiquitous and ferocious. Everyone was on top of everyone else in an infinite skyscraper—you looked down and it went as far as you could see, you looked up and it went as far as you could see, you spent years climbing the stairs, all the while wondering if you had moved up at all or if it was just an optical illusion.

In the summer of 1994, Thiel, his roommate, and some other friends rented a time-share in the Hamptons. It turned into a nightmarish weekend, with everything costing too much, the service bad, the whole vacation a fight with other people from start to finish—a classic example of something generated without regard to its real value. New York was too expensive—that was what it came down to. Lawyers had to wear good suits and ties, bankers had to eat and drink really well. In 1996, Thiel was making about a hundred thousand a year at Credit Suisse, and his roommate was making three hundred thousand. The roommate was thirty-one years old, three years older than Thiel, and he ran out of money. He had to call his dad for a loan.

That was when Thiel left New York and moved back to Silicon Valley for good.

The Valley was no longer the place Thiel had left four years earlier. What had happened in the meantime was the Internet. Between the midseventies and the early nineties, the personal computer had spawned countless hardware and software companies in Silicon Valley, and in other high-tech centers around the country; during the seventies and eighties the population of San Jose doubled, approaching a million, and by 1994 there were 315 public companies in the Valley. But none of the newer ones had been as important as Hewlett-Packard, Intel, or Apple. In the years since the Macintosh, the computer industry had seen more consolidation than innovation, and the undisputed winner was in Seattle.

The most important Silicon Valley company to come along since Apple was originally called Mosaic, started in 1994 by Jim Clark, a former Stanford professor and founder of Silicon Graphics, and Marc Andreessen, a University of Illinois graduate who, at twenty-two, had just the year before developed the first graphical browser for the World Wide Web. In 1995, the year that the last restrictions on commercial use of the Internet were lifted, their company went public as Netscape, headquartered south of Stanford in Mountain View. Its breakthrough product was a Web browser called Netscape Navigator. Over the next five months, while the company remained unprofitable, Netscape's stock rose tenfold. Between 1995 and the turn of the millennium—the period of the browser wars— the number of Web users around the world doubled every year. Yahoo! went public in 1996, Amazon in 1997, eBay in 1998. Netscape set in motion a tidal wave of technology companies in Silicon Valley, companies that didn't require prohibitive amounts of capital to get going, because

they were based on the Internet—companies that could be started by college grads, students, and dropouts.

The dot-com boom was just beginning when Thiel returned in 1996.
He moved into an apartment in Menlo Park and set up a hedge fund,
Thiel Capital Management, raising a million dollars from friends and
family. But something else was in the air. People he knew were getting
involved in start-ups, and Thiel wanted to do the same. He wanted, he
said, "to build constructive noncompetitive relationships with people.
I didn't want to work with frenemies, I wanted to work with friends. In
Silicon Valley it seemed possible, because there was no sort of internal
structure where people were competing for diminishing resources." Unlike New York, Silicon Valley wasn't a zero-sum game.

It took two more years. In the summer of 1998, Thiel gave a guest
lecture at Stanford on currency trading. It was a hot day and around six
people showed up. One of them was a twenty-three-year-old Ukrainian-
born computer programmer named Max Levchin. Just out of the University of Illinois, he had come to Silicon Valley that summer with a vague
notion of starting a company, sleeping on friends' floors—on the day of
the lecture he was looking for an air-conditioned room to cool off in. As
Levchin listened, he grew excited. Thiel was young, smart, he dressed in
a T-shirt and jeans, he was more than a step ahead of the game, what he
was saying sounded more like chess than investing. And he was a libertarian, like Levchin. Afterward, Levchin went up and introduced himself,
and they agreed to have breakfast the next morning and talk about
Levchin's ideas for companies.

They met for smoothies at a greasy spoon across El Camino from
Stanford Stadium called Hobee's, a hangout for students and young dot-
com entrepreneurs. Levchin, who annoyed Thiel by arriving late, pitched
two ideas—one having to do with online retailing, the other with encryp-
tion for handheld digital devices. Thiel quickly tossed aside the first
pitch, but the second interested him—cryptography was harder, not a lot
of people could do it. He asked Levchin how much money he'd need
to get started, and Levchin said two hundred thousand dollars. Thiel
revised it upward to half a million. In their next conversation, he said
that he would invest two hundred forty thousand and help Levchin raise
the rest.

They began to spend time together, getting to know each other by
trading puzzle challenges, mostly math puzzles. How many digits did the

number 125^{100} have? (Two hundred ten.) One of Thiel's puzzles involved a hypothetical table in the shape of a circle: In a game in which two players took turns placing a penny anywhere on the table without overlapping the others, with the winner the last one to put down a penny that didn't hang over the edge of the table, what would be the best strategy for winning? And did you want to go first or second? It took Levchin fifteen minutes to figure it out—the key was that the best strategy depended on disrupting the other player's strategy (*disrupt* was one of Thiel's favorite words).

The two puzzle jockeys were trying to figure out if the other guy was smart enough to hang out with. One night, at Printer's Inc. Café on California Avenue in Palo Alto, the duel went on for four or five hours, until Thiel threw out a puzzle that was so hard Levchin could solve only a small part of it. That ended the marathon evening, which cemented the friendship and partnership. (Even Thiel's constructive noncompetitive relationships were pretty competitive.)

Combining *confidence* and *infinity*, they named their new company Confinity. Levchin's cryptography idea was a little vague, but Thiel, who soon joined the company as its CEO, refined it: Confinity would store money—essentially in the form of digital IOU notes—on devices like the Palm Pilot, which seemed to be on the verge of taking over the world. With the necessary password, the infrared of one Palm Pilot could beam the note, linked to a credit card or bank account, to another Palm Pilot, using a software application called PayPal. It was a cumbersome and perhaps pointless service, but at a time when venture capitalists were pouring money into kibu.com, an online community for teenage girls, and DigiScents, which tried to transmit smells through the Web, the idea's weirdness made it seem innovative and therefore attractive. One angel investor heard the pitch over Chinese food near Hobee's and, with only the foggiest understanding of what the company did but a keen interest in the identities of other investors, came on board (his fortune cookie sealed the deal).

In July 1999, Thiel scored $4.5 million in financing. Levchin and his engineers stayed up coding for five nights to get ready for the announcement, which took place in front of a dozen journalists at Buck's, a restaurant in Woodside that was already a legendary site of big Silicon Valley deals. As the TV cameras rolled, venture capitalists from Nokia successfully beamed their preloaded millions from one Palm Pilot to another.

"Every one of your friends will become like a virtual, miniature ATM," Thiel told the press.

His strategy was to scale up as quickly as possible, in the belief that the key to beating competitors on the Internet was viral growth. Each new customer was given ten dollars for signing up and another ten dollars for every referral. Confinity kept track of users via a counter linked to its database that the company called the World Domination Index—every few minutes, a pop-up box on company computers would refresh the number with the sound of a ding—and by November 1999, just a few weeks after its launch, it was growing by 7 percent a day. But it became clear that setting up an account on the PayPal website, which enabled transactions with anyone who had an e-mail address, was a far more popular way to send money than trying to get Palm Pilots to mate on a restaurant table (the mobile Internet was in its earliest, glitch-ridden stage). The e-mail idea seemed so simple that it would be only a matter of time before competitors figured it out. The pace grew even more frantic, with hundred-hour workweeks. The most dangerous competitor, X.com, founded by a South African immigrant named Elon Musk, was located just four blocks up University Avenue. Confinity held daily meetings on the war with X.com. One day, an engineer displayed a schematic of an actual bomb that he'd designed. The idea was quickly shelved.

With his funding Thiel went on a hiring spree. He wasn't looking for industry experience but for people he knew, people who were incredibly smart, people who were like him, Stanford friends like Reid Hoffman, *Stanford Review* alums like David Sacks and Keith Rabois, and Confinity's cramped, spartan offices above a bike shop soon filled with carelessly dressed, badly groomed men in their twenties (Thiel was one of the oldest at thirty-two), chess players, math whizzes, libertarians, without distracting obligations like wives and children or time-wasting hobbies like sports and TV (one applicant was turned down because he admitted to enjoying shooting hoops). Some employees lived on junk food at their desks, others were on life-extension calorie-restricted diets. The company took out an ad in *The Stanford Daily*: "Think kick-ass stock options in a cool start-up are worth dropping out of college? We are hiring right now!" It became the first company in the history of the world to offer cryogenics as part of its employee benefits package.

Thiel was trying to build a successful business that would make him rich, but he also wanted to disrupt the world—in particular, the ancient technology of paper money and the oppressive system of monetary policy. The ultimate goal was to create an alternate currency online that would circumvent government controls—a libertarian goal. The summer he met Max Levchin, Thiel read a book published the previous year, *The Sovereign Individual* by Lord William Rees-Mogg and James Dale Davidson. It described a coming world in which the computer revolution would erode the authority of nation-states, the loyalty of their citizens, and the hierarchies of traditional professions, empower individuals through globalized cybercommerce, decentralize finance by moving it online with electronic money, and bury welfare-state democracies, while accelerating inequalities of wealth (which, in the madcap late nineties, seemed almost inconceivable). At the same time, local mafias would have wide latitude to inflict random violence. The book sketched out a libertarian apocalypse, a dream with dark edges, and it was part of the inspiration for PayPal.

Thiel disliked the human complication and friction of day-to-day management, which he left to others, but at company meetings he let his employees in on his larger vision. "PayPal will give citizens worldwide more direct control over their currencies than they ever had before," he told his staff. "It will be nearly impossible for corrupt governments to steal wealth from their people through their old means"—hyperinflation and wholesale devaluations—"because if they try, the people will switch to dollars or pounds or yen, in effect dumping the worthless local currency for something more secure." He concluded, "I have no doubt that this company has a chance to become the Microsoft of payments, the financial operating system of the world."

PayPal was growing exponentially, approaching a million users, while burning through ten million dollars of operating capital a month with hardly any revenue coming in. Was it the biggest thing since Netscape, or a Dutch tulip likely to die at any moment? Netscape itself was all but dead by 1999. Throughout that year, Thiel watched the dot-com whirl spin faster and faster—the Idaho billionaires showing up in the Valley looking for someone to give their money to, the brunches at Buck's and dinners at Il Fornaio, the thousand-dollar meals that broke entrepreneurs tried to pay for in company shares, the select e-mail invitation list to nightly launch parties that were rated with a starred ranking system determined by the fame level of the rock band playing. There were more than four hundred companies in Silicon Valley, and the average house in Palo Alto cost $776,000. The parking lot of the Stanford Shopping Center

was full of Audis and Infinitis whose owners were shopping at Blooming-
dale's and Louis Vuitton.

Thiel sensed that the end might come suddenly and soon. On the last
night of the millennium, at PayPal's New Year's Eve party, he listened
to Prince singing "1999," an early-eighties song that had been like the
soundtrack to the whole crazy year—for Prince had somehow seen it
coming years before:

> *Cuz they say 2000 zero zero party over, oops out of time*
> *So tonight I'm gonna party like it's 1999*

In February 2000, *The Wall Street Journal* gave PayPal a rough valua-
tion of five hundred million dollars. Others in the company wanted to
hold out for a larger figure before the next finance round, but Thiel told
them, "You're crazy, this is a bubble," and in March, with a sense of time
running out, he traveled abroad to raise another hundred million. On
March 10, the NASDAQ hit a peak of 5133—it had breached 3000 only
the previous November—and then it began to drop. In South Korea, still
reeling from a financial crisis, investors were so desperate to get in on Pay-
Pal's secret that one tried to eavesdrop from behind a palm tree on a
conversation Thiel was having in a hotel lobby. When Thiel's credit card
failed to work at the Seoul airport—he had reached his monthly limit—
a group of investors, instead of taking this as a worrying sign about the
health of an online payments company, bought him a first-class ticket on
the spot. The next day, they wired PayPal five million dollars with no
terms negotiated, no paperwork signed, and when the company tried to
return the money, the Koreans refused: "We've given you the money and
you will have to take it. We're not going to tell you where it came from, so
you can't send it back."

On Friday, March 31, Thiel closed the hundred million dollar round.
On Tuesday, April 4, the NASDAQ plunged below 4000, heading south
toward 1000, and the dot-com bubble burst.

PayPal was one of the few survivors. Just before the crash, it had
merged with X.com. Thiel stepped down as CEO, then returned later in
2000 when Musk was forced out. In February 2002, PayPal went public,
the first company to do so following the September 11 attacks (which
proved fatal to PayPal's libertarian ambition—electronic currency systems suddenly seemed like ideal ways for terrorists to hide money). At the

IPO party, Thiel took on a dozen employees simultaneously in a round of speed chess. In 2002, PayPal became the method of payment for more than half of eBay's auction customers, and after doing everything possible to create a more successful alternative, eBay purchased PayPal in October for $1.5 billion. Thiel quit the same day, walking away with $55 million on his $240,000 investment.

What came to be called the PayPal mafia went on to found a lot of successful companies: YouTube, LinkedIn, Tesla Motors, SpaceX, Yelp, Yammer, Slide . . . Thiel moved out of his one-bedroom apartment in Palo Alto to a condo in the Four Seasons Hotel in San Francisco. Within a week of leaving PayPal, he started a new fund called Clarium Capital Management. The end of his career as the CEO of a Silicon Valley start-up marked the start of his life as a technology mogul.

1999

WILD RIDE TO THE TURN OF THE CENTURY . . . **ELOQUENT CLINTON ALLY CHOSEN TO GIVE CLOSING ARGUMENT** . . . when you hear somebody say, "This is not about sex," it's about . . . Bill and Hillary Clinton are experimenting with a trial separation, the DRUDGE REPORT has learned. . . . **Party like it's 1999. Smell like it's 1959.** . . . Investigators, meanwhile, were hunting for a mystery man who fired two shots from a 40-caliber handgun inside Club New York during the dispute between Puffy's posse and . . . **IS THE INTERNET THE NEW HEAVEN?** . . . **FOR TALK MAGAZINE, ECLECTIC PARTY AND A "HIP" LIST** . . . Tina must have struck a deal with the gods of weather. It was an incredibly perfect night for dining alfresco, under the stars, with Manhattan as a dazzling backdrop and everything dominated by the dramatically lit Lady Liberty. The American flag billowed magnificently as the crowd danced . . . **CONE MILLS TO CLOSE PLANTS AND TRIM STAFF IN REVAMPING** . . . **THE COMMITTEE TO SAVE THE WORLD The inside story of how the Three Marketeers have prevented a global economic meltdown—so far** . . . **MILLIONAIRES? DIME A DOZEN. MARTHA STEWART'S DOMESTIC EMPIRE HAS MADE HER WORTH A BILLION** . . . Fuck Martha Stewart. Martha's polishing the brass on the *Titanic*. It's all going down, man. So fuck off with your sofa units and Strinne green stripe patterns . . . **COUNTRYWIDE BEEFING UP SUBPRIME MORTGAGE LOANS** . . . Today's postfeminist era is also today's postmodern era, in which supposedly everybody now knows everything about what's really going on underneath all the semiotic codes and cultural conventions, and everybody supposedly knows what paradigms everybody . . . **US BANKS UNLEASHED Imminent Death of Glass-Steagall Act Will Create Giant US Financial Firms** . . . The United States seems keener than most countries to celebrate the new millennium in style: maybe the nation is wealthy and optimistic enough that big parties seem apropos. . . . **COAST-TO-COAST FIREWORKS** . . . "This is a unique moment for our country," Clinton told a crowd assembled just off the National Mall, where a gala public celebration was scheduled for later Friday night. "Light may be fading on the twentieth century, but the sun is still rising on America."

DEAN PRICE

In 2003, Dean's younger son, Ryan, who was eight, began begging his mother to let him go live with his father in North Carolina. She finally told Ryan, "If you can remember your father's phone number, you can call him and have him come pick you up." Ryan stayed up all night trying to remember. Around 6:30 in the morning it came to him and he called his father. By ten o'clock Dean was at the doorstep.

Dean was in the middle of divorcing his second wife, and he and Ryan moved into the main house while Dean's mother took the apartment in back. Dean realized that it was just like *The Andy Griffith Show*, with Andy, Opie, and Aunt Bee living together under one roof. Dean made his family house, the house where his father had slapped him down, into his own. He hung carved mottoes around the rooms: DREAM on the fireplace mantle, SIMPLIFY SIMPLIFY SIMPLIFY on the stone chimney above it, SEE THE POSSIBILITIES over the opening between the living room and study. The Gettysburg Address hung on the wall over his bed, Robert E. Lee's definition of a gentleman stood on a table in the living room, and in the study there was a framed tobacco leaf. His mouse pad showed a picture of white-haired Thomas Edison from the eyes up: "There is always a way to do it better . . . find it!" On his bookshelves were classics like Emerson's essays and *Tobacco Road*, biographies of Carnegie and Lincoln, books on entrepreneurship, and *Think and Grow Rich*. A couple of old but functional twelve-gauge shotguns leaned in doorways. For heat he burned wood pellets in a woodstove hooked up to the chimney. His garage was cluttered with farm machinery, vintage signs, and a framed copy of his favorite Bible verse, Matthew 7:7. It was the house of a man with his eyes turned to the future and the past.

By 2003, Dean was starting to hate the convenience store business. He was better at conceiving and starting a business than running one, and the daily operation of the stores bored him. He had gotten into this business to be able to farm and sell his own produce, but no one had told him about the fifteen-hundred-mile Caesar salad. This wasn't real entrepreneurship—all it took was a calculator and a good profit-and-loss statement. He had two hundred employees, poor blacks and white trash, many of them single mothers, and he hated paying them close to minimum wage with no health benefits—how could you raise kids on that?—but when he tried to get a better class of workers by pushing the pay up to ten or twelve dollars an hour, the performance never improved and it took him two years to get the wage back down by attrition. You were totally taking advantage of people in this business, but there was no way around it—fast food drew the lowest of the low, people with no ambition, and the quality of the food reflected it. He knew that some of his employees were stealing from him, and a lot of them were doing drugs. They would stay up all night and come to work high at six in the morning.

Once, a customer called Dean and said, "I just left one of your restaurants."

"Really?" Dean said. "How was it?"

"I went in, got me a cup of coffee, asked the waitress, 'How you doing today?' She said, 'I'm doing just fucking great. I'm working at a damn Bojangles'."

Dean always relied on a partner to oversee the stores and take care of the books. That had been his brother-in-law, but after he and Dean's sister divorced, Dean had to buy him out for fifty thousand dollars, and he needed a new partner. His closest friend was Chris, the guy he'd lived out of a VW bus with in California. They had been each other's best man, and Chris had gotten into the bar business and lost everything when he developed a drug problem—bar, wife, child. Chris was a kind, bighearted guy, and Dean tracked him down in Florida and asked if he wanted to come back to North Carolina and make a new start by helping to build Red Birch into a southeastern chain. He always felt that a good bartender would be a good fast-food person because of the speed of the work.

Dean and Chris were business partners for several years, until June 6, 2003, which was Chris's thirty-seventh birthday. That day they played golf together, and then they went out for dinner with another guy to a restaurant in Martinsville. Dean was the designated driver, and Chris had been drinking beers much of the day. In the middle of dinner, Chris got up and left the table. Dean thought that he had gone to the bathroom, but after fifteen minutes Chris hadn't returned, and Dean started to worry. He checked the bathroom, but Chris wasn't there. He walked outside and looked around the parking lot—no sign of Chris. He got in his truck and drove the roads around Martinsville for two and a half hours, and he still couldn't find his best friend. He called Chris's wife, his second wife, and said, "You're not going to believe this but I have lost your husband." The wife came to meet Dean and said, "Why don't you just go on home and I'll call you tomorrow, let you know what happened."

"No," Dean said, "I want to know tonight. I'm responsible."

So Chris's wife got in Dean's truck and she directed him to a broken-down house on an abandoned street near the center of town, with rotting boards nailed across the windows and two black guys sitting on the front porch, smoking what looked like a joint. It was one in the morning and Chris was inside and Dean couldn't get him to come out.

It was worse than a sucker punch to the gut, because Dean loved Chris. He drove home to Stokesdale and stayed up crying the rest of the night. It turned out that Chris had left the crack house after Dean went away and in the middle of the night he let himself into the Red Birch office behind the Bojangles' restaurant in Martinsville. There, Dean believed, Chris took some cash and a check out of the safe to cover his fix. Dean concluded later on that Chris had been stealing from him for quite a while. Early the next morning, he called Chris: "I want you to meet me at Fairy Stone State Park." That was a park near Bassett where Dean planned to whup the shit out of Chris with a peachtree stick. Chris was messing with the lives and families of all the people who worked for them, along with his own and Dean's, and he needed to be taught a lesson. But Chris wouldn't meet him.

Dean agonized about what to do. Napoleon Hill had a theory that he got from Andrew Carnegie, about the "Mastermind," which was the co-ordination of effort between two people for a definite purpose. Just as hydrogen and oxygen combined to make something new—water—the blending of two like minds created a third mind, which had a divine power or force. With the Mastermind alliance, ideas could be caught out of the air that wouldn't have appeared to someone working alone. Dean and Chris had been like that. But Napoleon Hill didn't have instructions for what to do if one of the minds turned out to be a crackhead.

Then Dean remembered a story about Abraham Lincoln. One day, Lincoln was sitting under an old oak tree outside his log cabin and he saw a squirrel run down from a branch into the middle of the tree. That seemed strange, and Abe climbed up to look down into the place where the squirrel had disappeared, and he found that the whole center of the tree was hollow. He had to make a decision. Should he leave the tree standing, because it shaded his house from the sun? Or cut it down in case a strong wind toppled it? It pained him, for he loved the tree, but Lincoln cut it down. "And that's what I had to do with Chris. I had to cut him loose. It devastated his life."

Dean and Chris never spoke again. Last he heard, Chris had gone back to Florida and opened a shoe store around Fort Myers, but within a few years he disappeared again, one step ahead of his creditors.

When Dean looked back on that period, losing Chris was the first of a string of blows that came one after the other. In a way they ended up getting him out of the convenience store business. But first came the only windfall he ever enjoyed, and it appeared in the form of two brothers from India, Dave and Ash. They had been in the country for twenty years, living in Burlington, North Carolina, and they owned a hot dog stand in Florida called Hot Diggity Dog. One day not long after Dean sent Chris away, Dave and Ash stopped by the store in Stokesdale and left their names and number. Dean called, and the Indians said that they were interested in buying the Stokesdale truck stop. This led to a series of eight-hour meetings at Red Birch, with Ash compulsively punching numbers in his calculator the whole time, even when numbers weren't at issue—it was his security blanket. But there was a sparkle in his eyes.

Dean wanted to sell. He had always been overleveraged, playing the same game that people were playing with houses but on a commercial scale, taking on more debt as he built his stores from the ground up. He and the Indians went back and forth, going over every detail of the business. In the end, Dave and Ash paid him a million and a half dollars. It would have taken Dean twenty years to make that kind of money.

He might have gotten out of convenience stores right then—sold his other two truck stops to Dave and Ash, or found some other Indians looking to buy a piece of the American dream. Instead, he turned around and spent part of the money on a Back Yard Burgers franchise across from the Piedmont Mall in Danville. Back Yard Burgers was oriented more toward a white middle-class clientele than other fast-food chains, with a charcoal grill taste. Dean hired his three sisters to run the restaurant and sent them to corporate headquarters in Nashville for training. He planned a grand opening two weeks before Christmas in 2004.

That Thanksgiving, Dean and his sisters and mother brought a plate of food to his father where he worked, in a guard's booth at the entrance to the parking lot outside Unifi Manufacturing in Mayodan. His father had been divorced by the wife in Burlington, and at age sixty-five he was living alone in a rental apartment in Mayodan, in a little yellow house next to a shuttered mill. Unifi, a windowless concrete building hundreds of yards long, was the last mill in the area still doing any volume. His father was lucky to hold on to a job there. He was slobbering, barely coherent, and had to wear Depends because the painkillers had worn away his stomach lining.

Dean opened the Back Yard Burgers in Danville on December 13. Three days later, his father shot himself in the heart with a .357 in his bed. His last words were left behind on paper in chicken scratch hand-writing: "I can't take it any more."

Pete Price was buried on the Price tobacco farm, in the grave next to his father Norfleet's, under a stone cross inscribed with the words "Just a sinner saved by grace." Years later, Dean stood over the grave and said, "That was his whole mind-set. That was what was wrong with it. He thought he was a sinner. When he was really a child of God—could have done anything, and had powers he didn't even know."

A few months before the suicide, Dean and his father and Dean's boys had gone on a family vacation to Walt Disney World in Orlando. One day, Dean and his father were sitting under the Tree of Life, and they began talking about religion and the Bible. One thing that always struck Dean was where the Bible said, "And the word became flesh and dwelt among us." At Disney World he told his father, "And what that means is that your thoughts and your words become your reality, and you need to protect your thoughts and guard your words, and never say anything you don't want to see come to fruition in your life. You stay positive." And perhaps be-cause Dean seemed like a big success, with a lot of cash on hand from the sale of the Stokesdale store, and perhaps because his father's way of be-lieving had led him downward to this point, they sat there under the Tree of Life and his father listened—for the first and last time in their lives together, he listened.

Hurricane Katrina hit New Orleans on Monday, August 29, 2005. That morning, seven hundred fifty miles away, Dean watched on TV. By Friday, with oil refineries shut down all along the Gulf Coast, the price of diesel had spiked from $2.25 to $3.50 a gallon, and Dean was running out of fuel at his truck stops in Martinsville and Bassett. Commerce on Route 220 pretty much came to a halt, and the North Carolina public schools nearly closed for lack of fuel in school buses. Dean struggled to keep fuel in the ground any way he could, selling off-road diesel from his on-road diesel tanks. Independents like him were accused of price gouging, but they were only protecting what little fuel they had—if they kept the price low they'd run out in a matter of hours. It took two months for the region to emerge from the crisis.

Dean called Katrina "my come-to-Jesus moment."

He had long known that independent truck stop owners like him were hog-tied. Margins were so low that a small-scale distributor made less than a dime on the gallon. "From day one I've struggled with the business, always undercapitalized, always trying to leverage everything I had. Between the credit card companies, the big oil companies, the taxes, the employees stealing, with twenty-something percent unemployment around here, I just never had a chance." But Katrina almost put Dean out of business, and it drove him to realize that he had to do something different to survive. He had to make his truck stops energy independent—that would be his competitive advantage over all the other truck stops up and down 220. He was startled to learn how dependent America was on foreign oil, imported from countries that didn't like the United States, countries that sent terrorists to kill Americans, countries where Americans were now fighting and dying. "And it pissed me off that our government, George W. Bush and all the rest of 'em, would let this country get into a position where it is actually threatening our very existence. And all because of greed, and the almighty dollar, and putting our faith in these multinational corporations that clothe us, feed us, and fuel us."

A month before Katrina hit, Wal-Mart had opened its first Supercenter in Rockingham County. Two more were coming within six months, including one that would occupy 158,000 square feet in a mall on the highway between the center of Mayodan and Route 220. Three Wal-Marts for a poor rural county of just ninety thousand people: that would wipe out just about every remaining grocery store, clothing store, and pharmacy in the area, and because Wal-Mart also sold discount fuel, eventually it would kill the truck stop owners. Two thousand five hundred people applied for the 307 "associates" positions at the Mayodan store, which paid an average of $9.85 an hour, or $16,108 a year. On January 31, 2006, the mayor of Mayodan and Miss Rockingham County were on hand to roll out the red carpet for the grand opening on Highway 135.

Dean began reading around on the Web and found that when a big-box retailer came into your community, eighty-six cents of every dollar spent there went somewhere else. Very little money stayed home to benefit the people who lived, worked, and shopped there—just like with the local truck stops that kept only a dime on every gallon sold. Even before Wal-Mart showed up, the main streets of Madison and Mayodan were emptying out, the center of economic life moving to the highways where Lowe's and CVS had already arrived. "And if you think about it," Dean said, "the people that ran the hardware store, the shoe store, the little restaurant that was here, they were the fabric of the community. They were the leaders. They were the Little League baseball coaches, they were the town council members, they were the people everybody looked up to. We lost that." The rest of the country was supposed to be booming—Wall Street and Silicon Valley had more money than ever—but Rockingham County and the Piedmont were sinking into something like a depression. Anyway, how many investment bankers and software designers were there around the country? Then think of how many farmers.

A lot changed in Dean's mind very quickly. He had always voted Republican, except in 1992 when he went for Ross Perot, but after Katrina he realized that Bush was teamed up with the multinationals and the oil companies in the worst way. Even Reagan, his idol, had made a big mistake when he cut deals with the oil countries—wasn't Iran-contra about that?—and kept America on fossil fuels for thirty more years. History would judge Reagan harshly for that.

One day, Dean was sitting on a bar stool at his kitchen table, surfing a website called "Whiskey and Gunpowder: The Independent Investor's Daily Guide to Gold, Commodities, Profits and Freedom" on the lousy dial-up connection that was all you could get in Stokesdale, when he read the words "peak oil." It meant the point when petroleum extraction would reach its maximum rate and begin to fall off. A geologist with Gulf Oil named M. King Hubbert came up with the theory in 1956. Hubbert predicted that the United States, the world's largest oil producer, would hit its high point in domestic production around 1970—which was what

happened, and which explained why oil prices became so volatile throughout the seventies. Hubbert's theory was that the rest of the world would
reach peak oil right around 2005.

Dean stood up at the table, went weak in his knees, and stumbled
backward. He had a vision of what peak oil would mean where he lived
(Katrina had already given a glimpse): long-haul trucks coming to a stand-
still, food stranded on the highways, local people unable to eat or get to
work or heat their homes. Riots, revolution. At least, things getting very
chaotic very fast. People around here had guns, they had the Scotch-Irish
mentality to fight. Then something like martial law, maybe a coup d'état.
This was what America was facing. He knew that this moment would
stay with him, just like discovering Napoleon Hill. Napoleon wrote about
the power of concentration—that if you concentrated your mind on one
subject for an extended period of time, things would start popping into
your head and what you needed to know would be illuminated to you.
Dean could feel that happening to him now. He immediately called his
mentor, Rocky Carter—the contractor who had built the truck stop by
the Martinsville Speedway and turned Dean on to Napoleon Hill—and
told him about this discovery.

In the spring of 2006, around the time Dean found out about peak oil,
his friend Howard saw a story on CNN about a man in Tennessee who
was making ethanol that he sold for fifty cents a gallon. Howard was
twelve years older than Dean and had grown up in a house that his family
rented for twenty-five dollars a month on the Price tobacco farm. He was
stocky and irascible, with a thick white mustache and powerful forearms,
and he had spent most of his adult life stringing television cable, drinking, fighting, and riding motorcycles. He lost several front teeth in a bar
fight in High Point after he ran out of pool balls to throw at the bikers
coming after him. Then, at age fifty-three, he married a tough little slip of
a woman—"harder than a raw bone on a ladder knot," Howard said. She
had been his first love in his teens but she'd married someone else, so
Howard had to wait most of his life to settle down. They lived in a trailer
in Madison with his wife's daughter, who was obese and drew a disability
check.

The ethanol man lived outside Lynchburg, Tennessee, home of Jack
Daniel's. One day, Howard and Dean drove eight hours and found him by
a creek at the bottom of a crooked, foggy road—a short, beady-eyed man
with a big gut, making moonshine and adding gasoline. The man sold

them a still—a long copper tube, like an oversized bassoon, with several valves—for $2,100. Dean and Howard weren't his only customers. What with Katrina, the gas price spike, and the CNN clip, the ethanol man sold ten or eleven stills that day.

Dean and Howard drove back to North Carolina, bought some corn from local farmers, and started fooling around with sugar and yeast. They soon found out that making ethanol was too costly, in terms of the energy needed to separate the water and alcohol and also the number of government permits required. But Dean had also been reading about another alternative fuel: biodiesel. Before Katrina, he'd never heard the word, had no idea how it was even spelled, but biodiesel was appealing for a number of reasons. Transesterification—that's what the production process was called—took much less energy than making ethanol: for every unit of energy you put in, you created almost five units of fuel. Biodiesel was made from fat compounds called triglycerides, and the oil could come from various feedstocks, like soybeans or crushed canola seeds or animal fat, or even the waste cooking oil that restaurants got rid of. It could be manufactured on a small scale for relatively little money. Blended with regular number 2 diesel at a concentration of up to 20 percent biodiesel, it could go straight into an engine that needed no conversion. With slight modifications, a diesel engine could run on 100 percent biofuel. Politicians worried about the price of gas because that's what went into the voters' cars, but diesel ran the economy, got the food to market.

Dean and Howard drove back to Tennessee. The ethanol man had hooked up with two Germans who were making what they called "bee-o-diesel." Dean bought one of their portable reactors mounted on skids for twenty thousand dollars, having secured an investment from Rocky Carter. The reactor could produce a thousand gallons a day. Dean and Howard drove it back home and traded the ethanol still to a farmer in Harrisburg, Virginia, for two crops of canola harvested on fifty acres. Canola—it stood for Canadian Oil, Low Acid—was a winter cover crop derived from rapeseed. Forty-four percent of the crushed seed became oil, the rest meal for feeding livestock. Dean read that canola oil had 93 percent of the BTU value of number 2 diesel and took less energy to convert to fuel than other feedstock, because the fatty acid chains melted down at lower temperatures. Canola was a mustard seed. There was a parable about the mustard seed in the Bible—Jesus compared it to the kingdom of heaven: "Though it is less than all the seeds that are on the earth, yet when it is sown, grows up, and becomes greater than all the herbs, and puts out great branches, so that the birds of the sky can lodge under its shadow."

Dean harvested some canola seeds, tiny black balls like peppercorns. He ran the seeds through a small crushing machine twice, caught the stream of oil, filtered it, poured the oil into the reactor, and turned up the heat. He began making biodiesel. Unlike the Germans, he gave the first syllable a full, high, open-mouthed lift, as if it were the opening phrase of an old Baptist hymn. This was the stuff that was going to set him free.

"All I've ever wanted to do all my life," Dean said, "is farm and be left alone."

TAMMY THOMAS

In the late nineties, Tammy's high school sweetheart, Barry, reappeared. She had run into him a few times over the years and would never talk to him, once even fled with her kids when she saw him approaching at a festival. Then, at her godmother's son's wedding reception, Barry's aunt was the caterer and Barry was working with her. He pursued Tammy and cornered her and asked for five minutes to explain that he had never stopped caring for her, always loved her, regretted marrying the pregnant girl Tammy had seen him with the summer after their daughter was born. "If I could just give him five minutes," she said, "and it cost me seven years."

For a while it was a for-real fairy tale, as if God had wanted them back together. Her older daughter was told that the Time Warner Cable serviceman her mother was going to marry on July 3, 1999, was her father. She graduated the next year and left to study theater at Ohio State, so it didn't matter so much that she didn't like her mother's new husband. But Tammy's other two kids didn't have a great relationship with their stepfather, either. And within a few years, Tammy and Barry began to quarrel, and the marriage fell apart.

Tammy stopped going to the church on the south side where Barry's family was prominent. For a while she didn't want to be seen around the city. "Youngstown is very, very small," she said. "A lot of people were surprised that we were together anyway, so it was even harder being separated." So many things from her life that she'd repressed came back to hurt her. God and her cousin led Tammy to an interracial megachurch in Akron, the House of the Lord, where a sign in the sanctuary said RELATIONSHIPS ARE EVERYTHING. She decided that this was where she needed to heal, and she began attending services several times a week, and for two or three years church was her life.

She had lived in four different places on the south side, and it was now worse than the east side. She never felt safe getting into her car in the middle of the night when she worked the midnight shift, or leaving her younger daughter home alone after dark. She let Barry have the house, since there was already enough turmoil (he lost it to foreclosure a couple of years later). She could have moved to the west side, which was the last part of the city where homes were holding their value, but that was where white people from the east and south sides had fled. It would have felt wrong for her to join them there. In July 2005, she and Barry decided to divorce, and in August Tammy bought a modest house for seventy-one thousand dollars, with an attached garage, on a safe street in a township on the northern edge of Youngstown called Liberty. For the first time she had an easy drive to work.

In October she moved in. That same month, Packard Electric, going under a new name, declared bankruptcy.

For the two decades that Tammy worked there, Packard steadily chipped away at the labor force in Warren, going from more than thirteen thousand employees in the early seventies to seven thousand in the early nineties to three thousand by 2005. During the same years, the foreign workforce expanded to more than a hundred thousand, and Packard's auto parts factories became the largest employers in the maquiladora belt of Mexico. At some plants, like Plant 14, Tammy came to see that nothing was locked down, and over time all the machinery was moved south of the border, and with it the jobs on those lines. It was like a repetition of the steelworkers' agony, but in slow time, by attrition.

Tammy watched the union get weaker and weaker. The company's 1993 contract with Local 717 established a new third tier of workers who would never receive full wages and benefits. Tammy noticed how management treated the 93s differently, with stricter work rules, wouldn't let them talk to Tammy's line at Thomas Road, stood behind them and watched them work in a way that would make anyone nervous. The contract also gave incentives to do twelve-hour shifts, which was impossible for someone with a family, like Tammy, or for someone with health problems. It seemed like a way to get the more senior employees to retire, and then hire more workers as 93s.

In 1999, having consolidated its parts divisions, including Packard, into one entity called Delphi Automotive Systems, General Motors spun off Delphi into an independent corporation, with a public stock offering and a prospectus for investors that promised to "improve operating performance" with "a 'fix/sell/close' plant-by-plant analysis through which we seek to improve our cost competitiveness, and various other sourcing, labor, and cost reduction initiatives." Wall Street had been pushing GM to spin off Delphi for at least a year, thinking there would be more shareholder value in a smaller automaker and a separate parts company than in one vertically integrated GM.

Tammy found the whole spin-off suspicious. "At the time, Packard Electric was profitable. As soon as we came under Delphi, we were no longer profitable," she said. "I had a feeling then that something was not right about this. I'm not a conspiracy theorist, but I think the writing was on the wall. There was a plan to get rid of some of the long-term workers, so you spin these people off, you put them under an umbrella, and then you don't have to deal with them, because now they are not going to be GM employees."

The new corporation was independent in name only—Delphi's fate remained tied to its biggest customer, GM. Over time, it became clear that the spin-off was a tactic to break up what remained of the company's American workforce. From the outset, Delphi claimed to be profitable. But the profits turned out to be bogus—for three years, top management had engaged in accounting fraud. The company was investigated by the SEC and sued by two pension funds, and its senior executives quit. When GM went into a deep slump in the early 2000s, Delphi took billions of dollars in losses, before filing for bankruptcy under Chapter 11 in 2005.

But the bankruptcy was also tactical. It applied only to the company's North American operations. Delphi argued that reorganization under Chapter 11 should allow it to tear up contracts with its workers, and to oversee the winding down, the board hired a new CEO, Robert S. "Steve" Miller, who specialized in taking troubled companies and slashing them to pieces in order to make them profitable for new investors. He had done it before at Bethlehem Steel, and in 2008 he published an autobiography called *The Turnaround Kid*. Delphi's board gave Miller a compensation package that was worth as much as $35 million, while a group of senior executives got $87 million in bonuses, and stock options that were ultimately valued at half a billion. Two Wall Street banks, JPMorgan Chase and Citigroup, lent Delphi $4.5 billion and positioned themselves to stand first in line to be paid back, with interest and fees, when the company emerged from bankruptcy. Miller, his senior executives, and the banks would be the winners. The losers would be Delphi's American workers. No one was telling them what was going to happen, but Delphi had a confidential written plan, code-named NorthStar, to pursue "aggressive cost reduction via product exits, site consolidation, and legacy cost reduction." The plan was leaked to *The Detroit News* and published a month after the bankruptcy.

Still, Tammy didn't see it coming. She was making close to twenty-five dollars an hour, bringing home fifty-five thousand a year with overtime before taxes. She had her ten years in, so they couldn't lay her off for more than six months, and when she was off they had to pay her 80 percent of her wages. Her younger daughter was going to graduate from high school, and after that Tammy could focus on herself, maybe even travel. She was about to turn forty, and her last twenty or so years on earth were going to be smooth sailing. She was thirteen years away from early retirement, and when she got there she could finally grow up and decide what she wanted to be—something that fulfilled her and made her feel good, and it wouldn't matter how much it paid. She had given up the wedding business and was taking some classes at Youngstown State, thinking of going into counseling. By the time she retired she could have a Ph.D. Or go live in some third world country on her pension.

Tammy had seen jobs leave, seen the work getting condensed—you went from working one machine to two—and she could imagine Warren becoming a smaller plant. But the whole plant closing? "No. I never imagined that. Even seeing what happened to the mills. As long as GM was doing okay, we would probably be okay. We worked so much overtime, we literally could not keep up with orders. No one could have ever told me my job would go away." Three decades earlier, the workers at Sheet and Tube had never imagined it, either.

In March 2006, Delphi announced that it would close or sell twenty-one of its twenty-nine American plants and get rid of twenty thousand hourly jobs, two-thirds of the total. Warren would remain open but with a drastically reduced workforce, and the survivors would take a 40 percent pay cut. Tammy's wage would drop to $13.50 an hour. Workers were encouraged to accept a buyout with a lump sum of pay, because Delphi intended to retain fewer than six hundred fifty of Warren's three thousand remaining hourly employees. The buyout meant that they would lose most of their pension. The message was delivered via PowerPoint in a large conference room to groups of a hundred workers at a time. Everyone received a packet of information and was given until August to sign up for the buyout. People walked out of the room crying. Tammy was stunned.

But then something changed in her. She felt a calming spirit, like she knew it was going to be okay. This feeling had come over her at other hard moments in her life, when she had to live in a closet at age ten, when she became a mother at sixteen, when she lost her fiancé at twenty-nine. Her coworkers were in a panic, asking one another, "What are you going to do?" Tammy told them, "You know what? There is a whole wide world outside of Packard." She was actually a little excited. With the buyout money she could go to college full-time and become the second person in her family to get a degree—because her older daughter was already the first. After that, Tammy didn't know what she was going to do, but for the first time since she was a girl, she could dream.

Her friend Miss Sybil had always seen something of herself in Tammy: east side girls, single mothers, factory workers, women with ambition who had stuck it out in Youngstown. In a way, Sybil had it harder because she started working at GE in 1971, when black women were the lowest of the low in a factory. On the other hand, when Tammy came up a generation later, everything was falling apart. Sybil had stayed at GE until she retired in her sixties, but Tammy was making a great change at forty. Sybil knew exactly what she was risking. "Tammy had to make her own way and to be determined," she said. "I'm sure those three mouths looking at her were a great incentive. Packard was a darned good job. When she left Packard by the wayside she was taking an awful chance. She had that determination and drive. Most people I know who left Packard lost their luster. You step out on that limb and you can't fail."

Tammy took the buyout on the last day of 2006. She thought of the saying that God closes one door and opens another. "No. God is going to open *patio* doors for me."

2003

CITIES JAMMED IN WORLDWIDE PROTEST OF WAR IN IRAQ . . . A brutal dictator, with a history of reckless aggression, with ties to terrorism, with great potential wealth, will not be permitted to dominate a vital region . . . *I lift my lamp beside the golden door to pee, / And make a vow to make men free, and we will find their WMD.* . . . **BUSH ORDERS START OF WAR ON IRAQ** . . . If the end is near, the Green and Miller family, who are spread out across the country, want their relatives close by. So they've hatched an emergency plan in case the phones are knocked out: Meet in Wichita, Kan., at the confluence of the Big and Little Arkansas Rivers, under the outstretched arms of the Keeper of the Plains, a 44-foot steel sculpture of an Indian warrior. . . . **MOUNTING ANGER WITH FRENCH NOT ENOUGH TO STEM THE FLOW OF BORDEAUX** . . . These bastards who run our country are a bunch of conniving, thieving, smug pricks who need to be brought down and removed and replaced with a whole new system that we control. . . . **LATINOS NOW LARGEST MINORITY GROUP IN U.S.** . . . **POPE TO GAYS: YOUR WAYS ARE EVIL Slams Homosexual Marriage, Adoption** . . . In an emotional press conference at L.A.'s Staples Center, Bryant, 24, clutched his wife Vanessa's hand and apologized for his betrayal six months after the birth of . . . **THE "BUSH DOCTRINE" EXPERIENCES SHINING MOMENTS** . . . The laughs come from finding out just how isolated the overprivileged can be from the rest of the country. So much so that the 22-year-old Hilton, a fixture in society columns, doesn't quite know what a well is and has never heard of Wal-Mart. . . . **WALL STREET GIANTS PROSPER AMID DOWNTURN** . . . He displays other Master of the Universe attributes, including a fabulous art collection, a power wardrobe, and an attractive, blond second wife several inches taller than he is. . . . **HOUSING HOLDS AS SAFEST HAVEN FOR INVESTORS** . . . be glad that you own a house in Florida . . . But because I signed the contract and fulfilled my obligation to fight one of America's wars, I am entitled to speak, to say, I belong to a fucked situation. . . . **U.S. COPTER IS DOWNED IN IRAQ, KILLING 16** . . . "It was a tough week, but we made progress toward a sovereign and free Iraq," he said. . . . *Sir, I supported the war. / I believe in who we are. / I dedicate red wine to that today. / At Montrachet, near the Franklin Street stop, on West Broadway.*

INSTITUTION MAN (1): COLIN POWELL

Once upon a time in America

there was a family of light-skinned immigrants from the islands who lived in the city of immigrants, the New York of La Guardia, DiMaggio, and Coney Island, where mothers served oxtail soup for Sunday dinner or challah by candlelight on Friday night and fathers yelled at the newspaper in Sicilian or Polish while boys with condoms in their wallets and girls snapping gum became American in the streets.

On the third floor of 952 Kelly Street in the South Bronx, President Roosevelt's portrait hung on the living room wall, the flag and the Capitol behind him. Outside their tenement, the parents and two children were absorbed into the vast and generalizing wash of American institutions.

The mother was a proud member of Dubinsky's ILGWU (three hundred thousand strong), sewing buttons and trim on women's suits at Ginsburg's in the Garment District, where the father was the shipping room foreman and there was always work, even in the Depression. On Sundays they sat in the family pew at St. Margaret's Episcopal Church, where their younger child, a boy, was an acolyte in love with pageantry and incense. The boy went from PS 39 to PS 52 to Morris High School, and by virtue of his diploma, his New York City residence, and ten dollars, in spite of being a mediocre student he was admitted to the City College of New York, founded in 1847 on a hill overlooking Harlem as the Free Academy, whose first president, Horace Webster, said, "The experiment is to be tried, whether the children of the people, the children of the whole people, can be educated; and whether an institution of the highest grade, can be successfully controlled by the popular will, not by the privileged few."

And beyond the lights of the city, across the republic, stood the structures that held up the postwar order of middle-class democracy:

General Motors, the AFL-CIO, the National Labor Relations Board, the urban boss, the farm bloc, the public school, the research university, the county party, the Ford Foundation, the Rotary Club, the League of Women Voters, CBS News, the Committee on Economic Development, Social Security, the Bureau of Reclamation, the Federal Housing Administration, the Federal-Aid Highway Act, the Marshall Plan, NATO, the Council on Foreign Relations, the GI Bill, the U.S. Army.

The last of these became the boy's American home. He joined ROTC his first year at City College (he was going to be drafted anyway) and pledged the Pershing Rifles. A uniform and discipline gave the new pledge a sense of belonging. He needed structure to thrive. "I became a leader almost immediately," he later wrote. "I found a selflessness within our ranks that reminded me of the caring atmosphere within my family. Race, color, background, income meant nothing."

In 1958 he received his commission as a second lieutenant. The army had been integrated for just ten years, but the most hierarchical institution in America was also the most democratic: "Less discrimination, a truer merit system, and leveler playing fields existed inside the gates of our military posts than in any Southern city hall or Northern corporation." Hard work, honesty, courage, sacrifice: the young officer practiced the Boy Scout virtues in the sure belief that they would bring equal opportunity.

His American journey took him to South Vietnam in 1962, Birmingham in 1963, Vietnam again in 1968.

The captain stepped on a punji stick and escaped a mortar round in the A Shau Valley. Stateside a few months later, he was refused service at a drive-in burger joint near Fort Benning, Georgia. The major survived a helo crash near Quang Ngai and rescued several men. None of it upset his carefully calibrated balance.

He collected a chestful of medals and the admiration of his superiors. He refused to be undermined by the humiliations of racism or the folly of a war in which the fighting was done by America's have-nots. Both offended his democratic values. "Of the many tragedies of Vietnam, this raw class discrimination strikes me as the most damaging to the ideal that all Americans are created equal and owe equal allegiance to their country." But he was building his life on that ideal, so he remained practical, and his self-control became almost inhuman. The institutions showed their health by lifting up a man of his qualities, and even when they went off course, their ultimate power lay in self-correction.

And he would show anyone who doubted him.

Promoted to lieutenant colonel. Made a White House Fellow, just in time for Watergate—but even the worst political scandal in American history proved the institutional strength of democracy: Congress, the courts, the press, and the popular will cut out the cancer.

Battalion commander in South Korea, where he began restoring good order and discipline to the army after Vietnam. Brigade commander at Fort Campbell. Carter administration Pentagon. First star in 1979, age forty-two, the youngest general in the army. Fort Carson, Fort Leavenworth. Reagan administration Pentagon, where "the military services had been restored to a place of honor."

In 1986, the major general sat at his desk outside the office of the secretary of defense and placed a reluctant call on orders from the White House to transfer four thousand antitank missiles from the army to the CIA. They were destined for Tehran: arms, a Bible, and a cake for hostages. Iran-contra was the first blot on his résumé, but it sent him to the Reagan White House as deputy national security adviser, detailed to clean up the mess. "If it hadn't been for Iran-contra, I'd still be an obscure general somewhere. Retired, never heard of."

Restoring the National Security Council to good order and discipline was the perfect job for the lieutenant general. He loved to fix up old Volvos and Saabs. He was efficient, inspiring, a master of bureaucracy, the world's greatest staff officer. The institutions were at the peak of power. After all, they were about to win the Cold War.

In 1988, in the Hall of St. Catherine at the Kremlin, Gorbachev looked straight at him with a glimmer in his eye and said, "What are you going to do now that you've lost your best enemy?"

The next year the general got his fourth star the day before his fifty-second birthday. Chairman of the Joint Chiefs of Staff a few months later, the youngest ever. Without its best enemy America could fight wars again, and he ran the first since Vietnam—Panama (a drug dealer with a face like a pineapple), then the big one, Desert Storm. The ground campaign took four days to drive Saddam out of Kuwait. America was back, and the chairman did it by turning the agony of Vietnam into a doctrine: clear goals, national interest, political support, overwhelming force, early exit. (The Kurds and Shia were on their own; the Bosnians would be, too.)

By the time the general retired after thirty-five years in uniform, he was the most admired man in America. No one knew his political party—he had voted for JFK, LBJ, and Carter once, then he started voting Republican. Both sides trusted him because he embodied the bipartisan center. (A few people distrusted him for the same reason.) He was an Eisenhower internationalist, cautious to the core. As long as the center held, his prestige kept rising. History performed jujitsu and turned race and Vietnam in his favor, giving him an authority no one else in Washington had.

He made everyone feel that America still worked.

In 1995 he declared himself a Republican. His friend Rich Armitage, a known party member, had warned him not to: it was no longer the party of Eisenhower—it was no longer even the party of Reagan. Something had been set loose, a spirit of ugliness and unreason, even in foreign policy. (The Cold War had been clarifying and moderating—maybe Gorbachev was right.) The establishment still held the reins, but the horses were Know-Nothings. But he said that he wanted to broaden the party's appeal.

He could have been the first black president. Instead, he took himself out of the running and volunteered his time for poor kids in poor schools. His message was always the same: hard work, honesty, courage, sacrifice.

When he was called back to service, the new secretary of state took the stage and towered over the barely elected, bewildered-looking president. No one was more experienced, more able, more popular. He would open the hood, fix Russia and China, tinker with the Balkans, lubricate the Middle East, tighten up Iraq, and restore a demoralized department to good order and discipline. But his friend Armitage, who became his number two, thought Bush had picked his secretary of state for his approval ratings, not his views.

For two years the secretary represented the best face of America to the world.

When the planes hit the buildings he was at a meeting of Latin American leaders in Lima, and he had the presence of mind to linger long enough to vote for the Democratic Charter and reaffirm the values behind it. "They can destroy buildings, they can kill people, and we will be saddened by this tragedy. But they will never be allowed to kill the spirit of democracy. They cannot destroy our society. They cannot destroy our belief in the democratic way."

He assembled a coalition against the Taliban, bringing Pakistan into the fold. He let the world know that America was not going rogue—its friends still mattered. He didn't have to say that a country that had made the son of black immigrants in the South Bronx its emissary to the world was worth supporting.

And when the president turned his sights on Iraq, the secretary was the voice of caution. He didn't say no, but he tried to steer the car while stepping on the brake. His department was skeptical of the intelligence. He articulated a new doctrine: you break it, you own it. He wanted the UN involved. He didn't want to lose the center.

He was holding together the foreign policy establishment without knowing that it was gone. He needed structure to thrive, but the structures that held up the postwar order had eroded. The Council on Foreign Relations and the Ford Foundation no longer mattered. The statesmen and generals had become consultants and pundits. The army was composed of professionals, not citizens. The public schools were leaving the children of the whole people semiliterate. The parties were locked in a war of attrition.

He was trying to function inside institutional failure, but that was incomprehensible to the stellar product of great American institutions. The administration was rotten with ideologues and operatives who showed contempt for the institutions. He didn't see that they had him isolated and defeated.

The most popular man in America was alone.

The president wanted his approval ratings. The White House wrote a speech for him to give, forty-eight single-spaced pages. He had a week to get rid of all the lies, and that wasn't enough time, and there never could have been enough time, for he didn't stop to challenge its premise.

On February 5, 2003, the secretary went to the United Nations building on the East River, twenty minutes away from 952 Kelly Street, which had long ago been burned out and demolished. He sat down at the Security Council table with audiotapes, photographs, drawings, and a vial of white powder, and while the world watched on live TV, he spoke for seventy-five minutes about the threats posed by Saddam's regime. He spoke with all the authority and self-control of a lifetime, and a great many Americans were convinced, for this was the man who showed that America still worked.

Then he stood and walked out with the erect bearing of a soldier.

He had hurt himself far more than any punji stick or Southern bigot could hurt him.

When the war began, the president said that he was sleeping like a baby. "I'm sleeping like a baby, too," the secretary said. "Every two hours, I wake up screaming."

JEFF CONNAUGHTON

Connaughton's timing in politics hadn't been great, but in lobbying it was nearly perfect. When he first got into the business in 1997, companies were spending around $1.25 billion a year exercising their First Amendment right to petition the United States government for redress of grievances. Twelve years later, when he left, the amount had almost tripled. (This was just the fees paid directly to lobbyists—public relations fees added unreported billions more.) This pot of cash drew a horde of politicians: between 1998 and 2004, 42 percent of the congresspersons and half the senators who left office went on to lobby their former colleagues. Thousands of congressional aides also decamped for K Street, as did several hundred of Connaughton's ex-colleagues in the Clinton administration. When he first passed through the revolving door in 1997 and joined Washington's permanent class, the practice was still called "selling out." By the time he pushed through the other way in 2009, it had acquired the air of something enviable, possibly admirable, certainly inevitable—it was known as "cashing in."

In January 2000, Connaughton's boss Jack Quinn left Arnold & Porter—partly at Connaughton's urging—to set up a new firm. The moment was right: Quinn was known in Washington as an Al Gore guy, and Gore had a good chance to win the presidency in the fall. Quinn's political career went back to Eugene McCarthy's campaign plane in 1968, plus five years at the highest levels in the Clinton White House, where he'd kept his head in all the crises. When clients sat down with him, they believed this was how the White House thought about the big issues. The surprise was Quinn's new partner: Ed Gillespie, a Karl Rove guy. Gillespie had worked for Dick Armey in the House and helped draft the Contract with America, and he was positioned to be one of the Republican Party's main fixers if George W. Bush won the White House.

Quinn Gillespie & Associates rented elegant fifth-floor offices on Connecticut Avenue between M and N, up the street from Morton's, where the firm did its drinking. Connaughton came on board as principal and vice chairman, with a corner office and a 7.5 percent equity stake on top of his salary. Quinn and Gillespie divided the rest.

Other lobbying firms were either Democratic or Republican, and they lost clients when the wrong party took power. At QGA, the lobbyists were all strong partisans—Quinn and Gillespie first met as combatants on Fox News—but when they got off the elevator in the morning their loyalty was directed exclusively toward the firm and its clients. Congress was fracturing on ideological lines, voters were growing more polarized with every election, and states were turning red or blue, but at QGA they liked to say that they were all members of the Green Party, even though the division of labor was clear: the Republicans at the firm wrote checks to Republican politicians and hosted fundraising events for them; the firm's Democrats did the same on their side. As the 2000 election drew near, Connaughton realized that he wasn't quite as passionate as usual about his team winning—Bush or Gore, Quinn Gillespie would come out all right. On election night, Quinn was in Nashville with the Gore team and Gillespie in Austin with the Bush team, and as the Florida vote tipped back and forth, the two partners shared the latest news by BlackBerry. Gillespie played a major role for the Republicans during the Florida recount, and after the Supreme Court made Bush president, he became one of the hottest insiders in Washington. The firm now had ties to every power center in government.

Connaughton couldn't provide access to the top people in Washington. He wasn't a deal-making D.C. lawyer or party power broker. His highest rank in government had been special assistant to the White House counsel. What he brought was a capacity for hard, skillful work, a few years' experience in the Senate and White House (staff would return his calls), cable news exposure on behalf of Clinton during impeachment, and the cachet of being a Biden guy, though in truth he was more of a Kaufman guy and was becoming a Quinn guy. Soon he was making more than half a million dollars a year. A wave of cash came pouring in over a retaining wall and hit him in the face every two weeks. In Washington there were plenty of other people no one had heard of who were making more than a million a year.

Quinn and Gillespie considered themselves the smart guys in the business. Lobbying was no longer about opening one door for a client—power in Washington had become too diffuse for that. It was about waging a broad strategic campaign, hitting different audiences through different channels, shaping the media's view of an issue, building pressure on legislators in their home districts. Quinn Gillespie was expert at forming temporary "grasstop" coalitions—enlisting local citizens in a cause as if there had been organic grassroots support. The firm didn't flinch from controversy. When Quinn's legal client Marc Rich, a billionaire fugitive living in Switzerland, received a presidential pardon on Clinton's last day in office, the uproar consumed Quinn for weeks. But an alternative view of the affair was available: Quinn had gotten a tough thing done for a client. Old Washington—the press, the social establishment, the upholders of high standards—pretended that its moral sensibilities had been scandalized. New Washington understood that the Marc Rich pardon was good for business.

The firm's clients included the American Petroleum Institute, the nursing home industry, the British Columbia Lumber Trade Council, Verizon, Bank of America, Hewlett-Packard, and Larry Silverstein, the leaseholder of the World Trade Center. Quinn Gillespie helped Enron beat back attempts to regulate the electricity markets in California shortly before the company went bankrupt, and it represented the families of Pan Am Flight 103 in their effort to collect reparations from Libya. Connaughton had one of his biggest successes with online advertisers. He became the spokesman for a grasstop group called the Network Advertising Initiative, spent half a year working up a self-regulatory system for the industry, met with all five commissioners at the Federal Trade Commission and the attorneys general of seven states, and headed off a bill in Congress that would have helped consumers prevent websites from collecting data on their Internet spending habits. This was the kind of complex work that partners at big-time law firms did—and Joe Biden had never cared to know his opinion about anything.

At Arnold & Porter, Connaughton had drawn the line at representing Allianz, a German insurance company that had been accused of cheating Jewish policyholders after World War II. Quinn had helped negotiate the tobacco settlement under Clinton and wouldn't work for the cigarette companies. But Quinn Gillespie represented (for a reputation-hit premium) the Republika Srpska, the Bosnian Serb entity spawned at the end of the Balkan War, and Ivory Coast, which was enmeshed in its own civil war and whose government was rumored to be operating death squads. Connaughton found international work fascinating, and he believed that the firm was trying to get the Ivorian regime to do the right thing by holding elections (anyway, France and Poland never wanted to sign you up, only the bad boys). In 2005 he flew to Abidjan and was driven through terrifying checkpoints to the presidential palace, where he was seated in a chair next to President Laurent Gbagbo. But the president paid no attention to what his lobbyist had to say and showed no interest in democracy—he just wanted good PR. Connaughton bought a large carved elephant from a beachfront vendor and lugged it back to Washington for Gillespie, the firm's top Republican. Six months later the Ivory Coast account was terminated.

A colleague at the firm once said that when Quinn Gillespie hired a new lobbyist, only two things mattered: "One, is he comfortable asking his friends to do favors for him? And two, is he willing to do this?" The colleague made a show of spreading his legs. "Does he understand that we're here to make money? If he's not hungry to make money, he's not going to come to work every day doing what he needs to do."

After so many years in Washington, Connaughton was hungry, and not just to make money. He wanted to get things done and play at high levels. He'd never made it there with Biden—public service seemed to bring more humiliation than triumph—but the private sector was closer to a meritocracy: you got rewarded according to what you produced, not the whims and flaws of the boss. The job came with tremendous pressure—the heads of trade associations were particularly demanding—but no one was "dumb fuck." Quinn, Gillespie, and Connaughton were three Irish guys from modest backgrounds who believed in hard work and loyalty. They weren't crooks like Jack Abramoff. Connaughton loved his partners and what they built together, and his years at Quinn Gillespie were the happiest he spent in Washington. So he got a little defensive when people talked about lobbying as if it were something dirty. Hell, almost all of Washington was suckling at the corporate tit (he had seen that at Covington & Burling), most of them doing the exact same thing as the few thousand registered lobbyists who got slammed for everyone's sins.

He opened a brokerage account and lived in a few custom-made suits. After a few years he bought his first house, a town house in Georgetown, then a condo in Playa del Carmen, Mexico, right on the Gulf, for $420,000, then a beautiful thirty-nine-foot Italian powerboat that cost him $175,000 secondhand. But he kept his shitty American car.

A friend of Connaughton's, whom he'd met on the Biden presidential campaign, once told him, "This would sound strange to ninety-nine percent of Americans, but four hundred thousand a year doesn't go as far as it used to. I've got my mortgage on the house in Great Falls, two kids in private school"—everyone in Washington sent their kids to private school—"and I'm lucky if I save any money on four hundred grand." Connaughton had met his best Washington friends on that campaign, and some of them had made it like him, but the ones who stayed in public service longest painted themselves into a corner financially. In Washington there were no crosscurrents, no career opportunities that came along other than the one business of the company town. It was the capital of the planet and unimaginably richer than at any time in American history, but still an isolated town, a world apart.

In a certain way, lobbying was based on the web of Washington friendships. This was one reason congressional aides were in such demand on K Street. A senator's chief of staff would return a lobbyist's phone call if he knew and liked the guy, thinking: "I kind of want to help him. If I need him to do an event he'll do one for me, and I get good poop from him." Lobbying provided a valuable flow of information and analysis back and forth between corporations and government officials. If a senator was a sort of judge, a lobbyist was an advocate giving him the best arguments on one side of a case.

There was a problem, of course, which was that usually no one made it into the room to argue the other side—and never anyone able to put up anything like the kind of money the corporations paid to lobbyists and campaigns. Anyway, a senator wasn't a sort of judge. Maybe once, maybe Proxmire or Javits. But now senators were looking beyond the briefs—to the cash as well as the politics—to decide the case. The lobbyists were just intermediaries, hired guns. Blame the special interests, with all their money and the access that came with it, and beyond them the campaign finance laws that allowed cash to flood elections. "I'm in the room because I've raised money for you, and I can help you find positions that are going to raise more money," Connaughton said. "If that were stopped, then you get back to what Jack and I believe we are: smart guys who were good advocates."

Connaughton later developed a "universal theory" of money in American life since the 1980s: "When the benefits exploded on both Wall Street and Washington, when it became possible to make millions of dollars in corporate booty—I'm a living example of it, no one's ever heard of me and I walked out of Washington with millions of dollars—when the cost of certain behaviors diminished, when norms began to erode and disappear that had held people back at least from being garish about the way they made money, the culture changed. It changed on Wall Street and it changed in Washington."

Without meaning to, Connaughton had become a Professional Democrat. This was what he called the class of Washingtonians—lobbyists, lawyers, advisers, consultants, pundits, consiglieres, fixers—who shuttled between the shower of corporate cash ever falling on the capital and a series of increasingly prominent positions in Democratic Party politics. (There were Professional Republicans, too, of course—Ed Gillespie was one—who moved through Washington at least as easily as the Professional Democrats, because their party affiliation didn't require them to pretend that they disapproved of corporations and big-money politics.) Wealth added to their power, power swelled their wealth. They connected special interests to party officials using the adhesive of fundraising. They ate breakfast with politicians, lunch with the heads of trade associations, and dinner with other Professional Democrats. Behind their desks were "power walls"—photo galleries showing them smiling next to the highest-ranking politicians they knew. Their loyalty was to the firm first, then their former boss in politics, then their party, and then—if he was a Democrat—the president.

Washington was a small town where everyone was one or two degrees away, and you had better be nice to whomever you met at the telecom happy hour or the financial services get-to-know-you function, because if you weren't, it would get back fast. Quinn Gillespie encouraged its lobbyists to go out every night—the information generated through networking was valuable. Connaughton did his share, less over time—he disliked big parties, and eventually he had done so many events that he would valet-park his car, walk in, break out in a rash, and decide to leave. After a couple of questions, he and someone new would have each other sized up in the city's hierarchy—Biden guy, Clinton White House, works for Jack Quinn, telecom accounts—which determined how much they wanted to know each other. With the Alabama chip still on his shoulder, he was incapable of bullshitting about his own importance.

He remained single, though he came close to marrying a couple of times. If he had, his lobbying business might have increased exponentially. Power couples could switch off between government and the private sector, one spouse bringing in money while the other climbed the rungs of government, sharing whatever intelligence they picked up along the way. Connaughton dealt with a Senate chief of staff on a whole series of financial issues before finding out that he was married to a high-level banking executive. In Washington, pillow talk could be worth millions.

Certain couples belonged to the subset of Washington's permanent class having to do with the financial sector, the Wall Street–Washington axis—Treasury officials, Banking Committee staffers, regulators. Connaughton called it the Blob. (There were other blobs—for example, in defense, the military-industrial complex—that he never got to know.) Members of the financial blob were unusually tight with one another. In the case of one couple, the husband was an ex-lobbyist who worked on a key Senate committee, the wife an ex-Treasury official who went over to the SEC. They networked night and day, playing the long game, and when the two of them decided to cash in for good, they would be worth a lot of money.

Quinn Gillespie set out to do as little fundraising for politicians as possible. Hosting events downtown was the second-rate way of bringing in business—the firm thought it could win by being smart and strategic. But the politicians wouldn't leave it alone. Connaughton would secure a meeting for a client with a senator through the chief of staff. A few days later, he would get a call from the senator asking him to attend a thousand-dollar-a-head fundraiser. There was nothing to say except "I'd be delighted." Before long, the partners were maxing out on their fifty-thousand-dollar limit in contributions per election cycle, and Quinn Gillespie was bundling its share of campaign money, though never as much as the biggest players, like Patton Boggs and the Podesta Group, which did events almost every week.

A Quinn Gillespie fundraising event was typically a breakfast in the firm's conference room, a bacon-and-eggs buffet on a Tuesday, Wednesday, or Thursday, the only mornings when senators were reliably in Washington. It would start around eight, but Connaughton couldn't count the times a senator would come in at 7:45 and he would think, "Oh shit, we're both half awake and I have to entertain him for fifteen minutes." As host, he or Quinn would give the senator an over-the-top introduction: "One of the great public servants of our time and personally a wonderful human being, he called me when my child was sick . . ." Over to the senator, who would tell a couple of lame jokes, the clients would laugh, and then they'd get down to business. When Connaughton started out in lobbying, it was considered unseemly to combine raising money with discussing issues, but that line eroded over time like everything else, and eventually a pro like Chris Dodd, who was always loose and fun, with his red face and dark eyebrows and thick white senatorial hair, would just go around the conference table and ask each donor, "What do you care about?" Three weeks after an event, Connaughton would call the senator's chief of staff, who would say, "Hold on, the senator wants to talk to you directly"—for he was now part of the senator's political family. After a year without an event, it would become almost impossible to get the senator on the phone, and Connaughton would have to schedule another breakfast.

In 2001 he and Quinn organized a fundraiser for Biden, who had just become chairman of the Senate Foreign Relations Committee and was up for his sixth Senate term in 2002. The event raised almost seventy-five thousand dollars for his former boss. Two years later, he hosted another event. On both occasions, Biden failed to thank him. It was too much, and he complained to a close friend who had been working for Biden since before the speech in Tuscaloosa in 1979 and who'd taken Connaughton to lunch as a thank-you for the second fundraiser. Two weeks later, Biden sent him a note. "Jeff, you've always been there for me," it read. "I hope you know I will always be there for you."

Connaughton never really sold himself as someone who could get to Biden—in twelve years he only once asked Biden to meet with a client—but he made a cold calculation that it was worth maintaining the illusion of closeness, which meant enduring the slights. No one except Biden still thought Biden was going to be president—that part of the myth had become something of a joke—but chairman of Foreign Relations was a powerful position, and during the 2004 campaign, Biden was on John Kerry's short list for secretary of state, and anyway, it wouldn't have been worth very much to be known around Washington as an "ex–Biden guy." Being a Biden guy gave him stature with corporations trying to navigate the capital. So, publicly at least, he remained one.

In late 2003, Quinn Gillespie was bought by WPP, a London firm that was the world's largest advertising and public affairs company. The partners' share of the sale would be paid out in three installments over the next four years, and the eventual price would depend on Quinn Gillespie's profitability. Every dollar of profit would be multiplied in the price. Connaughton began to work harder than ever, and at night, in bars and restaurants, he would figure out his expected millions on the back of a napkin, constantly recalculating as the firm's income statements changed. From 2005 to 2007 Quinn Gillespie made almost twenty million a year, and toward the end of the earn-out period, maximizing revenues and minimizing expenses became such an obsession that Quinn would say they were digging for change in the sofas. When Connaughton finally cashed in, he was rich.

PART II

DEAN PRICE

A two-lane asphalt road ran past the woods—white oak, shagbark hickory, Carolina ash—and in the shadows of the trees a tobacco barn was year by year collapsing on itself, the metal roof sloping inward, pieces of bare siding hanging loose from nails. Nearby, a white clapboard house with empty windows squatted at the roadside half smothered in tree branches and vines, while a fire-scorched handwritten sign on the outside wall still advertised CRUSH. Farther along, the road took a turn and a tidy brick ranch house with a big satellite dish mounted on top stood in the golden sunlight of a red-brown field. Another bend, a gentle hill, deep woods again, then an abandoned metal warehouse alone in a clearing. The road straightened and flattened and came to a stoplight where a pair of strip malls faced each other, parking lots full, a Walgreen's across from a McDonald's, Shell opposing BP. Another light, a shuttered car dealership, a vast scrap yard with a mountain of twisted metal and stacked timbers next door to a spinning mill that was being methodically gutted like a great whale and sold off one part at a time. Then downtown, the lonely little main street, a tae kwon do studio, a government benefits office, a closed restaurant, a nameless corner store for rent, two pedestrians in four blocks, a Dollar General that marked the far end of town. On the other side the country opened up at once, the road passing fields, corn planted on one, nothing on the next—weeds and clods of dirt—then a residential development with two-story look-alike houses in neat rows laid out across someone's former tobacco farm. And beyond the subdivision, isolated on acres of grass behind a split-rail fence and a man-made lake, the supersized faux château of a celebrity NASCAR driver.

The landscape Dean had returned to, where he planned to live out his life, was very old and also new, as particular as anything in America and also as generic, as beautiful and as ugly. In his imagination it had become a nightmare, so profoundly wrong that he called it sinful, and he hated the sin more than any casual visitor or distant critic possibly could, yet he also saw here a dream of redemption so unlikely and glorious that it could only fill the mind's eye of a visionary native son.

Once, driving through Cleveland County, Dean happened to pass the hard-shell Baptist church that his father had once tried to get but failed, the failure that had broken his father's will. Dean had gone down with him to Cleveland County and heard the sermon that his father had given for his audition, back around 1975, so that decades later he recognized the church—and he also noticed that there was now a fucking Bojangles' right next door. For Dean, Bojangles' had come to represent everything that was wrong with the way Americans lived: how they raised their food and transported it across the country, how they grew the crops to feed the animals they ate, the way they employed the people who worked in the restaurants, the way the money left the community—everything about it was wrong. Dean's own business, gas and fast food, had become hateful to him, and he saw the error of his ways as his father never had, and the conjunction of his father's legacy and his own struck him with bitter irony as he drove past.

He was seeing beyond the surfaces of the land to its hidden truths. Some nights he sat up late on his front porch with a glass of Jack and listened to the trucks heading south on 220, carrying crates of live chickens to the slaughterhouses—always under cover of darkness, like a vast and shameful trafficking—chickens pumped full of hormones that left them too big to walk—and he thought how these same chickens might return from their destination as pieces of meat to the floodlit Bojangles' up the hill from his house, and that meat would be drowned in the bubbling fryers by employees whose hatred of the job would leak into the cooked food, and that food would be served up and eaten by customers who would grow obese and end up in the hospital in Greensboro with diabetes or heart failure, a burden to the public, and later Dean would see them riding around the Mayodan Wal-Mart in electric carts because they were too heavy to walk the aisles of a Supercenter, just like hormone-fed chickens.

The traffic on 220, the lifeblood of his chain, made him think about all those engines burning all those millions of gallons of gas that came from America's enemies overseas, and the millions of dollars leaking out of the local economy to the oil companies and big-box retailers. He would pull his truck into a Marathon gas station to fill up and notice the logo above the pump, with the words ALL ROADS LEAD TO LIBERTY written across a flag in the shape of the U.S. map, and it would make him a little crazy to think of people around here buying into such hypocritical bullshit. They'd grown dependent on the corporations and lost their independent spirit. They were supposed to be Americans, not Americain'ts, but democracy was in one of those stages of decline. It would take something big to rouse people in the Piedmont and make them act. Something as big as peak oil, which, in Dean's opinion, was the biggest thing in the twenty-first century. The age of cheap energy had begun when Colonel Edwin Drake drilled the first oil well in 1859 in Titusville, Pennsylvania, and it had created the greatest industrial power the world had ever known, and now it was coming to an end.

In the last lines of *Think and Grow Rich*, Napoleon Hill quoted Emerson: "If we are related, we shall meet." Dean, in his awakened state, met a writer named James Howard Kunstler, through his books and his weekly blog, Clusterfuck Nation. Kunstler, who lived in upstate New York, predicted the coming of what he called "the long emergency," drawing an apocalyptic picture of America in an age of oil scarcity, with the collapse of the suburban, automobile-based way of life, breakdowns in public order, scattered guerrilla uprisings, devolution of the country into semi-autonomous regions and localities, and immense hardships forced on a people who had been living for half a century in "the greatest fiesta of luxury, comfort, and leisure that the world has ever known." Those best equipped to survive would be Americans living on the land or in small towns, with local attachments, useful vocations, practical skills, and a grown-up sense of civic responsibility. The losers would be the exurbanites who chased the American dream in four thousand square feet of house forty miles away from an office park, drove everywhere, shopped at Target and Home Depot, and had long since lost the know-how to make their own fuel and food. For reasons of geography, history, and culture, southerners would fare badly in the long emergency, which would bring particularly high levels of delusional thinking and violence to the South. It was a future that the author, who stood in the old native line of puritan prophets, seemed to welcome, even desire.

All this resonated deeply with Dean. The sweeping statements, the all-or-nothing forecasts, the sense of possessing a secret that most people couldn't stand to hear, suited his frame of mind. But a worldview was only the projection of psychological inclination onto reality, and Dean was an optimist, a latter-day Horatio Alger. There was no Armageddon without the Rapture. He fervently believed that out of this collapse would come a new birth—a whole new way of life would emerge, right here in Rocking-ham County, and around the country. In a decade or so, the whole land-scape would be different. There might be no more Wal-Marts. Exxon and Archer Daniels Midland would be moribund, brainless, obsolete. With gas up to six or seven dollars a gallon, instead of centralization and long-distance transportation and everything on a huge scale, the new economy would be decentralized, local, and small-scale. Rural areas like the Piedmont were on the cusp of revival, and everything they needed was right at hand, riches in the fallow fields. In the age of riverboat travel there had been a gristmill every fifty miles or so, where people produced flour using water power. In the coming years, small fuel refineries and meat processors would spring up every fifty miles on Route 220. Instead of mass production, it would be production by the masses. The future would take America back into its past. In twenty years nothing would be recog-nizable. It would be a difficult transformation, but on the other side lay an absolutely beautiful America.

"If this is a one-hundred-fifty-year anomaly," Dean said, "where we took all the cheap, affordable oil out of the ground, and used it to get us to where we are today—when that starts to unwind, we will go back to where we were before, but yet we will have learned so much in the pro-cess of all this new technology that we take with us." And the key, he believed, was biofuel. "This is the model that will go forward, this green new economy. Unless they come up with something that will run these vehicles on air, or something that is infinite in availability, this will rule for a thousand years. It will be an agrarian economy, but locally. Who's to say what the future holds, but when these farmers can grow their own crops and power their own diesel tractors and not be subjected to anybody and be their own boss, that's a big change. And instead of us thinking that we are going into the unwinding, to me this is the greatest economic explosion that's ever going to hit in our lifetimes, because all that money that's being concentrated at the top, with food, fuel, clothing—what else do they control? banking—it might go back to little towns. I can see that happening."

In the grip of this vision, Dean's politics were taking a strange turn. He rejected his own, his family's, and his community's conservative views.

Now he believed that the country's problems had started with the Republicans. He lost his reverence for Reagan, and he had never had any for
Bush. But he wasn't exactly a Democrat, either. He was working things
out on his own, using the Internet, without a political party or trade association or labor union or newspaper, without any institution to guide
and support him. None of them had any credibility. He hated the banks
and corporations but he didn't trust the government, which seemed to be
in a conspiracy with big business. If anything, his opinions were becoming more like those of the rural populists in the late nineteenth century.
"Sometimes I think I was born a hundred years too late," Dean said.

On the other side of Dean's kitchen wall, his mother had Fox News on
all day. When Dean was a boy the family watched Walter Cronkite together, and back then his mother had no strong political views to speak
of, but now she was getting more and more conservative. Her politics
were based on "Bible principles," which meant opposing abortion and
homosexuality, and since Fox and the Republican Party tied all their positions to religion, there was nothing you could say to pry her away from
them. So she and Dean avoided talking about politics.

In 2007, Rocky Carter introduced Dean to a man named Gary Sink.
Silver-haired, heavyset, and conservative, Gary was retired from the printing and packaging business and serving as president of the Piedmont Off-
shore Sport Fishing Club of Greensboro. But he saw biodiesel as a smart
investment in the future, and he saw Dean Price as a charismatic entrepreneur, with an original vision, who knew how to talk and listen and
figure out how other people thought. In February 2007, Gary, Rocky, and
Dean traveled out to Oregon to look at a local farmer's seed-crushing machines, and they ended up buying three and having them shipped back to
Virginia. The trip tied the three men closer together and affirmed the
venture they were about to undertake. In September, they incorporated
Red Birch Energy as equal partners, with Gary as president and Dean
vice president. The idea was for each of them to invest around thirty
thousand dollars. Rocky's portion went into renovating a storage facility,
which sat on a piece of undeveloped property Dean owned next to his
truck stop in Bassett, Virginia, into a biodiesel refinery, housed in a structure of sheet metal and knotty pine boards, alongside a grain tower. To
design the refinery they hired an engineer from Winston-Salem named

Derrick Gortman, who had grown up on a two-hundred-acre tobacco farm. After the family's tobacco barn burned down, Derrick tried corn, then strawberries, but he could barely break even, and the farm was now sitting fallow. Derrick joined Red Birch and installed the reactor. On the walls Dean hung some of the old soda, ice cream, and bread signs that he'd collected at antiques shops and flea markets. For 2009, its first year of full production, Red Birch contracted to buy twelve hundred acres of winter canola from twenty-five local farmers, paying nine dollars a bushel, more than twice the price of corn. Dean also planted a small patch of canola right there between the refinery and Route 220, to show local farmers that this unknown crop grew easily in the Piedmont's red clay soil. The fuel would be sold to Dean's truck stop next door—a 20 percent biodiesel blend would go straight into the trucks filling up at his pumps. Everything would be in one place, a closed-loop system, from farm to pump, cutting out all the middlemen and transportation costs, staying competitive with or underselling the price of regular diesel.

Nothing like it existed anywhere in the country, and when the refinery was finished, in the early summer of 2008—an auspicious moment, with fuel prices across the country soaring to $4.50 a gallon, the roads around the Piedmont turning desolate, and the presidential candidates trying to appease an angry public—the sign Dean and Gary put up outside the plant proudly declared RED BIRCH ENERGY: AMERICA'S 1ST BIODIESEL TRUCK STOP.

They raised a giant American flag high above the grain tower. The canola patch by the highway was a field of velvety yellow flowers blooming on waist-high stalks.

That summer, local newspapers began to notice that something interesting was happening up on Route 220. They sent reporters to Bassett, where Dean Price had the quotes they needed. "We grow it, we make it, we sell it," he explained to the *Winston-Salem Journal*. "Everything is within house. We don't have to go anywhere else to get the fuel." "Canola will take the place of tobacco as the cash crop of the future," he told the Greensboro *News & Record*. "The best thing that could happen to this country is eight-dollar gas, because that would cause us to get off of it." "A lot of truckers are farmers and a lot of farmers are truckers," he told the *Richmond Times-Dispatch*, "and they'll patronize each other." He gushed to the *Martinsville Bulletin*, "This industry is laden with high-paying green-collar jobs"—seventy-five or a hundred jobs per truck stop, some of them paying twenty-five dollars an hour, jobs that couldn't be outsourced to China, jobs that would go to people in Henry County, Virginia, where unemployment was over 20 percent, and to people all over the countryside if the Red Birch model were franchised: jobs farming the crop, manufacturing the equipment, constructing the refineries, making the fuel, regulating it in state and federal agencies, teaching the technology at community colleges. "We are advocates of small-scale, farmer-owned biorefineries," he told the *Carolina-Virginia Farmer*. "For every dollar you spend on biofuel that is produced locally, ninety cents of that dollar stays local. Now think about the economic impact that would have if you circulate that through the economy, locally, five or six times. It could be huge—an economic boom for this country." It was good for the environment and improved the fuel mileage of eighteen-wheelers. Dean quoted Jefferson on the cultivators of the earth and talked about reviving the civic values of the country. He appealed to patriotism and American independence. If Iran and Iraq started fighting over an oil field, or America went to war with China, or a Muslim terrorist with a dirty bomb took out the power grid on the East Coast, Red Birch would stay on line, and the trucks on Route 220 would keep rolling. "It's win-win-win-win-win," Dean said.

One thing Dean never mentioned was global warming. There were too many doubters in his part of the country—as soon as they heard the words, they'd stop listening and start arguing. Dean himself wasn't at all sure it was true. He was much more convinced about peak oil, since there was an example right here in America. He didn't need global warming to make the sale.

Gary sometimes worried that Dean was getting ahead of himself, overpromising what they might not be able to deliver, and he started to resent the amount of attention Dean was hogging. He also wondered when Dean was going to pony up more money—so far he had invested only twenty-eight thousand dollars. Red Birch Energy had borrowed two hundred fifty thousand to buy the piece of property from Dean where the refinery was built, and it bothered Gary that Dean, though he poured in plenty of sweat equity and never saved his receipts for reimbursement, didn't invest a penny of his profit in their new company. But Dean was under pressure from his truck stop next door, which was financially hurting, and he used the money to shore it up. Then came the news that Dean's map of the property was wrong. He had taken land away to refinance the store without telling his partners, and the refinery had lost half its road frontage, its parking area, and some of the ground where the storage tanks stood. The smaller footprint reduced their collateral.

But Dean put Red Birch Energy on the regional map. He knew how to pitch the idea better than anyone else, and Gary learned to talk like him. In August, they started refining biodiesel out of waste vegetable oil, soybean oil, and animal fats bought on the market, blending it with highway diesel, and selling it at the pumps next door. There were a few sleepless nights as Dean and Gary waited to hear how the truck engines performed on their new fuel. Everything ran smoothly, and they revved up the crushers and began processing the canola seed they'd bought from an experimental farm in North Carolina. The machines squirted a jet of oil into a basin and sheared off flat black pieces of meal that would be sold for livestock feed. It took two days to break down the triglycerides with chemical additives and wash glycerin from the mixture before the oil was converted to biodiesel. The refinery began selling two thousand gallons of fuel a day at Dean's truck stop next door. The plan was to ramp up to ten thousand a day, or two and a half million a year.

That summer, Red Birch Energy began to make money. They were able to sell a gallon of biodiesel blended at 20 percent for four dollars at Dean's pumps, which gave them the dime's edge they needed over other truck stops. Dean thought they had the whole thing licked. It would be a Pandora's box for big oil—and once it was open, Katie, bar the door! People in the area would see the need, they'd see how the oil companies and foreign countries had them hog-tied. The next step would be to license the model all over rural Virginia and North Carolina.

But simultaneous with the materialization of Dean's dream—for that's what all this was, he knew, it was the fulfillment of that dream about the old wagon road—his other business, the one he had turned against, the fast-food-and-convenience-store chain, headed in the other direction. For during the same months of 2008 when Red Birch Energy was starting up, housing prices were dropping all over the country, and in the Piedmont, where the economy had been depressed for a decade, the crisis was forcing people to choose between paying their mortgages and putting gas in the car—at a moment when gas prices were at an all-time high—to drive to work. Foreclosure signs started appearing on properties that had never been worth very much. Dean saw the crisis as a ripple effect of the rising cost of fuel—a consequence of peak oil. But what was good for the new economy was bad for the old. And like a line of dominoes, his overlever-aged businesses began to fail, one after another.

The first to go was the Back Yard Burgers in Danville. Almost imme-diately, weekly sales dropped 30 percent, from $17,000 to $12,000. In fast food, the break-even was around $12,500. As his customers' disposable income dried up, they decided that they couldn't afford $5.50 for a cheese-burger and fries and went across the mall to pay $4.50 at McDonald's. That dollar difference was all it took, and the collapse happened in less than sixty days. The next year, Dean lost $150,000 on the restaurant and had to get rid of it.

But Dean had made a big mistake, which was to put all his stores and restaurants under one corporate entity—Red Birch of Martinsville, Inc.—on one banknote. So when a crack appeared in one wall, the whole edifice started to fall down, and because he was in trouble with one res-taurant, he couldn't get a loan to keep the others going. The next one to go was the truck stop near the Martinsville Speedway: Bojangles' exer-cised its option to pull the franchise in late 2009, and he had to close the truck stop in early 2010. After that, he closed the stand-alone Bojangles' restaurant in Martinsville. He made enough on the sale of both to pay off the bank, but some of his vendors became his creditors. Whatever money had been left from the sale of the Stokesdale store to the Indians went up in smoke. "I made a million dollars," Dean said, "and I lost a million dollars."

The economic crisis wasn't the only culprit. Dean had lost all interest in the stores and delegated the management to an accountant in Martins-ville, and his employees were ripping him off. Dean's friend Howard said, "Dean wouldn't check on those people—they was stealing him blind. He was bringing it in the front door with a damn teaspoon, they was taking it out the back door with a shovel. They just robbed him blind. The one in Bassett was one of the main culprits. He just didn't have sense enough."

"I was concentrating on biodiesel," Dean said. But it turned out that his dream of the future depended on his past. When his businesses started to fail, the domino standing at the end of the line was America's 1st BioDiesel Truck Stop.

RADISH QUEEN: ALICE WATERS

Alice was passionate about beauty—she wanted it around her all the time. She lived intensely through her senses and arranged fresh flowers everywhere and knew to leave the western windows uncurtained to flood the restaurant with golden afternoon light. Her palate was infallible, her food memory indelible. If she said, "This needs a little more lemon," it did. And the dishes were pure simplicity and delight: winter root-vegetable soup, mesclun salad with goat cheese, roast pork, asparagus vinaigrette, tarte tatin.

Her favorite word was *delicious*, and her favorite poem, which once hung above her kitchen table in Berkeley in the sixties, was by Wallace Stevens: while Huns are slaughtering eleven thousand virgins and her own martyrdom is imminent, Saint Ursula makes an offering of radishes and flowers to the Lord, who

felt a subtle quiver,
that was not heavenly love,
or pity.

Instead of the slaughter, Alice, too, saw radishes and flowers, and in them she saw her heart's desire. She was always falling in love—with a dish, a coat, a man, an idea—and she seldom failed to get what she wanted, sparing no expense (she was forever careless about money), because the tiny frame and rushed-off-her-feet manner and nervous girlish voice and hands on your arm concealed an iron will.

There were two major epiphanies in Alice's life. The first was about beauty, and it came to her in France, the country that represented everything that was pleasing to the senses. In 1965, she took a semester off from Berkeley just after the heady rush of the Free Speech Movement and went with a friend to study in Paris, where they soon drifted away from their coursework and lost themselves in onion soup, Gauloises cigarettes, outdoor markets, and Frenchmen. On a trip to Brittany, Alice and her friend dined in a little stone house with a dozen tables upstairs under pink tablecloths. The windows gave out onto a stream and a garden that had just yielded their trout and raspberries. At the end of the meal, everyone in the restaurant burst into applause and cried out to the chef, *"C'est fantastique!"*

That was how Alice wanted to live—like a Frenchwoman, in a tightly wound cloche from the 1920s, baguettes with apricot jam and café au lait in the mornings, long afternoons in a café, spectacularly fresh dinners like the one in Brittany. In fact, she wanted to run the restaurant herself, feeding her friends while they sat for hours and talked about film, flirted, laughed, danced. But she would bring her Francophilic dreams back to puritanical, mass-produced America.

Alice loved the revolutionary atmosphere of Berkeley in the late 1960s, but hers was going to be a revolution of the senses, a communal experience of pleasure. Around 1970 eating in America was a mix of fussy French restaurant cuisine and Swanson's frozen dinners. McDonald's served its five billionth burger in 1969, its ten billionth in 1972. And between those landmarks, in the summer of 1971, Chez Panisse, named for a character in an old Marcel Pagnol film, opened its doors on Shattuck Avenue in Berkeley.

The menu offered only one choice of meal, written on a blackboard:

> *Pâté en croûte*
> *Canard aux olives*
> *Plum tart*
> *Café*
> $3.95

The line stretched out the door. Some people had to wait two hours for their entrée. Others were never seated that night. Inside the kitchen all was chaos, but the dining room was gastronomic heaven. All the ingredients came from local sources—the ducks from Chinatown in San Francisco, the produce from a Japanese concession—and the plums, from local trees, were at their ripest. Alice, at age twenty-seven, had started something.

Chez Panisse was an ongoing celebration of food of a particular kind—grown locally and seasonally. Alice and her staff foraged around the Bay Area for ingredients, sometimes literally in streams and along railroad tracks for the greens and berries they wanted. She was appalled by the thought of serving food that had been frozen or trucked in from out of state. Once, the frozen food industry held a contest to see if expert panelists could tell fresh from frozen—twenty versions of the same ingredient, fresh or frozen, cooked in various dishes. Alice got every single one right.

The restaurant celebrated something else: bohemia. The atmosphere was open and informal, within the extreme snobbery of fresh ingredients and simple cooking. The staff had affairs with one another (none more than Alice—she liked her attachments without obligations), the restaurant was financed with hippie drug money, chefs did coke to keep themselves going, waiters took a toke on their way into the dining room, busboys stuffed opium up the ass before their shift (to avoid nausea), and at the end of the night there was dancing in the dining room. Alice was an inspiring, critical, and chaotic leader, and years went by in the red, and several times the whole thing nearly came crashing down, but always the little delicate-featured woman with the hair cut short would say, "It can be done, it will be done, it's going to happen, you'll see."

And Chez Panisse celebrated one other thing: itself, endlessly.

It took years for Chez Panisse to become the best-known restaurant in America. In the 1980s, the food scene took off around the country, and young people with new money wanted to eat only the best things, or at least be told they were doing so. Alice's restaurant became a place where wealth and celebrity went to be seen. By the 1990s she was a national figure. She embraced the gospel of virtuous food, insisting that her produce be strictly organic and that her meat come from animals that had been reasonably happy before their slaughter. She spread the good news of sustainability everywhere she went, telling anyone who would listen, "Good food is a right, not a privilege," and "How we eat can change the world," and "Beauty is not a luxury." Alice became a moralist of pleasure, a bohemian scold, holding delicious fundraising dinners for Bill Clinton, then following up with hectoring letters to the young president and First Lady urging them to plant a vegetable garden on the White House lawn as a model for America. To her dismay, they never did, but the country seemed to be catching up with her message as couples in big cities frequented farmers' markets on Saturdays to buy their heirloom tomatoes and porcini mushrooms. Among people who could afford to care, no word was held in higher esteem than *organic*. It carried a sanctifying power.

In the midnineties, Alice had her second epiphany. This one began with ugliness. One day, a local reporter interviewed her at Chez Panisse, and as they discussed agriculture in empty urban lots, she suddenly said, "You want to see a great example of how not to use land? You should come look at this enormous school in my neighborhood that looks like nobody cares about it. Everything wrong with our world is bound up in that place." It was the Martin Luther King Middle School, whose concrete buildings and blacktop playground she drove past every day, thinking they might be abandoned. The quote made it into the paper, the principal saw it, and before long Alice was invited to see the school, and maybe do something about it.

What Alice did was to ask if she could plant a vegetable garden on a neglected acre of land at the edge of the school grounds. She had seen the food sold to the kids—something called a "walking taco," a plastic bag full of corn chips drowned in a beef-and-tomato mess spooned from a can—and to her it symbolized a completely broken culture. Fast food wasn't just unhealthful, it spread bad values. She had a grand idea: the students would grow kale and bok choy and dozens of other things in the garden; prepare a nutritious, delicious meal in a school kitchen (currently closed for lack of repair money); and sit down together to eat it in the communal way that had disappeared from their hectic, dysfunctional homes, learning basic table etiquette as they ate and awakening their senses to a new relationship with food.

Alice believed nothing could improve what was wrong with California's miserable public schools so radically as a vegetable garden, and if there was something of the temperance crusader in her, walking through the slums asking why the men drank so much, Alice didn't let the thought trouble her for a moment. If a question about priorities was raised— should schools that didn't have funds for substitute teachers and classroom supplies spend money on "sustainability education"?—Alice got a steely look in her eye. "It can be done, it will be done, it's going to happen, you'll see."

This was the start of her transformation from restaurateur to evangelist. It took a couple of years to raise the money privately and get the official approval, the personnel, and—hardest of all—the participation of the students. But once the Edible Schoolyard got going, it was such a success that other cities around the country adopted the idea. In 2001, Alice brought it to Yale, where her daughter was an entering freshman. Four years later, Alice's idea took root on the National Mall.

And when Barack Obama arrived at the White House, Alice immediately wrote to him: "At this moment in time, you have a unique opportunity to set the tone for how our nation should feed itself. The purity and wholesomeness of the Obama movement must be accompanied by a parallel effort in food at the most visible and symbolic place in America— the White House." When Michelle Obama announced in May 2009 that there would be a vegetable garden on the White House grounds, everyone regarded Alice as its godmother.

In the sixties, most Americans ate more or less the same, bad things. Chicken à la king with a wedge of iceberg lettuce was a popular dish, while fondue made its way among the more daring. But in the new millennium, food divided Americans as rigidly as just about everything else. Some people ate better, more carefully than ever, while others got grossly overweight on processed foods. Some families, usually intact, educated, prosperous ones, made a point of sitting down together to a locally sourced, mindfully prepared dinner at home several nights a week. Others ate fast-food takeout together in the car, if at all. Alice helped make food into a political cause, a matter of social change and virtuous lifestyles, but in the age of Chez Panisse, food could not help being about class. Her refusal to compromise her own standards led others to turn her revolutionary spirit on its head.

For some Americans, the local, organic movement became a righteous retreat into an ethic defined by consumer choices. The movement, and the moral pressure it brought to bear in parts of society, declared: Whatever else we can't achieve, we can always purify our bodies. The evidence lay in the fanaticism of the choices. A mother wondered aloud on a neighborhood Listserv whether it was right to let her little girl go on being friends with another girl whose mother fed them hot dogs. This woman was sanitizing herself and her daughter against contamination from a disorderly and dangerous society in which the lives and bodies of the poor presented a harsh example. Alice hated the word *elitist*, but these were elite choices, because a single mother working three jobs could never have the time, money, and energy to bring home kale with the right pedigree, or share Alice's sublime faith in its beneficence.

Alice wanted to bring people to a better life, but she had trouble imagining that the immediate comfort of a walking taco might be exactly what a twelve-year-old wanted. When she heard the criticisms, she turned away, to the radishes and flowers. Anyone who was passionate enough about organic strawberries, she believed, could afford to buy them. "We make decisions every day about what we're going to eat. And some people want to buy Nike shoes—two pairs!—and other people want to eat Bronx grapes, and nourish themselves. I pay a little extra, but this is what I want to do."

TAMPA

Tampa was going to be America's Next Great City. That was what the 1982 book *Megatrends* said—Tampa would be one of ten "new cities of great opportunity," all of them in the Sunbelt—and in 1985 the Chamber of Commerce decided to aim higher than the city's hedonistic motto from the seventies, which had been "Tampa: Where the good life gets better every day," and replaced it with "America's Next Great City." The words appeared on billboards, bumper stickers, and T-shirts, and who could doubt that they would prove true when Tampa had a new international airport, it had the 1984 Super Bowl, it had the NFL Buccaneers, it had the eleven million square feet of the Westshore business and shopping district, it had sunshine and beaches, and it was growing as fast as anywhere in the country? Fifty million new people came to Florida every year, and since the sunshine and beaches weren't going anywhere, Tampa would continue to grow, and by growing, become great.

It grew and grew. It grew in order to grow. It grew throughout the eighties, in good economic times and bad, when pro-growth conservatives ran the Hillsborough County Commission and when pro-planning progressives ran the county commission. It grew throughout the nineties, when Tampa Bay got the NHL Lightning and the major league Devil Rays, plus another Super Bowl. After the millennium it grew like gangbusters. Florida's governor, Jeb Bush, was a developer, so he understood all about growth, and the county commission became majority Republican, with one or two votes safely in the pocket, and maybe the pay, of the developers, the land use attorneys, the builders, and Ralph Hughes. Hughes was a former boxer with a conviction for felony assault who, until he died owing more than three hundred million dollars in taxes, owned a company, Cast-Crete, that made all the precast concrete beams for all the doorways in all the subdivisions that were going up all over Hillsborough County.

For it was really the county that grew. While the city of Tampa inched past three hundred thousand people, Hillsborough County, with its vast tracts of unincorporated farmland and ranchland and wetland, surged beyond a million. The selling point wasn't America's Next Great City after all—Tampa was an old port with a defunct cigar industry, a history of labor trouble, a high crime rate, and an uneasy mix of Latinos, Italians, Anglos, and blacks. No, the growth was actually hostile to urban life. What it offered was the American dream in a subdivision, the splendid isolation of a new homestead an hour's drive from downtown. A developer's brochure promised thousands of square feet "a comfortable distance from the higher prices, taxes, and congestion of big city living. Come enjoy the home Tampa residents can only dream about." That was the ethos of the Sunbelt, and since the seventies it had made the Sunbelt the model for the country's future.

As long as more people came this year than last year, and next year than this year, there would always be more houses to build, and more jobs in construction and real estate and hospitality. Property values would continue to go up, and the state could continue to do without an income tax, financing its budget with sales taxes and real estate fees. To encourage more growth, friendly county commissioners would waive the impact fees that were supposed to be assessed to the developers in order to help pay for new roads and water lines. In the exurbs going up around Tampa Bay, property taxes could remain low, with new schools and fire stations funded by bond issues floated on the projection of future growth. So in a sense everyone was getting returns from investments that would come in tomorrow, or next year.

A few local critics pointed out the strategy's resemblance to a Ponzi scheme. But everything kept growing and no one paid attention.

The growth machine cleared out the pine trees and palmettos and orange groves along State Road 54 up in Pasco County. It cut down the mangroves on Apollo Beach and laid asphalt over the strawberry farms around Plant City. Farther south down Interstate 75, in Lee County, the growth machine built a university on the wetlands near Fort Myers (Senator Connie Mack put in a call to the Army Corps of Engineers), and it sold quarter-acre lots on the installment plan between the drainage canals of Cape Coral. Farmers and ranchers cashed out and suddenly, where there had been orchards or pastures or swampland, developers put up instant communities—they were called "boomburgs"—and christened

them with names that evoked the ease of English manor life: Ashton
Oaks, Saddle Ridge Estates, the Hammocks at Kingsway (even the trailer
parks had names like Eastwood Estates). Overnight, it seemed, the
growth machine paved empty fields of wiregrass into straight flat suburban streets called Old Waverly Court, Rolling Greene Drive, and Pumpkin Ridge Road, and along the curbs, driveways with small treeless yards
appeared, and two-story concrete block houses went up, with stucco walls
painted yellow or beige and a columned archway over the front door to
lend an illusion of elegance that would jack up the price. The developers
promised recreation centers, playgrounds, and lakes, and they sold the
houses on spec for $230,000, unless you got in six months later, when it
might cost you $300,000—you were buying or you were dying. Shopping
malls and megachurches sprang up nearby, and the two-lane highways
got so crowded that they had to be widened.

No place was too remote or unpromising for development. Gibsonton
was a little town on the eastern side of Tampa Bay, where carnival freaks
used to spend the winters—old rural Florida, bait shops and shotgun
shacks and Spanish moss hanging from live oaks. A builder out of Miami
called Lennar Homes wanted to bury a tropical fish farm in Gibsonton
under dirt and concrete and put up a new subdivision of 382 houses.
There were no nearby schools except in trailers, no shopping besides a
Wal-Mart a few miles away, and no jobs within a forty-five-minute drive.
But it was growth, so the county commission ignored the warnings of its
own planners and gave Lennar every possible break on impact fees and
taxes, and in 2005 Carriage Pointe opened for business.

There were no town centers out among the subdivisions, no towns at
all, no hills to relieve the flatness, so that you never quite knew where you
were without GPS, or what time of day it was without a clock, since the
bright tropical light hardly varied. A landmark would be a four-way stoplight at the intersection of two eight-lane roads, with a Publix in one corner, a Sam's Club in the next, a Walgreen's in the third, and a Shell station
in the fourth. There was a Town Center in Brandon, a vast unincorporated boomburg of a hundred thousand souls, but it was the name of the
biggest shopping mall. Brandon's main street was West Brandon Boule-
vard, or U.S. 60, and in the half mile between stoplights, the shops
passed by in an uninterrupted blur: *Einstein Bros Bagels Florida Car Wash
State Farm Dairy Queen Express Lube Jesse's Steaks McDonald's Five Star*

Paint Ball Aquarium Center Sunshine State Federal Credit Union Mister Car Wash Weavers Tire + Automotive Wendy's.

The growth machine became the employment agency. Other than minimum wage jobs at restaurants and big-box stores, it was hard to find work outside the real estate industry. In the hierarchy of the boom years, the poor were Mexican day laborers on construction sites; the working class had jobs in the building trades; the lower middle class were bank tellers; the middle class were real estate agents, title insurance agents, and civil engineers; the upper middle class were land use attorneys and architects; and the rich were developers.

Some of the buyers were refugees from Tampa, leaving the city behind on that promise of a dream home in a place they'd never heard of called Country Walk. Most came from out of state. But the area wasn't Miami or Palm Beach, a destination for upscale snowbirds. It was settled mainly by lower-middle-class people, many of whom followed the I-75 trail down from Ohio, Michigan, and other midwestern places that nurtured frugality and prudence. Hillsborough and the neighboring counties became conservative, churchgoing country, with antiabortion signs and prophecies of Judgment Day scattered among the highway billboards advertising model homes and liposuction. But those older values went soft in the flat light that stared down like a constant high noon.

There were the Luxes, Richard and Anita, from Michigan. Anita's father had worked in Ford's River Rouge plant long enough to remember Henry Ford and Walter Reuther, and Anita had a job with the city of Dearborn, until Richard's architectural firm asked him to start a new Florida office in the eighties. Anita brought her father's frugality to St. Petersburg and remained a coupon queen. But she went to work at Wachovia Bank, which got heavily into subprime loans after acquiring World Savings, out of California: the loans were called "Pick a Pay," and the customers were invited to design their own mortgages, choosing an interest rate and a payment plan. These loans were squeezed into the spectacularly profitable juice that fueled the growth machine.

There was Jennifer Formosa, also from Michigan, but raised by her mother in Florida. After high school she went to work as a bank teller in Cape Coral and married her baby's father, a local guy named Ron, who didn't have a high school diploma but made decent money pouring concrete foundations. Ron and Jennifer took out a $110,000 mortgage and built a three-bedroom house, refinanced to pay their bills, took out an equity line to put on a new roof, then refinanced again to pay off their cars, put in the patio, buy a boat, and blow the rest on cruises and trips with the kids to Disney World.

There was Bunny—"just Bunny"—who grew up on Utopia Parkway in Queens, New York, then chased the sun and the good life to Hawaii, Arizona, and West Palm Beach, before ending up in a subdivision called Twin Lakes on State Road 54 in Pasco County, where she bought for $114,000, then watched her house go up to $280,000 in six years.

And others came from farther afield. There was Usha Patel, the daughter of a successful contractor in Gujarat. Usha grew up a spoiled brat who was driven around by a chauffeur and never had to clean her dinner plate. But everything changed in 1978, when she was eighteen and her family married her off to an Indian engineer who worked in London. In 1991, because of her husband's back problems, they decided to move with their two children to sultry Tampa, where her brother practiced medicine. In Tampa, Usha learned once again to start from scratch and work herself to the bone. From six in the morning till two in the after-noon she ran the cash register at a gas station her brother had bought in a drug-ridden area in southern Hillsborough County (she was robbed twice at gunpoint), making three hundred dollars a week. From the gas station she drove home to Brandon in time to meet the kids after school, feed them, make sure they did their homework. Then she put on the uniform of a Mexican restaurant where she waitressed from four until eleven. "That is how the money came."

Usha saved and saved, and she raised her children to do the same. When her little boy wanted a pair of Air Jordans, she told him, "You're paying for Michael Jordan's name, that is all." She didn't even buy a house until the children had graduated from college.

Once the kids were working, she faced the choice that confronted other immigrants before her who were named Patel and came from Guja-rat: a gas station or a motel. She knew about the dangers of late nights behind a cash register, so in 2005 she set her sights on a Comfort Inn, just off I-75 where it crossed State Road 54 amid the boomburgs of Pasco County, less than three miles from Country Walk. It was a two-story mo-tel, sitting between a Cracker Barrel and an Outback Steakhouse, painted green and beige, with sixty-eight rooms at fifty dollars a night and a tiny swimming pool next to the parking lot. Usha paid $3.2 million, half a million in cash. The rest came in two loans, one from the Small Business Administration for $1.2 million, the other from a commercial lender called Business Loan Express for $1.5 million. Looking back, she came to believe the deal was fraudulent, based on a wildly overstated appraisal, but the lenders told her what to write on the application, and she wrote it.

"They get you into debt like putting butter in your mouth," she said. The motel was as unremarkable as any Comfort Inn around the country, maybe more so—but it was hers.

A lot of the buyers were speculators, from all over—flippers who aimed to clear fifty thousand dollars in six months—secretaries who made thirty-five thousand a year and juggled five or ten investment homes worth a million dollars, car salesmen who made their real money when housing doubled in two years. At the peak of the madness, in 2005, a house in Fort Myers sold for $399,600 on December 29 and $589,900 on December 30. Flippers were the ones driving prices to crazy heights. Mike Ross was a flipper.

Mike grew up in Newport Beach, California, and moved to Florida at age eleven. He came from a long line of boat builders, and after dropping out of ninth grade he went to work at the Pasadena Yacht and Country Club in Gulfport, across the bay from Tampa, repairing the boats of very wealthy people. He worked on a crew at first, and then for himself, and over time he made a hundred fifty dollars an hour sandblasting aluminum engine intake vents and refinishing the factory's lousy varnish work— varnish was a lost art. One of his clients was the CEO of duPontREGISTRY ("The World's Premier Luxury Marketplace"), who flew Mike and his wife on his private jet to wax his boats in the Bahamas. Another was Jim Walter, a Tampa multimillionaire who built cheap and quick houses all around the country. Mike took pride in his skill, and there was no end to the work—within three years of going solo he had 60 percent of the marina, he was making seventy grand a year—but it was backbreaking and brutal in the heat, with chemical compounds from the high-speed buffer flying into his face.

One day in 2003, Mike began shaking and vomiting from heat exhaustion. That's when he decided to stop working on boats. He was forty-two and overweight, and his body was tired. He'd always wanted to flip houses—he was just too chicken to do it. A lot of the guys whose boats he'd worked on made their money that way, or dabbled in it, and they encouraged him to try. Mike and his wife bought their first investment property with a loan from Swift Funding Corp. at 3 percent above the normal rate—a liar's loan, a subprime loan. It was the easiest thing in the world. He thought he'd clear 7 or 8 percent. The house cost them $50,000, and after working on the kitchen and bathroom for two months, they turned around and sold it for $68,000. Next they spent six months fixing up their own house in St. Petersburg, which they'd bought in 1985 for $48,000. At 5:00 p.m. on a Friday, Mike put up a sign outside: FOR SALE BY OWNER. The phone started ringing off the hook, and within three days they'd sold it for $169,000—amazing money. Then they bought a hundred-year-old farmhouse in rural Georgia, near Mike's parents, and moved up there to work on it. There was no fear anymore. It was the height of the market and it was so easy.

And there was Michael Van Sickler.

Van Sickler grew up outside Cleveland in the seventies and eighties, when the city was bankrupt or close to it. His father was an engineer with General Electric in Nela Park, in charge of GE's holiday lighting program—the Van Sicklers always had the best Christmas lights on the block. Life in suburbia bored Mike out of his mind—on summer days he'd sit around thinking, "God, where are the people?" Escape became possible in high school, when he and his friends would ride the Rapid, the light rail line, from Cleveland Heights to downtown and watch the Indians play a night game at Municipal Stadium, which was always empty in those last years before it was torn down. Then they'd walk over to the Flats, a factory zone by the Cuyahoga River that had been abandoned and then converted into a bar district where everybody congregated, and they'd try to meet girls. "That was probably when I understood the magic of what a city could do," he said—even a dingy Rust Belt city like Cleveland. "It starts with people."

After college, in the early nineties, Van Sickler followed his parents to Florida, where they had retired in New Tampa. He went to Gainesville for a master's in journalism—a college class on Woodward and Bernstein, Didion, and other classics of the genre had lit his imagination. When he got out, he was hired by a series of midsize papers around the state. He learned his trade covering city hall, a great sandbox because he made a lot of mistakes. His first story for the Lakeland *Ledger* was all quotes, because he felt no authority to say anything himself. That was what he wanted to aim for—the certainty of having a subject cold, so that his readers would finish a story knowing what to think.

In 2003, Van Sickler was hired by the *St. Petersburg Times*, the best paper in the Southeast—a dream gig. The landscape for newspapers was starting to look bleak. They were shedding jobs, and, in a few cases, folding under pressure from the Web and lost advertising. The *Times* was doing better than a lot of other papers, and it was destroying its cross-bay rival, *The Tampa Tribune*, which had been stripped down by its owner, a media conglomerate in Richmond, Virginia, to the level of fishwrap. The *Times* was owned locally, and it wasn't a for-profit enterprise—Nelson Poynter had willed his stock to the Poynter Institute for Media Studies upon his death in 1978—so it didn't have to make the same margins as wounded giants like the *Chicago Tribune* and the *Los Angeles Times*, which would soon be carved up by private equity investors in search of bigger profits.

Van Sickler and his wife, who also worked at the paper, bought a 1930 brick bungalow in Seminole Heights, a historic neighborhood just north of downtown Tampa that was starting to get funky after a period of blight. It brought a taste of those nights walking around the Cleveland Flats, but Van Sickler found the whole "Next Great City" business suspect.

When he was covering city hall at *The Palm Beach Post*, he'd gotten deeply interested in urban planning—for a while he even thought about switching careers, until he realized that city planners had even less clout than reporters. But his bookshelves filled up with titles like *A Field Guide to Sprawl*, *The History of the Lawn*, *Suburban Nation*, and the pair that were his bibles: *The Power Broker* and *The Death and Life of Great American Cities*. Van Sickler became a Jane Jacobs disciple. She gave a vocabulary to the desire he had felt growing up in Cleveland Heights with no one around on those excruciating summer afternoons: short blocks, pedestrian permeability, mixed uses, safety in eyes on the street, density. Life was richest and most creative where people of different backgrounds could meet face-to-face and exchange ideas. And that happened in cities—cities of a particular kind.

Moving to Tampa clarified all this, especially after 2005, when the paper created a beat for Van Sickler as its planning and growth reporter. The city had seemed fun and full of promise when he was twenty-two, in the early nineties, but by the 2000s it didn't look to him like much of a city at all: a nine-to-five downtown with about fifty residents, until a pair of huge condo towers that had no relation to the streets but would suck up demand for years to come went up, while all the shopping and Class A office space were miles away in Westshore, near the airport. Tampa had tried to take a shortcut to greatness, but that never worked; its downtown had no coherence, nothing to attract people beyond an office job, a hockey game, or a court case. Riding a bike around town was dangerous, and so was trying to walk across one of the broad, high-speed streets— Tampa ranked second in the country in bicycle and pedestrian fatalities. If you saw someone on foot, his car had probably broken down, and a woman crouched on the roadside for an hour without shelter had to be waiting for a bus. Commuter rail initiatives never got past the county commission, and Tampa Bay remained the second-largest metropolitan area in America, after Detroit, without one. As a result, strangers were never obliged to engage with one another. "No encounters happen by accident in Tampa," Van Sickler said. "Or if they do, they're traumatic."

A strain of thought said that urban life was un-American, and Van Sickler felt its presence in the growth machine out in Hillsborough County. The corporate-built houses in the subdivisions looked like bunkers, with tiny windows, no breezeways or courtyards to suit the climate, air conditioners running all the time in cavelike darkness. Inside, families sat in their carpeted living room before a large-screen plasma TV, with the blinds drawn against the sunlight. Outside, the long, long streets of identical houses without shade gave people no reason to want to walk anywhere, so they went from car to driveway to house and never got to know their neighbors. They were retreating from the world, and their isolation was deepened by a pervasive paranoia. Signs advertising accident attorneys, fast cash for houses, and get-rich-quick schemes were everywhere, and auto insurance was higher in Florida than elsewhere— insurers called it "a fraudulent state." Florida drew the transient and rootless on the eternal promise of a second chance, with more than its share of scammers and con men. So who was to say the guy living next door wasn't one of them?

A subdivision like Carriage Pointe was Jane Jacobs's vision of hell.

In 2006, Van Sickler wrote a story about the people buying houses around Tampa. A lot of them lived in other places, and when he tracked them down by phone, he would ask, "Are you living in the home? Oh, is it a vacation home? Why would you be vacationing in Ruskin—it's not a vacation destination." It turned out that at least half the sales were going to investors—a huge number. The whole concept of home ownership had been warped beyond recognition. These houses were disposable commodities. That was what drove the demand.

Van Sickler never quite fit in in Tampa. He was tall and pale, with strawberry blond hair, and he wore dress slacks and long-sleeved shirts. His voice sounded a little formal, like an old-fashioned radio reporter's, and his midwestern earnestness made him awkward amid the glad-handing of the Sunshine State, which was the other side of its fraudulence. He was especially earnest about his job. An investigative reporter had to be an idealist—Van Sickler didn't buy the idea that journalists were cynical. The press didn't help itself or its readers when a story gave both sides and left it at that, because some things were objectively true and reporters should say so.

Van Sickler sometimes feared that his style as a reporter was too abrupt and prosecutorial. Mark Sharpe, a Republican county commissioner, would get a call from Van Sickler about campaign donations from a developer and know immediately that there was going to be trouble. The questions would begin, innocent-sounding at first, simple matters of fact, but they would keep coming, one question after another, and Van Sickler remembered everything that Sharpe had ever told him, and eventually the reporter would spring his trap, arrive at the question that Sharpe had seen coming from the start: "If this guy's a major contributor, do you think there was anything wrong with your vote to waive impact fees?"

Van Sickler believed that there were two kinds of journalists—the ones who told stories, and the ones who uncovered wrongdoing. He was definitely the latter. But the only person he ever took down was Sonny Kim.

In the spring of 2006, Van Sickler began to hear about a man named Kenny Rushing. He was a black real-estate salesman, which was unusual in Tampa. His name and face appeared on billboards and TV ads as the caped superhero Captain Save-a-House, a play on the rap song "Captain Save-a-Hoe." He held jam-packed tent shows, where he showed up in a white Bentley and a Kangol cap, trailed by a convoy of Hummers festooned with his picture. He preached that the city's black poor could get a piece of the housing action just like everyone else, by buying up distressed properties and selling them for huge profits. "It's time to do for self," Rushing told an audience in Ybor City. "Black folks dominate what? Sports and entertainment. I want them to say that blacks dominate real estate, which has produced more millionaires than anything else I know."

It was all about empowerment, civil rights, and getting rich. Rushing had been a drug dealer as a teenager in Des Moines and done four years in a Florida prison. He made his story part of the motivational pitch, telling young dealers that they, too, should turn their smarts to the legitimate pursuit of flipping, enriching themselves while benefiting black homeowners who needed financial relief. "It was Carnegie crossed with Jay-Z," Van Sickler said. "The thing about the economy in Florida back during the boom years—it was hardly booming. It was only booming in one sector, and that was real estate. If you weren't on the inside, you were struggling just like everybody else."

Van Sickler began looking into Kenny Rushing. In his self-presentation he was just a low-level drug dealer, but in fact he had been a major crack distributor for the Crips. His stories of Golden Gloves titles were fabrications. And Captain Save-a-House turned out to be exactly the kind of predator that he denounced at his sold-out seminars. He had persuaded a seventy-three-year-old black grandmother in an aging, mixed neighborhood called Tampa Heights to let him take her dilapidated house off her hands for $20,000. The woman owed almost all of it on a loan from the city and ended up with just $1,729. Three weeks later, Rushing sold the house to an investment trust called Land Assemble for $70,000.

Van Sickler asked Rushing about the deal.

"If I had known the house was worth seventy thousand dollars I would have paid her a lot more," Rushing said, "sixty thousand easy. Don't slant this, I'm not taking advantage of a woman."

Van Sickler, in prosecutorial mode, asked if Captain Save-a-House would give her some of his profit.

"I'm not about to say, 'Here you go, here's all I made on the property.'"

In four years, Rushing and his partners had cleared well over a million dollars. Fifteen of the deals were in Tampa Heights, which, not coincidentally, was the planned site for a huge five-hundred-million-dollar redevelopment project, called Heights of Tampa, with nineteen hundred upscale condos and townhouses. Rushing was acting as the front man for two of Tampa's most powerful developers. He minimized the relationship, and the developers denied knowing him.

Van Sickler was intrigued by the connection between a former crack dealer and the city's elite, and he published his story in May. It introduced him to the vast underside of the hottest real estate market in the country. A broker he talked to while reporting the story passed along a tip: "If you think Kenny is something, you should check out Sonny Kim."

By the time Van Sickler caught up with Sonny Kim, the music had stopped.

Some people in the Florida real estate business could identify the precise moment when it happened. For Marc Joseph, a broker in Fort Myers and Cape Coral—the eye of the madness—there was a week in December 2005, with the average price per unit at a peak of $322,000, when the phone didn't ring as much as usual. It felt like a car slowing to a halt as all the air went out of the tires. Others timed the moment a few months before or after that and compared it to the lights being switched off. At some point in late 2005 or early 2006, with the housing market at its dizzying mid-decade height, speculators suddenly lost confidence, the faith that kept Florida aloft gave way, and the economy plummeted like a Looney Tunes character who, suspended in midair, looks down. Prices did what borrowers, lenders, flippers, Wall Street traders betting long, credit default swap desks, Fannie Mae, Asian bankers looking for 8 percent, antic boosters on CNBC, and Alan Greenspan somehow never imagined possible: they started to decline.

It took a year or two for the effects to be seen across the landscape of boomburgs, brokers' offices, construction sites, and retail malls. In early 2007, an official of Allied Van Lines reported to the Florida Chamber of Commerce in Tallahassee that the company was moving more people out of the state than in. Between 2007 and 2008, the number of electrical hookups in Florida decreased for the first time in the forty years that records had been kept. And for the first time ever, the state's net flow of immigration, the engine of the growth machine, dwindled to zero.

Lumberyards sold off equipment. Car dealerships laid off salesmen. Developers filed for bankruptcy, and their wives filed for divorce. By early 2008, the concrete company where Ron Formosa worked in Cape Coral started getting rid of guys. First Ron saw his hours cut in half, then he lost his job. At the same time, adjustable interest rates went up and balloon payments on subprime loans came due, which meant that borrowers like the Formosas, who were already watching their incomes and property values melt away, had an even harder time keeping up on their mortgages. Ron and Jennifer filed for bankruptcy, but they couldn't afford the fourteen-hundred-dollar fee, even after Ron found a job working for a locksmith, making nine dollars an hour changing the locks on foreclosed houses. The Formosas went a full year without making a mortgage payment before the bank put an ugly yellow auction sticker on their door. They found a nearby rental and vacated the house. Jennifer vowed to save her money next time instead of spending it. "I don't think I'll ever want to buy a house again," she said. This was how the foreclosure epidemic began.

On State Road 54 in Pasco County, the developer stopped work on Country Walk midproject, leaving behind streets whose pavement ended in wiregrass after a few feet, streets with signs and lights but no houses, streets with houses but no occupants. The promised tennis pavilion and beach volleyball court hadn't materialized. In a front yard, there was a FOR SALE sign next to a collapsed inflatable Santa Claus. Three yellowing copies of *The Tampa Tribune* lay on the front pavers at 30750 Pumpkin Ridge Drive, with trash in the kitchen and the fridge door open, and a FOR SALE BY OWNER sign in the yard. Half or two-thirds of the houses were vacant, but the residents who hung on in Country Walk parked their cars in the empty driveways and kept the neighboring lawns of San Augustine grass mowed to avoid an appearance of decline. On the more forsaken blocks the change was obvious—six inches of grass, weeds in the driveway, copper wiring ripped from the air-conditioner boxes, a rash of green mold spreading across a beige stucco wall, a VACANT or ABANDONED notice tacked to a front door. But the collapse of the Ponzi scheme was unspectacular, with no demolished factories or abandoned farms. The ghost subdivisions were pretty, in a way. Under the brilliant aquamarine sky the houses looked like perfect cardboard cutouts, the surfaces smooth and regular, the blinds drawn, the landscape almost untainted by human life.

The prices that had rocketed skyward dropped just as fast to earth. Up State Road 54 from Country Walk, Bunny's house in Twin Lakes, which had gone from $114,000 to $280,000 in six years, fell to $160,000 in two years. Some of the houses on Bunny's street had been owned by flippers, and some had been owned by people who could no longer afford to live in them, but in both cases nobody was there, and on a weekend afternoon Bunny from Utopia Parkway was watering her lawn, in hip-hugging Capri jeans, a sleeveless top, and silvery-green eye shadow, without another soul in sight.

Usha Patel's Comfort Inn earned a million dollars in her first year, eight hundred thousand her second. She found Americans to be hopeless employees. They lived day to day, collecting their paycheck on Friday, clubbing and partying even if they had kids, skipping work Monday, showing up late Tuesday, refusing some tasks because their pay was too low, always full of complaints and excuses—"My son took my keys." They might give her a week of hard work and then demand a vacation. Or a cigarette break every ten minutes, even if they didn't smoke. When Usha talked about American workers, her nose scrunched up and her mouth turned down and her eyes narrowed as if the subject was physically unpleasant. They were spoiled, as she had once been spoiled, and it was by all the foreigners doing cheap labor. The only good people she ever hired were immigrants like her, who were trustworthy and willing to work hard for low pay—a night manager from the Islands, a guy from India, the Spanish housekeepers.

But her optimism about the country was undimmed. It was the land of opportunity for everyone. "I love America," she said. "If any foreigner can come and get success, the people living here don't want to work." She liked America's rules and laws, the lack of corruption, the fact that anyone could get justice. Her son had become a young businessman—he owned his own computer shop in a Tampa strip mall and drove a BMW and lived on the twenty-sixth floor of a condo tower downtown. Compared to India, America was a dream.

In her third year, 2007, Usha's earnings dropped to half a million dollars, with occupancy at just 25 percent—you needed 50 percent to survive. Two things conspired against her motel. The first was the housing crash, which was beginning to bring down the wider economy (she blamed it on strict border enforcement, which kept out all the good foreign workers). The second was construction work on a new shopping mall along the access road between her Comfort Inn and I-75, which began around the same time as the downturn. The work closed her exit at night and took away her highway sign, which killed her business (the mall was never finished). She started having trouble making her twenty-five-thousand-a-month payments. Her son helped out, but before long she was falling behind.

Mike Ross got caught by the collapse in the middle of a family crisis. He asked a court to grant him custody of his grandchildren because his daughter and her boyfriend in St. Petersburg were abusing them—the boyfriend threw the one with cerebral palsy into a swimming pool and laughed, Mike said. By the time Mike and his wife, who was on disability from an auto accident, got custody, they were two years behind on the renovation of their old farmhouse in Georgia. Before they could finish, the market turned, and their $180,000 property ended up selling for $110,000. Mike's former clients in the yacht business advised them to move to Northern California, far away from the abusers, and flip houses there, but when they arrived in Vacaville with the grandkids, the economy was tanking and there was no work, not even in gas stations or 7-Elevens. Plus the financing rules had all changed, so it was impossible to get a loan and start flipping. The move cost them fifty thousand dollars, half their savings. After six months in California they moved back east, to a nice little town outside Raleigh, sort of like Vacaville with trees, but North Carolina was California all over again, no jobs in construction, auto body work, or anything else Mike tried. They were running out of money, and Mike began to fear they'd end up homeless. There was no choice but to move with the grandkids back to St. Petersburg, where the daughter and her boyfriend still lived.

Mike tried to get work with his old customers in the yacht business, but they were all well cared for by the repairmen he'd turned them over to. He hung around the Pasadena Yacht and Country Club for a while but didn't get a single call. That life was over. He borrowed money from a former client to put his family into a rental apartment in a ghettoish neighborhood, where the kids in the parking lot picked on the grandson with cerebral palsy. They were living on food stamps, his wife's disability, the grandson's SSI, and charity. Mike was deteriorating psychologically, his mind racing three hundred miles an hour—he was afraid of homelessness, suicide, the loony bin, running into the boyfriend, who didn't know they were back in St. Petersburg—afraid all the time, making up stories in his mind about what could happen to him and then finding that the things *did* happen. And he had once been so calm, so steady, varnishing yachts in the marina under a blue sky. His torso ballooned, and though he could still laugh at himself, his eyes stared out through rimless glasses in medicated sadness. He was on painkillers for back pain and Xanax for anxiety, and once, tired of it all, wanting to put his load down and sleep, he took thirty Xanax and four Vicodin and fell into a two-day coma.

"The economy triggered it all," he said. "It just ripped me apart, it took away my will to live. That's the way I see it."

They locked Mike up in the loony bin for three days. When he got out

he threw himself on the mercy of a Tampa crisis center, where he was
given counseling and help with the electric bill. He had always thought of
himself as middle-class, and it amazed him to come so close to living in
a homeless shelter. But the mental ward and the crisis center sort of
snapped him out of it. He read a book called *Finding Life Beyond Trauma*
and started taking deep breaths, got in touch with his spirituality, learned
to turn away from his worst thoughts. Since the medical field was reces-
sionproof, he signed up for a training course, paid for by the government,
as a home health aide. He found a job making $10.50 an hour, without
benefits, helping a ninety-one-year-old World War II vet with dementia go
to the bathroom. It was no harder than repairing millionaires' yachts.
Mike was glad to be of use.

Van Sickler and some colleagues at the paper crunched a lot of data about
foreclosed houses in Hillsborough County. They were everywhere, but
they clustered in two places: the older city slums and the ghost subdivisions. Van Sickler's mapping software showed a bright red dot at Carriage
Pointe, the development built on top of a tropical fish farm in Gibsonton:
the foreclosure rate was 50 percent, the county record. Van Sickler and
a photographer from the paper, Chris Zuppa, started driving out to Carriage Pointe in the evenings to find out what was happening there.

It was one of the weirdest places in Van Sickler's life as a reporter.
One night, he and Zuppa saw emaciated cows standing in the fields between the rows of single-family houses. The cows had been brought in so
that some homeowner could claim agricultural land use for a tax break,
and now they were starving because no one was feeding them. Van Sickler and Zuppa knocked on a lot of doors, but it was hard to find anyone
home, or anyone who would talk. The owners stranded here were mostly
families that had viewed Carriage Pointe as a starter home on their way to
someplace else. When prices dropped by 50 percent, they were trapped,
and furious with Lennar, the developer, which had promised them a pool,
a community center, and a limit on investment homes of 20 percent. As it
turned out, a lot of the owners of record lived in places like Fort Mill,
South Carolina, and Ozone Park, New York, and they didn't care what
life was like for people stuck in Carriage Pointe. Some of the foreclosed
houses were being used by drug dealers or traffickers in stolen goods,
littered with contraband. There had even been a shooting. Sheriff's

deputies were making nightly visits out to Carriage Pointe. Paranoia was running high, and one man proudly showed Van Sickler the security cameras he'd installed on his driveway.

"In suburbia," Van Sickler said, "no one can hear you scream."

A Ponzi scheme was a confidence game that succeeded only when enough people were willing to put aside common sense. Everyone involved was both being taken and taking someone else. The result was universal credulousness and universal fear. Carriage Pointe was supposed to be a little slice of the American dream, but it felt like the end of days. Van Sickler's reporting there led him to conclude that the bust wasn't all the fault of feckless homeowners, and he wrote a hard-edged piece exposing the role of developers and elected officials in creating the disaster.

Sang-Min Kim, nicknamed Sonny, had come to Tampa from South Korea. He was the owner of Body Design Tattoos, a piercing and tattoo parlor with an Asian theme. At one time or another in the middle years of the decade, Sonny Kim also owned a hundred houses around Tampa, most of them in the bad neighborhoods north of downtown, the same area where Kenny Rushing operated. In fact, Kenny and Sonny were business partners, selling houses to each other. By the time Van Sickler got on Kim's trail, in the summer of 2008, Sonny had cleared four million dollars' profit, and more than a third of his houses were in foreclosure.

Van Sickler drove around Belmont Heights and Sulphur Springs, two of the poorest neighborhoods in Tampa, to take a look at Sonny Kim's properties. There was a decaying two-story stucco house at 4809 North Seventeenth Street, with a blue tarp over the roof, boarded windows, and mattresses piled in the overgrown yard. Kim had received it in 2006 for a hundred dollars with a quitclaim deed witnessed by a convicted drug dealer. Three months later, Kim sold it for three hundred thousand dollars to a buyer named Aracely Llanes, who borrowed the entire amount from Long Beach Mortgage, a subsidiary of Washington Mutual Bank. Van Sickler stood in the yard and looked at the house and thought about that loan. It was incredible. Did anyone from the bank do a drive-by to eyeball the place? Eighteen months later, the house was in foreclosure and the bank was asking thirty-five thousand. Van Sickler went searching for neighbors to find out whether anyone was living in the house, but it was nighttime in a dangerous neighborhood, and people didn't answer his knock. Finally, a Tampa police car pulled up and a cop got out. "Someone around here doesn't like you," he said. A neighbor had called to complain about the tall white guy snooping around.

Van Sickler tried to track down Aracely Llanes. She had an Opa Loca address but no phone number—she was unreachable. Some of Kim's other buyers were drug dealers, arsonists, the mentally ill. Van Sickler looked at dozens of the houses he'd flipped, and it was always the same: a derelict property, a minimal purchase price, a swift resale for a ridiculously large sum, a no-questions-asked loan, little or no money down, the buyer nowhere to be found, the house never occupied, the loan in default. An expert told Van Sickler that some of the buyers—they were known as "straw buyers"—might not exist, or might be victims of identity theft. Or they might be Sonny Kim's partners in mortgage fraud. So might the brokers, appraisers, notaries, title agents, and ultimately the bankers who were in on the deals, some of them showing up again and again. Everyone was making money on Sonny Kim's business, and the business of all the other Sonny Kims out there, while the bad loans seemed to vanish into the air.

Van Sickler kept reporting into September. In the middle of the month, Lehman Brothers went down. Lehman was one of the banks making loans to Sonny Kim's straw buyers. So were some of the other big players that were suddenly all over the news and facing ruin—Washington Mutual, Wachovia, JPMorgan Chase, Countrywide, Bank of America, Fannie Mae, Freddie Mac. The headlines sent a shudder and a thrill through Van Sickler. It dawned on him that his local story about a tattoo parlor owner (which had already taken too long—his editors were showing a lot of patience) was connected to the story of the biggest financial crisis in decades. Down in Tampa he had the goods—the authority of his own eyes—that better-known reporters covering it from New York and Washington didn't have. You could trace the Wall Street collapse right back to the house at 4809 North Seventeenth Street, and to the houses in Carriage Pointe and Country Walk.

The banks had thrown money at fraudulent borrowers to overpay for crappy houses because the risk was immediately passed on to someone else. There was a new term in finance, at least one that Van Sickler had never heard before: "mortgage-backed securities"—bundles of loans that were sold by the lenders to Wall Street, where they were packaged as bonds and sold again to investors for huge profits. The term inspired dread, like the name of a new virus. Now Van Sickler understood: here were the mortgages backing the securities. Here were the defaulted loans that were threatening to bring down the global financial system.

The conventional wisdom among journalists was that everybody was responsible for the financial crisis. "Greed just got out of control. We don't know why, we just got really greedy, and everybody wanted a house they couldn't afford," Van Sickler said. "I think that's lazy journalism. That's a talking point for politicians who want to look the other way. We're not *all* to blame for this." He hated the kind of reporting that tried for a false balance and refused to draw clear conclusions even when they were staring the reporter in the face. His own work had led him not to "everybody," but to certain institutions—government agencies, real estate businesses, and especially banks. Sonny Kim was just a front man. "It was systemic. Banks were approving these loans without human eyes looking at them, because the appetite was so huge. They couldn't make these mortgages fast enough."

Van Sickler's story filled the front page just after Thanksgiving. Within a week the FBI got on the case, and soon after that Sonny Kim was co-operating, wearing a wire. Van Sickler waited for the feds to make their way up the food chain to the guys at the top.

SILICON VALLEY

Peter Thiel and his friend Reid Hoffman had been arguing about the nature of society ever since Stanford. Over Christmas in 1994 they had spent a few days on the California coast brainstorming about how to start an Internet business. Hoffman had Thiel read a new sci-fi novel called *Snow Crash*, by Neal Stephenson—a dystopia in which large parts of America have been privatized into sovereign enclaves run by powerful entrepreneurs and mafias, a kind of fictional precursor to *The Sovereign Individual*. The novel's characters escape the violence and social breakdown around them into virtual reality through a successor to the Internet called the Metaverse, where they represent themselves through avatars. *Snow Crash* gave Hoffman an entrepreneurial idea, and he soon left his job at Apple to start a dating website called socialnet.com, perhaps the first social network on the Web. It didn't succeed for various reasons—people turned out not to want to interact through avatars, they wanted to be themselves—but Hoffman continued to refine the idea, and after the sale of PayPal to eBay in 2002, he took his proceeds and launched a social network for businesspeople called LinkedIn. It was through LinkedIn that Hoffman met Sean Parker, and it was through Hoffman and Parker that Thiel met Mark Zuckerberg.

In the spring of 2004, Thiel and Hoffman were trying to talk their hyperkinetic twenty-four-year-old friend Parker out of suing Sequoia Capital, the investors in his online address book company, Plaxo. Owing to his libertine ways, Parker had been driven out of his own company, just as he'd been driven out of Napster, the music sharing site, a few years earlier. Thiel told him that rather than entangling himself in a lawsuit, he should start a new company. Three months later, Parker came back to Thiel with the news that he'd just become president of Thefacebook, a college social network with four employees, and that the Harvard sophomore who had founded it needed money because the number of students clamoring to get on was increasing and would soon overwhelm the computers. Hoffman, who had been tracking Thefacebook and Mark Zuckerberg all year, recused himself from becoming the lead investor because it might be seen as a conflict of interest with LinkedIn. The natural choice was Thiel.

Thiel liked to say that, on principle, a hard-core libertarian shouldn't put his money in social networking. If there was no such thing as society, only individuals, how could there be any return on the investment? Ayn Rand wouldn't have invested in Thefacebook. But Thiel, placing rational selfishness ahead of ideological purity in a way that wasn't completely inconsistent with the principles of Objectivism, had been interested in social networks for a while. This one looked like it might succeed where others, such as Friendster, had failed. The consumer Internet was still in its postcrash doldrums, and for once there were more good ideas around than investors chasing them. Thefacebook was already on about twenty campuses, operating under a benign version of the Brezhnev Doctrine: once a college was targeted for a takeover, pretty much the entire student population was captured in a matter of days, and the process became irreversible. With such an intense user base, it seemed that Thefacebook could go reasonably far. Hoffman had talked to the engineers and they had seemed quite good. So in midsummer 2004, Thiel agreed to meet Zuckerberg at Clarium Capital's offices in the heart of San Francisco's financial district, on the forty-third floor of 555 California Street, a granite skyscraper that had been the headquarters of Bank of America until it moved to Charlotte in 1998.

Parker did most of the talking for Thefacebook, but Thiel gathered a strong impression of Zuckerberg. He was only twenty, wearing a T-shirt, jeans, and rubber flip-flops, and already stubborn about what he wanted, with an intense focus, a coder's introversion, obtuse to the point of Asperger's about other people (something of a paradox in the founder of a social network). He matter-of-factly described Thefacebook's dramatic growth while making no effort to impress Thiel, and Thiel took that as a mark of seriousness. By the end of the meeting—which stretched on for most of the afternoon—Thiel had made up his mind to become an angel investor in Thefacebook. He would lend the company half a million dollars—"seed money"—which would convert into a 10.2 percent stake and a seat on its five-man board.

As the meeting concluded, Thiel told Zuckerberg, "Just don't fuck it up."

Years later, after Zuckerberg did not fuck it up, and the number of people using Facebook passed half a billion, and the value of Thiel's stake rose above $1.5 billion, and the story of its early days was made into a Hollywood movie that portrayed Zuckerberg and Parker in a less than flattering light, freaking out both of them, Thiel went to see *The Social Network* at a movie theater in San Francisco with a small group of friends. The meeting between his character and Zuckerberg's took thirty-four seconds of screen time, and although he came off well, relatively speaking, he also felt that his character looked too old, too much like an investment banker type—Thiel normally wore T-shirts at work, not button-down blue shirts. Later still, after Facebook went public in May 2012 and its stock price immediately began to fall, Thiel sold off most of his remaining shares, for a cash total of over a billion dollars from his original five hundred thousand.

The same year as his meeting with Zuckerberg, 2004, Thiel cofounded a company called Palantir Technologies (the name came from a crystal-ball-like stone in his beloved *Lord of the Rings*), which took software that had been used at PayPal to combat fraud by Russian gangsters and developed it for complex data analysis, finding subtle patterns in torrents of information to make it easier for government agencies to track down terrorists, fraudsters, and other criminals. Some of the seed money came from the CIA's venture fund, but in its early stages, Palantir depended heavily on Thiel's thirty-million-dollar investment. He became chairman of the board, and after Facebook got too big for its offices at 156 University Avenue in downtown Palo Alto, Palantir moved in—right across the street from where PayPal had its start. Eventually, Palantir would be valued at $2.5 billion. Thiel was on his way to becoming one of the world's most successful technology investors.

Clarium Capital was doing every bit as well. Thiel's was a global macro fund—it depended on analysis of world markets and government actions at the highest level. In 2003, its first full year, with $250 million under management, it returned 65 percent on investments. Thiel's strategy was to take the big-picture view of long-term trends and place bets that went against conventional wisdom: long on Japanese government bonds when others were selling; long on energy, because he was convinced that peak oil was real and global supplies were running out; long on U.S. treasuries, because he foresaw an anemic economy following the Bush recession of 2001. Year by year, Clarium enjoyed meteoric growth, topping out around seven billion dollars by the summer of 2008, a seven-hundred-fold increase in six years. The financial press began to talk about Thiel as an investing genius of a contrarian. To him, that only meant he thought for himself. Most people outsourced their thinking and deferred to the majority, the herd. There weren't enough Robinson Crusoes in the world.

Clarium moved to the fourth floor of a brick-and-glass building at the edge of Presidio Park, with splendid views of the Golden Gate Bridge and the Pacific. From his corner office Thiel could see Alcatraz and the Marin hills. The building was on the grounds of the San Francisco headquarters of Lucasfilm, the first floor decorated with statuary, from Thiel's favorite movie, of Darth Vader and Yoda. Clarium's sitting area was divided by bookcases of dark hardwood containing leatherbound editions of Madame de Sévigné, Dickens, Darwin, and George Eliot, along with books on structured finance and quantitative research. At the center stood a table with a chessboard that awaited players.

There was a hundred-dollar penalty for arriving late at the weekly 10:30 a.m. trading meeting. One Tuesday morning the subject was Japan. Eleven men in blue, white, or striped shirts without ties sat around a long conference table. Thiel presided from the end.

"The secret of Japan is that nothing ever happens," he said. "If I were Japanese I'd be fed up with years of stagnation, but I'm not Japanese, so who knows?"

Thiel's top trader, Kevin Harrington, a former Stanford Ph.D. candidate in physics, weighed in. "The old people in Japan are satisfied. Their assets have been going up. It's like the boomer class in the United States that thinks everything's going to be fine."

"Do you think we should be short?" another trader asked.

"It's been a mistake to be short Japan for the past twenty years," Thiel said. "I don't have a strong view on it. But if something goes wrong it could keep going. The political question is: Is Japan an authoritarian country, or is it a country where there's no government at all? I don't think it's a democracy—you can set that aside. Is it the Japan of the seventies, an authoritarian corporate state where you can force people to save a lot of money? Or is it like California and the United States, where the deep secret is there's nobody at the steering wheel at all? People pretend to be in control, but the deep secret is there's no one."

For half an hour the meeting turned into a seminar on Japanese history and culture. Finally, Thiel asked, "What are people optimistic about?"

"Enhanced oil recovery in the United States and Canada," a young trader said.

A trader named Patrick Wolff, who was participating by speaker-phone, said, "I will betray my libertarianism, but the state's monopoly on energy is rapidly eroding."

"Next week," Thiel said, "it would be useful for people to think about what they are optimistic and hopeful about."

As at PayPal, Thiel hired people who were like him. Clarium developed the reputation of a Thiel cult, staffed by young libertarian brains who were in awe of their boss, emulating his work habits, chess playing, and aversion to sports. Because Thiel saw a housing bubble, he was adamant that his employees not own their homes. He rented a ten-thousand-square-foot white wedding cake of a mansion in the Marina, a short drive from Clarium, with a terrace view of the illuminated dome and arches of the Palace of Fine Arts.

He began to live the life of a Silicon Valley billionaire. He employed a staff of two blond, black-clad female assistants, a white-coated butler, and a cook, who prepared a daily health drink of celery, beets, kale, and ginger. At his private dinner parties, guests were given a menu printed with a choice of entrees. He flew everywhere on private jets. One year he took his closest friends on a surfing trip to Nicaragua, another year on a river rafting trip to Zimbabwe, security guards in tow. Thiel was emotionally opaque, in an amiable way, but he showed a taste for decadent display while keeping his personal indulgence to a minimum, like Gatsby making phantom appearances at his own parties. He bought a Ferrari 360 Spider for fun and speed (his everyday car was a Mercedes SL500), paid for driving lessons at the Las Vegas Motor Speedway, and started a magazine called *American Thunder*, dedicated to stock car racing and the "NASCAR lifestyle" of hunting, fishing, and country music. (Despite being carried in two-thirds of Wal-Mart stores and featuring Dale Earnhardt, Jr., on its first cover, *American Thunder* folded after four issues.) He bought a San Francisco restaurant-nightclub called Frisson, where he hosted Facebook's million-users party. He threw other parties—fundraisers, book or company launches—at his mansion, for fifty or a hundred guests, and at the most outré the male servers sometimes went shirtless or wore nothing but aprons. He contributed millions of dollars to conservative causes and candidates. After the housing bubble burst, he bought the San Francisco mansion for $6.5 million, then an oceanfront spread on Maui for $27 million, and he rented a loft above Union Square in Manhattan. His houses were decorated in impeccably contemporary fashion for no one in particular.

"There is this strange way in which the amount of inequality just kept growing," he later said. "In the seventies, I didn't know anyone who was a millionaire. That would have been really rich, that was unusual. In the late eighties at Stanford, there were a few people who were wealthier, but something like the twenty-to-thirty-million range was colossally wealthy. Their parents had that much money—that seemed really extraordinary." Then, in 1997, a Silicon Valley novel called *The First 20 Million Is Always the Hardest* was published. "Twenty million seemed like a crazy amount of money. The theory I had was that it would seem counterproductive to have more. Maybe twenty million would be good, but way more would create all these problems." But, year after year, "somehow it just kept going."

In a really unequal world, if you tried to keep up with the Joneses (defining the Joneses as the average of the people who were better off than you), then you would surely get lost, always feeling that you were falling farther behind—because, no matter how much you had, the Joneses would always be ahead by an ever-increasing amount, forever eluding you, a fata morgana on the desert horizon. In a really unequal world, you needed a place to anchor yourself.

As a libertarian, Thiel welcomed an America in which people could no longer rely on old institutions or get by in communities with longstanding sources of security, where they knew where they stood and what they were bound for. All that was anathema to Thiel's worldview. He believed in striking out into the void alone, inventing oneself out of ambition, talent, and abstractions—so the unwinding allowed him to thrive. But he also stood at the center of a tight-knit group of friends, almost all men, most of them young, like-minded Silicon Valley successes who had gotten rich around the same time, in the binary-step-function way of the Valley—one day they suddenly had more money than God, but they kept wearing jeans and T-shirts—though none as rich as Thiel. These friends kept him connected to his old reality and screened out the more ephemeral and toxic status markers. When an online gossip sheet outed Thiel in 2007, he called it "the Silicon Valley equivalent of al Qaeda" and continued to keep his personal life private, disdaining intimate conversation even with his closest friends. Over dinner they did not talk about sex, religion, or other people's lives. Instead, they talked about ideas, world events, and the future of technology. Asked to name the investor he most admired, Thiel pointed to the billionaire recluse Howard Hughes.

During the 2008 presidential campaign, Thiel was interviewed by *Reason*, the libertarian magazine. "My optimistic take is that even though politics is moving very antilibertarian, that itself is a symptom of the fact that the world's becoming more libertarian," he said. "Maybe it's just a symptom of how good things are." In September, having passed the milestone of seven billion dollars, Clarium moved most of its operations and 90 percent of its staff to midtown Manhattan. Thiel was approaching the level of the world-class hedge fund managers, and he wanted to be closer to the action on Wall Street.

That same month, the financial markets collapsed. With everyone else in a panic, Thiel tried to catch a falling knife, but this time contrarianism became his enemy. Expecting coordinated intervention by governments to calm the global economy, he went long on the stock market for the rest of the year—but stocks continued to plummet, and his fund lost a lot of money. In 2009, when he shorted stocks, they rose, and Clarium's losses grew. Investors began redeeming their money. Some of them grumbled that Thiel had brilliant ideas but couldn't time trades or manage risk—he'd been predicting a crash in real estate for years, but when the moment came he was unable to take advantage. In mid-2010, with the bleeding unstanched, Clarium had to close its New York office and return to San Francisco. The moves were costly disruptions. By 2011, the fund's assets were down to $350 million, two-thirds of it Thiel's money, the entirety of his liquid net wealth. Clarium became a de facto family office.

For the first time in his life, Thiel had failed at something he prized, publicly and spectacularly. He was humbled by it, and unlike at PayPal, where setbacks had triggered outbursts, he took losing well and kept an even keel with his staff. During the same period, his view of America began to darken. As he reconsidered the years since the seventies, years that had seemed so bright and hopeful, especially in Silicon Valley, even Facebook lost its glow. But Thiel's pessimism also led him to form radical new ideas about the future.

2008

BAM SLAMS HILLARY IN HISTORIC VICTORY He's First Black to Win Iowa Caucus as Voters Embrace Message of Change . . . REAL ESTATE AP-PRAISED: FROM MALAISE TO CRITICAL . . . GM POSTS RECORD US AUTOMOTIVE LOSS OF $38.7B FOR 2007 Offers Buyouts to 74,000 US Workers . . . OIL SHOCK: ANALYST PREDICTS $7 GAS, "MASS EXODUS" OF US CARS . . . DEPRESSION QUESTIONS RETURN IN NEW CENTURY . . . IN WEEK OF IRAQ WAR ANNIVERSARY, OBAMA'S RACE SPEECH DOMINATED MEDIA COVERAGE . . . Obama's entire campaign is built on class warfare and human envy. The "change" he peddles is not new. We've seen it before. It is change that diminishes individual liberty for the soft authoritarianism of socialism. . . . *that there is something happening in America, that we are not as divided as our politics suggests, that we are one people, that we are one nation* . . . LEHMAN FILES FOR BANK-RUPTCY, MERRILL SOLD, AIG SEEKS CASH . . . BUSH ASKING FOR $700 BILLION BAILOUT . . . McCAIN PICKS FAILING OHIO FACTORY TO LAUD FREE TRADE He used his own recent political fortunes—a dramatic fade followed by an unexpected comeback to secure the Republican presidential nomination—to illustrate that depressed Rust Belt cities such as Youngstown can rebound. . . . PALIN REIGNITES CULTURE WARS . . . We believe that the best of America is in these small towns that we get to visit, and in these wonderful little pockets of what I call real America, being here with all of you hard working very patriotic . . . I bet bin Laden feels like a real asshole now, huh? "What? I bombed the wrong America?" . . . Heath Ledger passed away on Tuesday, sources reveal exclusively to PerezHilton.com. . . . SILICON VALLEY BARELY TOUCHED BY FINANCIAL CRISIS—SO FAR . : . How are you? You gotta love Face Book! YOU LOOK WONDERFUL. Hopefully I will get some pics of me and family downloaded soon . . . I can only imagine how anxiously you are awaiting election day? Are you still a strong Republican? Regardless, I always cherish our friendship . . . "CHANGE HAS COME" Barack Obama Elected First Black President; Economic Anxiety Propels Democrat to Electoral Landslide . . . *and together we will begin the next great chapter in the American story with three words that will ring from coast to coast, from sea to shining sea: Yes. We.*

INSTITUTION MAN (2): ROBERT RUBIN

Much to his surprise, Robbie Rubin, the new boy from Manhattan, was elected president of his fourth-grade class in Miami Beach in 1947, despite knowing nothing about how to be class president. He got good grades in high school, but he never would have gotten into Harvard if a lawyer friend of his lawyer father's hadn't introduced him to the dean of admissions. At Harvard he assumed that he would be part of the 2 percent of his freshman class that was going to flunk out, but his grades that year were excellent, and in 1960 he graduated Phi Beta Kappa, summa cum laude.

Bob Rubin never expected a girl as beautiful and talented as Judith Oxenberg to date him, so he introduced her to his Yale Law School friends in the hope that they would reciprocate by setting him up with women closer to his own level—but within a few months Bob and Judy were married at Branford Chapel.

Because his odds of making partner at Cleary, Gottlieb weren't great, in 1966 Robert Rubin looked around for a job on Wall Street. Going from a law firm to an investment bank was very unusual in those days, but his father landed him introductions at Lazard Frères and Goldman Sachs, and to his surprise they both made offers. He joined Goldman's arbitrage department, even though he didn't know what risk arbitrage was, and he doubted that he had the audacity to get executives on the phone to question them about prospective deals. The head of Goldman, the legendary Gus Levy, regularly yelled at Rubin for asking stupid questions, but Levy also thought that he would one day run the firm—which seemed far-fetched to Rubin at the time. In spite of doing well in arbitrage, he never in a million years thought he'd be offered a partnership, so he looked around for another job and was surprised, to say the least, when Goldman made him partner on the first day of fiscal year 1971. Within a few years he was on the management committee.

All his life he carried around a yellow legal pad, writing down notes and numbers, analyzing the likelihood of different outcomes, calculating risk and expected value. He found that he was interested in trading as an exercise in thinking about probabilities. Thinking probabilistically meant that he took even remote contingencies into account. The stress and flux of arbitrage left others nerve-racked and blinded by their own fear or greed, but he was always able to take the pressure of high-stakes trades in stride. He was a reasonably commercial person, but he didn't find his purpose in making money—he had learned that people found fulfillment only within themselves—and his identity wasn't job-dependent. This freed him to think more clearly about risk.

He took the long view, keeping in mind that the result of a trade wouldn't matter in a hundred years and that, while he enjoyed his membership in the establishment, he could always walk away into a different existence—sitting in a Left Bank café reading *Tropic of Cancer* and talking about the meaning of life, or fly-fishing at Spruce Creek or Tierra del Fuego. His core belief was that nothing could be proven to a certainty, so he functioned well in the uncertain world of markets. (He was also a reasonably good poker player.) This philosophical detachment made him a surprisingly successful arbitrageur.

Goldman Sachs in those years was a very different place from what it would become—much smaller and tamer, a boutique private partnership dominated by investment banking, not trading, a place where the senior partners spent their time tending to the needs of clients. In the 1970s, calmly and rationally, Rubin pushed Goldman to get into over-the-counter derivatives—options trading—and commodities, which grew exponentially and proved extremely profitable. In 1981 he was part of a small group that persuaded the firm to make its first major acquisition—J. Aron, a commodities trading house. When the new division ran into trouble, he turned it around by taking on more risk, which he found very interesting. (Over half the people at Aron had to be fired, a delicate undertaking.) From there he rose to the top of Goldman's huge fixed-income division, where he and his partner, Steve Friedman, had to stanch large losses on illiquid positions. To raise more capital they wanted to take Goldman public, following the other big Wall Street firms, but the younger partners with smaller stakes said no. With Friedman, Rubin became vice chairman of the firm in 1987, and in 1990 he reached the top. He got there, much to his own surprise, by maintaining the modesty of his ambition and the calm of his daring.

Rubin stood in the political center, looking in both directions, but he was a Democrat, because he was concerned about the plight of the poor. He was also worried about the growing deficits of the Reagan years. He wanted to get involved in politics—few things were more attractive to him than the thought of seeing the world from inside the White House—so he began raising money for the Democratic Party. In 1982, his friend Bob Strauss asked him to chair a congressional fundraiser. Rubin wasn't at all sure that he would be able to raise enough money—in those days there weren't that many Democrats in finance—but the dinner took in more than a million dollars. Party leaders began to solicit his support in tapping Wall Street money, and he raised almost four million dollars for Walter Mondale in 1984, and the same amount for Michael Dukakis in 1988.

As Rubin aged and grayed, his hair, parted on the left, still grew thick on top, while his hooded, pouched eyes got sadder and more skeptical. As Wall Street became an ever larger and more volatile juggernaut, he stayed steady and whippet-thin. As financial services were deregulated, he remained well regulated. He avoided the limelight, while his peers bought fifth homes and second wives and appeared regularly in Sunday Styles. After half a life at Goldman Sachs he was worth well over a hundred million dollars and lived in a Park Avenue penthouse, but he still wore plain rumpled suits to the office, walked around his neighborhood in an old pair of khakis, and always made time to read and fish. Colleagues heard him say "just one man's opinion" a dozen times a day. He was careful to hedge his ambition with humility, his risk-taking with expressions of worry.

When Bill Clinton was elected president in 1992, Rubin wasn't at all sure that he would be offered a position in the new administration, but he became the first director of the newly created National Economic Council. He had no idea how to function in the White House—didn't even know what a "decision memo" was—but he brought down his yellow legal pad, moved into rooms at the Jefferson Hotel, and sought advice from Washington veterans like Brent Scowcroft and Jody Powell. At meetings in the Oval Office or the Roosevelt Room, he didn't try to get as close as possible to the president; he liked to stay away from the head of the table, read the people in the room, and speak from a slight remove.

Self-effacement worked as well for him in Washington as it had on Wall Street. "You're going to be the strongest person in the White House," the president once said, which Rubin thought was ridiculous. He was just hoping to be relevant.

From the foot of the table, Rubin told Clinton that he would have to sacrifice his campaign promises on education, job training, and middle-class tax cuts and instead establish credibility on deficit reduction (cutting spending and raising taxes on the top 1.2 percent) in order to reassure the bond market. If deficits remained at Reagan-Bush levels, interest rates would go up, and if interest rates went up, economic growth would be stifled. (This wasn't just Wall Street's view—it was basic Rubinomics.) Clinton, all the while fuming that he was being turned into an Eisenhower Republican, assented. Nor did the president refuse when, from the foot of the table, Rubin further advised (not out of class solidarity, but in fear of undermining business confidence in the president) against using polarizing, class-laden terms like "the rich" and "corporate welfare." Even "corporate responsibility" was over the line. When the secretary of labor, Robert Reich, argued for more populist policies and language, Rubin would say—calmly, without raising his voice—"Look, I spent most of my life on Wall Street. I can tell you, you're just asking for trouble." In the Clinton White House, most of a life on Wall Street trumped any other experience, because the bond market was reality and everything else was an interest group.

Rubin was giving his best economic advice, always disinterested and on the merits. (If it happened to be Wall Street's view too, well, the economy had become dominated by the financial sector, and any Democratic president would be destroyed if he lost its confidence, especially after the party began to raise most of its money on the Street.) So Clinton, elected as a middle-class populist, governed as a pro-business centrist, and Rubin, after moving over to the Treasury Department in 1995, became one of its most admired secretaries, defusing financial crises in Mexico, Asia, and Russia, reducing the deficit to zero, and guiding the country through the longest period of economic growth in its history.

In 1998, the head of the Commodity Futures Trading Commission, a woman named Brooksley Born, floated the idea of regulating the enormous and shadowy market in over-the-counter derivatives—the market that Rubin had led Goldman Sachs into twenty years earlier. During a one-hour meeting at Treasury, Rubin was angrier than his colleagues had ever seen him (Brooksley Born was too strident, he felt, she didn't defer enough), and he lectured her to stay out of derivatives—she should listen to the banks' lawyers, not the government lawyers at her agency. He teamed up with Larry Summers, his deputy, and Alan Greenspan, the Fed chairman—called "the Committee to Save the World" on the cover of *Time*—and persuaded the Republican Congress to block Brooksley Born. (Not that Rubin wasn't worried about derivatives. In fact, he had always been worried about the size of Goldman's derivatives book, though he reluctantly agreed whenever traders wanted to make it bigger. And he continued to worry about the risks of derivatives as Treasury secretary, the way they could entangle financial institutions and magnify excesses in the market. He had no objection in principle to derivatives being regulated—just not by Brooksley Born—though he never got around to doing anything about it because of the opposition he would have faced from Wall Street and the rest of the Committee to Save the World.) In 2000, Congress passed and Clinton signed into law a bill—the last one the president signed before leaving office—that prevented derivatives from being regulated by any agency. (By the time the Commodity Futures Modernization Act became law, Rubin was no longer in government, so he couldn't be held responsible for any negative effects it might have had, as he would point out in later years.)

The same was true of Gramm-Leach-Bliley, passed by Congress and signed by Clinton in 1999, which repealed the 1933 Glass-Steagall Act and allowed commercial and investment banking under one roof. (Yes, Rubin vocally supported Glass-Steagall's repeal, mainly because the wall between commercial and investment banks had already eroded—a fait accompli that the most admired Treasury secretary since Alexander Hamilton was powerless to fix.)

In 1999, Rubin returned home to New York. He took out his yellow legal pad and began jotting down questions about his next move, taking notes in conversations with people like Henry Kissinger and Warren Buffett. He wanted to stay involved in public policy, but he saw no reason to become a monk financially, though he didn't care to take on the responsibilities of a CEO. In other words, he wanted to be a wise man, like Douglas Dillon or Averell Harriman in another era, the kind of figure who moved seamlessly between Wall Street and Washington, serving the interests of shareholders as well as the American people. (In fact, working on Wall Street would keep him current on financial issues so that he could remain useful to policymakers and give his customary disinterested advice based on the merits.)

Every firm in New York wanted Rubin's golden name, but Sandy Weill of Citigroup pursued him relentlessly with just the right offer: Rubin would sit at the top of the bank's empire as chairman of the executive committee, the in-house consigliere, shaping strategic decisions but bearing no responsibility for day-to-day operations. For this he would be paid fifteen million a year in salary and guaranteed bonus plus stock options (he was a reasonably commercial person), and he would get to use Citigroup's corporate jets for fishing trips and other expeditions. (Citigroup, the world's largest financial services company, had been created the year before from the merger of Citicorp and Travelers, a deal that would not have survived under Glass-Steagall, but Glass-Steagall no longer existed, though Rubin had nothing directly to do with its repeal and no one could justifiably accuse him of being paid back handsomely by Citigroup, though critics inevitably did.)

Rubin fished and read and advised senators and talked with foreign leaders and wrote his autobiography while he ran meetings of Citigroup's executive committee. He was a wise man, and his hair remained thick and his body thin. He had fingers in all parts of the establishment, joined the boards of Ford, Harvard, and the Council on Foreign Relations, became an important figure at Brookings, advanced the careers of his many disciples in business and government. He warned against fiscal recklessness and short-term investing. He basked in the glow of the longest economic expansion in American history, even as it faded out.

For it turned out that Rubinomics had not made much difference after all. The years 1993–99 barely slowed trend lines that had been in place for a generation. Between the late 1970s and 2007, years when Rubin held positions in senior management at Goldman Sachs, the White House, the Treasury Department, and Citigroup, the financial sector grew spectacularly, and the rules and norms that had kept it in check collapsed. Financial companies doubled their share of corporate profits in America, and salaries in finance doubled as a share of national earnings. The top 1 percent more than tripled its share of national income, while the income of those in the middle rose by only 20 percent, and the income of those at the bottom stayed flat. By 2007, the top 1 percent owned 40 percent of the nation's wealth, the bottom four-fifths just 7 percent. The period when

Rubin stood at the top of Wall Street and Washington was the age of inequality—hereditary inequality beyond anything the country had seen since the nineteenth century.

In his capacity as resident wise man, he urged Citigroup, as he had once urged Goldman Sachs, to take more trading risks with its huge balance sheet. He also advised that the risks needed to be carefully managed. After that, he didn't pay much attention while, between 2003 and 2005, Citigroup tripled its issuing of collateralized debt obligations and mortgage-backed securities stuffed full of bad loans from places like Tampa, where people whose incomes had been flat for years had all their wealth in their houses and used them as cash machines. By late 2007, the bank had forty-three billion dollars in CDOs on its books.

Most of it turned out to be worthless, and in 2008, when the financial crisis hit, Citigroup practically became a ward of the state. Its losses reached sixty-five billion, it needed two huge helpings of bailout money, and it was the only bank that the U.S. government seriously considered nationalizing.

Rubin had spent his career trying to harmonize his and Wall Street's interests with America's, and when that became impossible in 2008, he disappeared. He refused almost all interview requests, and on the few occasions when he spoke publicly, he brushed aside any blame. "I don't feel responsible, in light of the facts as I knew them in my role," he said. "Clearly, there were things wrong. But I don't know of anyone who foresaw a perfect storm." Even Alan Greenspan admitted that he had been wrong, but the pride that had always been masked by humility would not allow Rubin to do it.

In January 2009, having earned $126 million for his decade of advice, doubling his net worth, Rubin resigned his position at Citigroup. In April 2010, he was called to testify before the Financial Crisis Inquiry Commission in Washington. The panel included Brooksley Born, and when she asked Rubin about regulating derivatives, Rubin hastened to agree with her every word. He did not appear calm and steady. Sitting in his rumpled suit at the witness table, he looked anxious and red-eyed, as if he hadn't slept well. He explained to the commission, "The executive committee of the board, which you just referred to my being chairman of, was an administrative body. It didn't have a decision. What it did was it met between board meetings. Those meetings were very infrequent. And it wasn't a substantive part of the decision-making process of the institution."

"I don't know that you can have it both ways," said Philip Angelides, the chairman of the commission. "You either were pulling the levers or asleep at the switch."

Rubin said that, as a board member, he couldn't have known all the positions held by the biggest bank in the world.

"You were not a garden-variety board member," Angelides replied. "To most people, chairman of the executive committee of the board of directors implies leadership. Certainly, fifteen million dollars a year guaranteed implies leadership and responsibility."

Rubin mentioned that he had refused a bonus in 2007 (not out of any sense of guilt, but selflessly, so that the bank could use the money for other purposes).

Angelides said, "You'll be the only one in the end who can make an assessment of your responsibility."

When the three-hour hearing was over, Robert Rubin hurried from the room.

JEFF CONNAUGHTON

Connaughton didn't notice the bubble. In 2007 he sold his Mexican condo, tripling his purchase price for a huge profit. With that and his big payday from the firm's sale, he began looking for another vacation property, another condo to flip. He kept hearing about a stretch of coastline in Costa Rica called Mal País, a surf paradise with world-class beaches. Gisele Bündchen, the Brazilian supermodel, had built a house there, and it was becoming an off-the-map vacation sanctuary for Hollywood stars. Prices were soaring. He flew down that summer and looked at a pair of spectacular adjacent properties on a hillside over the Pacific. He decided to buy both, thinking to build a house on one, flip it, and, with the profit, build a villa for himself on the other lot.

One of Connaughton's clients at Quinn Gillespie was Genworth Financial, a private mortgage insurer. People there began telling him about an epidemic of foreclosures around the country. They warned him not to buy real estate until 2009 at the earliest. Biden was running for president again, and Connaughton joined the campaign and traveled to Des Moines, where a city councilman told him that one of the top three issues in Iowa was foreclosures. Connaughton relayed the message to a Biden staffer: the growing housing crisis should be a focus. (In the seventies, when Biden was still a freshman senator, Hubert Humphrey advised him, "You have to pick an issue that becomes yours. You should become Mr. Housing. Housing is the future.") The idea went nowhere. The candidates weren't talking about foreclosures.

Connaughton ignored the warnings, too. In the fall of 2007, at the top of the market, he closed on the Costa Rican lots for almost a million dollars. He knew that the land was overvalued, but he expected it to become even more so. When the price of Dutch tulips is doubling every month and you think you can get in before it quadruples, is that rational or irrational behavior? "It was greed," he said.

For fifteen years, Connaughton had raised more money for Biden than anyone else in Washington, and he joined Biden's second presidential campaign as treasurer of its political action committee, Unite Our States. The effort was doomed from the start. Biden was basically winging his stump speech, which was essentially his résumé—outstanding at one stop, disjointed the next. And he still hated the money game. When a young staffer got into his car one day, holding a list of names, and announced, "Okay, Senator, time to do some fundraising calls," Biden said, "Get the fuck out of the car." He believed that strong debate performances would bring him more money than personal calls. The politician who had converted Connaughton to his cause thirty years earlier with a speech in Tuscaloosa was a consistently powerful presence onstage with his more popular rivals, Hillary Clinton, John Edwards, and Barack Obama. But he was nowhere in the polls.

Connaughton spent December in Iowa. Every two years, members of Washington's permanent class migrated to various spots around the "real America," where "real people" lived, and campaigned for their team. They built chits that way, and they got back in touch with what it meant to be a member of a party. In 2000, Connaughton held a Gore sign at an intersection in Wassau, Wisconsin, at six in the morning, while all the black motorists and half the women gave the thumbs-up, white men shot him hateful looks, and a school bus driver with a load of children in back actually flipped him off. In 2004, he spent three weeks knocking on doors around South Dakota for Tom Daschle, the Senate minority leader—ten hours a day, bone-tiring work. The poverty shocked him: many trailers in Rapid City had rotted-out floors exposing the dirt below. The nicer mobile homes were voting Republican: "Daschle's gone Washington." He met Lutheran women who thought the senator's position on abortion was hypocritical—one thing in South Dakota, another in Washington—and who were so passionate that they came closer to converting him than he did to converting them. Abortion was one of the very few issues that could blow up on a politician back home—no one knew or cared how a senator voted on the Private Securities Litigation Reform Act.

Near the Pine Ridge reservation, a Native American woman told Connaughton, "You only care about us once every four years." It burned a hole right through him because he knew it was true—the plight of people like her moved him every presidential election cycle, and then he forgot about them. He tried to organize a donation of computers to community centers in the poor areas, but no one in the Daschle operation followed up. Out here in the middle of the country he felt no energy, none of the entrepreneurial spirit of the coasts and big cities, as if all the molecules had come to a rest. At night he would collapse at his hotel, where the bar was crowded with Washington lobbyists who were temporarily in South Dakota for the same reason. That November, Daschle lost.

On the campaign trail in 2007, Connaughton began spending occasional time with Biden. Once, before a fundraising event, they were alone together—Connaughton mustering his usual smile, saying how good it was to see the senator, crisply informing him about the group he was about to address. Biden suddenly looked at Connaughton with a question in his eyes, as if to ask, "Why are you like this with me? Why aren't we friends?" And he even started to say something. "Why are you, why can't we . . . ?" Connaughton left Biden's words hanging in the air. In three seconds the hosts would walk in, and, more than twenty years after "Just gimme what you got," there was too much to say, and it was probably too late.

A campaign like Biden's was an exercise in collective self-delusion. Ted Kaufman, who was a senior adviser to Biden, told Connaughton, "In a presidential campaign, you're either faking it or you're dead." On January 3, 2008, Connaughton monitored the Iowa caucus vote at a high school near Waterloo. About eighty people stood in Barack Obama's corner, sixty in Hillary Clinton's, and six in Joe Biden's. He finished fifth in Iowa, with 0.9 percent, and dropped out that night. He requested from his staff a list of the people who had helped his campaign the most. Connaughton ranked third.

He had been faking it for a long time, and what he felt was overwhelming relief. He closed an imaginary ledger on three decades of his life. He was done with Biden.

Later that month, Connaughton flew down to Costa Rica and went out for dinner with his architect and an American developer. The developer had just come from meetings of the loan committees of Lehman Brothers and Merrill Lynch in New York. "Both companies are technically insolvent," he said.

"What? I don't believe it," Connaughton said.

The developer explained that the banks were sitting on assets whose current value was exceeded by their liabilities. Connaughton still resisted. If it was true, everything he had learned in business school about efficient markets, everything he had learned in law school about the standards of disclosure at banks, about the professional duty of the lawyers and accountants they hired to reveal material information and protect investors, was bullshit. He believed in those institutions—he had to.

"I predict we're going into a three-year recession," the developer went on. Connaughton continued to argue. Much later, he wished that the man had reached across the table, seized him by the jacket, and shouted, "I know you just met me, but think hard about this: both firms are technically insolvent. Believe me, you need to act! Sell everything you own before it's too late!"

When he returned to Washington, Connaughton picked up a new book titled *The Trillion Dollar Meltdown,* by a former banker named Charles R. Morris. It argued that overleveraged banks and debt-strapped consumers with unaffordable mortgage payments were creating a credit bubble that would soon pop and create a global financial calamity. Connaughton read the book and tossed it aside.

That March, Bear Stearns failed. Connaughton kept an eye on his stocks, where he had most of his wealth in a globally diversified portfolio. The markets were falling, but not precipitously. He expected at most a 10 percent correction. It was never easy to time getting out and back in just right. He stayed put as the Dow dropped toward 10,000.

In September, Lehman Brothers went bankrupt, the rest of Wall Street poised to perish with it. Charles R. Morris's meltdown—now two trillion dollars—happened faster than anyone could have imagined. Within a few months, Connaughton's stock portfolio and his property in Costa Rica had lost almost half their value.

But during the same months, his political stock rose to its peak. On November 4, Joe Biden was elected vice president of the United States. By the end of the year, Connaughton was headed back into government.

TAMMY THOMAS

In early 2008, a little over a year after Tammy lost her job at the factory, a man named Kirk Noden asked her to meet him for coffee. Noden was a professional organizer. He had grown up not far from Youngstown, gone to college at Kent State, and worked organizing neighborhoods in Chicago and Birmingham, England. When he returned from overseas in 2006 and came to Youngstown, he tried to do what he had done in other places, following the Saul Alinsky model of community organizing: round up the troops in your group, march down to city hall or the local developer's office, and shake the tree to get resources for the neighborhood. That approach came out of an earlier era, the middle of the twentieth century, when power was more consolidated and centralized in the cities. After a year of trying, Noden realized that the model was irrelevant in Youngstown. There were no resources to be shaken loose. The tax base had collapsed. The mayor had very little power. Industry was a ghost of its former self. The centers of power were elsewhere—in some ways, they were spread around the globe. Youngstown was so damaged, beyond anything he had expected, that it forced Noden to think in a new way.

He consulted with the Wean Foundation—old steel money from Warren—which, unlike other elites and institutions, had moved beyond nostalgic illusion and was pursuing rather radical ideas for the resuscitation of the Valley. In the summer of 2007, Noden and Wean decided to start a new community organization, the Mahoning Valley Organizing Collaborative, which would become the basis for a statewide effort to fight the causes of decline—the loss of jobs, inequities based on class and race—as well as the effects. All the large institutions in Youngstown were distrusted, because they had failed: industry, unions, banks, churches, every level of government. The only way to bring about change in the Valley was block by block.

Noden began looking for organizers to hire ahead of the formal launch in the spring of 2008. Joel Ratner, the president of Wean, told Noden about a woman he had met through her work at the Salvation Army, where she was leading workshops for single mothers in an internship funded by the foundation while pursuing her bachelor's degree in sociology at Youngstown State. "You ought to meet her," Ratner said. "She might be a gold mine."

Noden got in touch, and he and Tammy arranged to meet one April afternoon at the Bob Evans restaurant near her house.

The first thing Tammy noticed as Noden drank his coffee was that this fresh-faced white guy looked like a thirteen-year-old (he was in his thirties). When he mentioned the possibility of a job at a new organization, she was skeptical. She still had a year to go for her degree, she was struggling in her classes, and to be honest, she was already a little disillusioned with the world of social services. There was so much infighting—they seemed to be about maintaining their existence instead of serving folks.

Noden explained what it would mean to be a community organizer: she would teach other people to hold those in power accountable. It was something Tammy had never imagined doing. "What do you mean?" she said. "This is the kind of place where the congressman goes to jail, the sheriff goes to jail. You're going to hold them accountable?" And then she thought about it and added, "Somebody does need to do it."

Noden asked about her childhood, the neighborhood she grew up in, did she remember the mills, what was it like to work in the factory while raising three kids. She wasn't used to talking about herself this way but she did her best to answer his questions, saying how her neighborhood had been safe when she was coming up because of the mob, how that changed with the street gangs and crack—though she assumed he knew some of the answers already.

And what made her angry?

Well, people liked to say the east side looked like Beirut, and she would think—without saying—"What do you mean? This is where I'm from." And she told him, "I'm pissed that I have to raise my kids, get them educated, and get them out because there's no opportunity here." Her older daughter was living in Orlando, her son was thinking of moving to North Carolina, and the younger daughter wanted to go live with her sister. After the Delphi buyout the girls tried to get their mother to move to

Florida. "I am going to have to get on a plane to go see my kids. It shouldn't be like that. They should be able to grow up and buy a home in this community. My grandmother worked too hard for my neighborhood to look the way it does. She cooked and cleaned in a lot of houses and now they're going downhill. I remember when I was little my grandmother would take me downtown to go shopping."

She had never once thought about who was really responsible. Or that she could hold their feet to the fire. She really was getting angry. So he had her. He was offering her a different way to help people. He talked about Chicago and told her stories of the campaigns there, with people who were serious about building power and pushing for change, connecting some of it to the civil rights movement. She thought it all sounded exciting.

They sat together for a long time, and while she was talking about herself Noden watched her and saw something that he would describe to her later, something that she herself couldn't quite see: a kind of raw power. It came from her passion about the east side and how it had been forgotten. He saw it as the pilot light that would get her up day in and day out for a job that would not be easy. She was taking a brave leap to re-make herself, and she might come and go quickly, but she would be like-lier to stick it out than someone coming to Youngstown from Columbus or out of state. She knew the story of the black community here because it was her story. He invited her to a formal interview, and she agreed.

It took place at the Unitarian Church on Elm Street, near Youngstown State. Tammy had never heard of that kind of church. Since the divorce she had been steeped in her church in Akron. She asked the cousin who had brought her there about the Unitarians.

"They accept all religions and all beliefs," her cousin said.

"But what does that mean?"

"That means you could be a Satanist and still be welcomed into the Unitarian Church."

"No way."

"Just be careful," her cousin said. "I'm going to be praying for you."

On the day of the interview, Noden met her at the church door and told her to have a seat in the sanctuary until they were ready for her. Back then Tammy had her hair in long dreads, and she had put on weight in the past few years, and she couldn't help thinking how black she would seem to whoever was going to interview her. She sat down and glanced around.

There were no crosses anywhere. In alarm she thought, "I ain't never been in no church without a cross." To calm herself down—on top of everything else, this was her first job interview in twenty years, and the last one was for an auto parts assembly line—she picked up a hymnbook and leafed through its pages. Her eyes fell on a song about the summer solstice. She was in a devil-worship church!

As she was stashing away the hymnal, Noden came back and led her to the office where two women and a man were waiting. Tammy was so shaken up that an instinct to pull herself together made her take over the room, going from one person to the next, introducing herself, "How are you doing? I'm great!" When Kirk asked for an example of a time that she stood up to authority because of an injustice, she told them the story of the girl at Packard who had been down on the floor scrubbing oil, and she could tell they were moved. She sailed through the interview, she wowed them. But part of her was thinking that if she did get the job, her new colleagues would wonder why the doorknobs were always greasy since Tammy started working, because she would be anointing them every day.

She became one of the first hires. She could stay in school and still hold down an exciting job making reasonable money with benefits. She thought, "I knew God was going to open up these doors."

Noden gave his new organizers their marching orders: go out and talk to every church, neighborhood group, and potential leader they could find, recruit seventy-five people to attend a meeting, organize some kind of action, or they were fired. Noden assumed that Tammy would work on the east side since she knew it so well, but she refused, because that was just the problem—she knew too many people there, family and friends, knew what her brothers were doing, and it would be a conflict of interest. Instead, she began organizing on the north side, most of which no longer resembled the place where Granny had gone to work in white people's homes—it was starting to look like the rest of Youngstown.

One day, Tammy was canvassing a neighborhood on the north side on foot, carrying a yellow notepad on a clipboard and going door-to-door, introducing herself to anyone she could find, trying to keep it under five minutes. "How is your neighborhood? How long has that house over there been empty? Why do you think it hasn't been torn down? I just talked to someone down the street who feels the same way you do. There are a lot of homes in the city that are abandoned and need to be torn down and I'm going to tell you, there are some things that really need to change. Would you come to a meeting? Because it doesn't do a whole lot of good for just one person to call the city, but if we all get on the same page . . . Yes, I'm from Youngstown, born and raised, and I have watched how this city has changed, and know what? I'm at a point where I'm like, no more, it's time for it to stop. If you come to this meeting with about fifty or sixty of your neighbors then we'll discuss it. Can I get your number?" The goal was to recruit local people and train them as leaders, so that they would bring others along, and slowly the disempowered would gain a sense of agency and the voiceless would begin to speak.

She turned down a street and heard two women talking and laughing on a front porch. The porch was covered with Pittsburgh Steelers banners and paraphernalia, and the front lawn had so many doodads scattered around that it looked like a yard sale was going on. The women were having what Tammy called a pity party—one of them complaining that she couldn't afford her health insurance. Tammy took this as her cue to approach. "What are you saying about health care?" She introduced herself and gave her pitch. The woman with the health insurance problem was the owner of the house and Steeler fan, Hattie Wilkins. She was in her late fifties, short and heavyset, with long dreads colored gold, a big husky voice, and a boisterous manner. Hattie turned out to be a distant relative of Tammy's stepfather. As far as Hattie was concerned, Tammy had just popped up out of a crack in the sidewalk.

Tammy asked Miss Hattie if she would be willing to have a one-on-one with her and then be trained by MVOC as a leader.

"I'm already a leader," Hattie said. "I don't need no training." For twenty years she had been the head of her union local in a pillow factory on the west side. Then the company paid her to quit because she caused so much trouble—that was why she had to cover part of her health insurance. The three houses to her left were vacant—she kept the grass cut next door—and then there were two empty lots where the houses had been torn down. Hattie had turned one of the lots into a cut-down-flower garden—she called it that in memory of her granddaughter, Marissa, shot in the heart at sixteen while leaving a party. Hattie scavenged the tulip and daffodil bulbs and rosebushes from the yards of abandoned houses, and she would never cut any of the blooms because Marissa was cut down like a flower.

Leaving her job had cost Hattie her power base, the hundreds of work-ers at the pillow factory. Now she was down to just four or five people in her neighborhood. Maybe she wasn't a leader after all, maybe she needed what Tammy was offering. She agreed to a one-on-one.

It wasn't long before Tammy became Miss Hattie's role model. Tammy had a talent—Noden noticed it early on—for forming deep bonds with her leaders, inspiring them with her energy and focus on the task until they were willing to throw themselves in front of a bus for her. Hattie loved the way Tammy spoke, how she could get people's attention and keep it. Hattie was taking classes at the college in order to use proper grammar around the neighborhood kids so that they would learn to speak like the TV newscasters instead of using the slang of the hood. She told Tammy, "When I grow up I want to speak just like you."

The organization's first big project was to map Youngstown—to con-duct a survey, going block by block, of every house in the city, finding out which ones were occupied, which empty, which had been torn down or needed to be. The surveyors assigned a grade to each house in their area. If Tammy had surveyed the east side, she would have given the aban-doned and stripped property at 1319 Charlotte an F. On the north side, not far from the park where she and Granny used to feed the swans during the year they spent in the Purnell mansion, she surveyed two blocks that had thirteen abandoned houses out of twenty-four. She talked to the mail-man about which houses were occupied, and when winter came she waited for a snowfall to see if there were tire tracks on the driveways.

Forty percent of the parcels in Youngstown turned out to be vacant. Almost a quarter of the empty houses were owned by random people in other states like California, and even foreign countries like Austria or China, house flippers caught in the real estate downdraft, Internet shop-pers who hadn't grasped the sorry state of their purchase on Craigslist or pennyforeclosure.com. The most common complaint Tammy heard in her travels was vacancy and the crime it always attracted. MVOC compiled the results of the survey in a color-coded map of the city, with green for empty lots and red for abandoned structures. On the map the east side was vast and green, with bright red spots scattered through it.

Youngstown's black mayor, Jay Williams, had made it a policy to speed up the demolition of abandoned buildings, but there were too many to keep up with and no one knew where they all were, for the job of city planner was also vacant. MVOC's color-coded map became the only functional model for the physical condition of the city. In 2005, after convening fourteen hundred residents in Stambaugh Auditorium to talk about Youngstown's future, the city had produced an ambitious document called 2010 Plan. It was the first rational effort to deal with the fact of the city's decline—the fact that it had *shrunk*. That's how Youngstown looked, like a man who'd lost a lot of weight in an illness but was still wearing his baggy old clothes—big open spaces without enough people and structures to fill them. The imbalance between scale and inhabitants made the city feel empty, except for a few lonely figures wandering the streets. The term "shrinking cities" was coming into vogue—it was often applied to Detroit—and because 2010 Plan discussed the need to reduce municipal services to a realistic level given the reduced population, Youngstown was hailed as a pioneer. There was a lot of talk about community gardens, pocket parks, beekeeping, chicken coops. In 2005, *The New York Times Magazine* put 2010 Plan on its annual list of the year's best ideas. Youngstown was in danger of becoming a media darling.

No one outside the city knew that the plan was never acted on. It was too explosive, because it meant that some people would have to move. Who would those people be? Older black homeowners on the east side who had decided not to leave and were holding on to their history. Many of them believed that industry was going to come back. Where would they be moved to? White areas like the west side. When Tammy heard about the idea, she hated it. She immediately thought of people she knew—Arlette Gatewood, a retired steelworker and union activist who was still living way out on the east side near the Pennsylvania line in an area that was turning to woodland. Or Miss Sybil, her older friend from the east side. She thought about the house her great-uncle built. Yes, the city could no longer afford garbage collection and water lines throughout the metropolitan area. She got that. "But at the same time, why would Ms. Jones want to move out of the house she's paid for, she raised her children in, and go somewhere else?"

Instead of 2010 Plan, Tammy was focused on the small steps that her leaders, the neighborhood people she was training, could take. She organized an event at which a slumlord named Mark King was called out for buying three hundred properties all over the city during the housing bubble and allowing 20 percent of them to become uninhabitable. It was covered in the local media, and the next day King showed up at the organization's downtown office asking what he had to do to stop getting bad press. Tammy recruited Miss Sybil to speak at the event, telling her that the east side needed to have a voice, which was how she became vice chair of MVOC. Miss Sybil told Tammy that people on the east side were starting to organize neighborhood groups, feeling a few tremors of hope. "Anybody that comes and throws you a line," she said, "you're going to grab it."

The job let Tammy see Youngstown in a new way, as if by walking streets and knocking on doors and mapping neighborhoods she was able for the first time to get a broader view of the place where she'd lived all her life and see it whole. She had always put the blame on individuals for failing to help themselves. "One of the things that would frustrate me is when you see a person who ain't got nothing, ain't trying to get nothing, and don't want nothing. An unmotivated person who doesn't want to get better." There was a lot of that in Youngstown, but now she saw it as the problem of a community. Generational poverty, failed schools, the loss of jobs—"A lot of it is not that they don't want. It is because the system is designed in some instances like it feeds on people a little bit and messes up people's minds. People get caught in it and they don't know how to stop it." In her own life she had stopped it, but she had never thought about politics—the city, the state, the country.

Tammy might have been the last black person in Youngstown to hear of Barack Obama. She was so consumed with her kids, her job, her classes, her church, that she never followed the news and wasn't aware of a serious black contender for the presidency—who had once been a community organizer, of all things—until the start of 2008. When she had turned eighteen, Granny had told her to register to vote, to register as a Democrat, and to vote for the Democrat. So she always voted, without paying attention to the candidates. She knew more about the mayor's races than the presidential. They talked about politics a little at Packard, and in 2004 she couldn't understand why so many workers there—white women especially—everyday working-class people like her were voting for Bush because of their religious beliefs. Mostly, though, she thought of politics as a dirty business. Youngstown was one of the most corrupt cities in America—a judge went to jail, the sheriff went to jail, and the congressman for most of her adult life was James Traficant, a mob politician who remained popular in Youngstown even after he was expelled from Congress and went to prison for bribery and racketeering, because Youngstown was populist, anti-institutional, and Traficant made a flamboyant career of telling powerful people to kiss his ass.

Her friend Karen from Packard was the one who got her interested in Obama. Tammy didn't think America was ready for that—she thought Hillary Clinton would be the nominee because they'd accept a white woman before a black man. But she went with Karen to hear Obama speak at Youngstown State in February, and Tammy was so impressed that she went home and wrote up some notes on what he'd said. Over the summer she knocked on a lot of doors on the east side in MVOC's get-out-the-vote campaign. Some people were saying, "We got a chance for a black man to be president," and other people were saying, "They ain't going to elect a black president," but she had never seen such excitement about an election. Even her father volunteered for the Democratic Party, making phone calls from the local office—he had never done anything like that. He drank, ate, and slept Barack Obama. Her divorce and her new job had opened up a big rift between her and her dad, but they came back together over Obama, phoning each other to swap stories about can-vassing. Once, her dad called and said, "If another person tells me they are not going to vote for Barack Obama because they think he's going to get assassinated, I might kill myself."

On election night there was a pizza party at the MVOC offices. It was the first time Tammy had ever tasted Jameson's. When Obama won, and he came out with his family to give his victory speech, Tammy couldn't quite shake a sense of disbelief. When she was little, Granny had bought her the three-volume Ebony Success Library, about the achievements of black people throughout history, and in turn Tammy always tried hard to make her children proud of being black. During Black History Month at school, she made sure they wrote their reports on people who weren't the usual suspects. In fifth grade her older daughter wrote about the civil rights activist Ella Baker, but the teacher, who had never heard of Baker, rejected the report.

People could pick and choose whether someone was an important inventor or activist, but a black president—nobody could deny that. It wasn't just black history, it was American history. Afterward, Tammy hung a framed picture of the forty-fourth president on the wall behind her office desk. It showed Obama on election night, waving to the throng in Chicago, above words he had spoken during the campaign: "Our destiny is not written for us, but by us."

DEAN PRICE

Barack Obama was the first Democrat Dean ever voted for. It was a no-brainer—if Obama had been a white man, 80 percent of the country would have gone for him. Obama, not John McCain or Sarah Palin, came to Martinsville, Virginia, in the August heat of that election year and told a crowd in the community college gym, "I will fight for you every single day. I will wake up in that White House thinking about the people of Martinsville and the people of Henry County, and how I can make your life better." Obama understood that the old system had failed, and whether or not he knew about biodiesel, he kept talking about a new green economy. That was music to Dean's ears.

In 2008, the rest of the country started to catch up to the Piedmont. After the Wall Street collapse in September, millions of people lost their jobs, and January, the month when Obama took the oath of office and promised "a new era of responsibility," was the worst month in decades. Huge companies like General Motors were on the verge of extinction. Wachovia Bank, which had once been a pillar of Winston-Salem, went under, along with other banks from Wall Street to Seattle. One establishment institution after another trembled and fell. Writers were using terms like "the Great Recession" and "the end of the suburbs." It was the worst time since the worst time of all. Dean believed that the American people were ready for radical changes. Electing a black president was just the first of them.

Dean's congresswoman in North Carolina's Fifth District was a Republican in her sixties named Virginia Foxx—a stout woman with short gray hair and a degree in education who had been a reliable backbencher for George W. Bush. The district ran from the Blue Ridge Mountains on the Tennessee border to just west of Greensboro, with no town larger than twenty-five thousand people, and 90 percent of the residents were white. In other words, Foxx represented what Sarah Palin (speaking at a campaign fundraiser in Greensboro three weeks before the election) called "the real America," by which she did not mean fallow farms and disability checks and crack. Foxx was reelected easily, but in 2008 she seemed like a relic of the past, and so did her constituents, and maybe even her party.

On the other side of the state line, in Virginia's Fifth District, a small earthquake was taking place. Virgil Goode, the anti-immigrant, pro-tobacco, conservative Democrat turned Republican incumbent, was opposed by a young lawyer and self-described practitioner of "conviction politics" named Tom Perriello. Perriello was thirty-four but looked like a college wrestler preparing for the opening clinch—short and broad-shouldered, with a wide flat face, a muscular jawline, and an edgy stare. On the day he was supposed to decide whether to run, he was stung by fifty yellow jackets, went into anaphylactic shock, and staggered into the woods outside his parents' house near Charlottesville. His father, an obstetrician, happened to see him from across the lawn, grabbed the EpiPen that was on hand because of his mother's recent allergic reaction, ran out to the woods, and injected his son as Tom's eyes rolled back in his head. Perriello didn't know if it was a sign from God, but he chose to take it that way and declared his candidacy for Goode's seat.

No one really understood what Perriello did for a living—he called himself a "national security consultant," a "social justice activist," and a "public entrepreneur." He listened to "conscious hip-hop" music and raised his glass of Jack Daniel's to "a better world." The fact that he was single, once wore a beard, and had spent much of his short adult life in New Haven, New York, Sierra Leone, and Darfur gave the Goode campaign a fat target for the modern version of sectional-cultural warfare.

For a long time the great mystery for the half of America that voted Democratic was why white people living in small, obscure places and getting poorer year by year were simultaneously getting more Republican— why the kind of Americans who, a century before, had passionately supported William Jennings Bryan were now voting in overwhelming numbers for the party that wanted to deregulate Wall Street and zero out the capital gains tax—why, along Route 29 south of Charlottesville, there was a great big GOODE sign outside an overgrown shack. But in 2008, times had gotten bad enough in the Piedmont for some people to turn in the other direction. Perriello made it easier for them because he didn't use the typical language of big-city liberals—he talked constantly about God, was for guns, hedged gay marriage, and sounded radical on economics, denouncing the "corporate capture of government" and the big banks and multinationals whose collusion with Washington made it impossible for the little guy to compete. Perriello sounded for all the world like a twenty-first-century Bryan. He wasn't—his friends were human rights activists and Washington think tankers and *New Republic* writers, eastern elites who spoke the language of insider baseball and progressive causes—but in the Fifth District he raised his voice with genuine passion for the hard-pressed farmer, the out-of-work seamstress, the small merchant. He didn't find the great mystery in American politics very mysterious. "The core assumption is that somehow these poor working-class people are benighted for voting against their self-interest," he said. "Tell me a rich Democrat that doesn't vote against their pure self-interest."

On November 4, Perriello swept the better-educated precincts around the university town of Charlottesville, where turnout among young people was high because Obama was at the top of the ballot (Perriello said that Barack Obama was the first politician in his lifetime who inspired him), and he cut into Goode's advantage in the worse-off towns and rural areas of Southside, down along the North Carolina border. On election night the polls showed Perriello ahead by 745 votes out of 315,000 cast. Goode demanded a recount. Six weeks later, Perriello was certified the winner.

His victory in a conservative district was one of the biggest upsets of the year, and one of the races that made 2008 look like a watershed election. Perriello was Dean's kind of politician, and Virginia's Fifth was the district where Dean had built America's 1st BioDiesel Truck Stop. In retrospect it seemed inevitable that the two men would cross paths.

One of Perriello's first moves in office was to send an aide around the district, which was bigger than New Jersey, to find out what his new constituents needed from the stimulus bill that was moving through Congress. Around the farms and small towns of Southside, the aide found signs of life in renewable energy: a dairy farm outside Danville that was making electricity out of manure; a nursery just across the road where a former Goodyear engineer was testing crops for energy yield; a landfill in Martinsville where officials wanted to turn methane gas into electrical power. No one had told these people to do any of it, and they were just the kinds of businesses that Perriello wanted to highlight, tangible examples of a new economy in the Piedmont that didn't look like the past. Instead of enormous factories and big-box stores that sucked the wealth out of a community before abandoning it, these were small-scale projects that created five or ten jobs at a time and kept the money local.

Eventually, Perriello found out about Red Birch Energy.

Dean had worked up a pitch, a PowerPoint slide presentation, and he was taking it to any audience that would listen. He always brought along three jars, one containing canola seed, the second canola oil, and the third biodiesel fuel, with a golden liquid in the upper half and a sediment of dark-brown glycerin waste below. He started with his come-to-Jesus moment, the week Katrina hit the Gulf Coast. He told the story of Red Birch Energy and gave the quote from Jefferson about the cultivators of the earth, along with a lot of figures about energy yields from canola and the advantages of biodiesel over regular diesel, and made a strong case for smallness over bigness and the need to keep money local. The farmers and truck stop owners would be the new oil barons! Let the wealth trickle down from *them*, not from Wall Street! He asked how many people in the audience had heard of peak oil—never more than 15 or 20 percent. Dean firmly believed that there would be one Red Birch or there would be five thousand, and he closed with the story of Roger Bannister, the first man to break the four-minute mile: within five years of his feat, more than a hundred other people had done it. "He walked through a threshold. He showed 'em that it could be done. That's the way we feel about Red Birch Energy."

Over time, he fine-tuned the pitch, making slight adjustments for different audiences. To the monthly speaker's breakfast of the Greensboro Kiwanis at the Starmount Country Club, he talked about the potential for investment in biofuels. Sometimes he got out ahead of his audience and later realized what had happened—too many quotes from Democratic presidents in a Republican county, not enough explanation of the refining process to a group of government officials. But every time—and he must have given the pitch to a hundred different audiences—Dean sounded as if the exciting novelty of his words was occurring to him right then for the very first time, *because it was*, and that this and only this was the road to collective salvation, *because it was*. A salesman had to believe in what he was selling, and Dean believed with the fervor of a convert. He was a

Johnny Appleseed for biodiesel, spreading the good news from town to town.

Dean always said there was a thin line between an entrepreneur and a con man. What made Glenn W. Turner the latter and not the former? He probably believed every word he said with "Dare to Be Great." Maybe Turner was in it for the money and fame, but Dean wanted to make his fortune, too. So what was the difference? "When I first started, I had to check myself," Dean said. "Are they with me? Am I a shyster? Am I trying to sell snake oil in the form of biodiesel?" But the oil he was selling wasn't snake oil, and that was the difference. Biodiesel was as real as the earth. It made complete sense to anyone who listened: this was the way out of depression and into the future. Then he would pinch himself, thinking, "Am I in this position? Has my journey taken me to this place where we're on the cusp?" It was mind-boggling.

One day in early February 2009, Dean was at the Omni Hotel in Richmond, preparing to give his pitch to the Virginia Agricultural Summit, when he went to get a Starbucks and saw a familiar-looking person sitting at a laptop. It was Tom Perriello—Dean knew his face from TV ads. Introducing himself, Dean said, "Please wait just a minute," and he raced up to his room, where he had three copies of the January/February issue of *U.S. Canola Digest* with a lead article about changes in Washington and rural America: "Red Birch Energy could almost be the poster child for the Obama administration as it is energy independent, sustainable, community-focused and inspirational." Perriello waited, and when Dean returned with a copy of the magazine and showed him the quote, the new congressman loved it. They talked for twenty minutes, and before leaving, Dean invited Perriello to visit Red Birch.

As for Perriello, meeting Dean Price confirmed something that he had come to believe over the past few years and had made a tenet of his campaign: the elites in America didn't have answers for the problems of the working and middle class anymore. Elites thought that everyone needed to become a computer programmer or a financial engineer, that there would be no jobs between eight dollars an hour and six figures. Perriello believed that the new ideas for making things in America again would come from unknown people in obscure places.

Two months later, in early April, Perriello visited the Red Birch refinery with the governor of Virginia, Tim Kaine, and an entourage of local officials and aides and reporters. Dean wore a brown coat and a tie, his black hair parted neatly in the middle, looking like an uncomfortable farm boy among men in dark suits (Gary Sink wore a navy-blue one). He gave his pitch to the assembled guests inside the refinery. Kaine actually fell asleep in the front row, and Dean almost called him on it, remembering the time his father had done that to him when he was a boy and fell asleep in church. But Perriello really listened. He wasn't like other politicians Dean had met or would come to meet, who made him feel like a shoe salesman trying to squeeze his pitch into a few available seconds. After the formal event, Dean took Perriello to the back of the plant and showed him the crushing machines, which were going full tilt. The congressman gave Dean his cell phone number and told Dean to look him up in Washington for a beer. Dean called once, but Perriello didn't answer and he hung up without leaving a message.

They met again in July, on a farm north of Danville, where two members of Obama's cabinet—Tom Vilsack, the agriculture secretary, and Stephen Chu, the energy secretary—were appearing as part of a tour of rural America. The month before, Perriello had voted for the administration's energy bill—it was known as "cap and trade," or "the climate change bill"—a vote that made him much less popular among some of his constituents, who had been persuaded by energy companies and conservative groups that it would raise their electric bills and kill jobs in coal. At the farm, Vilsack and Chu talked about how renewable energy could tap the work ethic and the values of rural America, which had been neglected and even lost, and Dean felt that the highest officials in President Obama's government were thinking along the same lines that he was. At one point Red Birch was mentioned, and Perriello had Dean stand up to be recognized.

Dean once said that Perriello could be president someday, and Perriello once said that if there was one American he wished the president would spend five minutes talking to, it was Dean. The congressman put Red Birch on the White House radar, and on a Thursday in August, an e-mail addressed to "Dear Friend" arrived at Red Birch, inviting "a select group of regional and national energy leaders" to "engage with Cabinet Secretaries and White House staff to discuss the ongoing debate over our energy future and how we can all contribute to a positive outcome." The event would be held the following Monday. On Sunday, Dean and Gary took the train to Washington and spent the night at a hotel next to Union Station. The next morning, Dean put on his only suit—a black one that he had bought back in December 2004 to escort his third wife's daughter to her homecoming dance and instead ended up wearing to his father's funeral that same week—and a green tie, and he and Gary took a taxi to 1600 Pennsylvania Avenue.

They never actually set foot in the White House. The event was held next door, on the third floor of the massive, French Second Empire–style Old Executive Office Building. Mark Twain called it "the ugliest building in America," but Dean was overwhelmed with a sense of awe he'd never felt anywhere else. The granite halls and marble staircases, the history in those rooms named after presidents! The last speaker at the conference was the president's young green-jobs czar, Van Jones, who was also the most dynamic. He had a way with phrases—when it came to employing inner-city youths to weatherize buildings, Jones said, "We're going to take away their handguns and give them caulk guns!"

Dean happened to get the last question of the day. He stood up and said, "Since we're all here advocating the same thing, and we're going to go out and preach the gospel, one of the things that needs to be talked about is peak oil—because without it, nothing of what we're doing makes any sense. How does the administration feel about peak oil?"

Jones didn't appear to be familiar with the Obama policy on peak oil, or even what peak oil was. He handed the question off to a woman from the Department of Energy, who spoke for half a minute, demonstrating that she didn't know any more than Jones. Afterward, Dean decided that peak oil was just too hard for politicians to handle. It meant the end of suburban, fast-food, industrial America, including Wall Street—no wonder the White House didn't have a position. But Dean was taken with Van Jones, who exchanged high fives with him and Gary at the end of the event. And he was sorry when, two weeks later, Jones resigned after Glenn Beck and other conservatives tied him to extreme views on the 9/11 attacks and the imprisonment of Mumia Abu-Jamal, along with the word "assholes" as applied to congressional Republicans. But Van Jones was never going to recruit the farmers in Rockingham County to the cause of green energy. They weren't going to listen to a radical black man from San Francisco, and they didn't like Obama any better—after Dean's trip to Washington, some men at the local diner said, "You went to see that nigger?" The one man they might listen to was T. Boone Pickens, the billionaire corporate raider, who was old and white and had been appearing in ads for natural gas and renewable energy.

On his trip to Washington, Dean got nowhere near Obama, who was vacationing that week on Martha's Vineyard. But a few months later, he actually met the president. In March 2010 an event was held at Andrews Air Force Base to announce the first biofuel fighter jet, and Dean was invited. He brought his son Ryan, and they waited in line as Obama greeted the crowd. There was no time to say anything, but Dean was struck by the feel of the president's hand. It was the softest of any man he'd ever shaken hands with. It told him that Obama had never done a lick of physical work in his life.

Red Birch Energy was looking for a piece of the stimulus money that had been passed by Congress. The company needed help. In the last weeks of 2008, the price of fuel had plummeted, farther and faster than ever before. Below four dollars a gallon, Red Birch saw its competitive advantage disappear and started losing money. In the spring of 2009, when the canola farmers drove to the refinery with their load of seed, Dean and Gary had to tell them that the company couldn't afford to pay for the crop it had contracted to buy. All they could do was cover the 6 percent interest on the money owed. Most of the farmers were understanding, but some of them threatened Gary and Dean and others vowed to sue Red Birch. One North Carolina farmer named John French—a Harley-type dude—pulled up in his big dually truck, the kind with four wheels on the rear axle. Before he unloaded his seed, Dean told him, "We don't have the money."

Dean was sure the farmer was going to kick his ass right then and there.

"Leave it here, let us crush it and try to sell some fuel," Dean went on, talking fast and straight, "or take it back to your farm and try to sell it somewhere else."

Once Dean opened his mouth, it was impossible not to like him a little. The farmer got in his dually and drove the load back to North Carolina. But the company's reputation took a big hit around the Piedmont.

Without five-dollar gas, it was impossible to make Red Birch profitable. This was the hard lesson that Dean and Gary learned from the fiasco of the 2009 canola crop. And they realized that the answer lay in changing their business model and using the canola not once but twice: first converting the feedstock into food-grade cooking oil, selling it for ten dollars a gallon to local restaurants, and collecting 70 percent of it back as waste oil, then making biodiesel from that. If they could get to food-grade, they could pay farmers eighteen dollars a bushel, which would increase the volume of seed coming in and raise their profits. But it would cost almost half a million dollars to buy new crushing machines and bring the plant up to Department of Agriculture code. Perriello's office put them in touch with officials in Richmond, who said that food-grade canola wouldn't qualify for a stimulus grant. Instead, Red Birch was encouraged to apply for a grant toward the purchase of a microturbine, which could generate electricity from the glycerin waste left over from making biofuel, take the refinery off the grid, and create a new income stream when Red Birch sold some of the power to other users. Dean got the application in just a few minutes ahead of the deadline. In January 2010, Perriello came to Martinsville to announce the award of $750,000 in federal stimulus funds for Red Birch to buy a microturbine.

The ceremony took place in the main hall of a natural history museum, under the suspended skeleton of a fourteen-million-year-old whale. There were other dignitaries besides Perriello, and other recipients besides Dean and Gary (on this occasion Dean wore a yellow jacket, a yellow shirt, and black pants), and by the time Perriello got up to speak, most of the energy had seeped out of the room. Wearing a flag lapel pin on his charcoal suit, and looking half the age of every previous speaker, Perriello took the podium with a kind of angry restlessness.

"The next big thing this area can be known for is clean energy," he said, and he gave a shout-out to Red Birch, calling Gary and Dean "freedom fighters and entrepreneurs." "Instead of driving by their truck stop and leaving three or four cents on a dollar spent, you leave ninety cents at theirs. When things are 'too big to fail,' maybe they're a little too big to be the model in the first place. We are right on the cusp of a transformation, and that's why it's so exciting. This is a kind of industrial revolution moment." He blamed both parties for policies that favored big corporations and made America's small producers less competitive. "I'm sick of it, I'm *sick* of buying everything from China and overseas, and sending our dollars to petrodictators. We're the only country in history to fund both sides of a war!" His voice was getting louder. "Politicians from both parties have never been to a farm—only for a photo op. They think it's the jobs of the past, but I'm here to tell you they're the jobs of the future. This is a region that's been hit hard, but it's a proud area that wants to stand tall and compete again."

News crews shot video. Reporters swarmed around to interview Dean and Gary. The grant was like an affirmation from on high that a biodiesel truck stop was not a harebrained scheme, that some of the most powerful people in the country found it worthy. That day—January 14, 2010—was the high-water mark for Red Birch Energy.

After the ceremony, Dean drove back to North Carolina, and Gary went to the plant to have lunch with Flo Jackson, a black woman in her midforties whom he had hired to write a new business plan and who was visiting Red Birch for the first time. Flo was a former college basketball star with an MBA from James Madison. She had managed a Target and a Wal-Mart, and Gary wanted to bring her on to whip Red Birch into financial shape.

The most pressing problem was the truck stop next door, which was the refinery's main customer. Dean had long since stopped paying attention to his store, where half the employees were stealing from him and would have failed a drug test if they'd been given one. In October 2009, Dean had filed for Chapter 11 bankruptcy, which allowed him to keep his truck stop business—Red Birch of Martinsville, Inc.—open and reorganize its debt. Flo Jackson's contract said that she wouldn't be responsible for managing the truck stop, but she ended up spending most of the year on Dean's business—first trying to save it, then unwinding it. The books were a mess—two entries totaling a quarter of a million dollars were marked simply "withdrawal by owner." The truck stop owed the bank two million dollars, and no buyer would assume that debt. Flo told Dean that he was running his business like a dreamer. And Dean began to resent her, for here was the reality principle in the person of a tough, blunt-spoken woman, brought in by Gary from the outside, telling Dean what he didn't want to hear. Over time, he went to the refinery less often. As far as he was concerned, the new regime was squeezing him out.

One bad thing followed another in the year 2010. Because of red tape, the first half of the stimulus money took nine months to arrive, and in the meantime the news of the grant brought Red Birch Energy to the attention of officials in Henry County. They went after Dean for eighty-five thousand dollars in back taxes owed on the truck stop between 2007 and 2009. Dean swore it was political, because Red Birch was so identified with Perriello and Henry County was deep red. The county also cited the refinery for a grease spill, and the fine kept going up. "The county manager has done everything he can to get us out of here," Gary said. He and

Dean, being North Carolinians, would never be accepted in a narrow, closed-up place like Martinsville.

From the highway, the biodiesel refinery and the truck stop appeared to be part of the same operation, sitting on the same couple of acres carved out of the same red hillside and separated by just a hundred fifty feet of pavement. In 2008, when the future looked bright, the arrangement was celebrated as a "closed-loop system." But in 2010, financial troubles made it clear that these were different businesses whose interests were in some ways opposed. The truck stop—Red Birch of Martinsville—was entirely Dean's. The refinery—Red Birch Energy—was a partnership that was falling more and more on Gary's shoulders. When the refinery became one of the truck stop's creditors, Gary had to take out an eighty-thousand-dollar line of credit to keep fuel in the ground. Dean paid him by relinquishing stock in Red Birch Energy.

On September 16, the U.S. Bankruptcy Court in the Western District of Virginia ordered Dean's truck stop business into Chapter 7. There were thirty-six other debtors in court that day. Red Birch of Martinsville was completely liquidated, and the truck stop was sold off to a national chain, WilcoHess, which tore down the store's two-level front porch, with its balustered wood railings—the old-fashioned country-market appearance that Dean's customers had loved when he introduced it back in 1997—and replaced it with a façade of brutal whitewashed concrete. The gas station stopped pumping biodiesel and went back to regular number 2 diesel, the imported fuel that had been cut off by Katrina in 2005, leading Dean to his come-to-Jesus moment. So Red Birch Energy lost its main customer, and soon the refinery was making biofuel at just 10 percent of its capacity. The sign outside the plant was still, strictly speaking, true: Red Birch remained "America's 1st BioDiesel Truck Stop." But its claim to fame was gone. Red Birch no longer grew it, made it, and sold it.

Four days after the bankruptcy order, Dean was indicted by a Henry County grand jury for failing to turn over almost ten thousand dollars in meals taxes that his business had collected on behalf of the state.

He had always feared the power of government, almost as much as he had feared poverty. Government could put you in prison, and prison was one of his nightmares. He didn't think he could stand losing his freedom. He often dreamed about it—a feeling of anxiety, that he had messed up somehow, though not intentionally, and they were coming for him—and he would wake up from these dreams overwhelmed with relief, thinking:

"Thank God that wasn't real." Once, in 2007, around the time he was getting into biodiesel, Dean had to spend a night in jail. The divorce settlement with his second wife had required him to send her thirty-three hundred dollars a month for five years (Dean worked it out to eight hundred dollars for every day of their marriage), but when his ex remarried he assumed that he was off the hook and stopped paying. It turned out that Dean still owed the money, and the judge at the Rockingham County Courthouse in Wentworth ordered him put in shackles. Ryan, who was twelve, was with Dean and saw his father led away as a prisoner. Dean spent that night in a cell with a dozen other men, and he never wanted to go back.

Dean didn't like to talk about these things. If someone asked him a difficult question about the state of his business affairs, or his personal finances, or his legal troubles, he would answer, "Ummm . . . ," a high elusive syllable that floated away into the air, implying that the thing wasn't so serious, would be taken care of, was already being taken care of, and then he would turn the conversation to the wisdom of Napoleon Hill or the promise of the new green economy. In 2010 it was easier living in his imagination of the past and the future than on the stretch of Route 220 that was his life, and so there were many calls that went unreturned, pressing matters ignored, reckonings deferred.

That was one of the hardest years of Dean Price's life, and 2011 would be even worse. Yet he always swore he'd never quit. He never lost faith in his vision. He would not be like the gold prospector in Colorado that Napoleon Hill described, who stopped drilling and sold off his machinery when, as things turned out, he was just three feet short of the mother lode.

JUST BUSINESS: JAY-Z

Everything has to be put in context.

Shawn Corey Carter, born in '69, Marcy Houses, country of Bed-Stuy, planet of Brooklyn (New York and the universe came later). Fourth and last child of Gloria Carter, employed as a clerk; father Adnis Reeves, a preacher's son. Marcy was a fortress in brick, twenty-seven buildings, six floors each, four thousand people, living to the left of him, right of him, on top and bottom of him—parties and stress, a birthday one day, a shooting the next.

At four Shawn got on a ten-speed bike, put his foot up, and coasted sitting sideways. The whole block was amazed—"Oh God!" First feeling of fame and he liked it. Fame felt good.

Mom and Pop had a million records stacked in milk crates: Curtis Mayfield, Staples Singers, ConFunkShun, the Jackson 5, Rufus, the O'Jays . . . He loved Michael Jackson the most, and when Gloria got home from work and put on "Enjoy Yourself," Shawn sang and spun around the room, his sisters singing backup. The seventies weren't bad in Marcy, kind of an adventure for a kid. Dice games on the concrete, football in fields strewn with glass, junkies nodding off on benches—kids would dare each other to tip them over. "We were able to smuggle some of the magic of that dying civilization out in our music and use it to build a new world," he later wrote. "We found our fathers on wax and on the streets and in history."

Summer of 1978, he came upon a Marcy kid no one ever noticed before in the middle of a crowd, rhyming, throwing out couplets about anything, about the benches, the people listening, his own rhymes, how good he was, the best in New York, for half an hour, and Shawn thought: "That's some cool shit. I could *do* that." Home that night he wrote down rhymes in a spiral notebook. It filled up, rhyming took over his life, in front of the mirror every morning, on the kitchen table while he banged out a beat past bedtime, driving his sisters crazy—he could *do* that. When an older boy named Jaz-O, the best rapper in Marcy, taped their voices with a heavy-ass recorder and played them back, Shawn's sounded different from the one he heard in his head. "I saw it as an opening, a way to re-create myself and reimagine my world. After I recorded a rhyme, it gave me an unbelievable rush to play it back, to hear that voice."

I'm the king of hip-hop
Renewed like Reeboks
Key in the lock
Rhymes so provocative
As long as I live

People in Marcy started calling him Jazzy.

Sixth grade, he tested off the charts—reading like a twelfth grader. School never challenged him, but he scoured the dictionary for words to use. One day, Miss Louden had the class take a field trip to her brownstone in Manhattan. The refrigerator door produced water and ice cubes. That was the first time he knew he was poor. People in the projects spent half their lives sitting on plastic chairs in dirty government offices waiting for their name to be called. Kids snapped on each other for every little sign of poverty, so they talked about getting rich by whatever means, and he got that hunger, too—no way he was going to sit in class all day. When he eventually got his hands on enough cheese to buy an off-white Lexus, "I could just feel that stink and shame of being broke lifting off of me, and it felt beautiful. The sad shit is that you never really shake it all the way off, no matter how much money you get."

That same sixth-grade year, 1980, his pop bounced. Worse than a father he never knew was a father who was around the first eleven years, teaching his boy how to walk fast through the hood and remember which bodega sold laundry detergent, whether it was owned by Puerto Ricans or Arabs, how to observe people in Times Square (what was that woman's dress size?), and then disappeared and never came back. The boy never again wanted to get attached to something and have it taken away, never wanted to feel that pain again, never let anyone else break his heart. He became guarded and cool, eyes flat, stopped smiling, harsh laugh: "Hah hah hah."

Next year, when he was twelve, his big brother stole some of his jewelry. Shawn got a gun, saw the devil in Eric's drugged eyes, closed his own, and squeezed. He hit his brother in the arm and thought his own life was over, but Eric didn't go to the cops, even apologized for using when Shawn came to the hospital. Just another shooting in Marcy and there'd be more, but he never again hit, never got hit. He was lucky.

Crack showed up in 1985, a few years behind rap, and it took over Marcy. Crack immediately changed everything and was irreversible—brought coke out of bathrooms and hallways into public view, turned adults into fiends, kids into hustlers, made parents fear their children. Authority was gone and the projects went crazy. Shawn Carter saw another opening.

He got in the game at fifteen. He was just following—kids went to college where college grads were everywhere, kids sold drugs where hustling was everywhere. His friend Hill lined him up with a local dealer, and they went in for what turned out to be a job interview. The dealer told them how serious the hustle was, that it required dedication and integrity. The dealer was later murdered—balls cut off and stuffed in his mouth, then he was shot in the back of the head. That was how serious the hustle was. It didn't stop Shawn. He wanted in.

He was helping his mom with the light bill. He was buying the right gear for himself, the Ewings, the gold teeth, the girls. He was feeling the adrenaline rush. With a cousin of Hill's he got a piece of a dead-end street in Trenton and started taking New Jersey Transit over on weekends—pretty soon he was living there. He hid his work and weapons in baggy jeans and puffy coats, construction boots kept his feet warm on winter nights. He was all business. He put the hurt on the local competition with lower prices because he got his supply cheaper from the Peruvians in Washington Heights. The squeeze made him unpopular, and one afternoon there was a face-off in the park, guns drawn, nobody shot—it was win or go home. Another time, an arrest—his first, no charges—cost him his stash and he had to work sixty straight hours in Marcy to get his money back, staying awake eating cookies and writing rhymes on brown paper bags.

His dream was to be the rich guy in the nice car with the big gun, Scarface—"Say hello to my little friend!" The hustle was a paranoid fever, one eye always open, "excited with crime and the lavish luxuries that just excited my mind," and he got addicted to the rush just like the fiends got addicted to what he sold. Kids who put on their orange uniform and walked past the hustlers on the corner to a job at McDonald's were suckers trying to play by the rules. They didn't have a dream, they had a check, surviving nine to five, but he wasn't trying to survive—he was trying to live it to the limit. Better die enormous on the street than live dormant in a little box called Apartment 5C. He rarely smoked weed and stayed sober when he drank—being conscious let him focus on the money. He was always about the money. Second best wasn't worth the ultimate price on the street, so he learned to compete and win as if his life depended on it.

The crack game didn't end the rap game. He would go back to Marcy for a few weeks at a time and get with Jaz-O to work on rhymes. But his months on the streets took him further and further away from the notebook, so he learned to memorize longer and longer rhymes without writing them down, and that became his method. He had one foot in rap, one foot out. His cousin B-High thought he was wasting his talent hustling and stopped speaking to him. "These rappers are hoes," his crew told him. "Some white person takes all their money." Secretly, he was afraid he might not make it in music. And the business looked like a pay cut—especially after EMI offered Jaz-O a record deal in 1988, flew him to London for a couple of months with Shawn tagging along, then cut him loose when his first single bombed.

Shawn switched over to Big Daddy Kane, a legendary Brooklyn rapper with a bus tour, and was given the mic at intermissions, rapping as Jay-Z for his meals. Everyone who heard Jay was blown away by his verbal cleverness, his confidence, his speed-rhyming in that high outer-borough deadpan—so good so easy he didn't take it all that serious. When the tour was over he went back to hustling.

His crew extended their distribution chain down to Maryland and D.C. where the profit margins were high, riding Lexuses up and down I-95, moving a kilo of cocaine a week. His loyalty was to his money, but he had a fear of running the streets into his thirties, of being nothing. One day in Maryland in 1994 a rival fired three shots at him point-blank and missed—"divine intervention." After a decade of hustling he decided to see if he could make as much money selling records as he did selling rocks.

> I figured, "Shit why risk myself I just write it in rhymes
> And let you feel me, and if you don't like it then fine"

A Brooklyn producer named DJ Clark Kent put him with a Harlem promoter named Damon Dash, who was skeptical until he saw Jay's Nike Air Force 1s. But none of the labels wanted Jay-Z—maybe it was too crafty, maybe too real—so he took his hustling profits and started his own label with Dash. They called it Roc-A-Fella, in case anyone doubted their intentions. They were going to take over the world.

Reasonable Doubt came in 1996, twenty-six years in the making. It was complex and sinister, dense with rhymes laid over lush samples from the records his parents had loved in the seventies, a portrait of the rapper as a young hustler from the next, lost generation, ready to kill and live with regrets and sick thoughts or die trying for big money, diamonds, Rolexes, fine champagne, fine girls, escape.

This shit is wicked on these mean streets
None of my friends speak
We're all trying to win

It didn't take over the world, but it was big. Jay-Z swept the clubs and sold tapes to corner stores until he landed a distribution deal. He gave Marcy a voice, and the nightmare that America had locked in the basement was suddenly playing in kids' bedrooms. They wanted to live the American dream with a vengeance, like Scarface, like Jay-Z, they wanted to break the laws and win because only fools still thought you could do it in an orange uniform or a cheap suit when that game was fixed, and there could be a shortcut with a big payoff. It was paying off for the former Shawn Carter. Everyone who knew rap understood that Jay was going to be huge.

Music was just another hustle. He was a reluctant artist, still about the money and not apologizing for it, but to make this hustle work over the long run you needed art. He was as cold and focused as he'd been on the streets—seven more records in seven more years, all platinum. He softened the tracks and dumbed down his lyrics—more large living, less regret—to hit a bigger audience and double the dollars. It turned out lots of young whites could relate to *money cash hoes Gs cream Cristal Lexus mackin poppin pimpin bitches grams rocks nines niggaz*. Jay-Z told rap's eternal story—"why I'm dope, doper than you"—a hundred different ways, no two couplets alike, and the kids believed him, so they wore what he wore, drank what he drank, and made him rich.

He launched a clothing line and it brought in more revenue than his music company, hundreds of millions. Started his own movie studio, got his own Reebok sneaker, distributed his own vodka, put out his own cologne, trademarked his own shade of Jay-Z Blue, cross-promoted everything. Stabbed a record producer in the VIP section of a Times Square club in 1999 for bootlegging his fourth album and quoted Pacino in *Godfather II* as he drove in the knife: "Lance, you broke my heart." Holed up in the Trump Hotel with his lawyer and crew playing guts, a three-card game that rewarded self-possession. Vowed never to lose his shit again and later copped a plea, getting away with probation.

He became a corporate rapper, an outlaw entrepreneur, wearing sneakers to the boardroom like in a Silicon Valley start-up, working in the legit world while living the hustler's dream. He retired from rapping in 2003 at Madison Square Garden (but that didn't last long) and became a music executive, president of Def Jam, the biggest label in hip-hop. He cut his old partner at Roc-A-Fella loose, taking the name with him—"It's just business," Jay-Z told Damon Dash, sounding like another screen mobster. And he rhymed the point in his own words:

I sold kilos of coke, I'm guessin I can sell CDs
I'm not a businessman, I'm a business, man
Let me handle my business, damn!

It was the same hustle all the way up—he was doing the same thing on the twenty-ninth floor in midtown that he'd been doing on the corner in Trenton. The mainstream embraced rap while rap copied the mainstream, and Jay-Z played the game better than the suits because he'd learned it on the streets. When critics called him a sellout or materialist, he had the answer: selfishness was a rational response to the reality he faced.

Everything has to be put in context.

He did the things that top celebrities did: became a lifestyle brand, opened a sports bar chain, got sued by his workers for back wages, met Bono in a London cigar room with Quincy Jones, put his name to philanthropic causes, made the Forbes 400 (net worth 450 mil), hung out with presidents, carried on beefs with other stars, hooked up with a singer every bit as big as he was, bought her an island for her birthday, rented a wing of a maternity ward before she was due and made it their private suite, tried to trademark their baby girl's name for future use (the U.S. Patent Office refused), and released a single when Blue Ivy Carter was four days old, rapping: "My greatest creation was you . . . You don't yet know what swag is."

The more he won, the more they loved him everywhere, lived through him, celebrated his money and power as their own. At concerts fans raised their hands together and flashed his Roc-A-Fella diamond logo as if they owned a piece of the deal. He was a mogul and a revolutionary, an icon and a thug (that was the perfect hustle), worshipped for getting to the top with a big fuck-you and no standing in line, still telling the world why he was dope, doper than you. And if he ever failed—when his sports bar in Vegas went bust, or his summer tournament basketball team stacked with NBA ringers lost, or his deal with Chrysler to put out a Jay-Z edition Jeep Commander painted Jay-Z Blue fell through—every trace of failure was hidden, as if the revelation might be fatal to his spell. He had to keep winning. Success wasn't about anything except itself.

When Jay-Z bought a slice of the Nets and fronted the team's move to Brooklyn, he became the boss and the star, the black Branch Rickey, Jackie Robinson with sins. When the new arena opened, he sold it out eight straight nights. In the smoky dark he told sixteen thousand fans, "I don't think it's a coincidence that this is where Jackie Robinson was the first African American to play professional sports and break the color barrier. And I don't think it's a coincidence that I was part of the group that brought the Nets here from New Jersey. You'll hear people say I only own a small percentage of the team. It doesn't matter what percentage—the story is that a black kid from a single-parent house made it from the Marcy projects about six minutes away from here. So the fact that I have any ownership in this franchise is fuckin amazing. The fact that I have any ownership in this venue is fuckin amazing. Don't let them diminish your accomplishment or dim your shine." Jay-Z held up his middle finger. Sixteen thousand middle fingers answered him.

There were times when he looked around at his life and thought he was getting away with murder.

TAMPA

By the thousands and thousands the foreclosures came. They came to Country Walk and Carriage Pointe, to inner-city Tampa and outermost Pasco, to Gulfport and northeast St. Pete. They arrived at houses where three months of mail lay in a pile at the front door, and houses where children were watching *Dora the Explorer* and adults had stopped answering the phone, and motels with 20 percent occupancy, and obscurely named investment entities with no known street address. They came like visitations from that laconic process server, the angel of death.

The foreclosures started out as complaints, all of them the same complaint: *You owe me money!* The complaints were filed by such transparently named financial institutions as HSBC Bank USA, and EMC Mortgage Corporation, and BAC Home Loans Servicing, L.P., formerly known as Countrywide Home Loans Servicing, L.P., and LSF6 Mercury REO Investments Trust Series 2008-1, and Citibank, N.A., as Trustee for the Holders of Bear Stearns Alt-A Trust 2006-6 Mortgage Passthrough Certificates Series 2006-6, and Deutsche Bank Trust Company Americas f/k/a Banker's Trust Company, as Trustee and Custodian for IXIS 2006-HE3 by: Saxon Mortgage Services, Inc. f/k/a Meritech Mortgage Services, Inc. as its Attorney-in-Fact. The complaints of these institutions were drafted by foreclosure mills such as Law Offices of David J. Stern, P.A., and Marshall C. Watson, P.A., and Florida Default Law Group, and they were delivered as summonses by process servers such as ProVest, LLC–Tampa, and Gissen & Zawyer Process Service, and the Hillsborough County Sheriff's Office. The summonses were personally served on, or nailed to the front door of, or left with a neighbor of, or tossed in the trash near the empty house of, Olivia M. Brown et al., and Jack E. Hamersma, and Mirtha De La Cruz a/k/a Mirtha Delacruz, and Aum Shree of Tampa,

LLC, and LSC Investor, LLC, and John Doe, and Josephine Givargidze and Unknown Spouse of Josephine Givargidze. The summons stated:

> A lawsuit has been filed against you. You have 20 calendar days after this summons is served on you to file a written response to the attached complaint with the clerk of this court. A phone call will not protect you; your written response, including the case number given above and the names of the parties, must be filed if you want the court to hear your side of the case. If you do not file your response on time, you may lose the case, and your wages, money and property may thereafter be taken without further warning from this court.

Thus set in motion, the lawsuits converged on downtown Tampa, where they assembled on the fourth floor of the George E. Edgecomb Courthouse of the Thirteenth Judicial Circuit. Across the bay they gathered in hordes on the third floor of the St. Petersburg Judicial Building of the Sixth Judicial Circuit. They were transformed into millions of pages of legal documents, and the documents were crammed into thick dull-brown legal folders, and the folders were stacked in boxes, and the boxes were loaded onto carts, and the carts were wheeled into courtrooms by bailiffs who looked weary from the effort. There, the black-robed judges—some of them brought out of retirement for this purpose, their six-hundred-dollar per diem largely paid by foreclosure filing fees—went about the work of clearing Florida's backlog of half a million foreclosure cases, as earlier generations had cleared the mangrove swamps that made way for Tampa.

There were so many foreclosures, and the pressure from the state Supreme Court to dispose of them quickly was so great, that one senior judge, aged seventy-five or so, might carry three thousand cases at a time. A December morning's daily docket in Hillsborough County consisted of sixty cases, beginning at 9:00 a.m. with National City Mortgage vs. Christopher Meier and ending at noon with Chase Home Finance vs. William Martens, allowing each case three minutes, and usually less, for justice to be served. After lunch, starting at 1:30 with Wells Fargo Bank vs. Stephanie Besser, and ending at 5:00 p.m. with Deutsche Bank vs. Raymond Lucas, the judge ruled on sixty more.

If Ms. Besser or Mr. Lucas happened to be represented by counsel, the rocket docket—for so it was called—might temporarily slow down and fall behind schedule. Worst of all if Ms. Besser or Mr. Lucas appeared in person, for then the court would have to confront the human face of a foreclosure, the particular lineaments of anxiety etched there by the prospect of losing one's home, and embarrassment would settle over the proceedings, as if a terminal patient had wandered into a room where doctors were coldly discussing her hopeless prognosis, and the judge might be more likely to ask a few hard questions of the plaintiff's attorney. Fortunately, this almost never happened. Most of the cases were unopposed, the only lawyer present the bank's—almost always an attorney from one of several law firms around Florida, known as foreclosure mills, assigned the case by an automated computer system—who was sometimes not even physically there, just a voice with a law degree on the court's speaker-phone, knocking off fourteen cases in a half-hour call, and each case ended with the judge asking, "Anything unusual about this file? Anything missing?" and then setting a date for the foreclosure auction, two floors down in Room 202. At times the courtroom was empty except for the judge, a court assistant or two, and a bailiff wheeling the cartloads of cases back and forth. And, to save time, and perhaps to keep this judicial stockyard out of public view, many hearings weren't even held in a courtroom, but confined to the obscurity of the judge's private chambers.

In the summer of 2010, in Courtroom 409 of the George E. Edgecomb Courthouse, officers began to notice a woman at the daily foreclosure docket who had no apparent business there. She sat in the back row, never saying a word, but taking copious notes. If she had a case it never came up, and she looked more like a legal secretary than a lawyer, in her snakeskin-patterned V-neck top, black slacks, embroidered jacket, and tortoiseshell glasses. She was a short dumpling of a woman in her sixties, with dry straw-colored hair cut to her neck and a tired expression—the kind of person no one noticed, unless she happened to do something unusual.

Sylvia Landis—that was the woman's name—was just a civilian, a private citizen, but she had a personal interest in how the courts were handling the torrent of foreclosures and the people swept up in them. Like nearly everyone in Tampa, she came from somewhere else—Doylestown, Pennsylvania. Her father had been a salesman, chronically unemployed, and she had grown up in financial chaos. She was in her thirties before she stopped having nightmares about starving to death, but she earned a master's degree in personnel administration and pulled herself up into the middle class from which her parents had fallen. She worked as a career trainer with the Los Angeles Police Department for two decades. In 1999, Sylvia began to prepare for her retirement by joining the growing subculture of middle-class people who got involved in real estate. She took a class with a Southern California investment guru named Marshall Reddick, who laced his seminars with godly inspiration and whose motto was "helping to wipe out middle-class poverty." The course was like a revival meeting, with people running out of the room to buy houses. Sylvia caught the spirit, and at one time or another she owned five houses: two in California, which she sold for a profit; a condo in Asheville, North Carolina; and two in Florida—one in Tampa, which she used for rental income, and a brand-new one in Cape Coral, where she planned to live after she retired.

It didn't work out that way.

In 2004, ovarian cancer forced her into early retirement from the LAPD with a pension. She moved to the Asheville condo in 2007, thinking she would start a new career. In early 2008, when the market was tanking, she found herself unable to breathe and had to be hospitalized in the cardiac ward. She owed $157,500 on the three-bedroom house in Cape Coral—the epicenter of the crisis, with the single highest foreclosure rate in the country—and the rent she was collecting had dropped in half. She knew that she was going to lose the house, and before Bank of America could foreclose, she tried to get rid of it in a short sale, selling the property for less than she owed on it. That was when Sylvia became acquainted with the ways of the banks.

She found a buyer in early 2009 (she was going to lose half her investment), but she seemed to be on the phone with B of A every day, always passed from one person to another, and the sale didn't happen, and meanwhile she believed that the bank was padding her costs. The term "robo-signing" wasn't yet in use, but she received documents that didn't seem authentic—computer-generated copies, with erroneous dates and suspicious signatures, of the assignment and transfer of her mortgage note to Bank of America after it bought Countrywide, the original lender. She wrote to bank vice presidents, to state attorneys general, to Gretchen Morgenson of *The New York Times*, to anyone who might care. She ran out of money for attorney's fees and had to represent herself. All this while she was still recovering from cancer, and needless to say the stress wasn't good for her health.

At the end of 2009 she completed a short sale on the house in Cape Coral. As if this had never happened, two weeks later, the bank's law firm, David J. Stern, sued Sylvia for default. (Stern was the biggest and most notorious foreclosure mill in Florida, run like a legal sweatshop with a hundred thousand cases a year, most of them from Fannie and Freddie, earning profits that its boss spent on four mansions, ten luxury cars, two private jets, and a 130-foot yacht, before being shut down by a state fraud investigation.) It took Sylvia four more months to find someone at the bank who would straighten out the wrongful foreclosure mess, but her credit was shot.

By then she had moved to Tampa. She had fifty thousand dollars' equity in her house there, with a ninety-one-thousand-dollar fixed-rate mortgage. It made financial sense to get rid of the Asheville condo, even at a steep loss, and claim the Tampa house that she'd used for rental income as her residence. And her one companion, a hyperactive little shih tzu—Sylvia had no children—needed a yard. It was a very modest place, in a working-class subdivision called Sugarwood Grove where her neighbors drove trucks and fixed their own houses. All the same, she needed a roommate. In 2007 she'd had a million dollars in assets. Now she had zero. Her savings were gone—she would have been on the street if not for her government pension. Along the way, she had given a big chunk of money to Wajed "Roger" Salam, a Tampa "joint-venture expert," "founder of the Mastermind Forum," and onetime associate of the motivational speaker Anthony Robbins. Needless to say, she never saw that money again. Back in L.A., some members of the real estate guru Marshall Reddick's club had filed a class action lawsuit against their mentor for fraudulent home sales in Florida (according to Sylvia, Reddick created more middle-class poverty than he'd ever ended). Still, though she regretted not having trusted her instinct and gotten out of the market with a lot of money when she saw the crash coming, Sylvia wasn't ashamed of getting into real estate in the first place, even though investors were now vilified for causing the crash, consigned to the same status as subprime mortgage lenders. Wasn't it the American way to take the initiative and help yourself?

A phrase that she once read in a *New York Times* column described her perfectly: "the formerly middle class." She knew that countless others were making the same downward journey. Sylvia had grown up apolitical, with unquestioning respect for authority—she didn't even know the name of her union at the LAPD—but the experience with the bank changed her. She called it "outright fraud," something she had never imagined possible. A very conservative impulse that came from Doylestown, a fear of chaos and longing for law and order, led her downtown to the George E. Edgecomb Courthouse of the Thirteenth Judicial Circuit. She wanted to see what happened to foreclosures when they reached the bar of justice. She thought that her observations might be helpful to others.

Sylvia felt a certain awe on the Monday morning when she first went to court. Her instinct was to be polite and not make any fuss, but she had trouble finding the foreclosure court—there was no public schedule of hearings. She was told by a receptionist on the sixth floor that cases would be heard in Room 513, but she found that Room 513 was in a locked section of the fifth floor, with no court officer in sight. She went down another floor to Courtroom 409, where the receptionist had suggested there might also be hearings (though nothing seemed certain, because nothing was written, and the law was nothing if not written). The door to Courtroom 409 was open. Inside, there was a bailiff. She told Sylvia that there was nothing to watch, just administrative procedures.

"Are there any rules against my sitting in?" Sylvia asked.

At the bench, Judge Doug Little was presiding over a telephone and a cartful of file boxes. Present on speakerphone was an attorney from the Law Offices of David J. Stern, Esq. "Good morning, Your Honor," the phone squawked, in keeping with the solemnity of the proceedings. As the rocket docket got going, Sylvia began taking notes. The original mortgage document was often missing from the file, and the judge would tell the lawyer on the line to get it in by the end of the week. In some cases the entire file was missing. Several defendants showed up or had a lawyer represent them. There was Michael Mcrae, who had lived in his house for eighteen years, with two sons and a new job, and who was trying to refinance the loan (the judge extended the sale date). There was Howard Huff, a black man with little education, who didn't seem to know where the house in question was located, since he had simply agreed to put his name on a mortgage as an investment vehicle with a broker he knew, and now found himself being sued by the bank. (Sylvia, in distress, ran out after Huff and urged him to contact Legal Aid. Huff looked at her in bewilderment.) But the overwhelming majority of the cases went uncontested. Sylvia knew how it was, how the banks beat them down, lied to them, gave them the runaround, didn't answer calls, until, by the time their day in court finally came, most defendants had long since given up. Justice was delivered in their absence, in the blink of an eye.

"I spend more time at the McDonald's drive-through window," Sylvia said later, "than people who were losing their homes got." Present in their stead, she felt something different from the stress of her own ordeal, something more like empathy.

Near the end of the morning session, Judge Little suddenly addressed her. "Is there anything you need?"

"Could I have a copy of the docket of cases?"

The judge looked uncertainly to the bailiff. The bailiff firmly shook her head: "The docket is shredded every day." Later, Sylvia saw the bailiff whisper something about her to one of the court officers.

But by that point in her life, Sylvia was not as easily deterred as she might have appeared. She waited till the end of the day, then asked again for the docket, and this time she received a copy from the judge's clerk. With the docket, she was able to attach the names of homeowners and banks to the cases that she'd witnessed and jotted down. That night, she wrote up her notes in a report and sent it to a network of Florida lawyers active in foreclosure defense. That was how she became, without pay, their eyes and ears in court. That was how Sylvia Landis joined a movement— the first movement she was ever part of, "a middle-class movement," she said, of people concerned about law and property rights and transparency and democracy, with all the middle-class naïveté of Americans who had always believed in the system and never fought it in their lives. And that was how she came to know Matt Weidner.

MATTHEW D. WEIDNER, P.A. ATTORNEY AT LAW, said the sign on the plate glass window. REAL ESTATE CIVIL LITIGATION FAMILY LAW CORPORATE LAW. Basically, Weidner took anything that walked through the door—he was a door lawyer, the subsistence farmer of the legal world, a couple-grand retainer up front. He worked out of a crappy storefront office between a saloon and a bikini bar on a sketchy strip of downtown St. Petersburg, his messy curved desk taking up most of the available floor space. Weidner seemed a little sketchy, too, at first.

He was in his late thirties, Florida-born. An old debit card showed that he'd once been fat, but he got into triathlons and trimmed down, and the wall behind his desk filled up with framed medals beneath his degrees. He was divorced, having left a house with a big mortgage to a wife who didn't want to sell. He knew the fall was imminent when Hummers started appearing in their subdivision—the arrogance, the absurdity of it all. Weidner himself leased a white Cadillac, his contribution to the U.S. auto industry, with a camouflage survival backpack in the trunk. He had an animated pink face, a bowlegged walk, and a quick throwaway line for every situation he walked into. He would enter Room 400 of the St. Petersburg Judicial Building, his pale blue eyes widening in mock horror at the assortment of dark-suited attorneys present, and announce: "Bunch of thugs in this courtroom." Once he got going, the sentences rolled out in fluent waves of excitement and indignation. "We're consuming crap from wherever but we're not making anything. How are we supposed to make mortgage payments here in the United States when we don't make anything else? What if we have a brownout or a blackout that's completely accidental but shuts down New York City or Chicago? How long do you think it's going to take before absolute panic sets in?" Then, at his hyperbolic height, he took a verbal step back to check himself: "Am I being hysterical?"

Weidner hadn't always held apocalyptic views about America. He had started life as a Boy Scout in the home of spring break, Daytona Beach. His uncle, Don, was director of the Florida Republican Party when the state was still largely Democratic—under him the party was established in all sixty-seven counties and held its first state convention, in 1979. Matt was suckled at the breast of Ronald Reagan, attended Young Republican events, devoutly believed in God and country, American exceptionalism, self-reliance, and small government. In college, during the Gingrich revolution in Congress, he named his boxer Newt. He was all for invading Iraq—"We'd do a good deed and get a forward operating base of a gas station." And yet, looking back, he now saw that the rot had already set in with his parents and their generation, in the seventies. Weidner's grandparents busted their asses after World War II and died with their house paid off—hell, his granddad was still working while his dad, with his reverse mortgage, had been retired and screwing off for a decade. "Our parents were fat and lazy," he said. "Our grandparents would never have mortgaged everything and lived off the credit. If you look at the gross domestic product in the past twenty years, in particular the last ten years, it's not off anything we've produced. It's trading on the paper of what was produced thirty years before that."

Weidner got his law degree from Florida State in 1999, then went to work as a lobbyist for the Florida Academy of Pain Medicine. His job was to fly around the state entertaining doctors and getting drug reps from Pfizer and Novartis to write fifty-thousand-dollar checks at the academy's annual conference. He would attend meetings in Tallahassee where the room was set up so that the flow of lobbyists proceeded smoothly past the food table to the waiting lawmaker. The moment of truth came with the handshake, when Weidner would lock eyes with the state rep and pull the envelope stuffed with checks from his pocket, and the state rep would palm it, feel its thickness, determine how much time Weidner had to explain why it was important to defeat a law requiring patients to visit a doctor every time they refilled their hydrocodone prescription because moms wouldn't be able to get cough syrup for their kids—then Weidner would be cut off midsentence, time to move on.

Over time, these events made him physically sick. He would leave the room thinking, "I want to get into an honest profession, like the fucking practice of law."

In 2001, he began working at his uncle Don's law office in Jacksonville. On December 12, Weidner was supposed to fly to Fort Lauderdale and back with his uncle, another lawyer, and two clients on Don's single-engine Piper Cherokee. A last-minute phone call from a judge kept Matt at the office. That evening, in a heavy fog, the plane crashed into a pine swamp near the Jacksonville airport, killing everyone.

With his chilling reprieve, Weidner fled to St. Petersburg, where he set up a one-man practice. For the first few years he didn't even have a place to sit, would just grab a desk when one of the other lawyers in the storefront office suite was in court. He hustled and scraped by, mostly on divorce cases, until, around 2007, foreclosures started coming in—lots of them. The first cases were from poorer areas like south St. Pete. Then middle-class professionals showed up. It was carnage, but all in the shadows, because no one wanted to talk about it—shamefaced men who could hardly bring themselves to tell Weidner about the mortgage modification scam they'd fallen for. Couples sat down and lit into each other, the wife blaming the husband for losing his job, the husband blaming the wife for wanting a big house, until Weidner stopped them: "Hey, guys, it's us against them now, and it doesn't matter what happened, we've got to stick together." He would walk around to their side of the curved desk and roll up an empty chair between them: "I want you guys to focus on the impact this has on the kids."

Some clients came in the first time saying, "I'm not losing my home no matter what it takes," and Weidner told them, "I'm your guy. I'm going to fight for you." Through most of 2008 and 2009 he assumed that the government and the banks would work something out—split the defaulted loans, the Treasury paying the banks half the value, the banks writing off the other half as bad debt, the mortgages now belonging to the feds, who would start over with the homeowners and keep them in their houses. Something like the bank bailout—just evaporate all that phantom debt, which would never be paid off in the whole history of the world. But there was no bailout for homeowners. His clients would spend pointless months trying to get someone at the bank on the phone to agree to a short sale or loan modification, finally growing tired and coming back to Weidner: "I'm ready to go. Mom's got a place I can live at," or "We're going to rent somewhere downtown."

Weidner would tell them, "I've never lost a foreclosure case." It was true. Zero. Not because he was that good, though clients found him to be a fearless advocate. It was because the system was that bad.

Weidner found that as soon as he offered any resistance, the bank's case started to crumble. The original note was lost. A title search couldn't establish continuous chain of custody. The Mortgage Electronic Registration Systems had replaced the good old physical document at the recorder's office in the county courthouse with a digital facsimile, which, under Florida law, shouldn't qualify. The paperwork bore a fraudulent signature, a phony date, a bogus seal. No one noticed any of this while the economy chugged along, but as soon as things went into the toilet and people stopped being able to pay, America's mortgages turned out to be a hoax. A client named Arlene Fuino, a real estate agent and "short sale and foreclosure resource," was being sued for default by "U.S. Bank National Association, as Trustee for Structured Asset Securities Corporation Trust 2006-WF2." What the hell was that? Weidner took the case to a Sixth Circuit judge and demanded that the plaintiff's attorney show capacity: "All we're asking is for them to identify who is the entity that is asking my client to give them a couple hundred thousand dollars." Basically, Wall Street ("Gotham," he called it, "the anus, the black hole of the country, sucking all the money up there, the core of the apocalypse") had sliced and packaged the mortgages so many times through securitization, and then the banks had cut so many corners trying to recover the bad loans, that no institution could establish a clear right to someone's house. Which didn't stop the sheriff's deputies from banging on the door.

Weidner had never doubted the soundness of the courts, and he was staggered by the implications: "Our entire system of property ownership is in chaos and turmoil."

One day, he was sitting in Room 300 of the St. Petersburg Judicial Building, waiting for his case to come up, when a plaintiff's attorney in another foreclosure case informed the judge that she wasn't the plaintiff's attorney after all. She had been hired by a computer at a gigantic foreclosure mill called Lender Processing Services to represent Wells Fargo, but it turned out that Wells Fargo was not the holder of the note—U.S. Bank was—at least, that was what she thought. Judge Pamela Campbell told her to get it straightened out. When Weidner's case was called, he stood up on the courtroom's pale green carpet and said, "Your Honor, my head is about to explode because of what we just heard in the last case."

Judge Campbell smiled wanly. "Hopefully they'll figure out who the proper plaintiff is."

The judges heard Weidner's arguments, and the judges issued stays on foreclosure sales. But the judges refused to grant his motions to dismiss—because, after all, his clients *owed money*. So the cases languished in purgatory year after year, as the mortgages went unpaid, the courts remained clogged, the banks rejected applications to modify loans, and the clients got no resolution. But at least they stayed in their homes.

There was, for example, Jack Hamersma. When Jack first walked through Weidner's door, he was a burly boat salesman, a man's man, who had once owned a collision shop and had also done some house flipping. He was just past fifty and owed six hundred thousand dollars on two loans on his house in St. Pete—a ridiculous amount, because by the time Jack retained Weidner, it was worth maybe half that. Jack wanted his lawyer and anyone who would listen to know that he had worked all his life, had been able to afford the house when he bought it. Once Weidner got involved, the banks couldn't put the first piece of paper together, and the suit dragged on for years, during which Jack lost his job with the boat company, his savings dwindled, and he came down with three types of cancer—colorectal, liver, and lymph. That happened to a lot of Weidner's clients—the job, the house, their health, usually in that order. Weidner watched Jack shrink before his eyes, dropping a hundred pounds, until, three years after that first consultation, he limped into the office one afternoon to discuss his case, wasted legs sticking out of his shorts, a canvas bag hanging over his shoulder, from which a drip tube extended under a bandage on his chest. He had just come from five hours of chemo and was at the start of forty-eight hours of pumping.

"I find that a lot of my clients are sick," Weidner told Jack after inviting him to sit down. "I don't know what the connection is. Do you know?"

"The stress level is obviously high," Jack said, in a voice that sounded clotted. From the neck up there were still traces of rugged good looks. "When you can't work, you have no income over a period of years, then it does bad things to you. You run out of money—it's nothing intentional, you just can't pay them."

"You're one of the guys that's been hanging around the longest," Weidner said.

"It's going to outlive me."

"Don't give up yet." It didn't take much to set Weidner off, and Jack's presence was enough. "We want to do our task, our vocation, we want to provide, and I'm just so fucking furious that our government has ripped away our ability to provide anything."

"I don't know if it's up to the government to create jobs," Jack said, "but it's up to them to help the situation. When I applied for some kind of aid they looked at me like I had three heads." Jack was pretty much broke, which disqualified him from the government's emergency homeowners' program. His treatment was costing thirty-five thousand a month, and if Medicaid rejected his application, the treatment would end. "I'm in this little tiny corner and I can't find my way out. Something is going to collapse sooner or later."

"They didn't give my mom any longer than they gave you, and she's still kicking."

"I'd like to think I can beat it. From an attitude perspective, I think I can—on the spiritual side. But on the clinical side, no, it's inoperable. The statistics say you live two years with what I've got."

The conversation turned to Jack's case. It seemed to have gone moribund. "I have not heard anything from Bank of America in probably a year," Jack said. "I get an occasional little FedExgram from Wells Fargo telling me that if I pay them a hundred and eighty-three thousand dollars today they will wipe it off."

"So if you receive it today and they receive it tomorrow—"

"Technically it's too late." Jack managed a little laugh. "I'm not going to stir the pot."

"Let sleeping dogs lie." Weidner was getting riled up again. How the fuck could fifty trillion dollars of debt in the United States ever be paid off? "It gets to that level of abstraction where the only people that are fucking paying anymore—why should you pay? This whole debt thing, we're just feeding this monster that, if everyone just stopped, then they'd really be in a fix."

"I don't pay anyone anymore," Jack said. "I can't, I have no way to." When somebody tried to serve him with a summons on his Home Depot card, he didn't answer the door.

"The only thing that is even remotely possible is massive worldwide debt repudiation," Weidner said. "It all gets fucking burned up, because, if not, your son works for his entire life and never accumulates anything, because he is busy paying off personal debt and government debt and institutional debt."

"From my side, I can't do anything about anything, so what do you do?"

"Nothing."

"Nothing," Jack said. "Which isn't my frame of mind, it's not my character, it's not my makeup, but I'm pushed into that corner to the point that I have no options left."

It was a mystery to Weidner why the banks didn't aggressively pursue Jack's house, which was still worth some money, but went after others tooth and nail. It seemed totally random, which was even scarier than the other scenarios—that the banks wanted to keep the debt on their books as assets to show their stockholders, or that they were getting perverse financial incentives, or that they actually thought the market was going to bounce back sometime soon. The other thing Weidner couldn't understand was why all the unemployed homeowners in foreclosure across the country didn't come together in a mass movement. He asked Jack about that, and Jack had an answer.

"It cuts you off from everything. Imagine getting up every day and not having a purpose. You're not working, your self-worth goes down the toilet. You don't interact with people. You stay in your house. You don't want to answer the phone. It isolates you. I can't even go out to get a bite to eat. I don't want to spend fifteen dollars."

Weidner leaned back in his chair and clasped his hands behind his head. "The good news is we've kept you in the house."

"That's a wonderful thing," Jack said. "Tomorrow is going to come."

"It is. And you'll be there greeting that day. You're not going anywhere."

"I'd rather be broke and still kicking than not kicking. They can kill you but they can't eat you, ain't that the law?" Jack and Weidner shared a laugh.

So the case of BAC Home Loans Servicing, L.P., f/k/a Countrywide Home Loans Servicing, L.P. v. Jack E. Hamersma dragged on, and Jack continued to live in his house, until, two months later, he died there.

Weidner's head was always about to explode. His mind filled with visions of a decadent kleptocracy in rapid decline, abetted by both political parties—America's masses fed on processed poison bought with a food stamp swipe card, low-skill workers structurally unable to ever contribute again and too dumb to know their old jobs weren't coming back, the banks in Gotham leeching the last drops of wealth out of the country, corporations unrestrained by any notion of national interest, the system of property law in shambles, the world drowning in debt. He was an NRA member with a concealed weapons permit, and he kept a Smith & Wesson AR-15 semiautomatic rifle with three forty-round clips at his bedside, but it didn't make him feel safer, in fact it scared the shit out of him, because he saw the orgies of collectors at gun shows and knew how many of his fellow Floridians were armed: constitutional patriots like himself, military vets and sportsmen in camo, and tattooed kids from the cities, who looked like the start of militias. The whole thing went crazy when Obama took over—there was a run on ammunition, and gun dealers started selling T-shirts that said "WARNING: I AM A VETERAN. Department of Homeland Security has determined that I may be radicalized and a threat to national security. Approach at your own risk. YOU HAVE BEEN WARNED!" So what would happen if the Tampa power grid went down? Chaos. That was the future—civil unrest, social disintegration.

Weidner planted a little victory garden in the courtyard of his condo in St. Pete, carrots and lettuce, tomatoes and peppers. It was amazing to taste real vegetables—even to touch them. He was thinking about buying a piece of land out in eastern Hillsborough County, in a remote area where he went for weekend drives with his girlfriend and stopped to buy raw honey and milk at the subsistence farms of people who lived off their crops and hunted deer and wild boar. That might be the only answer: Americans would have to farm again. All these brokers and investors would get dirt under their nails and go to bed sunburned and exhausted, and that would take care of their anxiety and depression. The simpler communities would inherit the earth. He would use the place as a refuge when the shit went down, maybe hire a couple of foreclosed vets with a military skill set to take care of it. You didn't want all of them wandering around, mentally fucked up, with nothing to do.

Weidner began blogging in 2009. At first he did it to drum up business, but before long he found a voice—bombastic, canny, mischievous, outraged—and became a leader in the foreclosure defense movement that had gotten started with a group of attorneys in Jacksonville, led by a Legal Aid lawyer named April Charney, who introduced Weidner to Sylvia Landis. Blogging under the slogan "Fighting for the American People, Speaking Out As Long As Political Speech Remains Protected," he wrote every day, in the early morning or late at night, often at great length. The week of Martin Luther King's birthday he posted an essay to "My Dear Fellow Attorneys," closely modeled on King's "Letter from a Birmingham Jail":

> While confined here in a foreclosure courtroom, I came across your recent statement calling my present activities "unwise and untimely" . . . Perhaps it is easy for those who have never felt the stinging darts of foreclosure to say "Wait." But when you have seen good families thrown into the street, when you have seen the banks kick down doors and change the locks with no court order, when you have seen law enforcement standing idly by and saying "it is a civil matter," when you have seen court rulings that are repugnant to fundamental laws, when you have seen the bank and corporate executives reap unconscionable profits, when you have seen clients become sick and die due to the stress and pain of foreclosure and their economic situation, when you have seen single women who live in mortal fear that her front door may be kicked down for the third time, when you see children who have only known their parents suffering—then you will understand why we find it difficult to wait.

Weidner was reprimanded by the Sixth Judicial Circuit for disrupting courtroom proceedings after he offered to help an old lady who was defending herself against foreclosure. The court said that he was soliciting clients; he said that senior judges were trying to punish him for calling on the federal government to take over the Florida rocket dockets. He was also sued for libel by a Palm Harbor company that he'd accused of robo-signing mortgage documents. Some reporters even credited him with popularizing the term. He began to get calls from *The New York Times* and *The Wall Street Journal* and was often in the pages of the *St. Petersburg Times*. He liked talking to reporters—the press was the last best hope for his cause, the only institution in which he still had faith, surpassing that of most of its practitioners. Weidner remained, though, an everyday attorney, practicing out of a crappy office, driving his white Cadillac the six blocks to the county courthouse. "I would love to be like a Gloria Steinem," he said, "because I've got a big mouth on me and for some reason I can get people to listen. But I have to earn a living." The one thought that held off the imminent explosion in his head was of the millions of dollars in legal fees that his office and his blog—where he posted the motions he filed for others to use—were costing the big banks up in Gotham.

One day, Weidner got a call from an Indian woman named Usha Patel. A commercial lender, Business Loan Express, was trying to take back the Comfort Inn that she owned in Pasco County. Usha e-mailed Weidner a sheaf of documents, and he read them and heard her out, but he declined to take her on—he was representing homeowners, and hers was a highly convoluted commercial case. Later on, when the case went to court, he got involved tangentially, and he was glad that he did, because Weidner never met a client like Usha Patel, one who fought so hard, who held such a fervent belief in the American dream that it was almost enough to restore his own.

Usha knew that she was responsible for the loan—after all, she had signed the note—and in early 2010 she was trying to negotiate a new payment schedule with Business Loan Express when she and her family traveled to London for a wedding. Upon their arrival back at the Tampa airport, her son looked at his phone and said, "Mom, we have an emergency hearing."

Usha's emergency hearing was a small sideshow in the great spectacle of frauds and failures that opened the new millennium. Business Loan Express, rebranded Ciena, was in bankruptcy and being sued by the Justice Department for fraudulent lending practices. A bankruptcy up on Wall Street was a threat to Usha's failing motel down in Pasco County as Ciena searched for ways to pay off its creditors. Weidner said, "The titans of finance are up there in Gotham fighting over the carcass of Ciena, while at the same time Ciena's tentacles are down here wrapped around Usha's neck." The lender had deceived Usha—it had no intention of working out a new payment schedule—and at the emergency hearing on March 19, the Pasco County circuit court ordered the motel into which Usha Patel had poured her whole life to be put into receivership, which meant stripping away its revenues on behalf of bankrupt Ciena and its creditors, leaving Usha without a business. In court she wept. Her son told her, "No—I have money, and I'm going to pay an attorney before the judge signs the order." That same day, Usha filed for Chapter 11 protection for her company, Aum Shree of Tampa, in the federal bankruptcy court downtown. The motel was granted a stay. Then things got complicated.

At the first bankruptcy hearing, Usha found that the plaintiff was no longer Ciena, or Business Loan Express, or any other name she'd ever heard since taking out the loan. Her new adversary was HSBC, the second-largest bank in the world—the "indenture trustee" of the mortgage-backed security that included Usha's loan. Suddenly documents were filed showing the mortgage assigned to HSBC, documents without a notary seal, documents without witnesses or dates, documents with suspicious signatures of supposed vice presidents, and Usha's case joined the great foreclosure mess that was sweeping across the country. Unable to force the bank to settle with her, Usha seized the paperwork as her only weapon to save her motel.

For almost two years, Usha fought HSBC and its army of lawyers. She read every document that entered and left her lawyer's office, learning everything she could about bankruptcy and property law. As the docket lengthened, the documents filled up box after box, which she loaded into the back of her Toyota RAV4, where she stored them and drove them between the motel, her house, and her son's computer shop. When her first attorney had to drop the case, she hired another, and when he stepped down, she hired a third, and then a fourth, and Matt Weidner came on as an adviser representing one of Aum Shree's shareholders, but Usha knew the case better than any of them—it was Usha who pushed her lawyers to keep fighting, not the other way around. Eventually her legal bills reached two hundred thousand dollars. Long before that, she ran out of money, and her son and the rest of her family, in the United States, England, and Gujarat, sustained Usha in her fight—because unlike Mike Ross, Sylvia Landis, and Jack Hamersma, Usha Patel was not a native-born American, which is to say, she wasn't alone.

"This is my bread and butter," she said. "My heart and money. If I don't fight I'll be on the street, after twenty years of hard work."

In the weeks before the trial, Usha, Weidner, and her latest attorney stayed up well past midnight at her son's computer shop, night after night, and went over every word of the case. Two days before the trial, HSBC, confronted with the possibility of losing, suddenly agreed to settle. Usha accepted a new schedule of payments, with $150,000 down and $10,000 a month at 6 percent interest. It hardly felt like a victory, but she spent several thousand more dollars celebrating with her many lawyers and other supporters at the oldest restaurant in Tampa.

Fighting a global financial services company to an exhausting draw caused Usha to revise her view of her adopted country. Justice, she concluded, was for rich people, not her. The bankers and lawyers benefited while she went broke. The banks made their money by bullying little people, first trying to intimidate her into surrender, and then, when she fought back, burying her in paperwork, hiring appraisers and inspectors who filed false reports about the condition of her motel, smearing her name. When she talked about HSBC, her nose scrunched up and her mouth turned down and her eyes narrowed in the same look of disgust with which she described the work habits of native-born Americans.

All the same, Usha hadn't reached the same conclusion as Weidner. She didn't believe that America was going down. She still saw a bright future, for her children if not herself. "Right now," she said when her case was over, "God bless America. I believe that."

PART III

JEFF CONNAUGHTON

Early every morning in 2009 and 2010, Connaughton drove his shitty American car down Massachusetts Avenue to his job on Capitol Hill, pissed off. He was angry at Wall Street for more reasons than he could name, bankers, lawyers, accountants—especially for kicking aside the laws and rules and institutional checks and codes of behavior that he had studied in business school and law school and naïvely believed in. He was angry at Washington—both parties—for letting it happen. He was angry at the regulators, the SEC, OTS, OCC, the ratings agencies, and the other enablers who hadn't done their jobs. He was angry on behalf of the American people—not the poor, to be honest, who were always with us, but the people in the middle who had (Clinton's words) worked hard and played by the rules and saw half their 401(k)s disappear in their late fifties just when they thought they'd saved for retirement and now were fucked. He was angry on behalf of his friends from school, men around fifty years old in Tampa, Austin, Madison, suddenly wondering if they could hold on to the house. And finally, he was angry on his own behalf. No one was going to cry for him, but he had lost a lot just when he had a lot for the first time in his life. "Maybe I felt it so much because I had so much personally at stake," he said. "I was just coming into huge bucks as the whole system falls apart. If you can't trust Republicans to protect wealth, what good are they?" He was surprised that more people weren't as pissed off as he was. Connaughton, a moderate Democrat, was in the process of being "radicalized by a stunning realization that our government has been taken over by a financial elite that runs the government for the plutocracy."

When Biden got the vice presidential nomination in the summer of 2008, Connaughton had suddenly found himself on the outer edge of the inner circle of the biggest game in America. It was so big that he didn't give a second thought to reopening the Biden ledger. The jockeying resumed, the nauseating ride of up and down, out and in, but this time much faster, dizzying. At the convention in Denver, he went from exile in a hotel fifteen miles outside town, with no role at all, to vetting the guest list for the Thursday night VIP party in the Biden hotel suite—letting other former staffers know that he could get them in, or keeping out people who pretended to bleed Biden blue. At the party, he waited his turn and received an arm around the shoulder. "We did it, pal," Biden said.

The ride continued in the fall campaign. He was nowhere; then he was helping Kaufman, who served as cochair of the vice presidential pretransition (two months compiling a massive VP bible on every aspect of the job, down to the office space); then, after the election, he was off the transition because lobbyists were summarily banned from the new administration for two years (except those who weren't), and it didn't matter that he'd never asked Joe Biden for a favor. It was a little cynical of Obama to single out Connaughton's particular subclass of the permanent class—most everyone he was hiring had made a ton of corporate money one way or another. Connaughton ended up with a lousy blue ticket to the inauguration, entry to a standing-only viewing area hundreds of yards from the stage, and even that was impossible because of the crowds, so he watched the swearing in of President Obama and Vice President Biden on television with another former Biden staffer at the Hawk 'n' Dove, one of his Capitol Hill haunts from his early days as a Biden guy.

Whenever Connaughton started slipping toward outer darkness, a call on his cell phone brought him back, and it was always Ted Kaufman, his indispensable ally in Washington. When Kaufman inherited the first two years of Biden's next Senate term, he asked Connaughton to be his chief of staff—or rather, he asked another Biden insider to ask Connaughton if he would say yes were the job to be offered, because nobody wanted to be told no at that level in Washington. Connaughton would have preferred a White House job like deputy counsel, but he bore the stigma of a registered lobbyist, and Biden was hardly using his scant influence to get his people into top positions. So he thought about it over a weekend, then informed Jack Quinn that he was going to leave the firm where he'd had his greatest success and made some of his closest friends. Just short of fifty and facing a huge salary cut, Connaughton went back to the Senate.

The financial crisis was the biggest issue in the country, and Connaughton and Kaufman saw it in similar terms. First, it represented a breakdown of the legal system. How else, other than unchecked fraud, could those banks have been "technically insolvent," with only a handful of insiders knowing the truth? But there were deeper causes—the dismantling of the rules that had kept banking stable for half a century. Connaughton saw Kaufman—seventy years old, with a musty MBA from Wharton—as Rip Van Winkle, waking up in the age of "synthetic collateralized debt obligations" and "naked credit default swaps." What the hell happened to Glass-Steagall, which maintained a wall between commercial and investment banking? (Passed by Congress in 1933, repealed by Congress in 1999, bipartisan vote, Clinton's signature.) What about the "uptick rule," which required investors to wait until a stock rose in price before selling it short? (Instated by the SEC in 1938, abolished by the SEC in 2007.) It was easy to overlook this denuded free-market landscape during the long boom years—Connaughton had done just that—but when the storms blew in and there were no walls to keep out the gale or trees to hold down the eroded earth, everyone howled.

Kaufman was going to be a senator for just two years. No election hung over his every move like a guillotine, so he didn't have to start half his mornings with a fundraising breakfast on K Street. Connaughton also felt liberated: he'd already cashed in once and didn't have to take calls from lobbyists while calculating his future employment prospects. They both had the luxury to go after Wall Street without a thought for the repercussions. "I'd be doing the same thing if I were running for reelection," Kaufman told the press, but Connaughton had been in Washington too long to believe it. This was their moment, the first year of the Obama presidency, with the economy hemorrhaging hundreds of thousands of jobs.

The previous October, in the last month of the campaign, Connaughton had picked up signs from Kaufman that the Obama team wanted to bring Robert Rubin on as Treasury secretary. "Don't you realize that half the country wants to hang Bob Rubin?" Connaughton asked when Kaufman expressed enthusiasm at the prospect. Kaufman would later say, "It was like a car had broken down and we needed a mechanic." Obama, inexperienced in government and a novice in finance, seemed to believe that Rubin and his followers were the only competent repairmen available.

No more proof was needed that the establishment (the one Clinton had invoked that night in his private study) would emerge from the disaster in fine shape. The establishment could fail and fail and still survive, even thrive. It was rigged to win, like a casino, and once you were on the inside you had to do something dramatic to lose your standing, like write a scathing op-ed (and even then you'd get a pass for expressing public-spirited views unless you actually named names). Rubin was no longer viable for Treasury, but his people were practically the only candidates under consideration by Obama, who, after all, had fought his way into the establishment from farther back than any of them. Michael Froman, Rubin's chief of staff under Clinton, later a managing director at Citigroup, introduced Rubin to Obama, and he continued working at the bank while serving on Obama's transition as personnel director, then collected a $2.25 million bonus before joining the administration. Jacob Lew, another Citigroup executive, became deputy secretary of state with a $900,000 bonus in his pocket. Mark Patterson, a Goldman Sachs lobbyist, was hired as chief of staff at Treasury despite the lobbying ban. Timothy Geithner, a Rubin protégé and the architect of the bailouts, was appointed Treasury secretary and survived the revelation that he had flagrantly underpaid taxes to the agency he was going to lead. Larry Summers, whose meaty fingerprints were all over the pro-bank policies of the late nineties, and who earned millions in speaking fees from various future bailout recipients, became the leading economic adviser at the Obama White House. Even Rahm Emanuel, Obama's chief of staff, a career public servant, had made a cool $16.5 million at a Chicago investment bank in the thirty months he spent between government jobs. All at the top of their field, all brilliant and educated to within an inch of their lives, all Democrats, all implicated in an epic failure—now hired to sort out the ruins. How could they not see things the way of the bankers with whom they'd studied and worked and ate and drunk and gotten rich? Social promotion and conflict of interest were built into the soul of the meritocracy. The Blob was unkillable.

Connaughton watched all this with unease. He knew something about revolving doors and mutual favors and the unconscious biases of the powerful. He, too, had steeped in these worlds throughout his career— investment banking, Congress, the White House, lobbying. Yet the financial crisis was a seismic event, causing substantial pain to millions of people, and for once an angry public was paying attention. Now was the time for Washington to take on Wall Street.

To have any impact, a senator had to choose just a few issues. He didn't have room in his schedule, or his head, for more. When they both worked for Biden, and Connaughton wanted to bring something new to the senator's attention, Kaufman used to say, "Jeff, every time you want to put something into the boat, you have to take something out of the boat." From the outset Kaufman, who wasn't even a member of the Banking Committee, focused on two things: fraud, and the problem of "too big to fail." He cowrote a bill that authorized $340 million for hiring more FBI agents and funding federal prosecutors to go after the fraudsters—not just petty mortgage originators in Long Beach and Tampa, but top Wall Street executives who had concealed the damage until the whole edifice collapsed. It was the Justice Department's job to decide who should be investigated, but presumably people like Lehman's Dick Fuld and AIG's Joseph Cassano and Merrill's Stanley O'Neal and, who knew, maybe Goldman's Lloyd Blankfein himself. When the fraud enforcement bill sailed through in May, and Kaufman (a mere freshman) was invited to join the president onstage at the White House signing ceremony, he and Connaughton thought they were getting somewhere.

In September, Kaufman and Connaughton asked for a meeting with one of Attorney General Eric Holder's deputies, Lanny Breuer, the assistant attorney general for the criminal division. (He and Connaughton went back a decade, when they briefly overlapped at Covington & Burling on Connaughton's way out of the White House counsel's office and Breuer's way in.) The pursuit of financial fraud hadn't turned up a thing, and Kaufman wanted to make sure that the Justice Department was on the case and using the money. He planned to hold an oversight hearing to make sure. They met in Kaufman's office on the third floor of the Russell Building. Breuer explained that he was operating under a lot of constraints, including a shortage of laptops. He said that he depended on the "pipeline" of FBI investigators from around the country to bring cases.

Connaughton saw his opening. "Lanny, you need to go down into your pipeline and make sure the FBI and U.S. attorney's offices are making this a top priority. Shake your pipeline hard and get it to bring you cases— don't just sit back and wait." Complex fraud cases were too hard to make in the normal course of an overworked federal prosecutor's business. The perpetrators were sophisticated at erasing the traces and constructing their defense even as they committed their crimes, abetted by well-paid lawyers and accountants, later blizzarding investigators with irrelevant paperwork. Instead, something like a task force should be set up to target each institution under suspicion, devote a year or two to the investigation, take the time to learn what to look for, examine every e-mail and IM. Connaughton referred back to his shared history with Breuer under Clinton: "You need to be like Ken Starr. You need to target some of these guys like they were drug kingpins, just like Starr targeted Clinton, and squeeze every junior person around them until you can get one to flip."

The meeting left him with the distinct sense that there was no great urgency at Justice.

Kaufman's oversight hearing came in December. Breuer sat at the witness table, joined by senior officials at the SEC and the FBI. They all said that they were on the case, but they needed insiders who could testify about motive and intent. Just give us time.

Connaughton wanted to believe them. But 2009 slipped into 2010, and nothing happened.

In mid-January 2010, Connaughton and Kaufman traveled to New York to meet Paul Volcker, the aging giant of the Federal Reserve. Volcker had crushed inflation under Carter and Reagan by driving up interest rates so high that he induced a major recession. The bankers loved him for it, and the farmers and construction workers blocked traffic in Washington to denounce him. But Volcker was an eccentric member of the establishment. He lived at the heart of the overlapping worlds of political and financial elites, yet he had become such a scalding critic of Wall Street—the too-clever engineering, the over-the-top pay—that he was now an internal dissident, officially respected, unofficially distrusted. He once told a group of executives, "The most important financial innovation that I have seen the past twenty years is the automatic teller machine . . . I have found very little evidence that vast amounts of innovation in financial markets in recent years have had a visible effect on the productivity of the economy. Maybe you can show me that I am wrong. All I know is that the economy was rising very nicely in the 1950s and 1960s without all of these innovations. Indeed, it was quite good in the 1980s without credit default swaps and without securitization and without CDOs."

Volcker made the perfect foil for Obama: he could be used to appease the reformers and give cover with the establishment. The president appointed Volcker to lead his economic advisory group, without taking the advice seriously. Volcker's main proposal—to ban banks from setting up hedge funds or private equity funds and from trading for their own accounts with depositors' money—was a half step back toward Glass-Steagall. After six months, nothing had come of it.

Volcker sat down in his midtown conference room with the visitors from Washington and said, "You know, just about whatever anyone proposes, no matter what it is, the banks will come out and claim that it will restrict credit and harm the economy." Long pause from the little round face at the top of the long body, eyes magnified by glasses, cagey creases running down either side of the mouth. "It's all bullshit."

Kaufman laughed. He admitted that his ambition was to restore Glass-Steagall fully.

"I won't stand in the way of someone who wants to do something more dramatic," Volcker said.

The next week, Obama announced his support for what he called the Volcker Rule. He was trying to jolt his presidency out of its lowest moment: Scott Brown had just been elected to Ted Kennedy's Senate seat, denying the Democrats their ability to defeat the Republican filibusters that now dogged every last move the majority tried to make on the Senate floor. The president's health care bill appeared to be doomed. And more Americans were unemployed than at any time since the Depression.

Connaughton thought the timing of the health bill was bad. For the better part of a year it had been sucking up all the air in Washington, and exactly what did it have to do with unemployment and the financial crisis? Maybe it was the southerner in him, but he doubted Washington's ability to write a multi-thousand-page bill that could fix something as vast and complex as the health care system while the country was falling apart. He would sit in on the Friday morning meetings of the Democratic chiefs of staff in the Hart Building conference room, and listen to presidential aides enthuse about the "optics" of White House health care meetings, the "messaging" campaign, how well phrases like *cost cutting* had poll-tested—and there were weeks when the word *economy* wasn't spoken once. But on health care Kaufman just followed the Democratic leadership. What Connaughton cared about was Wall Street, and on that issue he and Kaufman went their own way.

The senator in charge of the Wall Street reform bill was Chris Dodd, chairman of the Banking Committee. Connaughton had disliked Dodd ever since 1995, when Connaughton had urged Clinton to fight the corporations on the securities litigation bill (his first taste of taking on Wall Street) and Dodd had been the one fighting back. Having raised tens of millions of dollars in campaign money from Wall Street (almost a million dollars in 2007–2008), Dodd was so deeply in its debt that many of his constituents seemed to hold him personally responsible for the financial crisis. After it emerged that he had received a sweetheart mortgage from Countrywide and approved millions of dollars in bonuses from the bailout fund for executives at AIG, voters in Connecticut expressed outrage. Dodd got the message and announced that he would retire at the end of 2010.

That should have liberated him to go after Wall Street with Kaufman, but Connaughton saw it the other way around. If Dodd had to face the voters again, he would have felt pressured to shepherd through a tough bill. Instead, he was free to prepare for life after the Senate, where the power of money would still hang over his career. You had to think really hard before you took on the establishment, because there were a lot of ways to build a very comfortable life if you went with the flow (like become the top lobbyist for the movie industry, which was what Dodd would go on to do), but standing against the establishment closed off a big part of America that otherwise would have made room for you. You were in or you were out.

Dodd spent the entire winter negotiating with the Republicans behind the closed doors of the Banking Committee, making concessions, insisting that he wanted a bipartisan bill. But he never got anywhere—Richard Shelby of Alabama wouldn't play ball, and Bob Corker of Tennessee didn't have the clout. The Volcker Rule became expendable, Glass-Steagall was nowhere in sight. As the months dragged on, Connaughton began to suspect that Dodd was negotiating with himself, using the Republicans and the ideal of bipartisanship as a cover to weaken financial reform and end up with a bill Wall Street could live with. Connaughton began to understand the supreme power of the committee chair to decide what made it into a bill and what did not, whether amendments would be added in committee or on the floor, which would survive and which would die. Since his boss didn't sit on the committee, Connaughton had little insight into the state of play.

One day, he called up Jack Quinn at his old firm. "I can't get to the

Banking Committee," Connaughton said. "I assume you guys are having a hard time getting information about the bill?"

"I just spent forty-five minutes with Chris Dodd yesterday," Quinn told him. Along with the CEO of an insurance company he represented, Quinn had sat down with Dodd and found out exactly what was going on. Connaughton, the key deputy of a senator with a keen interest in financial reform, was clueless. He wrote to another chief of staff, "I came into government to effect change on Wall Street, and now I realize the profession I just left is having more input on the bill than I'm having from inside the Senate." The other chief wrote back, "That's really sad."

Connaughton cultivated a few reporters who agreed to protect his anonymity, and, as "a senior Senate aide," he began to go after Dodd in the press. "My understanding is that Dodd is moving forward with a bill that includes concessions," he told CNBC. "I thought you made concessions to gain someone's support. After four months of negotiations, Dodd has made concessions to get Republicans to *consider* it. I truly don't get it." The same senior Senate aide told *Newsweek*, "One can only hope the president realizes what's at stake."

Kaufman decided to take his case to the Senate floor. With Connaughton and another aide, he drafted a series of speeches on Wall Street excesses, the financial crisis, and the failure to punish any of the culprits.

When a senator stood at his desk and read the speech that a staffer had just placed on the mahogany lectern next to a glass of water, no one was listening. The presiding officer of the Senate, some freshman of the majority party, was perched up in the raised chair, reading his *New York Times* or scrolling through her BlackBerry. Otherwise, the senator gave his speech to an empty chamber. Halfway through, the next senator with floor rights might appear through the double doors at the back of the room and walk to his desk, where he would shuffle through a prepared text that he hadn't laid eyes on until that minute. No reporters listened and took notes in the press gallery above the presiding officer's chair—there were just the unmanned C-SPAN cameras programmed to swivel and focus in tight on the speaker, cutting out the rows and rows of empty desks. It was so rare for two senators actually to listen to each other's arguments and debate them that once, when Jeff Merkley, a freshman from Oregon, happened to enter the chamber while a Democrat and Republican were engaged in a lonely back-and-forth, he stopped and thought, "Wow, that's unusual—there's a conversation occurring in which they're making point and counterpoint and challenging each other." Thus the world's greatest deliberative body went about the business of the people in the year 2010.

Connaughton knew that no one would hear the speeches Kaufman gave, so they were written in the form of long, detailed essays, full of historical explanations and hard polemics, in the hope that they would be quoted on the Internet by allies—Arianna Huffington, the MIT economist and blogger Simon Johnson—and circulated widely.

On March 11, Kaufman demanded of the empty chamber, "Given the high costs of our policy and regulatory failures, as well as the reckless behavior on Wall Street, why should those of us who propose going back to the proven statutory and regulatory ideas of the past bear the burden of proof?" He went on, "The burden of proof should be upon those who would only tinker at the edges of our current system of financial regulation. After a crisis of this magnitude, it amazes me that some of our reform proposals effectively maintain the status quo in so many critical areas." He added that he didn't trust the regulators to do a better job of enforcing rules the next time a bank started to implode. Congress had to do the job for them, by writing a bill with clear and simple lines. Dodd's bill wouldn't solve the problem of too big to fail. "We need to break up these institutions *before* they fail, not stand by with a plan waiting to catch them when they do fail."

On March 15, after the release of the bankruptcy examiner's report on Lehman Brothers, which strongly suggested that fraud had led to the firm's demise, Kaufman took to the floor again. Sounding like Joe Biden in 1985, he said, "At the end of the day, this is a test of whether we have one justice system in this country or two. If we don't treat a Wall Street firm that defrauded investors of millions of dollars the same way we treat someone who stole five hundred dollars from a cash register, then how can we expect our citizens to have faith in the rule of law?"

On March 22, the bill made it out of Dodd's Banking Committee. There was a pale version of the Volcker Rule, weak regulation of derivatives, and no clear lines about how much liability banks could sustain. Connaughton and Kaufman drafted a biting critique.

"This is really going to piss off Dodd and the administration," Connaughton warned him.

"I'm speaking to the ages," Kaufman said.

The speeches began to be noticed. The *News Journal* in Wilmington covered them on its front page and quoted them favorably in its editorials, *Time* magazine profiled Kaufman, and Huffington praised him. Dodd was sufficiently annoyed to call from Central America, where he was leading a congressional delegation, and tell Kaufman, "Stop saying bad things about my bill." Connaughton spoke to Dodd's Banking Committee staff director, who reassured him: "Don't worry about being critical. Chris will be the one who gets to take the victory lap in the end."

It was true. For starters, Dodd had the other committee chairmen on his side. He also had the president's top advisers. In early April, Larry Summers paid a visit to Kaufman's office and explained why the senator was wrong to want to break up the biggest banks. Doing so would make America less competitive in the global financial race, and large banks would actually be less likely to fail than small ones. Kaufman was determined not to be steamrolled and kept interrupting Summers's interruptions with a friendly pat on the arm, citing Alan Greenspan to rebut Summers's claims. A month later, it was Geithner's turn. Connaughton chatted with the Treasury secretary while they waited outside Kaufman's door and found him to be witty and light on his feet. When they entered Kaufman's office, Connaughton told his boss, "I've patted him down—he's clean." Geithner was more conciliatory than Summers, explaining that the big banks would shrink anyway under new international capital requirements. Kaufman said that regulations had failed in the past, and the only foolproof way to prevent another bailout was to limit the size of the banks. In the end, they agreed to disagree.

Finally, Dodd had the White House on his side—he had the president. Connaughton had come back to the Senate imagining that Biden would be their key ally, and he urged Kaufman to pick up the phone and ask his old friend to push Justice about the lack of high-level prosecutions, push Treasury to get serious about financial reform. As always, Kaufman was protective of Biden. Wall Street wasn't Biden's issue—it would have taken up half the boat, and the boat was already full with Iraq, the stimulus, and the middle class. Connaughton couldn't get over the strangeness: their former boss held down the second-highest position in the country, a few steps from the Oval Office, and they couldn't do a damn thing about Wall Street. The Republicans were a lost cause, so Connaughton saved most of his bitterness for his own team. "You might as well be beholden to the permanent class," he said, "if you're going to pull your punches at a moment of national crisis."

In late April, Kaufman and Sherrod Brown of Ohio introduced an amendment to Dodd's bill that would limit the nondeposit liabilities of banks to 2 percent of gross domestic product. In effect, Brown-Kaufman would force banks that grew beyond a certain size to be broken up. The two senators took to the floor and went back and forth without a script. Spectacles perched on the end of his nose, Kaufman towered over his desk and chopped the air and his trembling voice declaimed, "In 1933 we made a decision that helped us through three generations. Why are we not passing legislation that'll work over the next two or three generations? Something that'll work whether we get a president who believes in the fact that we should have free markets or not? Whether we have a good regulator or a bad regulator? Why should not the Senate of the United States do its job?"

Connaughton was watching on TV in their Russell office, and his mind wandered back down the years and he said to no one in particular, "He's like Biden." Later, Connaughton sent Kaufman a note: "There's nothing more honorable than standing up as the sole dissenting voice on a matter of principle."

Those weeks in the winter and spring of 2010 were the most intense of Connaughton's working life. He would get into the office by seven-thirty and keep going even after he returned home at night, opening his laptop and reading till midnight. He spent one whole weekend devouring the two-thousand-page Lehman bankruptcy examiner's report and then drafting Kaufman's speech on it. It was as if an old idea of politics that somewhere along the way had eluded him now returned—the years of drift and frustration, the fundraising breakfasts and happy hours, the slow immersion in compromise, all of it faded away and he was back where he had started in Tuscaloosa, dedicating himself to the noblest calling of all.

But that had been three decades ago: years in which Washington was captured—*captured*—by the money power. He had been captured as well, and until now he hadn't fully grasped how much the "influence industry"—the lobbying, the media campaigns, the grasstops, the revolving door—had transformed Washington. "When you go back into government, you realize how dramatically asymmetrical it has become with the public interest. Virtually no one walks in your door trying to educate you about the public's argument." He had come to see himself as Jack Burden, the narrator of *All the King's Men*—tainted and disillusioned by politics.

Human nature remained constant, but when the money got so blown out of proportion, it corrupted human behavior in a thousand little ways. "Washington changed me," he said. "And if it changed me, it must have changed a lot of other people, too."

There were three thousand lobbyists swarming Capitol Hill, urging Congress not to do anything fundamental about the wreckage the banks had made. Who stood on the other side? An angry but distracted public that didn't know how to use the levers of power. A handful of bloggers with influence among the persuaded. Back in the eighties, a coalition of labor unions and trial lawyers and consumer advocates could put up a fight, but by 2010 they were largely spent. An organization called Americans for Financial Reform was pushing for a new consumer agency, but Connaughton had to call *them* and say, "Where are you guys? I don't feel your presence on the Hill." If the Brown-Kaufman amendment had been a boon to corporate America, Connaughton would have been working with a team of lobbyists, strategists, and industry leaders to build massive pressure on the Hill. Instead, he was practically on his own.

Kaufman and Connaughton decided to address the fragility of the stock market. Though it hadn't caused the financial crisis, the market remained the point of entry for millions of Americans into the world of finance, and it had taken their investments down with it. Like credit, stocks were no longer what they had been when Connaughton was in business school and on Wall Street. Instead of a few exchanges where men in blue coats waved trade orders and shouted to be heard on the floor, the stock market had become a computerized casino, with more than fifty venues around the country, dominated by high-frequency traders—the sharks at the poker table—using advanced algorithms to make thousands of trades a second and profit from tiny fluctuations in stock prices. Connaughton spent months researching these new markets and was stunned by the opacity of the electronic labyrinth. He was a pretty sophisticated investor, but he could no longer say what happened to the trade orders he placed— and none of the insiders seemed able to explain it, either. The ordinary investor was at an immense disadvantage, the market vulnerable to extreme volatility, and the SEC years behind in monitoring it.

Kaufman began pushing the SEC to improve its oversight of high-frequency trading, and at first Connaughton thought they were getting somewhere. Mary Schapiro, Obama's choice to lead the commission, said that she shared Kaufman's concerns and the SEC would review the structure of equity markets. At one meeting, an official at the commission told Connaughton, "Wow, it's great to hear from someone who isn't from the industry." No one walked through the commission's doors on F Street, next to Union Station, other than finance people with a gripe about a regulation. But as Wall Street aggressively fought any but the smallest changes, inertia set in at the SEC, and, once again, nothing happened.

May 6, 2010, was the day when Connaughton's second life in government began to end. In the early afternoon, the stock market suddenly plummeted seven hundred points in eight minutes before reversing itself, with the momentary disappearance of almost a trillion dollars in wealth. The flash crash, as it came to be called, was caused by the kind of automated trading that Kaufman had warned about. A few hours later, Kaufman was sitting in the presiding officer's chair when Mark Warner, the Virginia Democrat, explained to the Senate what had just happened. "I have become a believer," he said, and invited Kaufman to come down to the floor and essentially say to the world, "I told you so"—which Kaufman did. Then he spoke up one more time for his amendment, for a return to the rules and limits of the Glass-Steagall era.

The same afternoon, Chris Dodd, after refusing for weeks to allow Brown-Kaufman to come up, suddenly cleared the way for a snap vote that night. The amendment had been picking up momentum in the press and on Capitol Hill, with even a few Republican senators announcing their support, including Richard Shelby of Alabama, the ranking member of the Banking Committee. It was time to head off Brown-Kaufman.

Shortly before the vote, Dianne Feinstein of California, one of the wealthiest members of the Senate, asked Richard Durbin of Illinois, "What's this amendment about?"

"Breaking up the banks."

Feinstein was taken aback. "This is still America, isn't it?"

Just after nine in the evening, the amendment went down, 61–33.

After the result was announced, Dodd took the floor and told the Senate that it was Richard Shelby's birthday. Around four in the afternoon, Dodd said, the Banking Committee had brought out a cake and shared it. "So we celebrated in the midst of the debate. It's important that people in the country know we can have very strong differences, but we also can work together. While we disagree with one another on substantive issues, we can enjoy each other's company on a personal level, a civil level." And Senator Dodd wished Senator Shelby a very happy birthday.

Later that night, Kaufman returned to his office in Russell. Connaughton asked him what he should put into a press release. Kaufman could muster only three words: "I am disappointed." They had known it was doomed, but the size of their defeat was devastating. In the span of a few hours, they had been vindicated by the flash crash, then thoroughly whipped on too big to fail. The southerner in Connaughton, the romantic believer in lost causes, told the staff, "Some things are worth fighting for."

On May 21, the Dodd bill passed the Senate, and on July 21, President Obama signed the Dodd-Frank Wall Street Reform and Consumer Protection Act into law. The Volcker Rule was now a ghost of itself, with the details left to regulators. Kaufman at one point decided that the bill was too weak to earn his support, but in the end he voted with his party.

The main lobbying group in favor of a strong bill, Americans for Financial Reform, threw a party and invited Kaufman's staff to celebrate. The new law, after all, had created a federal agency called the Consumer Financial Protection Bureau—a place at the table for the American public—which was the piece of Dodd-Frank that Connaughton also liked. The event was held in a shabby rented theater far from downtown, and the spread included white bread, baloney, and Doritos. Connaughton thought back to all the corporate events he'd attended in plush downtown conference rooms, with shrimp and roast beef. He was happy to be here.

There were four months left in Kaufman's abbreviated Senate term, but the big fights were over. Most of them had been lost, or left in a limbo that was worse than losing. For his part, Connaughton would have tossed away all of Dodd-Frank, the Volcker Rule, and everything else for the simple act of enforcing the law. One fastball at Wall Street's chin, a few top executives going to jail, would have had more effect than all the new regulations combined.

Kaufman, who was going to take over from Elizabeth Warren as the head of the congressional panel overseeing the bailout fund, asked Connaughton what he wanted to do next. Find a job in the administration? Lead a Washington nonprofit for financial reform?

Connaughton imagined himself as an employee of the Interior Department, taking his lunch break out on C Street SW and going up to the

hot dog vendor: "You got any sauerkraut today, Harvey?" The idea of joining a nonprofit was just as dismal. It would be one thing if the Republicans were in power, but the guys in the White House were supposed to
be on his team. If he was going to take on the establishment, he didn't see
the point of doing it in Obama-Biden's Washington. One day in late August, he was channel flipping when Glenn Beck came on, telling an immense crowd on the Mall that change didn't come from Washington,
it came from real people in real places around the country. Beck was an
asshole, but Arianna Huffington wrote the same thing in a column two
days later. They were right. Connaughton felt a sneaking sympathy with
the Tea Party.

He could always go back to Quinn Gillespie, but if he spent another
day there it was going to be on his tombstone. Instead, the years with
Kaufman, the proudest of his life, could be the final stamp on his Washington career. He was approaching fifty-one, and he was tired of being someone's number two. If he stuck around, doing no matter what, he would
have to maintain the fiction that he was a Biden guy and perhaps again be
humiliated by the man to whom he'd been loyal for a quarter century.
"Honestly and painfully," Connaughton said, "with Biden as vice president I was tired of being a fraud. I don't care how much money it means,
I don't care how many people want to buy me drinks, I'm just not going to
do it. It would have been a look-in-the-mirror kind of thing." The more he
thought about it, the more it made sense: the only thing to do was leave
Washington.

He sold his Georgetown townhouse in a single September day, and
closed on November 1. The next day was Election Day. The Republicans
retook the House, and whatever chance of holding the banks and the
bankers accountable for the last crisis and so preventing the next one was
gone. That morning, Connaughton took the train to New York. He had
been asked to fill in for another Senate aide on a panel at the New York
Federal Reserve Bank, in lower Manhattan. His topic was "Financial Crisis and Financial Crimes." There were three hundred people in the sixth-
floor auditorium—Wall Street executives, regulators, lawyers from the
district attorney's office. He tried to distill two years of work into fifteen
minutes.

"First, was there fraud at the heart of the financial crisis?" Connaughton began. "Second, has the law enforcement response so far achieved
effective levels of deterrence against financial fraud? Third, are federal

law enforcement agencies sufficiently capable of detecting fraud and manipulation, particularly in markets that are increasingly complex? And finally, should Wall Street itself care about all this?"

He paused.

"In short, my answers would be yes, no, no, and yes."

He reviewed the Justice Department's failure to bring any high-level prosecutions, in spite of voluminous evidence turned up by the Lehman bankruptcy examiner and the Senate's Permanent Subcommittee on Investigations. He talked about the SEC's paralysis in the face of manipulation of the stock market by high-frequency traders. The auditorium was silent, the audience paying attention.

"Senator Kaufman's term, and my time as a Senate staffer, ends in twelve days," he said in conclusion, "but this is not a fight for one senator to wage. These are questions that go to the foundations of the rule of law and America's future economic success. For the common good, I hope you answer them well."

Outside, he stood at the corner of Nassau and Wall Streets, exhilarated. He had just blown himself up in the heart of American finance. He would never again be a member of the permanent class.

Connaughton's Senate job ended on November 15. He flew to Costa Rica and immediately went out for an eight-hour hike. When he came back to his hotel room, he turned on the shower and got in without taking off his clothes, standing under the stream and letting it soak him and soak him until he felt clean.

2010

INCOME GAP WIDENS . . . **TEA PARTY LIGHTS FUSE FOR REBELLION ON RIGHT** . . . **EXCLUSIVE DETAILS: SNOOKI DUMPED EMILIO— BELIEVES HE WAS USING HER TO GET FAMOUS** . . . @SenJohnMcCain: @Sn00ki u r right, I would never tax your tanning bed! Pres Obama's tax/spend policy is quite The Situation. But I do rec wearing sunscreen! . . . If you don't have money, you cling to your freedoms all the more angrily. Even if smoking kills you, even if you can't afford to feed your kids, even if your kids are getting shot down by maniacs with assault rifles. You may be poor, but the one thing nobody can take away from you is the freedom to fuck up your life. . . . . **IT'S THE LAW OF THE LAND: HEALTH OVERHAUL SIGNED** . . . **BANKS PREPARE FOR BIG BONUSES, AND PUBLIC WRATH** Goldman Sachs is expected to pay its employees an average of about $595,000 apiece for 2009, one of the most profitable years in its 141-year history. . . . **JUSTIN BIEBER FEVER HITS MIAMI** . . . **CHINA PASSES JAPAN AS SECOND-LARGEST ECONOMY** . . . **BOTH PARTIES SEEK WAYS TO CHANNEL POPULIST IRE** . . . I'm sure there will be times in the months ahead when you're staying up late cramming for a test, or dragging yourselves out of bed on a rainy morning, and wondering if it's all worth it. Let me tell you, there is no question about it. . . . you don't take the name Barack to identify with America. You take the name Barack to identify with what? Your heritage? The heritage, maybe, of your father in Kenya, who is a radical? Is—really? . . . **99 WEEKS LATER, JOBLESS HAVE ONLY DESPERATION** . . . I'm not a witch. I'm nothing you've heard. I'm you. None of us are perfect, but none of us can be happy with what we see all around us: politicians who. . . . Khloe Kardashian forgot to get a bikini wax before her husband, Lamar Odom, came to town, so her sister Kourtney—who has been waxing herself for years—offered to do the job. The story ended with a badly burned vagina. . . . **OBAMA SIGNS OVERHAUL OF FINANCIAL SYSTEM** . . . **REPUBLICANS WIN HOUSE OF REPRESENTATIVES WITH VICTORIES NATIONWIDE** . . . *I never thought about love when I thought about home / I still owe money to the money to the money I owe / The floors are falling out from everybody I know*

CITIZEN JOURNALIST: ANDREW BREITBART

In February 1969—when the *CBS Evening News* with Walter Cronkite, the most trusted man in America, was watched by twenty million viewers, or one in six households—a three-week-old baby boy of Irish descent was adopted in Los Angeles by a Jewish steakhouse owner and his banker wife, Gerald and Arlene Breitbart, and given the name Andrew.

When Andrew was two, *The New York Times* and *The Washington Post* published the Pentagon Papers, defying threats by the Nixon White House. The next year, Bob Woodward and Carl Bernstein were assigned by the *Post* to cover a break-in at Democratic National Committee headquarters in Washington. Andrew's toddler years coincided with the golden age of Old Media.

The Breitbarts were upper-middle-class Republicans (four bedrooms, a pool, a canyon view) living in rich, liberal Brentwood. Andrew grew up on American pop culture, British new wave, and Hollywood celebrity. "Which famous people come into the restaurant?" he would ask his father (the Reagans, Broderick Crawford, Shirley Jones and the Cassidy family, lots of other celebs). Andrew took tennis lessons from the top pro in Malibu and once spent fifteen unforgettable minutes looking for the instructor with Farrah Fawcett.

Andrew was eleven when the Cable News Network went on the air in 1980. He was thirteen when *The McLaughlin Group* and *Crossfire* introduced yelling heads to news analysis. From early on Andrew was a breaking-news junkie. At the Brentwood School he made up for being neither famous nor rich by cutting up in class and inventing droll quotations for stories in the *Brentwood Eagle* about high school social life. To keep up with his friends, he had to take a job delivering pizzas and pocketed big tips from the likes of Judge Reinhold. Basically, he was "the ultimate Generation X slacker," Breitbart later wrote, "not particularly political, and, in retrospect, a default liberal. I thought that going to four movies a week, knowing the network television grid, and spending hours at Tower Records were my American birthright."

In 1987—the year that the Federal Communications Commission voted 4–0 to repeal its own Fairness Doctrine, which had been in effect since 1949 and required licensees of the public airwaves to present important issues in an honest and equitable manner (a vote that paved the way the following year for a Sacramento radio host named Rush Limbaugh to syndicate his conservative talk show nationally)—Breitbart entered Tulane. He spent his four years in New Orleans partying with a group of wealthy, hilarious, debauched friends, drinking himself into oblivion, and betting his parents' money on football games and backgammon.

In his weakened state, Breitbart was exposed to the pernicious influence of his American Studies professors and their reading lists, which included Foucault, Horkheimer, Adorno, and Marcuse rather than Emerson and Twain. Fortunately, he was too drunk to be thoroughly indoctrinated in critical theory, but the prevailing philosophy of moral relativism inevitably eroded his personal standards. It wasn't such a big step from the Frankfurt School to getting shitfaced nightly.

Breitbart stumbled through graduation and returned home to L.A., where his parents cut off his stipend, giving him the shock of his life. He started waiting tables near Venice Beach. Hard work was fulfilling. "My values were returning from exile."

In the fall of 1991, he tuned in to the Clarence Thomas hearings, fully expecting to side with Anita Hill and the Democrats. Instead, he was outraged that porn rentals and a stray comment about a stray pubic hair on a can of Coke were being used to destroy an honorable man because he was conservative and black—with supposedly neutral journalists leading the mob. Breitbart's eyes began to open, and hatred was born in his fun-loving soul. He would never forgive the mainstream media.

Several more years passed before Andrew Breitbart found his mission in life. In 1992—the year Warren Buffett, a major investor in the Washington Post Company, warned that "the economic strength of once-mighty media enterprises continues to erode as retailing patterns change and advertising and entertainment choices proliferate"—Breitbart got a job delivering scripts around Hollywood. He preferred listening to FM radio in his Saab convertible to kissing ass in the outer offices of Michael Ovitz or going to parties where people said, "I work in the clothing room at *Mad*

About You." But when grunge took over the alternative rock stations ("Who were these whiny, suicidal freaks?"), he switched in disgust to the AM dial. There, talk radio was waiting for him.

He found that he would do anything to listen to Howard Stern and Jim Rome. He put on a Walkman and kept listening after getting out of his car to make his script deliveries. But he was still enough of an unthinking liberal that, upon seeing Limbaugh's book *The Way Things Ought to Be* on the coffee table of his girlfriend's father, a TV actor named Orson Bean, he scoffed.

"Have you listened to Rush?" Breitbart's future father-in-law asked.

"Yeah, he's a Nazi or something."

"Are you sure you've listened to him?"

Orson Bean, a game show regular from the sixties, was the seventh most frequent guest on *The Tonight Show*—his opinion counted. And after tuning in to Limbaugh over months during the 1992 campaign, Breitbart began to regard El Rushbo as his true professor. "I marveled at how he could take a breaking news story and offer an entertaining and clear analysis that was like nothing I had ever seen on television." The hidden structure of things was becoming clear.

That same year, a friend from high school who was worried that Breitbart was adrift paid a visit to his apartment and told him, "I've seen your future and it's the Internet."

Breitbart replied, "What's the Internet?"

One night in 1994, he vowed not to leave his room until he was connected. It took a rotisserie chicken, a six-pack of Pilsner Urquell, and several hours of sweaty effort with a primitive modem of that time, but at last he heard the crackle of a connection and suddenly Andrew Breitbart was linked to the Internet, the one place beyond the reach of the Democrat-Media Complex where you could say and think and be anything, and he was born again.

It wasn't long afterward that Breitbart found a one-man news digest called the Drudge Report—a mishmash of politics, Hollywood gossip, and extreme weather reports. He was hooked, and when Drudge began exposing Clinton sex scandals that the media wouldn't touch, Breitbart knew what he wanted to do with his life. Drudge and the Internet rescued him from the cynical irony of his generation and showed him the power of one individual to expose the corruption of the Complex. Breitbart was so awed that he sent an e-mail to the secretive Matt Drudge:

"Are you fifty people? A hundred people? Is there a building?" Drudge introduced him to a rich Greek-born L.A. divorcee and author named Arianna Huffington, who wanted to do the same kind of awesome Web-based muckraking as Drudge. In the summer of 1997—a year after MSNBC and Fox News launched—Breitbart was invited to her Brentwood mansion, and over spanakopitas and iced tea Arianna offered him a job. Pretty soon she couldn't get him to go home.

The Internet and the conservative movement fused together in Breitbart's brain. He read Camille Paglia on academic politics and saw his whole life as an illustration of the Complex's totalitarian power. He'd been living behind enemy lines ever since birth: the liberal fascism of the Hollywood elite, the left-wing bias of the mainstream media, the Nazi-fleeing German philosophers of his Tulane syllabi who had settled in L.A. and taken over higher education in order to destroy the coolest lifestyle in history and impose their Kurt Cobain–like depressive nihilistic Marxism. The left knew what the right ignored: New York, Hollywood, and college campuses mattered more than Washington. The political war was all about culture. A barely employed, autodidactic Gen-X convert with an ADD diagnosis and an Internet addiction was uniquely well armed to fight it.

For the next eight years Breitbart worked with Arianna and Drudge. He helped Arianna with her biggest coup, getting a Clinton crony who had fabricated his war record disinterred from Arlington National Cemetery. Who needed *The New York Times*? "We were all doing more from Los Angeles with minimal resources than the mainstream media were doing from Washington, D.C., with hundreds of reporters."

The terrain Breitbart sauntered onto was diminishing, crumbling, wide open to him. Pillars of the Old Media were turning to infotainment and opinion journalism to save money and hold on to a distracted audience. Reporters were spooked because Jayson Blair made up stories in the *Times* and Dan Rather aired phony documents on *60 Minutes*, while watchdogs on the right and left barked ferociously at their every hint of bias and upstarts of the New Media jeered the frightened gatekeepers, until no one knew who was right and what was true and no one trusted the press and the press stopped trusting itself.

It was the perfect environment for Breitbart to stake his own claim.

In 2005—the year Rather was sacked by CBS, *The Wall Street Journal* reduced its width from fifteen to twelve inches, the *Los Angeles Times* cut another sixty-two newsroom jobs, and Arianna, by then a liberal convert, started Huffington Post with Andrew's help (he later claimed to have thought it up as a fifth column in the Complex)—Breitbart.com launched. It was a news aggregation site for wire service stories (you could bash the Old Media and feed off it at the same time) and a forum for truth telling, in the spirit of the Swift Boat Vets and other citizen journalists. The great thing about New Media was *anybody could do it.* Breitbart would fly to New York all the time and make sure he got invited to mainstream media parties, where he drank their appletinis and pinot noir and made them think he was on their side, but at the end of dinner he would get in their faces and say, "You guys don't get it. The American people are now in control of the narrative, and you can't grab it for yourself and drive it off the cliff."

Everything changed for Breitbart on the August day in 2009—the year the *Chicago Tribune* eliminated its foreign desk and *The Washington Post* closed its three remaining domestic bureaus in New York, Chicago, and Los Angeles—when a young citizen journalist named James O'Keefe walked into his house with a batch of raw videos. They were the Abu Ghraib of the Great Society. They showed O'Keefe and another citizen journalist named Hannah Giles posing as a pimp and prostitute who wanted to set up a brothel using underage girls imported from El Salvador. James and Hannah brought their hidden camera into offices of the national left-wing organization ACORN, in Baltimore, New York, and other cities, where low-level staffers sat across the table and gave them useful advice on how to establish their business while making the federal tax code work in their favor. "It was like watching Western civilization fall off of a cliff."

Breitbart knew exactly what to do. Make news by breaking news. Feed the media like training a dog, one video at a time instead of the whole meal at once, catching ACORN and the news outlets off guard, exposing their lies and biases while keeping the story alive. Use a friendly network like Fox News to amplify the effect. Stay on offense, be outrageous. His real target was the mainstream media—honestly, who cared about the poor homeowners that ACORN protected from predatory lenders, or the low-income workers whose wages it fought to raise? Within a few months, ACORN ceased to exist and Breitbart was a Tea Party hero and media bigs were competing to publish profiles of him. It felt like he was doing every single banned class A narcotic simultaneously.

It was fun! Telling the truth was fun, having the American people behind him was fun, fucking with the heads of nervous journalists and helping the mainstream media commit suicide was fun. Breitbart went on *Real Time with Bill Maher* and stood up for himself and Rush to the politically correct hometown mob of an audience, and it was an incredibly committed moment in his life. He found himself the leader of a loose band of patriotic malcontents, and *right in front of him* was the same opportunity that the Founding Fathers had had—to fight a revolution against the Complex.

And if he happened to get an Agriculture Department official named Shirley Sherrod fired by releasing a deceptively edited video that seemed to show her making anti-white comments when in fact she was doing just the opposite—fuck it, did the other side play fair? Anyway, Old Media's rules about truth and objectivity were dead. What mattered was getting maximum bang from a story, changing the narrative. That was why Breitbart was winning, with ample help from his media enemies, and why he must have been at least semi-sober during his college classes on moral relativism.

In 2010 Breitbart was everywhere, Manhattan and D.C., the Tea Party Convention and the White House Correspondents' Dinner, Twitter and YouTube, working his BlackBerry while talking on the phone, turning his florid face and keen blue eyes and wave of graying hair toward every camera aimed in his direction, getting up close with righteous indignation and puerile humor, jabbing his finger. *Kate Zernike of* The New York Times, *are you in the room? You're despicable . . . Ted Kennedy was a special pile of human excrement, he was a fucker, a big-ass motherfucker . . . When people are like, "What do you think we should do on health care?" I don't have a fucking clue, it's too complicated for me . . . It's time for the allegedly pristine character of Representative John Lewis to put up or shut up . . . They think they can take me down, that they can hurt me. It just makes me bigger . . . Fuck. You. John. Podesta . . . Have you ever seen me on TV? I always change the subject to the media context . . . Media is everything . . . It's a fundamental flaw in my psyche—I don't do well with death . . . They want to portray me as crazy, unhinged, unbalanced. Okay, good, fine. Fuck you. Fuck you. Fuck—*

On March 1, 2012, in the full flame of glory, less than a year after scoring his biggest coup in the shape of Congressman Anthony Weiner's erect penis self-photographed behind gray briefs, shortly after leaving an evening of wine and talk in a Brentwood bar, Andrew Breitbart collapsed from heart failure and died at age forty-three.

TAMPA

At the start of 2010, the *Times* took Mike Van Sickler off the housing beat and sent him to cover city hall in St. Petersburg. He understood the reasons—the budget was tight, the paper was losing a couple of hundred jobs. He had hoped to take his work on Sonny Kim to the next level and look into the players who had made his deals possible, but he couldn't tell his editors exactly how he was going to get there and nail it in three months, and they couldn't afford to wait him out.

In June, Sonny Kim was indicted by the feds and pleaded guilty to money laundering and fraud. It was a big case for Florida's Middle District, but Van Sickler had handed it over on a plate. The U.S. attorney's office announced that Kim had been part of a conspiracy and the investigation wasn't finished, but months went by and no one else was brought in. Van Sickler wondered, "Where are the big arrests? Where are the bankers, the lawyers, the real estate professionals?" Kim was just one piece of a network—what about the institutions? It was the same in Washington and New York: not one criminal case brought against the big banks. Van Sickler was mystified. "It's going to be one of the great puzzles of history to figure out, when Obama became president, why Eric Holder didn't decide to make this a priority."

Around Tampa, 2010 was the rock bottom. Unemployment in Hillsborough County passed 12 percent. The residential housing market was dead in the water, and commercial real estate was starting to sink. Middle-class people were showing up at the crisis centers and social service agencies, clueless how to navigate the maze of government benefits. There were stories on TV about families of four sleeping in cars, schoolchildren who didn't want to tell their classmates where they lived. Radio ads for precious metals warned of collapsing stock markets and hyperinflationary depression in the new Washington–Wall Street economy. But no one seemed to have any solutions, other than to wait for the housing market to come back, which was supposed to happen around 2015. The county commission went back to cutting regulations and lowering impact fees on developers—anything to jolt the growth machine into gear, even though tens of thousands of units around Hillsborough County sat vacant. The sense of crisis would flare up, then wilt under the humidity. The sunshine and beaches were still here. It was a torpid apocalypse.

There was one idea that inspired some people in Tampa: rail. Back when Tampa was going to be America's Next Great City, none of its rivals around the Sunbelt—Charlotte, Phoenix, Salt Lake City—had commuter rail systems. Now they all did, leaving Tampa behind. Tampa had standing plans for a light rail line, funded by a sales tax increase, but the Hillsborough County Commission always refused to allow it onto the ballot. In 2010, the wind shifted. Mark Sharpe, the Republican county commissioner—a fitness buff, intense reader, and former navy intelligence officer with a crew cut—made light rail his cause, saying it would bring economic development and finally elevate Tampa Bay to the status that had eluded the area for a quarter century. Sharpe was a conservative—in 1994 he had tried to join the Gingrich revolution, running for Congress on Grover Norquist's no-tax pledge (he lost to the Democratic incumbent). But by 2010 he was appalled at how narrow and extreme the Republican Party had become. He aspired to be a John McCain–like reformer, and he talked in ways that other Republican elected officials didn't dare, quoting John Quincy Adams on the need for canals and roads to unite the nation, Lincoln on federal land grants to the railroads, Eisenhower on the interstate highway system, telling audiences with a chuckle, "It was *constitutionally okay* for the government at the federal level to be involved in building roads." But now those highways were jammed, gas prices chronically high, and you could widen I-275 only so much. Sharpe openly mocked the growth machine. "They build something, call it Lazy Oaks, and hope there's a canal running through it, put in a nine-hole golf course. I don't know about you, but after one or two times golfing I get bored."

Light rail looked like streetcars, slower and cheaper than regular rail or subway trains. The plans called for forty-six miles of track, a single line from the airport through Westshore to downtown Tampa and then up to the University of South Florida and New Tampa. The tracks would follow some of the long-defunct tram routes that had once crisscrossed Tampa.

In 2010, the Hillsborough County Commission finally voted to put a one-cent sales tax referendum on the November ballot.

Van Sickler had loved trains ever since he was a teenager riding the Cleveland Rapid to Municipal Stadium and the Flats. He saw in light rail the answer to the sprawl that had brought Tampa down. Building the tracks and stations would create jobs, but more important, light rail would change the pattern of living. People would get off the train and walk, and walking (without fear of traffic death) would change the urban landscape, away from the shopping plaza, the parking lot, the gas station, and the roadside sign to townhouses, cafés, bookstores, the kind of places that encouraged pedestrians to linger, and their presence would spur other businesses to cluster, and before long there would be density—Jane Jacobs's heaven. Strangers would meet in nontraumatic accidental encounters and exchange ideas. Tampa would become the magnet for educated young people, tech start-ups, and corporate headquarters that its counterparts with commuter rail had already become, putting the economy on a sounder foundation than real estate had. The center of gravity would move back to the city, away from Country Walk and Carriage Pointe, which would fade into irrelevance. If there was an answer to the fatal growth machine, it was rail.

Karen Jaroch grew up in Tampa, the daughter of a retired military officer. When she was sixteen, in 1980, she got up the nerve to hold a sign at the corner of Westshore and Kennedy for Reagan and Paula Hawkins, a Republican who became Florida's first woman senator in the conservative sweep that year. That was Karen's last public political act for almost thirty years. She married a fellow student at the University of South Florida who was the most liberal person she'd ever met, and at first they couldn't talk politics, but over the years, in her quiet, reasonable way, she brought him around to her side. They were both trained as engineers and they lived next to a golf course in New Tampa, an unincorporated boomburg on the northern outskirts of the city, and raised four kids while Karen became a stay-at-home mom, a churchgoer, a PTA member, and in every way an ordinary middle-class woman, down to her geographically indeterminate middle American accent.

She had a square face and wore her dark hair in teased bangs, eighties-style. She always voted Republican, though she didn't like what Bush did with the Medicare prescription drug bill and No Child Left Behind—too much government. She and her husband always lived within their means, owned a $250,000 home, and when a couple she met at a dinner party making far less than her husband said that theirs was worth $700,000, she was appalled. "They were trying to make a buck off the bubble. They were going to live in it a year and pay interest only. They had all these grandiose plans, and here we were doing everything right. You knew it was trouble." She blamed the government for that, too—not deregulation, Wall Street, or mortgage lenders. The Community Reinvestment Act of 1992 forced the banks to change their rules and give subprime loans to unqualified people so that more Americans could be homeowners. It was government driving the banks, not the other way around. Why would the banks want to lose money?

Still, Karen was never active in politics, until 2008. At the beginning of the year she got her stimulus check from Bush—six hundred dollars— and she thought, "What is this? Why are they sending this off to everybody? It's not the role of government to take money and redistribute it." But she stayed out of the election, because John McCain didn't interest her. Then came Sarah Palin in August. Palin electrified Karen. "I could relate to her in a number of ways—her spunk, conveying the views that I held and saying it and not being ashamed of it. She was the same age as me, she was married at the same age as me, her kids, being on the PTA, the way she viewed economics." Karen was a vegetarian, but it didn't bother her that Palin liked to hunt as long as she ate the meat. Palin wasn't an elite—that was what Karen could identify with. Tampa was under the control of a powerful business elite, people like Al Austin, who built Westshore, people who had been making the same mistakes over and over with too much government. Karen's first political experience had been Reagan, an outsider who came in and bucked the system. Like Palin. That was what Karen was looking for.

The bank bailout, then Obama's stimulus package, Cash for Clunkers, the auto bailout—spending was out of control, and it seemed like big business was in collusion with big government. Someone was making money, and it wasn't the little guy. Karen didn't know that a third of the stimulus was tax cuts, and she didn't need to, because she was against it as soon as she heard about "shovel-ready projects." People like her who had done what they were supposed to were being asked to bail out the freewheeling spenders, again and again, with no end. Judging by his actions, Obama didn't believe in the American ideal that hard work pays off and you get to keep what you earn. His communistic father, the one he wrote a whole book about, and his radical mentors painted other ideas into Obama's psyche.

Karen began to fear that her America, the country she'd grown up in, would not be available for her children. One day, she was helping her son study for his midterm exam, which was on ancient Egypt, and it got her thinking. At the beginning, everybody farmed the land along the Nile and gave rice to the Pharaohs, but then the Pharaohs wanted to build pyramids for their own glory, and they started taxing the people. The same thing happened in Rome. The same thing was happening in the United States. The country was in decline, and her kids might not have her opportunities.

Karen was a longtime listener to Glenn Beck—he got his break on talk radio in Tampa back in 2000—and because he was now saying so much of what she felt, she DVRed his new TV program on Fox News. The Glenn Beck show caught fire right after the election of Barack Obama, almost three million people tuning in every afternoon. In early February 2009, a few weeks after the inauguration, Beck told his viewers to meet one another: "There are more of you out there than you know." Hearing that inspired Karen to spend ten dollars and set up an online meet-up site to organize the first gathering of the Tampa 9/12 Project. Beck's crusade was based on nine principles, such as "America Is Good" and "I work hard for what I have and I will share it with who I want to," and twelve values, including Reverence and Hope.

On March 13, 2009, people gathered for viewing parties in Hebron, Kentucky, and Golden Valley, Arizona, and other towns all across the country. Eighty people met at the Tampa Ale House. It was five in the afternoon and the Glenn Beck show was on. There was a video about September 11, 2001, the bravery and unity that followed the attacks, and then Glenn Beck was standing backstage of his set, with his blond brush cut, pinstriped suit, and sneakers, close to the camera, his face filling the frame, choking back tears. "Are you ready to be that person you were that day after 9/11, on 9/12? I told you for weeks, 'You're not alone.'" Beck looked upward and extended his arms. "I'm turning into a frickin' televangelist!" and his voice was breaking, his eyes puffy, his features swelling with the hangdog hurt of the thousand failures and grievances that he carried for the millions of people watching him. He wiped away a tear.

"I'm sorry. I just love my country, and I fear for it. It seems like the voices of our leaders and special interests and the media, they're surrounding us—it's sounds intimidating! But you know what? *Pull away the curtain.* You'll realize, there isn't anybody there! It's just a few people that are just pressing the buttons, and their voices are actually *really weak.*" He leaned in closer and his eyes went hard. "The truth is, they don't surround us. We surround *them.* This is *our* country."

The strangers who gathered at the Tampa Ale House didn't watch the whole show. They were more interested in talking to one another. Karen had always been shy, right through adulthood—just taking on the school spelling bee for the PTA scared her—but now she found herself growing bold. "We all knew each other, in a way," she said. "We didn't know each other, but we all felt connected. We had never had a voice and we were starting to create our own voice." They were people like her—not country club Republicans, just people who felt something was wrong. And she had brought them together. That was the beginning of Karen Jaroch's life in politics.

Summer brought Obamacare and a nationwide rebellion. On August 6, Tampa's Democratic congresswoman, Kathy Castor, held a town hall meeting in a room that was far too small for the fifteen hundred people trying to get in. Things descended into chaos when members of the 9/12 Project, enraged by Castor, enraged by Obamacare, enraged that the doors to the jammed room had been shut on hundreds of protesters, started shouting, "You work for us! You work for us! Tyranny! Tyranny!" until Castor gave up trying to speak and had to be escorted out. Karen was there, and the next afternoon she received a call from a producer at CNN. Could she get downtown to appear that night on Campbell Brown's show? Three hours later she was sitting alone in a studio with a satellite link, the voice in her earpiece out of sync with the small video screen just beneath the black hole of the camera where she tried to keep her gaze, feeling like a deer in the headlights.

Campbell started in on her. "I'm all for civic engagement, but explain to me what the point is of shouting down your congresswoman, of yelling at them. What does that really get you?" Karen tried to answer, but Campbell interrupted. "I'll let you finish, but nobody was being heard there, that was total chaos, everyone yelling."

"People are frustrated," Karen said, bangs falling over her left eye. Her head shared a split screen with Campbell's, or occupied one-eighth of the screen alongside the three pundits—a Republican strategist, a cable analyst, and a Web writer—invited on the show to talk about the incident. "Middle America feels disenfranchised. We are not being listened to. Our congresspeople are rushing things through," she said. "People are scared they're going to lose their health care. It's going to create huge deficits that are going to outlast my children."

Campbell asked who her leaders were.

"We're grassroots," said Karen, soft-spoken but standing her ground. "We're local organizations. I'm not getting a dime from anybody." She felt that Campbell was twisting things against the Tea Party, making it seem as if they'd been rowdier than they were. It didn't matter—the people she knew got their news elsewhere. Afterward, her friends in the movement congratulated her on standing up for the forgotten Americans and making the mainstream media look biased and stupid.

Then came rail. Nothing Obama and Congress did got Karen as energized as the proposal for a taxpayer-subsidized light rail system in Tampa. The issue took over her life for the entire year 2010. She started a group called "No Tax for Tracks" and boned up by reading an antirail report from the Heritage Foundation. She argued that the system would cost too much, wouldn't create jobs, wouldn't have riders, had failed elsewhere, would burden the area with decades of debt. When a fact threatened to undercut one line of argument, she would switch to another, for Karen's real objection to the referendum went far beyond dollars per mile.

In the nineteenth century, rail was the future of transportation, the engine of American wealth. In the twentieth century it was a boring topic for public policy and budget experts. In 2010 it symbolized everything that the American right feared and hated—big government, taxes and spending, European-style socialism, a society in which people were forced to share public services with strangers and pay for them. Rail was a threat to the lifestyle of New Tampa, where the line was supposed to end. In New Tampa you drove to the supermarket once a week (instead of walking or taking the bus every day like in the city), then loaded up the minivan at Home Depot on weekends. Karen gave speeches decrying the influence of urban planners and warning against Agenda 21, a nonbinding United Nations "sustainable development" resolution from 1992 that many Tea Partiers regarded as a Trojan horse for world government, a danger to American sovereignty, and an ominous threat to its single-family homes, paved roads, and golf courses. The fact that President Obama made intercity high-speed rail a centerpiece of his stimulus bill only confirmed their worst suspicions. So streetcars were absorbed into the national fury and became the Tampa Tea Party's signature issue in 2010, as tax cuts and abortion had been to earlier generations of conservatives.

Once, backstage before a televised debate with Tampa's mayor, Pam Iorio, who was the main political force behind light rail, Karen mentioned that her husband had recently been laid off from his job as a civil engineer. They were about to lose their health benefits and were going through a tough time.

"Karen," the mayor said, "won't this initiative put him back to work?"

"No, your plan isn't going to create any jobs," Karen said. It was a sacred principle, and she wouldn't let her family's misfortune weaken her. The battle against rail felt to Karen like David against Goliath. There were a lot of powerful forces on the other side—the Chamber of Commerce, the South Tampa elite, the editorial page of the *St. Petersburg Times*, and Commissioner Mark Sharpe—and rail proponents spent more than a million dollars. On Karen's side there was another tireless Tea Party organizer named Sharon Calvert, whose Dodge Durango was festooned with bumper stickers declaring DON'T TREAD ON ME and TAKE AMERICA BACK! There was David Caton, an ex-pornography-cocaine-alcohol-Quaaludes-Ativan-and-masturbation addict turned Christian crusader against porn, homosexuality, and rail. And there was Sam Rashid, a Karachi-born businessman in Brandon, with the forbidding stare of a professional poker player (which he was), who funded right-wing political candidates, including Mark Sharpe—until Sharpe turned sellout, liar, and RINO by supporting the rail tax, an unforgivable breach, whereupon Rashid vowed to punish him by having him defeated in the midterms, along with his beloved rail.

On November 2, light rail went down in Hillsborough County by 58 to 42 percent. Karen Jaroch and the Tea Party had outhustled the downtown businessmen and politicians, as voters in the unincorporated boomburgs and ghost subdivisions didn't see a benefit in rail or want to pay another penny of taxes in the depths of the recession. Rick Scott, a Tea Party hero, who had refused to meet with any newspaper editorial boards and received none of their endorsements, was elected governor, continuing unbroken Republican rule in Florida that dated back to 1998. Soon after taking office, Scott decided to reject $2.4 billion in federal stimulus money for a high-speed rail line connecting Tampa and Orlando, on which work was set to begin within weeks (the money went to California). The seventy-acre site for Tampa's new downtown rail terminal remained a vast dirt field next to the interstate. A data company that studied statistics for fifty metropolitan areas, factoring in unemployment, commute time, suicide, alcohol use, violent crime, property crime, mental health, and cloudy days, announced that Tampa was the single most stressful city in the United States. Eight of the top ten were in the Sunbelt. Five were in Florida.

Mark Sharpe survived the challenge from a Tea Party candidate hand-picked by Sam Rashid. After being reelected to the county commission, Sharpe voted to put Karen Jaroch on the Hillsborough Area Regional Transit Authority board. After all, her side had won the rail war—and among his many Tea Party detractors, he found Karen to be the most reasonable.

A few weeks after the election, Mike Van Sickler was assigned to cover a meeting of the Pinellas County Transportation Task Force, which was taking place somewhere near the St. Petersburg–Clearwater airport, in a government-academic-business joint use facility called the EpiCenter. As he drove past two-story apartment buildings, strip malls, and office complexes with no street numbers, he couldn't find the EpiCenter to save his life. "Lost in Clearwater," Van Sickler muttered, gripping the wheel of his Ford Focus. "Talk about no sense of place. Give me a sign!" Rio Vista, Bay Vista—these faux names! He hated it out here. If he screamed, no one would hear him.

The defeat of light rail had depressed Van Sickler more than he expected. It seemed as if America was becoming a country that no longer believed in itself. "We can't, we can't, we can't. Let's not do that rail project because it's not going to work. We can't try to be the next great city. We're just going to settle for what we've got. We're not happy with what we've got, but we can't do any better." That wasn't the country he'd grown up in. He had grown up in a much more optimistic country.

Van Sickler arrived at the EpiCenter half an hour late, red-faced with irritation. The Pinellas County Transportation Task Force was debating whether to proceed with its own rail initiative after the defeat in Hillsborough. There were a hundred people in the room, including Karen

Jaroch. In the front row sat two men in their twenties, one in a green T-shirt with an Irish shamrock, the other in a red I'M STILL WAITING FOR MY BAILOUT! T-shirt. Whenever a member of the task force said something like "We keep talking about 'when the economy turns'—part of the reason to do this is to turn the economy," the two guys in T-shirts would cover their faces or throw their heads back in silent laughter.

After the meeting, Van Sickler, in his corduroy jacket and tie, notebook in hand, approached the one in the lucky Irish T-shirt and identified himself as a reporter from the *St. Petersburg Times*. The guy gave him a hard look. Van Sickler asked what he thought of the discussion.

"I think they're a bunch of communist sons of bitches who want to raise taxes. If you listen to everything they say, it's about how they're going to pull the wool over the eyes of the public. They want to push their agenda onto the people. Would you ride it? It doesn't go where I want to go. Who's going to ride it in Pasco—the cows or the fences?" The guy's name was Matt Bender. He was a jobless construction worker, looking for any kind of work, but he refused to apply for unemployment benefits. "I'll make my own way," Bender said. "We have the pursuit of happiness, not the guarantee. I'm tired of both parties not listening to what the people want, and the corruption, the inside deals, the backroom deals. We have to eliminate the political class bit by bit."

As Van Sickler drove back to the office to write up his story, he thought about the way Bender had looked at him. The contempt. Just like the comments that came in after one of his stories went up on the Web—they had nothing to do with what he'd written, minds were already made up, every local issue was drowned out by the shouting on national cable news. There were no longer any facts that everyone in America could agree on at the start. For example, his paper had gone to great effort and expense to dig up information about the benefits, as well as the costs, of light rail in Tampa, and none of it had sunk in. What had sunk in was "No tax for tracks"—maybe because light rail seemed kind of fanciful to people in Hillsborough County who just wanted to hunker down, raise their families, hang on to their jobs. And it had been the same with Sonny Kim, his big story from the financial crisis. Van Sickler had waited two years for heads at higher levels to roll, and instead the U.S. attorney's office had nothing to show but a low-life mortgage fraudster. Van Sickler was beginning to wonder about the relevance of newspaper work. The weeks and months it took for an investigative reporter to map the story out, get it right, and deliver, with the hope that something might change as a result—and then *nothing* happened. What was he doing it for—his ego? Because it didn't seem to matter to anyone else.

But he wasn't about to stop believing in journalism. "You've got to believe in something," he said. "I don't believe in God—I believe in this. I believe in the possibility that man can improve himself, that we as a civilized society can get better, and journalism is the part of it that makes sure things are working." For most of the twentieth century in America, things worked about as well as they ever had in human history. Even if that was no longer true, and most Americans no longer trusted reporters like him, what was the alternative? Who else was going to be the public's eyes and ears? He didn't see Daily Kos or Red State at city hall, he didn't see Google or Facebook at the county commission.

One Sunday morning, Van Sickler applied sunscreen (though it was still March) and drove out to eastern Hillsborough County. He wanted to see what was happening in Carriage Pointe, the county's most distressed subdivision, which he had visited a dozen times and written about at length. The place still seemed pretty deserted—houses where he'd once interviewed the owners were now abandoned. But as he walked along the streets—not a stick of shade—and stopped to talk with a Jersey woman who was working in her yard, and a black man from West Palm Beach who was sitting with his family in an open garage, a picture started to emerge: people were moving here again. Most of them couldn't afford to buy—instead, they were renting, because rent was cheap. They knew nothing about their neighbors, and if they depended on the after-school center up the road they were out of luck because it was shutting down due to county budget cuts, and the price of gas sucked up a big chunk of their wages since the nearest jobs were forty-five minutes away, and if their car ever broke down they were completely screwed.

But Carriage Pointe was still alive, and as Van Sickler drove away he had a vision of the place five or ten years in the future: a slum in the middle of nowhere. The rich would live in the cities, the poor would live in the exurbs, and Tampa would wait out the slump until the growth machine started up again.

DEAN PRICE

If you drove around Southside Virginia or the Piedmont Triad of North Carolina in the weeks before the 2010 midterms, you would see black billboards along the roadside that announced NOVEMBER IS COMING. The signs were vague and ominous, but everyone knew what they meant. A black "November Is Coming" bus prowled the region's roads, festooned with figures on the cost of the "Failed Stimulus," "Healthcare Takeover," and "Cap & Trade Energy Tax." The billboards and the bus were paid for by Americans for Prosperity, a group that Dean had never heard of, which was funded by the Koch brothers, a pair of oil and gas billionaires from Kansas who believed that President Obama was deliberately destroying the free enterprise system.

The Tea Party was so big in Dean's area that he didn't broadcast his personal views, but as far as he could tell, it was like the brownshirts. His neighbors never gave Obama a chance. They called him a socialist, a radical, and a Muslim, but the word that got to the main point started with *n*. People like that were easily conned by a huckster like Glenn Beck. Dean used to watch him when he had a show on CNN, and because it was a regular news channel, when Beck made all kinds of predictions after 9/11—there was another plot, a bomb would go off at such-and-such time tomorrow—Dean would think, "Lord have mercy, if that happens this country's screwed." After a couple of times, he decided that Beck was a nut—more entertainer than anything else, another snake oil salesman. But he had a following, including in the back of Dean's house. On the other hand, MSNBC was hopeless. Rachel Maddow looked too dykish, and Dean just couldn't relate to Keith Olbermann.

Dean had his own questions about Obama. He still liked the president and respected him, but he couldn't understand why Obama didn't do more to spell out his ideas for the new economy. Washington let the biofuel tax credit expire in 2009, and investors were uncertain which way things were going. Tying it all to global warming just muddied things up, made it too partisan. Obama still talked about renewable energy, but it seemed like he didn't have a clue what to do, or he didn't think the country could handle the truth, or he still had the old mind-set that bigger was better. His agriculture secretary, Vilsack, had a slogan touting small-scale production—"know your farmer, know your food"—but he wasn't going to turn his back on industrial farming. They were playing both sides. Everybody had believed that Obama would get in there and tell the truth and not side with the multinationals, but maybe they bought him off. Could that be it? Or did he just hire the people who helped cause the problems in the first place? Summers, Geithner—that was like the fox and the henhouse. But the American people were thinking radical change back in 2008, not the status quo.

Dean thought about Obama a lot, questioned him, argued with him, wondered about him, almost as if they knew each other. He kept dreaming about him, too—he didn't know why, but he tried to encourage those dreams. It was important for your very last waking thoughts to be only the things you wanted to see in your life. You almost had to will it. Because once you were asleep your subconscious would work on it, drawing to you the things you continuously concentrated on. That was Napoleon Hill. Lying in his bed, Dean thought about what he would do once he made his fortune. He had a very specific vision of it. Then he would fall asleep and dream about being with the president. They were sitting alone in a room, and Obama was listening while Dean spoke. He never remembered his words—it was just the cause, the cause, the *cause*.

In November the Tea Party was coming for Tom Perriello.

The first TV ads against him went up before he'd been in office a month—right around the time his Republican colleagues in Congress stopped returning his phone calls. "There was a decision made by the highest levels of leadership that they weren't going to have their fingerprints on anything," he said. "They were smart enough to know the economy couldn't possibly turn around before November 2010, and they could run against us. That was probably a smart strategic move but it was a fundamentally immoral and unpatriotic thing to do. To me that's more or less evil."

In Perriello's district, the recession was so severe that local officials were faced with a choice between closing schools and raising property taxes, and at first there was hardly any opposition to taking federal funds. A Republican banker in Danville, who had been the president of the Virginia Bankers Association, wondered why there was no money in the stimulus bill for public works, like overhauling the Depression-era post office downtown—that was how desperate things were. Perriello himself regarded the stimulus as "fairly milquetoast stuff"—he wanted something bigger and more visionary, like a "national smart grid"—but the Recovery Act did bring three hundred million dollars into his district, money that kept teachers in classrooms and paved roads that needed paving. But over time, as the months went by and the slump continued, and there was no sign of work starting on the stimulus project to rebuild the decrepit Robertson Bridge over the Dan River, and the Republicans in Washington and the Glenn Becks on the airwaves denounced everything the government did, endlessly repeating the lie that the stimulus hadn't created a single job, public opinion in the Fifth District began to turn against Obama and Perriello.

Then came the hellish summer of 2009. After Perriello and the House voted for the president's energy bill in June, outside money from anti-Obama groups like Americans for Prosperity poured into the district. The local Tea Party organized a protest in the parking lot outside his office in Charlottesville, fifty or a hundred people gathered, and when Perriello came out to talk to them, they denounced the federal energy police that they were certain the bill would empower to raid their homes in order to check the efficiency of their refrigerators. But this was just a warm-up for health care. In August, Perriello held twenty-one town hall meetings around the district—more than anyone else in Congress. Everywhere he went, five hundred, a thousand, fifteen hundred people would pack the senior center or theater, stoked with the talking points they'd downloaded from the Internet and brought on a sheet of paper, in some cases so angry that they kicked and spat at members of Perriello's staff. They lined up to rant against death panels and violations of the Constitution ("You want the government to control doctors' decisions? Are you insane, stupid, or just plain evil?"), and Perriello stood there with a microphone, looking twenty-two years old in his blue shirt and khakis and tie, sweating, nodding, taking notes, drinking water, listening until every last constituent was finished, and answering until he lost his voice ("The Supreme Court for the last couple hundred years has read Article I in an incredibly expansive way"), even if it took five hours.

"Nobody was getting converted," he later said. "This was about endurance."

The town halls appeared on TV news, and they gave the impression that everyone in the district opposed health care reform, even though many people who attended (and many who didn't) were in favor or undecided—but theirs were the quieter voices, and sometimes when they spoke up they were shouted down, and as the month went on, the people with quieter voices, having watched the raucous earlier meetings on TV, decided not to bother coming, so that by the end of August the Tea Party in Perriello's district believed that the congressman was ignoring nearly unanimous opposition.

The spectacle of the town halls was so ugly that the old civic groups, the Rotary Clubs and garden clubs, nonpartisan pillars of the community, stopped issuing courtesy invitations to their congressman to come meet them for fear of being embarrassed by protests. And Perriello also noticed that the traditional trade associations, like the ones for small businessmen and community bankers, which used to give their members useful fact-based information and explain how they were negotiating the best deal possible with the government, now wilted under the popular heat and refused to play ball.

By the end of that first summer of the Obama administration, one could have the impression that most of the country was in open revolt against a president who had won a resounding victory just nine months earlier.

Perriello cast a difficult vote for health care, and after the bill passed in March 2010, a Tea Party activist posted what was supposed to be Perriello's home address outside Charlottesville, urging people to go make their views known. It turned out to be the address of his brother, his brother's wife, and their four children, and the next day someone cut the family's gas line.

Perriello began to feel that the first politician to inspire him was also leaving him hanging out to dry. On the one hand, Obama had "an unbelievable willingness to do what I got into politics to do, which is to take on the problems that neither party has had the guts to touch for my entire life." On the other hand, the president spent his first year trying to cut deals with Republicans who were never going to give an inch, and he went out of his way to let bankers discredited by the financial crisis avoid taking a fall. The president talked about "a new era of responsibility," but it didn't seem to apply to those guys. The Obama team was full of un-imaginative advisers who were too friendly to Wall Street and didn't know how to create jobs on Main Street. "If you only know other people on Wall Street who make six or seven figures, all you're trying to do is get back to the nineties," Perriello said. "Well, in the nineties people in my district were losing a crapload of jobs." The elites were biased toward other elites, even after they had failed massively. "Empires decline when elites become irresponsible." Obama was a progressive insider, not a populist outsider, and Perriello got no cover from the administration when he went out to face his struggling, irate, misinformed constituents.

The din of shouting in town halls and on AM radio, cable TV, and the Internet; the hostile and anonymous commercials filling the airwaves, paid for by the coal and insurance companies and the Koch brothers; the entanglement of cash, interest groups, and spinelessness on Capitol Hill; the strangely ineffectual Obama White House; the ongoing depression in the Piedmont: amid all this, who would know or care about Red Birch, and Perriello's efforts on its behalf?

Six Republicans challenged him. The winner of the primary was a go-along-to-get-along state senator named Robert Hurt. One day in August, three months before the midterms, Perriello began vomiting and couldn't stop. For several nights he got no sleep. After two years of coffee and Diet Coke all day, and scotch or Jack Daniel's in the evenings, and never enough water, he was completely dehydrated.

November came. On the day before the election, Perriello was franti-cally campaigning alongside Senator Mark Warner in Martinsville. At the Sirloin House the two politicians went table to table greeting diners, some of whom didn't want to look up from their cheese fries. Dean Price was there—he'd shown up to say hi and good luck—and he and Perriello ex-changed a hug.

"You've put up with a lot, I've put up with a lot," Perriello told him, "but we're on the right path, the path of righteousness! You know I believe in what you're doing, keeping that money in the community instead of sending it to petrodictators."

The news cameras were rolling, and Dean picked up his cue. "It's what I call the leaky bucket effect. Ninety cents on every dollar of oil and eighty-six cents at the big-box stores leaves the community."

Perriello lowered his voice. "Once this craziness is over in a couple of weeks, let's sit down over a beer."

There wasn't time to say more. Perriello was on his way to the next joint—Pigs-R-Us—and the day had barely begun.

The next day a woman named Lorna voted at the Ridgeway Ruritan Club, a one-story cinder block building on a wooded side street near the speedway south of Martinsville. Then she positioned herself on the sidewalk with a sign that said HURT. Lorna was a retired schoolteacher, about seventy, short and round inside a green woolen coat with a peaked hood. The rims of her sunglasses had a leopard-skin pattern, and under heavy lipstick her mouth was tight.

"This country is not socialist, we are founded on Judeo-Christian principles," Lorna fairly spat, "and I will riot in the street if I have to. I have never been so ashamed of the way that man has diminished the presidency. He doesn't dress properly, he calls certain people enemies, and he talks about certain networks. He is just what he is, a Chicago agitator. He does not have presidential qualities, he doesn't represent all the people. We had statesmen—now all we have are politicians. I have never seen a president who has tried to change this country—this country does not need changing—fundamentally transform this country and we don't need that from a Chicago agitator."

Lorna listened to talk radio and watched Fox News because the others were so obviously biased—that David Broder column yesterday, saying Obama was so much smarter than everyone else! And then there was Al Gore, living in his mansion and flying on his private jet, yet Lorna was supposed to pay everything she had in taxes after she and her husband never went on a cruise and didn't buy extravagant cars and saved every penny he made working as a supervisor at the DuPont plant so they could enjoy life together and he could golf after retirement, but then they never had the chance. If he could hear her running off her mouth like this, he would turn over in his grave and say, "Lorna, shut up," but now that she was retired from the school she could say what she wanted, and she had a lot on her mind. "I want to eat what I want to eat, and for them to tell me I can't eat french fries or Coca-Cola—no way! They want to tell me what to think. I have thought for myself all my life and I've done okay. I came from nothing, and I have never been so despondent as I am now. You can't be the super force around the world if the economy is weak. I just hope and pray that this country can get back on the right track."

Lorna's fury was ebbing. She hadn't mentioned her congressman once.

That night, Perriello and his family and staff waited for the results in the offices of a small financial services company, above a wine bar in historic downtown Charlottesville, the prosperous apex of the Fifth District.

"All right, everybody," Perriello called out, "we outperformed in Danville by a thousand votes!" A cheer went up. At eight o'clock half the precincts had reported and Perriello was trailing 53 to 45 percent, but those were mainly rural areas. Charlottesville started coming in, but Hurt's lead held. Perriello's press secretary was trying to keep the networks from making a call. Perriello gave a wry smile. "We're surging back! Not really. But we're doing better. Let's keep closing that number." At eight thirty Henry County finally reported, and Perriello got killed there. Red Birch hadn't made a dime's worth of difference.

He lost, 51 to 47 percent. He came closer than other Virginia Democrats who were defeated, including long-serving ones, including ones who had taken safer votes. The aide who had traveled the district in early 2009 looking for projects to fund told Perriello, "We hit a gale force wind." Across the country it was a rout for the president's party.

Perriello gathered his family together. Some of them were crying. He was the most cheerful person in the room.

"I'll tell you this—I don't know why, but I feel great. We left it all on the table. Not everyone who lost tonight fought for forty million Americans to get health insurance coverage and cover preexisting conditions. Not everyone who lost tonight came up with a national energy strategy. This is the way we do things—high risk, high reward, leave it all on the table." Perriello was smiling. "I kind of feel a weight lifted."

Once, when Ryan was around thirteen, Dean took him to the big Labor Day flea market and gun show in Hillsville, Virginia. On Dean's recommendation, Ryan spent his money on a bubble gum machine. The idea was to put it in the convenience store next to the biodiesel refinery in Bassett and start making a little money. "It was sort of a lesson to teach him," Dean said. "The reason most people stay poor, in my opinion, is they don't know the difference between an asset and a liability. Most people thought their homes were an asset, but they were a liability. The best way to tell the difference is if something puts money in your pocket, it's an asset, and if it takes money out of your pocket, it's a liability, very simply. Buying a bubble gum machine and getting a return on that asset I thought was a very valuable lesson."

The next year, when Dean's truck stop company was liquidated and he lost the store, the bubble gum machine had to be taken home and put away in a closet. Dean hated for Ryan to lose his investment that way. But Napoleon Hill said that with every adversity there was a seed of equal benefit.

Dean was looking for that benefit.

He felt useless around the refinery. His shares in Red Birch Energy had been diluted to almost nothing, and Gary and Flo were running the place. Dean told Gary that his whole approach was wrong—Gary was trying to make a lot of money fast instead of building up the business. They were losing potential customers for licensing the Red Birch model because Gary was quoting exorbitant prices—it had happened with a businessman up in New Jersey. "A pig gets fat," Dean told Gary, "and a hog gets slaughtered."

"What did you say?" snapped Gary, who was quite overweight. He was now on the hook for the entire debt of the company, nearly a million dollars, which obliged him to sign over the deed to his house and boat as collateral. As far as Gary was concerned, Dean was always willing to spend anybody's money but his own. The third partner, Rocky Carter, wanted to be bought out because his construction business had taken a big hit with the housing bust, but Gary couldn't afford to pay him off. Debt had all three of them entangled like snakes.

Gary and Dean argued constantly. "I don't like you anymore," Gary told Dean one day. "You're not the person I started with." He began to question whether Dean was mentally stable, insinuated that Dean might end up like his father. That pissed Dean off more than anything else. He was down and his partner was undermining him.

In the winter of 2011 everything started to unravel at once.

First came the tax case. Henry County, Virginia, had indicted Dean the previous September for failing to remit almost ten thousand dollars in meals taxes. On January 27, 2011, he was found guilty of a misdemeanor and ordered to pay a twenty-five-hundred-dollar fine and a hundred dollars in court costs on top of the outstanding taxes. That same winter, Red

Birch was audited by the IRS. Because Dean was on the board, with his tax liability, the company's permit to make fuel was pulled, and Red Birch went out of business for seven weeks.

In March, Dean resigned his office, relinquished his remaining stock in exchange for ten dollars, and gave up his paycheck. The IRS lifted its hold, and the refinery started up again without him. That was the end for Dean Price and the biodiesel company that had taken from him its name and inspiration. Not long after his departure, a notice appeared on the Red Birch Energy website. It said, "Recent change in ownership and management," which linked to a "press release" that announced: "**Dean Price**, a former co-owner of Red Birch Energy, Incorporated, **is no longer associated with Red Birch Energy and has not been a part of the company since April 2011 in any way.**"

Yet Gary continued to get wind that Dean was talking about Red Birch and about himself as part of it. In July, Gary sent him a letter.

Dean,

It is really difficult for me to get to this point in our relationship and write this letter to you, but you have chosen this path for me to take and leave me with no choice. I have made several attempts to get you to communicate with me to no avail.

I realize your life is upside down right now and I really hate adding to that burden but again, I have no other choice but to come to the following conclusion.

The conclusion is that you are out there representing RBE as you see fit and that will not work for us . . . **I'm truly sorry, but I have to insist that you cease from representing Red Birch Energy in any way going forward.**

Dean, as you know, we have been providing Health Care Insurance for you and your family. As you will not be involved with us any more, we will have to cease providing that coverage to you effective September 1, 2011.

Dean, on a very personal note, I'm very disappointed it has come to this. I really wish it hadn't. When we first started, you were a great partner, but when the truck stop started to fail, you changed. Yes, you are still a nice person, but you have avoided all responsibilities to the company, cut off all communication with any of us, lied to us on many occasions . . . I could go on, but I won't. All I can say is I wish you well and hope you find a way to get your life back in order.

Sincerely,
Gary N. Sink
President

Dean never replied. "They kicked me when I was down," he said, "and they ran me off."

Meanwhile, the liquidation of his business had not resolved the problem of his debts. One of his creditors at the truck stop had been his fuel supplier, Eden Oil, a small company out of Rockingham County. Dean had considered the owner, a man named Reid Teague, to be a friend, but once Eden Oil got a judgment on Dean for $325,000 in unpaid fuel bills, Teague became his nemesis. First he cut off the fuel supply to the truck stop, which was what had forced it into Chapter 7. But the liquidation of Red Birch of Martinsville couldn't protect Dean, for Teague was coming after his personal assets, too. In February 2011 Dean learned that his house—the house his grandfather Birch Neal had built in 1934 on land he won in a poker game, where his mother had grown up and the Neals had raised tobacco for decades, where his father had slapped him down the last night they lived together under the same roof, where he had returned from Pennsylvania in 1997, the house that he had spent a year moving down the hill from the highway and rebuilding on a new foundation, the house that he had made into a home for Ryan when his son came to live with him, that was also his mother's house and that they jointly owned— his house was scheduled to be auctioned off on the Rockingham County Courthouse steps, in Wentworth, on May 15. He didn't tell his mother, but a notice appeared in the local paper. A cousin once removed dropped by the Sunday before the auction on the pretext of reminiscing, but as she was leaving she told Dean that she was there to check out the house for its sale value.

Dean had been thinking about declaring personal bankruptcy ever since the end of 2009, but for one reason or another—he was concentrating on biodiesel; his lawyer had stopped returning his calls after collecting his fifteen-hundred-dollar fee; no one wanted to face ruin—he hadn't done it. But on Monday, May 9, six days ahead of the scheduled auction, Dean filed under Chapter 7 as a "self-employed entrepreneur" in the U.S. Bankruptcy Court for the Middle District of North Carolina, in

Greensboro. He did it to save his house. Twenty-six other debtors appeared in court with him that day. Across the country, over the course of the year, there were 1,410,653 bankruptcies.

Dean's debts totaled a million dollars. His assets—his half of the house in Stokesdale, his quarter share of the forty-four acres that was the remnant of the Price tobacco farm, his furniture, tractor, clothes, books, and shotguns, his vintage signs, his 1988 Ford pickup truck, and the used Jeep Wrangler that he had bought for Ryan's sixteenth birthday—all fell within the exemptions allowed in North Carolina, so he was able to hang on to them. He had to undergo credit counseling and take a financial management course.

On July 25, he went to the courthouse in Greensboro for the meeting of creditors. It was held in a room on the first floor, and instead of creditors, who seldom attended a hearing, Dean found himself surrounded by his fellow debtors, old people, people sitting in wheelchairs or walking on canes, breathing through respirators, waiting for their name to be called by the bankruptcy trustee, and they reminded him of his father and how he had been broken by failure. He had never felt his father's shadow on him like that. The crease in his britches.

While he was in bankruptcy he actually thought a few times about ending it. But he could never do that to his boys—it would be the easy way out. And, in a way, bankruptcy was a wonderful thing because it allowed a fresh start. Thank God he didn't live in a country where they cut off your head if you fell into debt.

On August 30, Dean's case was closed. He had felt the Lord's hand on him the whole time.

By then he already saw the right way forward. After getting thrown out by Gary and them he came very close to quitting biodiesel, but it turned out to be one of the best things in his life. Otherwise, he never would have come up with the new idea. He would have stayed at Red Birch until he died trying.

There was a Henry Ford quote that he'd read somewhere: "Failure is simply the opportunity to begin again, this time more intelligently."

TAMMY THOMAS

Tammy loved doing actions. She loved the bigger stage, the larger movement. Public speaking freaked her out, but in 2009, when the organization joined unions and other groups in rallies for health care reform and other causes all over Ohio and in Washington, Tammy would be at the front of the bus leading the songs and chants. She had a sense of the drama, and how to keep it alive when it was fading. Once, outside a Chase Bank in Columbus, an organizer with a bullhorn kept trying to get a chant of "Si se puede" started, the Spanish version of Obama's "Yes we can," but there were hardly any Hispanics in the crowd. Tammy finally grabbed the bullhorn and got everyone singing. Another "Si se puede" and the action would have ground to a halt.

In Mason, Ohio, a conservative white town, they stormed the lobby of United Healthcare singing and chanting. In Washington, Tammy and others from Youngstown—local people she had recruited, like Miss Hattie—joined a national progressive group on K Street and shut down a whole intersection, and from there they marched to Bank of America to denounce Wall Street, then protested on the front lawns of bank executives. It was pouring and Tammy got soaking wet in spite of the trash bag she had turned into a poncho. She got sick afterward, but it was exhilarating. It made her feel, "Hey, take that! You've been giving it to us and everyone else forever. Take a little bit of it back." She was standing up and saying—whether it was true or not—"I'm not going to take this anymore." She thought about all the foreclosures she knew, and the redlining in black neighborhoods like the east side, and the payday lending abuses. "I just get sick of when people take advantage of other people. And you take advantage of the people who have less already? Isn't that America? That is the nature of the beast and it seems like we are getting so deeper into it." She thought about being forced to retire from Packard, and the CEO and

upper-level staff getting their bonuses while leaving all these people without jobs, decimating a community, and some of the banks getting bailed
out with her tax dollars, and she still couldn't get a loan from them while
she had to pay her mortgage every month. "That makes me want to say,
'What the F?' It's the injustice of it."

The actions put her leaders on a stage they had never dreamed of.
Miss Sybil, just retired from hauling cement at the Ohio Lamp factory,
went to Washington and met with Shaun Donovan, Obama's secretary of
housing and urban development. She told him that some of the stimulus
dollars to distressed cities should go for demolitions. She brought out
MVOC's map and explained that the problem in Youngstown wasn't gentri-
fication, like New York or Chicago—Youngstown didn't need low-income
housing to be built, it needed vacant houses to be torn down. After three
meetings the secretary got it, and he also remembered her name.

Miss Hattie became a local celebrity. Tammy had her speaking all
over town, about health care, vacant houses, what the banks were doing
to the neighborhood, until people would walk up to her at the store and
say, "You don't know me but I know you, I seen you on TV. You speak for
all of us that can't speak." Then Tammy took her to Washington, and
Miss Hattie nearly died of nervousness getting up in front of what looked
to her like thousands of people on Capitol Hill. When she started stutter-
ing and said some things wrong, Tim Ryan, Youngstown's congressman
after Traficant, hugged her. "You are a dynamic speaker," he said, "you need
to introduce me every time." It was like her mother patting her on the back
and saying, "It's going to be all right." After that she hit the ground running.
Miss Hattie said later, "Tammy molded me into the leader that I am."

Across the street from her cut-down-flower garden, in another vacant
lot Miss Hattie started the Fairmont Girls and Vicinity Community Garden. She put up a white picket fence, like in the suburbs, and built raised
beds out of scavenged wood and chipboard, and compost bins from factory pallets. Georgine's restaurant loaded thirty pounds of compost in her
truck every day, and her doctor gave her horse manure from his farm.
Tammy wrote a grant application to the Wean Foundation and Miss Hattie received thirty-seven hundred dollars to get started. She was trying to
beautify the neighborhood and teach the kids something nobody could
take away from them. "You might hate it at first, but you can cook with
greens and you don't have to eat meat all the time. You can eat for cheap
or nothing as long as you work hard. Hard work is the key to everything.

I didn't know that when I was young, but I guess I got wisdom with age." The garden was a serene thing—it reminded Miss Hattie of her father's garden. But the kids in the neighborhood were all teenagers now, and it was hard to get them interested. It didn't help when the house next door to her garden had an attic fire because a seven-year-old boy was playing with matches, and the owner immediately began stripping off the aluminum siding to sell for scrap.

Miss Sybil started a community garden on her block of the east side as well. It was an urban garden, black soil and green vegetable waste on top of concrete. "We all go back to dirt," she said, "everything goes back to dirt." She knew nothing about gardening, just eating, but she and her neighbors grew everything edible to man. The policy was come at will and pick what you want, just don't tear up the garden. Only the groundhogs and deer didn't abide by it.

Tammy and MVOC did a second survey of Youngstown, this time of grocery stores. Their map showed that Youngstown was a food desert—there were hardly any decent stores in the whole city. From certain parts of the east side it took a four-hour round-trip on the bus to buy fresh groceries, and it made a big difference when a Bottom Dollar opened up on the south side. A good corner store might carry a few potatoes, a few onions, and heads of lettuce starting to turn black, but most were like the F&N Food Market next to Vickie's demolished house on Shehy Street, selling fast food, liquor, and cigarettes. The organization pressured corner store owners to sign an agreement to stock fresh, nutritious food and keep their stores from becoming hangouts for dealers.

The food campaign put Tammy in touch with a white evangelical church south of Youngstown, where the minister, Steve Fortenberry, had started a cooperative farm on thirty-one acres. His congregation had some older and more conservative members who were skeptical of anything having to do with environmentalism, so he pitched the project as feeding the hungry, which was easier to sell. Teenagers, disabled people, and ex-cons from Youngstown worked on the church's farm over the summer, and Tammy and Fortenberry arranged to bring the food by truck to community centers and farmer's markets around Youngstown.

In her earlier life, Tammy never would have met someone like Steve Fortenberry. She wouldn't have met Kirk Noden. She didn't know there were people like Noden with such a passion for the underdog. She called him "the blackest white guy I know." The work was taking over her life. It stole time away from her family, she didn't go to church as often as before, she didn't get around to spring cleaning. But MVOC also opened her up to different people and experiences, even different cuisines (Kirk challenged her to eat octopus, and she learned to love Indian food). She used to look at white people wearing dreads and think, "Why are they trying to lock their hair like a black person?" That didn't faze her anymore, and neither did the peculiarities of the Unitarian Church—a woman opening up a meeting with a chant and a gong—or any other religion. It was all part of a cultural experience. After her divorce, when she got so deep into the House of the Lord, she'd stopped drinking, but now she and the other organizers held long strategy sessions over food and drinks, and they always ended up telling war stories, comparing victories and scars. She had never been around people who were so passionate about their work. There was so much more to life than she had known. And nothing burned her up more than when certain people she knew said that Kirk was trying to take advantage of black people, or that he was racist. "Are you kidding me? Do you know what he has done for me and my family? He didn't have to hire me. I didn't have any experience, I had no degree. He saw something needed to be done here and he had a couple answers. If you want to fix it and make it better, you haven't in the past twenty years. What are you waiting for?"

When Tammy left Delphi, her buyout was worth about a hundred forty thousand dollars. It sounded like a lot of money, until you figured that it was two and a half years of pay with no guarantee of another job. She lost more than half of her pension, but she ended up among the lucky ones with a good job. Her best friend, Karen, who was ten years older, took the buyout but didn't find another job, and she and her husband went through hard times, like just about everyone else Tammy knew at the plant. The company did too good a job of scaring workers into leaving, and so many took the buyout that Delphi had to bring a few hundred back to the Warren factory as temps to get up to six hundred fifty. Tammy knew some people who went back to work in the high-speed press area, running three or four machines for thirteen dollars an hour—double the work for half the pay.

The media predicted strikes over the threatened cuts, but the unions went quietly as they negotiated their members' steep loss of pay and

benefits. Delphi emerged from bankruptcy in 2009 with most of its operations sold off to GM, the company that had owned it from 1932 to 1999
(in 2009 GM was also reorganized under Chapter 11, with a $50 billion
investment from the U.S. government). Delphi's remaining assets were
owned by a group of private investors, which gave a new name to the company that had once been Packard Electric, then Delphi Automotive Systems, then Delphi Corporation: it was now DLPH Holdings Corp. The
hedge fund manager John Paulson, who had made almost $4 billion by
selling subprime mortgages short in 2007, unloaded 20.5 million shares
in the new entity and made a $439 million profit on a $14 million investment. By then, the company employed fewer than twenty thousand people
in the United States, out of a global workforce of almost a hundred fifty
thousand.

The factories where Tammy worked—Plant 8, Hubbard, Thomas
Road—were shut down. They soon joined the landscape of broken windows, weedy asphalt, and empty parking lots that stretched across the
Mahoning Valley. The restaurants and bars frequented by Tammy and her
coworkers lost most of their business.

Delphi was hailed as a model of cost cutting through bankruptcy.

After paying taxes on her buyout money in 2007, Tammy had eighty-
two thousand dollars left. She spent part of it helping her mother and
kids, and she put part of it into a CD that earned 3 percent. But in 2007
she hadn't yet been hired by MVOC, and she was thinking again about
leaving Youngstown. She wanted to make a little extra on the rest of the
money in order to position herself to leave, and to receive regular payments because she was in school. She had a relative by marriage who
was a real estate agent in the area, and who had helped Tammy and Barry
finance their house on the south side. He admired Tammy, called her a
hustler—someone who knew how to survive and didn't get too down—
and he was always asking her to come work for him (he also had a lawn
care business, a day care center, and a nonprofit that helped people coming out of prison). Sometimes he even called her "daughter." He offered to
invest her money in real estate. He wrote out a contract promising a 10 percent annual return in monthly payments, and Tammy gave him her last
forty-eight thousand dollars from the buyout.

The first year went great. The checks came every month and were
enough to cover her house and car payments. When the second year
began in mid-2008, with the housing market sinking, he asked her to

turn the money over for another year and negotiated the rate down to 8 percent. By that Christmas he was paying her only 5 percent, and the payments were arriving late. In 2009 they stopped coming.

Tammy's mother's health was declining, and Tammy wanted to get her out of a nursing home into a decent house. She asked the relative to bid fifteen thousand dollars of her investment on a house that was probably worth twice that. She won the bid, but when he couldn't come up with the five-thousand-dollar down payment, she knew something was really wrong. When she demanded her money back, he said that he didn't have it. "I'm sorry," he said, "I'm going to get it together. I'm trying not to file bankruptcy, because if I do ain't nobody going to get paid. I'm going to rebound and then you'll get your money."

She knew that he was trying. Without the payments she couldn't keep up on her house in Liberty and the bank was getting ready to foreclose, and somehow he gave her the twelve hundred dollars she needed to get a loan modification. But he still couldn't come up with the money that she had invested with him, and she began to think that he had been running a Ponzi scheme, using her money to pay other people, and he'd been caught by the collapse of the market, just like Madoff at the very same time. She began to hear stories about other people, some out in California, who had invested with him and never got their money back, and other stories that he had transferred mortgages to relatives using his broker's license and refinanced without letting them know. His employees weren't getting paid. She confronted him and told him that she was thinking of going to the police. The relative, who was a deacon in his church, said, "That is not what Christians do to each other."

She was trying to be a good Christian and do the right thing. Anyway, what would a police report get her? She didn't turn him in, and she told few people in the family. Finally, he wrote her a check for part of what he owed her. When she took it to a check cashing place, it bounced. That's when he stopped taking her calls and disappeared. She never heard from him again, and never saw her money again—money that she had counted on for the lean years after Delphi, then her retirement. She was furious with herself. She should have put the money in a safe CD with a low return, maybe set aside part of it to experiment with the stock market. "You're so damn stupid," she railed, "I don't know why you even did that. Why did you ever trust him?" She was angrier at herself than at him, and in spite of everything she felt a little sorry for him, because he was ruined.

In the midst of this fiasco, Tammy lost her parents. Throughout her life, her father had often been cutting and combative, and ever since her teens she had defied him, but toward the end she saw a buried softness in her father that allowed her to believe that he loved her. In September 2009 he died in his sleep of liver cancer, after leaving the hospital and going home to be with his wife and their children and enjoy a meal of barbecue, watermelon, grapes, and a beer.

But for Vickie it was different. Her health had been bad for years, with the disintegration of her bones, hepatitis C, and the ravaging effects of heroin. She was depressed, fading mentally, and Tammy was trying to figure out a way to bring her home and care for her. Over Thanksgiving, Vickie was hospitalized at St. Elizabeth's, where Tammy visited her. But Tammy had surgery scheduled for December 2, with a month of recovery afterward. She didn't feel that she could take time off from organizing the way she had done at Packard if someone covered for her. She spent the days before her operation trying to catch up on work, and though they talked on the phone three times, she wasn't able to go see her mother again. While Tammy was in the hospital, her mother, without telling her, asked for her own treatment to be stopped. Tammy was released from the hospital on December 4 and went home. Two days later, her mother was taken to the emergency room with congestive heart failure, and she died at the age of sixty-one. "She was alone," Tammy said. "I couldn't make it to the hospital in time. I promised her I'd be there with her. My mother needed me and I couldn't be there for her." This thought would not leave Tammy alone.

They still had so much living to do. But Vickie had been ready to go for a long time, even though she knew that Tammy wouldn't let her. And after she was gone, Tammy missed climbing into bed beside her, sitting next to her without saying anything, her hug, her hand stroking Tammy's hair, a comfort no one could replace, because in spite of everything it was her mother.

For a long time afterward, Tammy questioned herself, and her work, which had kept her from seeing her mother at the end, and God, who had filled her life with so much struggle and taken away so many things that she loved—everything except her children.

TAMPA

At the bottom of Tampa, where the peninsula died into the bay, South Dale Mabry Highway ended at the front gate of MacDill Air Force Base, the home of United States Central Command. World-famous four-star generals—Tommy Franks, John Abizaid, David Petraeus—drew up war plans for Afghanistan and Iraq there, commanded hundreds of thousands of troops in battle, took off in their personal jets to fly around their Area of Responsibility, committed huge strategic errors, and belatedly tried to correct them. They enjoyed the lavish hospitality of Tampa society hostesses while shaping U.S. foreign policy and the fate of nations across the most volatile region of the globe, from Egypt to Pakistan, with all the authority of Roman proconsuls. After the White House and the Pentagon, no parcel of America exercised more power during the War on Terror than MacDill. And four blocks away lived the Hartzells.

The Hartzells were Danny and Ronale, their kids Brent and Danielle, Danny's younger brother Dennis, and four cats. They lived on South Dale Mabry Highway, across from the MacDill Motel and Bay Check Cashing, in a two-bedroom apartment on the ground floor of a complex where the neighbors dealt drugs and got mad if someone looked at them wrong. The Hartzells regularly watched HGTV, which was devoted to real estate, but they were too poor to flip houses, lose them in foreclosure, or end up as clients of Matt Weidner. They didn't even have a car, which left them at the mercy of Hillsborough Area Regional Transit buses. Danny never made more than twenty thousand a year, and the only time they had spare money was at tax time—one year they spent their Earned Income Tax Credit on a computer, the next on a black vinyl armchair and sofa, then on a cheap flat-screen TV. They were estranged from their surviving relatives, most of whom were heavy drinkers. They had few friends, and no church (though they were Christian) or union (though they were working class) or block association (though they wished the area was safe enough for the kids to go trick-or-treating). They hardly gave a thought to politics. What they had was one another.

In 2008, when the recession hit Tampa, Danny was laid off from his ten-dollar-an-hour job at a small factory near the base called Master Packaging, which made plastic snack food bags. The worst thing about it was that his supervisor, who had gone to high school with Danny, made someone else give him the news. Danny brought the pink slip home and showed it to Ronale, and she said, "What are we going to do now?" That was in March. Danny spent the rest of the year searching for a job. He applied at Home Depot, Sam's Club, Publix, and sixty other places, taking long bus rides to interviews, but he was always the twenty-fifth applicant for one opening. He was in his late thirties, short, with a pot belly on him, a wispy goatee, and a nearly hairless head under his Steelers cap. He was missing a bunch of teeth and spoke in a loud hoarse voice because of deafness in one ear. He classified himself as a "blue-collar-type guy," not a "behind-the-counter-take-your-money-can-I-help-you-find-your-dress-size-type guy," but the only jobs left were in retail, and he lacked the right look and manner.

One evening just after Christmas, the family sat around their cramped living room, a teen game show on TV, the kids holding hands on the gray carpet, which had seen better days. Brent, who was twelve and small for his age, and Danielle, who was nine, still believed in Santa, had no trouble doing so because they didn't see how their parents could afford presents. In fact, Danny and Ronale had depended on charity for Christmas this year. Danny didn't like having to do that—other people out there were in worse shape than they were—and he hated not being able to put Danielle in dance class or Brent in soccer. He thanked God every day for Ronale, but, to be honest, he was actually starting to lose heart. "Why do all these people out there view me as such a bad person? They don't know me, they don't know my work history, they won't give me a chance. I start to wonder, what's wrong with me? You work for what you have, that's all anyone can do, and then all of a sudden the economy gets so bad and instead of thirty people looking for work there's three thousand."

And yet somehow Danny blamed himself. He had dropped out of high school his senior year and now regretted it deeply, and he felt that the world was singling him out for some terrible payback, that this trouble must have been his fault, that the failure was his alone and he had no right to anyone's help. From the bankers on Wall Street to the home-owners in Weidner's office, no one else seemed to take this view of themselves.

Danny came from outside Pittsburgh. His father, an alcoholic, had been a maintenance man for the railroad, then the power company, then a local college, before moving the family to Tampa when Danny was around twelve and the steel mills were closing in the early eighties. He drank even harder in Florida. He taught Danny to drive defensively and love the Steelers, but otherwise no one kept after Danny to brush his teeth or do much of anything else.

Ronale had it far worse. She was born in Tampa. Both her parents were drunks, her mother a spiteful woman with an evil look in her eyes. They split up when Ronale was seven, and she was dragged around Florida and North Carolina by her mom (who drank rubbing alcohol if she couldn't find booze and shacked up with any man who would have her), sometimes living in their car, missing a lot of school, stealing Reese's cups because her mother was too strung out and selfish to buy her food if Ronale said, "Mommy, I'm hungry." From an early age the idea stuck in Ronale's head that she'd never be that type of parent.

When Danny was in tenth grade and Ronale in ninth, they lived next door to each other in South Tampa, near the base. Danny's older brother, Doug, went after Ronale, and out of sheer jealousy Danny would barge into the room whenever they started to make out. He'd walk past Ronale on the sidewalk, look her in the eye, and say "Bitch," and she'd answer "You're such an asshole," and when they found out that they liked talking to each other it was the beginning of lifelong love. Ronale dropped out of high school earlier than Danny—she was sick of being bullied. "Quite a few people literally wanted to kill me," Ronale said. "Backed into corners and no one to help me and stuff, and everything." She went to work in a Laundromat, and he got a job as a grinder at a welding shop in St. Peters-burg. When she became pregnant with Brent at twenty-two, in 1995, they moved into a trailer together. In 1999, with Danielle on the way, they married.

Working against the Hartzells as they set out in life was their nearly complete lack of education or money or family or support of any kind, plus more than their share of health problems: Danny's deafness and tooth decay, Ronale's tooth decay, obesity, and diabetes, Brent's ADHD and growth hormone problem, Danielle's hearing disability and anxiety. Working in their favor: Danny had a trade, the parents didn't drink or do drugs, the kids were respectful, the family would stay together no matter what, they all loved one another. By conventional morality, the plus side should have kept them afloat, and at another time, in another place, maybe it would have.

The first disaster came in 2004. It was the usual downward spiral of circumstances and mistakes. First, the welding shop moved up the coast to New Port Richey, and Danny couldn't afford to move with it, so he lost his job. The Hartzells were renting a trailer in St. Pete, Danny doing odd jobs for the owner with the idea that they'd buy it as soon as they got their Earned Income Tax Credit. But the owner never paid Danny, and then he told the Hartzells to leave, claiming Danny owed him back rent. One night, Danny's father and brother Doug got drunk and decided to trash the trailer on his behalf. When the police were called, they arrested Danny at the motel where the Hartzells had checked in, and Danny spent the worst night of his life on a concrete slab in a jail cell with a hundred other guys. The next day the judge took a look at his spotless record and released him on his own recognizance, but now the family had nowhere to live.

They roamed around St. Pete for a month, sleeping in the car. Ronale stocked up on meal boxes at the food pantry, and when the kids got sunburned she rubbed them down with vinegar to speed up the healing. Brent was bored without his video games, and Danielle was afraid of night noises. Later, she remembered sitting in the car one night by the beach beneath the Gandy Bridge. "There were a bunch of food boxes in front of me, and I would look at the food boxes and then I would look out at the trail of sand up to the ocean." In the mornings, Danny and Ronale put the kids on the school bus as if nothing had happened.

They managed to move back to Tampa, found the apartment on South Dale Mabry Highway for $725 a month, and Danny was hired at Master Packaging. For the next four years things stabilized. Danny's younger brother Dennis slept on their living room sofa and chipped in his pay from a part-time job retrieving shopping carts at Wal-Mart. With Danny's wages, Danielle's SSI, and food stamps, it was enough to keep their heads above water. Then the pink slip came, and one thing led to another.

In the spring of 2009, Danielle was diagnosed with osteosarcoma— bone cancer in her left leg. For the next year and a half, the Hartzells' lives were absorbed in hospitals and tests and surgeries and chemotherapy.

Almost all the care was charitable. With a cash gift from a complete stranger they bought a 2003 Chevy Cavalier to drive to appointments. Danny stopped the job hunt to give his daughter his complete attention, and Ronale, who was always complaining about wrongs done by teachers, employers, landlords, and neighbors, loved Danielle's doctors and joined cancer parent groups, the first time in her life she felt part of a community. The apartment filled with framed inspirations:

WHAT CANCER CANNOT DO
It cannot cripple love
It cannot shatter hope
It cannot quench the spirit
It cannot destroy confidence
It cannot shut out memories

A prosthesis that would require regular four-millimeter adjustments as she grew was sewn inside the length of Danielle's skinny little leg. She went a whole year cancer free. They thanked God. Otherwise, nothing changed for the Hartzells.

In the late spring of 2011, Danny Hartzell had a dream: he would move the family to Georgia.

He'd lived in Tampa ever since he was twelve and now he felt trapped. The walls of the apartment were getting smaller and smaller, especially after the couple next door was arrested for neglecting their two small children, leaving their apartment filthy, with fast-food containers sitting around, and the roaches migrated through the wall to the Hartzells' place. They were the small, infesting kind—they left a black trail of larvae where the living room wall met the ceiling, they scurried over the vinyl furniture, got into the bathroom sink and the kitchen Tupperware, the air-conditioning ducts blowing the horrible smell of their poo throughout the apartment. Because of the roaches, Ronale stopped making pasta and instead bought frozen foods at Wal-Mart, pizzas, Velveeta Cheesy Skillets, six Salisbury steaks for $2.28, which was cheaper than cooking anyway— it cost less to buy a cake than make one from scratch—or else she boiled ramen noodles, which Danny called one of man's greatest inventions. There was nothing they could do about the roaches short of having the

place bombed, which would mean paying for three nights at a motel. The
roaches embarrassed Danny and Ronale, who prided themselves on keeping the place clean. Meanwhile, the new family that moved in next door
liked to scream and play loud music at one in the morning. One day, the
upstairs neighbors flushed their toilet and opened a hole in the plaster
ceiling over the Hartzells' toilet while Ronale was in the bathroom. The
super never fixed it.

For a while Danny had a part-time job at Target, unloading and shelving stock in the late-night hours before the store opened, making $8.50 an
hour. At first he got thirty or forty hours a week, just enough to get by, but
after the holidays the store cut back on his hours, and by spring he was
averaging ten hours a week, for a paycheck of $140 every two weeks after
taxes, while Target hired three new people in his department at lower pay.
He couldn't help thinking he'd make more if he got laid off and started
collecting unemployment, not to mention seeing their food stamps double.
One day Danny overheard his managers talking about the store's sales
figures from the day before, which were down to $52,000. He did a quick
calculation. "Almost four hundred grand a week, and they can't afford to
pay me? It's just greed."

When Target first hired Danny, they showed him a video on the evils
of unions and told him that if anyone approached him about joining one,
he should report it to management. Danny had never thought much about
unions, but he wondered what was so wrong with them. One night he
and Ronale watched a show on the History Channel that talked about
the Battle of Blair Mountain, a coal strike back in the 1920s. What got
Danny was the fact that miners from the rest of West Virginia went down
to help the ones in the southern part of the state who were trying to join
the union, and a lot of them got killed by hired thugs of the coal company.
That kind of thing didn't happen anymore. People were too scared to join
a union, and the corporations had too much money, they'd just threaten
to sue. These days it was hard to get people to agree to do anything together. He knew that it wasn't any better for poor people back in the day.
He could even remember being a boy in Pennsylvania and huddling
around the kitchen stove for heat, eating government beans and peanut
butter out of black-and-white cans. But what had changed since then was
people. In the world today it was dog eat dog, every man for himself.

On the morning that Target told Danny to come in when Danielle had
a doctor's appointment, he was a no-call no-show, something he'd never

done before, which pretty much invited them to fire him, and they did. He applied for unemployment benefits. He was right back where he started.

The Hartzells were sick of Florida. Five out of ten people were jerks, Ronale said. Neither Danny nor Ronale had voted in the last election, but they hated the new governor, Rick Scott, who was cutting everything poor people needed, including schools. The Hartzells wondered why Americans like them were sinking while new immigrants, like the Indians right across Dale Mabry, were able to buy convenience stores. Danny had heard that their first five years in America were tax-free. He wasn't a racist, but if that was true, it was unfair.

When Danielle was sick, Ronale had gotten on Facebook, and through her page Danny had reconnected with a childhood friend from Tampa. The friend was operating a forklift up in Georgia, in a small town called Pendergrass. The Hartzells drove up to spend one July 4 weekend with him and his daughter, and they loved the trees, the fishing, being able to walk outside the friend's door and not see another house. The schools up there sounded good, and housing cost less, and Ronale decided that only two out of ten people were jerks. There was supposed to be plenty of jobs. Even Wal-Mart was nicer in Georgia—Ronale heard they let people off over July 4 weekend. If the Hartzells ever wanted to move to Georgia, the friend invited them to stay with him until they found their feet.

And suddenly, at the beginning of June, they decided to do it. They wanted a fresh start. Their lease was up at the end of the month, but moving to another apartment in Tampa that didn't have roaches would only change their place, not their situation. "It's kind of like I've fallen in that non-climbable-out-of rut," Danny said. "Maybe it's partly me—maybe I stopped trying. I was struggling for so long I got tired and threw my hands up in the air. Maybe some people are better climbers. My whole thought process is, if you can't climb out, why not move?"

Danny's dream was exciting and scary. The Hartzells clung to it like a ladder at the bottom of a well. Danny didn't know if he was doing the right thing for his family, but not doing it seemed worse. Ronale was tired of reaching the end of the month with twenty-nine dollars and having to wait for Danielle's next SSI check to arrive so she could buy Diet Pepsi or Dr. Pepper. "Some people are afraid, but sometimes you've got to make that big leap," she said. "Keep your faith and say your prayers." She wouldn't miss a thing in Florida other than Disney World and Danielle's doctors.

Danny didn't have a job lined up, but Wal-Mart promised a spot at a local store in Georgia for Dennis, who was coming with them, and the kids were happy about going somewhere new. There was hardly anyone to say goodbye to.

On the last day of June, the day before their move, Danny and Ronale got new teeth. They drove with the kids to a walk-in dental clinic next door to a crack house in a bad neighborhood of East Tampa. Each of them had had infected gums and residual teeth that needed pulling, which took weeks, so that by the time they were ready to be fitted with new sets, they were completely toothless. "It's going to be strange," Danny said in the waiting room. "Daddy's going to eat a Dorito tomorrow. I haven't ate a Dorito in about eight years." He went into the dentist's office and emerged after half an hour flashing a smile of brilliantly white, perfectly even teeth, mostly paid for by Medicaid. The teeth made him look younger and less poor. Danielle sat in his lap and coached her father: "Say 'them.' 'Zebra.' 'Tycoon.' 'Dolphin.' 'Wal-Mart.'" Danny began to like the feel of his dentures. "I could get a girlfriend with these," he said, twitching his eyebrows suggestively.

Ronale's teeth took an hour to be fitted. Voices were raised in the office, and she came out furious. "The upper one hurts my gum!" she cried.

The dentist, a Hispanic woman, patiently explained that Ronale's mouth was still sore from the extractions. For a few days she should take the dentures out every fifteen minutes and rinse them in warm salt water. "If you could come back next week I would be very happy to make an adjustment."

"I'm leaving tomorrow," Ronale said. "This is pain. I'm sorry if your other customers don't mind pain, I'm not perfect. It's like a toothpick going into my gum."

"But it was too loose," the dentist said. "It was going to fall out."

"I want to go. I'm tired of being treated like I'm stupid."

On the drive home Ronale went on about the pain and the way the dentures pushed her lips out so that she looked like a gorilla. Danny's fit him better. "Lucky you," she said, "yours don't hurt. With mine it hurts to talk."

"Then leave 'em in," Danny cracked.

"You jerk."

Soon the kids were playing the word game with their mother, getting

her to pronounce "zebra" and "Wal-Mart." By the time they got back to
the apartment, the car was full of laughter, Ronale joining the rest of the
family between complaints. At home she took her teeth out and never
wore them again. Out of sympathy or inertia, Danny did the same.

The next morning, July 1, Danny rented a sixteen-foot Budget truck
with all the money he could scrape together and backed it up to the apartment door. He and Dennis spent the day loading their stuff. The TV,
computer, and sofa. Boxes of dried food. The kids' bikes. Danielle's
Hannah Montana school supplies. Danny and Brent's large video game
collection (Ronale was sick of seeing the back of her husband's head when
he disappeared into World of Warcraft for ten hours at a stretch). They
tried to get rid of everything that was infested, including the black vinyl
armchair, but Danny was resigned to some roaches making the trip to
Georgia with them.

In the middle of the day, an official letter came from Tallahassee: the
unemployment compensation board's appeals referee determined that
Danny had been terminated by Target for cause, and his benefits claim
was rejected. "I guess it's just all water under the bridge at this point anyway," he said, putting aside the letter. "Being that we're going up there to
stake a new claim. Right, Brent? I really think things will be better up
there. Everything will be fresh and new. I think this is the right thing to
do. Things aren't going to get any better for us here."

To escape traffic and heat, they waited most of the day to leave: Danny,
Brent, and one cat in the rental truck, Dennis, Ronale, Danielle, and the
other three cats in the Cavalier. By sunset the Hartzells had left Tampa
behind.

They lasted a little over a month in Georgia.

Danny's friend had a new girlfriend, and she didn't want the Hartzells
around. He was a surly host, demanding reimbursement for movie tickets,
dropping broad hints that they should move out as fast as possible, treat-
ing them as inferiors, even making fun of Ronale's weight, which greatly
offended Danny. One day, the kids went for a walk in the woods and
Brent came back with ticks. The next day, Dennis disturbed a hornet's
nest in the yard and was stung half a dozen times. They moved into the
first trailer they could find, off a busy highway. The A/C didn't work,
but the kids were afraid of the stinging velvet ants, so they stayed inside

the stifling trailer day and night. The good news was that Danny found a welding job, working on tractor trailers with a crew of Mexicans for $12.50 an hour, but on his first day he caught a falling piece of steel and aggravated an old back injury. The next day he could hardly get out of bed. After years of unemployment and retail he wasn't in shape for heavy work. Brent was doing fine—he could be anywhere as long as he had his family and video games—but Danielle missed her friends, and her parents belatedly realized that the regular eight-hour trips back to the hospital in Tampa for adjustments to her prosthesis were going to be arduous and expensive. In rural Georgia every drive was long—Dennis's new Wal-Mart was miles from the trailer, the milk began to spoil before Ronale could get it back from the store, and they were eating up all their money in gas. Worst of all was the isolation. They were no longer speaking to Danny's friend. In Tampa at least they had the doctors, the support group. Here they had no one.

By early August they were done. Returning to Tampa was less a decision than a collapse. A benefactor from the hospital found them a trailer park near Brandon called River Run. Ronale looked at the pictures online and put down a two-week deposit of four hundred dollars. They rented another truck and left Georgia just before midnight on a Friday. When they reached River Run the next morning and saw the holes in their trailer's walls, the jalousie windows that didn't open, the door without a lock, the lack of any appliances, they wanted to fall on their knees and cry. There was no way the children could live there. They drove into Tampa and dropped Dennis off at Wal-Mart to plead for his old $7.60-an-hour job back. Then they started looking for a motel. Some homing instinct led the Hartzells back to the area around MacDill, where they took a forty-five-dollar-a-night room at the Crosstown Inn off South Dale Mabry Highway, a few blocks north of their old apartment. There was a toaster oven, and they ate toasted hot dogs one night, little pizzas made out of buns, tomato sauce, and sliced cheese the next. All their stuff was in the rental truck, already a day late on the return, which meant half the deposit. They'd lost the deposit on the trailer in River Run. They had enough money for about a week at the motel. After that, there was a woman they knew from the hospital who might be able to take in Brent and Danielle while Danny, Ronale, and Dennis slept in the car.

Danny was at the end of his rope. He tried to put on a brave face, but he kept berating himself—he hadn't thought the whole thing through, all the consequences, and now the simplest decision left him paralyzed. One day, Danny and his daughter were sitting in their car in the Wal-Mart parking lot getting ready to go in and buy sandwich meats, bread, and potato salad for dinner at the motel, and Danielle started crying. She was afraid that if they became homeless again the cats would die. Danny always tried to be a strong father in front of his kids, but as he put his arms around Danielle he couldn't keep from crying with her.

In the middle of the crisis, Danny experienced a painful clarity. He knew two things: everything had to be about Danielle's health, and everything depended on his finding a job. Shaking off a numbness that had settled over him, he began driving all over Tampa, dropping off applications everywhere that was hiring, fast food or anything, it didn't matter. After Dennis's supervisor at Wal-Mart put in a good word for Danny, he was hired to unload and stock produce for eight dollars an hour. With his and Dennis's jobs at Wal-Mart, he was able to secure a $745-a-month apartment in public housing on South Lois Avenue. It had one more bedroom than their old place on Dale Mabry, which was only a mile away, bringing them full circle, as if God had meant for them to forget about going somewhere else to start over, and instead try to make things work here where they had their feet planted.

PRAIRIE POPULIST: ELIZABETH WARREN

She had two stories to tell. One was about herself, the other was about America.

Elizabeth Herring was a good girl from Oklahoma. Her folks were Dust Bowl survivors who never headed out to the coast, conservative Methodists clinging to respectability. They had three much older sons. By the time Elizabeth arrived in 1949, a business partner had run off with the money that her father had saved up for a car dealership. Mr. Herring had to work as a janitor in an Oklahoma City apartment building to pay his debts and feed his family.

The parents used good English and taught the children not to say *ain't*, and Liz made them proud with her grades. Despite her father's job, she was so convinced the family was securely middle class that it shocked her to learn that her mother hadn't been married in a nice wedding dress.

When Liz was twelve, her father had a heart attack. He was demoted at work, and between that and the medical bills, the Herrings couldn't make payments on their air-conditioned bronze Oldsmobile and lost it. In order to hold on to the house, which they had bought in Oklahoma City's best school district, Mrs. Herring had to take a job answering phones in the mail order department of Sears. On the first day of work, Liz watched as her mother, crying, squeezed herself into an old girdle and black dress.

"Is this dress too tight?" her mother asked.

Liz lied that she looked great.

Her mother railed at having to go back to work, hammered on her husband for failing the family. He withdrew into his humiliation. Liz stayed out of the way—throughout her life she had a habit of refusing to look a debacle in the face—and kept up appearances. She babysat and waitressed, sewed her own clothes, had her father drop her off a block away from Northwest Classen High School so that her classmates wouldn't

notice the condition of their old off-white Studebaker. She joined the Pep
Club and won the Betty Crocker Homemaker of Tomorrow award.

It was the midsixties, but none of the upheavals reached the Herrings.
Oklahoma City was still segregated. Liz's brother Don was fighting in Vietnam and of course they supported him and the war. Liz recited the daily
prayer at the start of school. She knew that a girl's two choices were nursing or teaching, and that she would choose the second.

She made the debate team and turned out to be very good at it. She
subscribed to *Time* and *Newsweek*, spent a year researching nuclear dis-
armament and Medicare, and won the statewide competition. Other than
a visit to her elementary school by one of its former students, the TV star
James Garner, when she was eight, debate was Liz's first intimation that
there could be a life for her in the wider world. At sixteen she won a full-
ride scholarship to George Washington University. By then, the Herrings
had regained their foothold in the lower middle class.

Within a few years, by the early seventies, she was Elizabeth Warren,
married to her high school boyfriend, a NASA engineer; she had a degree
in speech pathology from the University of Houston and a baby daughter.
A few years after that, following her husband from job to job, she got a law
degree at Rutgers and had a son. Her husband wanted her to stay home
and raise the kids, but she was restless. In 1978 she got divorced and
began teaching law at the University of Houston. She was a registered
Republican because the party supported free markets, which she thought
were under too much pressure from government.

That same year, 1978, Congress defeated a bill to set up a new consumer protection agency, but it passed another law making it easier to
declare bankruptcy. Elizabeth Warren decided to pursue scholarly research on this obscure subject. She wanted to find out why Americans
ended up in bankruptcy court. She took the attitude of her unforgiving
mother. "I set out to prove they were all a bunch of cheaters," she would
later say. "I was going to expose these people who were taking advantage
of the rest of us."

With two colleagues, Warren spent the 1980s doing her research. And
that was when the first story she told, her own story, ran across the second,
which went like this:

Starting in 1792 with George Washington, there were financial crises
every ten or fifteen years. Panics, bank runs, credit freezes, crashes, de-
pressions. People lost their farms, families were wiped out. This went on

for more than a hundred years, until the Great Depression, when Oklahoma turned to dust. "We can do better than this," Americans said. "We don't need to go back to the boom-and-bust cycle." The Great Depression produced three regulations:

The FDIC—your bank deposits were safe.

Glass-Steagall—banks couldn't go crazy with your money.

The SEC—stock markets would be tightly controlled.

For fifty years, these rules kept America from having another financial crisis. Not one panic or meltdown or freeze. They gave Americans security and prosperity. Banking was dull. The country produced the greatest middle class the world had ever seen.

Warren's life began in those years, and although she had seen her share of rough times as a girl, her parents and brothers were doing all right, and she managed to reach the age of thirty in good financial shape.

Then came the late 1970s, early 1980s. "Regulation? Ahh, it's a pain, it's expensive, we don't need it." So government started unraveling the regulatory fabric. What happened next? The S&L crisis.

In the late eighties, seven hundred financial institutions went under just as Warren and her colleagues were getting ready to publish their research on bankruptcies. What they had found was just the opposite of what Warren expected, and it upended what she had believed about markets and government. Most Americans in bankruptcy weren't deadbeats gaming the system. They were middle class, or wanted to be, and had done everything they could to avoid ending up in court. They were working hard to keep up, to afford a house (like Warren's parents) in a district that still had decent schools so that their children could stay in the middle class or reach it, but the loss of a job, a divorce, an illness had taken their savings. They lived more and more on credit and finally sought refuge in bankruptcy to avoid spending the rest of their lives deep in debt. Most people in bankruptcy weren't irresponsible—they were too responsible.

As a girl Warren had known what debt meant. Now she began to see financial ruin through her father's eyes rather than her mother's—not as a social shame, but as a personal tragedy that was seldom the result of weak character. If anything, it was the result of weak regulations. The more the banks pushed Congress to get rid of the rules, the more people went broke. The numbers were exploding.

This work changed Warren's life. She continued her research and writing for the next two decades (Harvard hired her in 1992). She was asked to advise a commission on federal bankruptcy law. She watched as the credit card companies and banks rolled over the consumer groups, pouring millions of dollars into Congress. In 2005, with the help of Democrats like Joe Biden and Chris Dodd and Hillary Clinton, Congress passed a law restricting the right to file for bankruptcy. It was a huge win for the business lobby. She learned something about the ways of Washington.

And the second story continued.

In 1998, Long-Term Capital Management collapsed and almost took the investment banks with it, showing that this increasingly autonomous financial world was perilously linked together around the globe. A few years later, Enron fell, revealing that the books were dirty. And the White House and Congress kept unraveling the fabric.

As wages stayed flat, debt kept more and more families afloat. As schools deteriorated, the struggle of parents to keep their children in the middle class came down to owning a house in the right school district. As the cost of those houses soared, parents worked harder than ever. (With her daughter, Warren wrote a book about this cycle of effort.) The banks realized that the middle class was the largest profit center of all. They started pulling at the threads supporting mortgages, credit cards, and consumer lending, and those, too, gave way. The regulators were spread out over seven agencies, moving in seven different directions, and none of them had the consumer as a main focus. It wasn't hard for the banks to get these cops off the beat and start selling increasingly dangerous mortgages, credit cards, even car loans. The banks turned the promises American families made to pay them back into tranches of debt, which they packaged and repackaged as securities, and sold off to investors.

Three things happened:

Profits soared.

Bonuses soared higher.

Risk entered the stratosphere.

Then everything fell to earth, and the bankers turned back to the American people and said, "Whoa, there's a real problem here, and you better bail us out or we're all gonna die." So the American people bailed them out.

It took Warren thirty years to be able to tell this story in five minutes on *The Daily Show*.

By then, the country was deep in crisis, and the crisis was the stuff of her life's work. President Obama had met her in 2004, and he knew his way around "predatory lending." He read an article that she published in 2007, at the start of the foreclosure crisis, proposing a new consumer financial protection agency. "It is impossible to buy a toaster that has a one-in-five chance of bursting into flames and burning down your house," Warren began the article. "But it is possible to refinance an existing home with a mortgage that has the same one-in-five chance of putting the family out on the street—and the mortgage won't even carry a disclosure of that fact to the homeowner." Warren's idea was for a new federal agency, independent of Congress, that would force the banks and credit card companies to disclose the risks and penalties in their financial products in clear terms. Obama liked the idea. Shortly after he was elected president, Warren was named the chair of the panel that oversaw the bailout fund.

So Warren went down to Washington. She was something unfamiliar there. First of all, she didn't look like a Washington woman. She had her hair cut in a simple bob. She wore rimless glasses, not much makeup, and a teacher's shapeless sweaters and turtlenecks hanging loose on her slight frame.

She didn't sound like a creature of the capital, either. She was a professor of bankruptcy law, but her language was as plain as her coiffure. She made no attempt to conciliate or ingratiate. She actually seemed to hate the banks. She had arrived at radicalism, like many conservatives before her, by seeing the institutions that had sustained the old way of life collapse. Sometimes she was cutting or angry, and spoke of leaving "plenty of blood and teeth" on the floor. Even though she badly wanted to run the new consumer agency that she had invented, she did nothing to help her own political cause, subjecting the very people whose support she needed to tough questions about the taxpayers' money. She didn't play the game.

She seemed to have walked into the hearing room and taken her seat at the dais out of the past, from the era when the American prairie raised angry and eloquent champions of the common people, William Jennings Bryan and Robert LaFollette, George Norris and Hubert Humphrey. Her very presence made insiders uneasy because it reminded them of the cozy corruption that had become the normal way of doing business around Capitol Hill. And that was unforgivable.

The bankers could never forgive her. They saw her as "the Devil incarnate," and they threw money all over Congress to keep her out of the consumer agency job. They called her naïve, but what they couldn't forgive was how well she knew their game.

The Republicans could never forgive her. She didn't back down or extend the usual courtesies, and so they hectored her, called her a liar to her face, and devoted themselves to killing the consumer agency almost as if they were pointing the knife at this woman who dared.

Some of the Democrats could never forgive her. The White House considered her "a pain in the ass." Dodd suggested that her ego was the problem. Timothy Geithner, aggravated almost to shouting in an oversight hearing, couldn't stand her.

And the president didn't know what to do with a woman like this. They had Harvard Law School in common, and Warren talked about the same things Obama did—the hard-pressed middle class, the need for a fair playing field, the excesses of finance. But she did not talk about these things as one of the elites. She did not say, in the same breath, "It's not personal, guys—let's be reasonable and get a deal." For that reason, some of Obama's most passionate supporters were moving away from him, and toward her.

In the summer of 2011, the president emerged in the Rose Garden from an extended negotiation with himself and, to avoid an unwinnable fight, announced that he would nominate Warren's deputy, Richard Cordray, to be chief of the new consumer agency. Then he bestowed an affectionate kiss on Warren's cheek.

But she was already gone, back to Massachusetts, to run for a seat in the chamber where the voices of Fighting Bob and the Happy Warrior had once stirred the souls of ordinary men and women.

WALL STREET

Kevin Moore* was born and raised in Manhattan, and he went to work at a top American bank right out of college, in 1998. That was the year Long-Term Capital Management went down, almost taking Wall Street with it, the year before Glass-Steagall was repealed. None of it meant much to Kevin then; it was years before he understood the significance. He was the last person hired for his training class—he only got the job because most of the competition out of college was flocking west to the gold rush in Silicon Valley—and he was voted most likely to be cut loose first.

But Kevin found out pretty quickly that banking wasn't that hard. Wall Street used this purposefully opaque language to intimidate outsiders, but to succeed you just had to be somewhat comfortable with math or else with bullshit—the former went into trading, the latter into sales, and a quant who could lie made the big money. To reach the top you had to be a fucking dirtbag and knife fifty-seven other people—that was the only thing separating them from the next ten guys down—and Kevin had no interest in getting there. His goal was to work as little as possible and live the life he wanted, which meant lots of foreign travel, good food, music, design, and funky friends. He started at the bank's offices in the financial district making eighty grand a year with an eight-thousand-dollar bonus. The most he earned in his first six years was maybe a quarter mil. The crazy money came after that.

On the morning of September 11, 2001, Kevin was at the office talking about the day's trades when he felt the ground shake. Suddenly all this paper started fluttering past the windows. From one side of the building there was a direct view of the flames billowing out of the North

* Not his real name.

Tower. All the TV sets at the trading desk were on CNBC, which had a monopoly on the Street—CNN wasn't robust enough on finance, the BBC was too soft and international, Reuters had no network, nobody took Fox seriously—and CNBC began showing video of the tower. They were saying it was a small plane, but Kevin could tell from looking out the window at the exit wounds that it wasn't a fucking small plane. The flight path wasn't normal—it didn't look right at all.

He went back to work, and he was on the phone when U.S. treasuries suddenly spiked—London was buying them. He told the guy on the line, "I think we're done here," and tore up the ticket. Outside the window it looked like a ticker tape parade, burning shreds floating past. The fire was getting worse. The TVs on the trading desk had been switched to CNN, and suddenly on the live video a second plane flew by. *Holy shit, another fucking plane!* And . . . boom. It felt like an earthquake.

"Everybody stay calm," said the head of the desk.

"I'm not staying calm," Kevin said. "I'm getting the fuck out of here." People were saying that the fire marshal was on his way, everyone should follow the fire drill procedure, but Kevin had already started toward the elevators. "Fuck you and your fire drill procedure," he said. "You want to fire me, fire me. I'm done." No one else moved. Brilliant traders making a couple of million a year, and they stood around waiting for directions from some buffoon who had no information. They mispriced the two planes.

On the street, crowds were coming up out of the subways without a clue. Everything looked normal. Kevin got on an uptown train headed toward his parents' apartment, and he was probably the only person on board who knew what had just happened. His coworkers eventually got evacuated, and they were standing on the street when the South Tower came down and covered them in dust. In a crisis you realized that society operated without anyone knowing deep down what the hell was really going on.

The bank had to move its operations out of the city for a couple of weeks. Markets were a buy surprisingly quickly, and they were right—the attacks didn't change that much. The airlines were fucked, but not necessarily that much worse than after four terrible plane crashes. The Fed kept cutting rates. Before long, a financial boom was on.

In 2004, Kevin left his safe and boring job to join the proprietary trading desk at a big European bank, with zero job security and huge potential—one of the ballsier and more correct decisions of his life. The

European bank was about to get into collateralized debt obligations. The stock market determined the size of your apartment and whether you had a Viking stove—who was rich and who wasn't. The bond market determined if shit worked or everyone was eating sand, who was alive and who wasn't. Ever since the eighties, credit had been the biggest driver. All the things that would later go wrong, structured credit, default swaps, were good inventions; they mitigated risk or offered financial solutions to companies and investors. The problem was the execution. In the mid-2000s, when there was just too much money on the table, the moral compass moved.

The culture of the prop desk was extremely aggressive. The dopey bankers in Europe wanted to leverage their deposit base, so they turned control over to the cowboys in New York and London, who started driving around drinking and shooting out the windows. The prop desk was on a lower floor—after 9/11 the trading desks were moved down there to keep the moneymakers alive, so the guys earning millions stared out at the sandwich shop across the street while the HR chicks making forty grand sat in cubicles on the upper floors with amazing views of the river. On the prop desk there was no team, just a bunch of guys all playing with a piece of the bank's balance sheet for a shot at enormous rewards. Kevin traded credit derivatives and corporate bonds—things like airline debt.

When you were on a prop desk and getting it right, there was nothing better on Wall Street, and for two years he got it right. He earned close to a million dollars a year, most of it his bonus—multiples of his previous pay—and he would have made more if he had cared more. He paid off the mortgage on his apartment in the East Village, lived off his salary, and saved the bonus. He didn't own a car or a boat. He became a connoisseur of New York's best restaurants and picked up the tab for his starving-artist friends. He didn't need more.

It wasn't just American mortgages that blew up the world—it was global credit. Kevin was part of that, and during the middle years of the decade he watched the credit bubble inflate. He wasn't doing anything wrong—he had a great deal going on the prop desk and didn't want to screw it up. He wasn't like the guys saying "Just print the fucking CDO, we'll get the bonuses this year and when it blows up in three years we won't even be here." But he knew that something was off kilter. He had a girlfriend in the European country where the bank was based, and on one visit he saw all these people using its ATM cards, and he thought, "This is a fucking regular bank. This isn't Bear or Merrill." For every dollar his girl-friend put in her savings account, Kevin was buying forty dollars' worth of bonds. At one point in 2005, he was shown a huge trade by a salesperson from Deutsche Bank. Greg Lippmann, the head of Deutsche's CDO desk, was short the housing market—he might have been the only bond trader at a big Wall Street firm who saw that everyone in Florida and Nevada was about to start defaulting on their mortgages—and he needed someone to take on some of his credit derivative risk. "Look, here's the deal," the salesperson said, "there's all these fucking mortgages and they're all full of shit." But Kevin passed. It all made sense—he never understood why all those houses in places like Tampa were worth anything—but he didn't know mortgages well enough to get in that deep and then time getting out right. And it turned out to be the right call, because he would have lost a ton of money at the start, and he left the prop desk well before the trade made Lippmann millions and Deutsche Bank $1.5 billion.

At the end of 2005, when Kevin was almost thirty, he followed his boss to the emerging markets desk, working between London and New York, trading corporate bonds and traveling to fun places like Buenos Aires and Kiev. He had platinum status on every airline and knew some foreign cities a lot better than the places in America where people filled their pickup trucks with subsidized gas and drove thirty miles to a job. In 2006 everything took off, people were buying any financial asset they could get. Prices in London were so retarded that Kevin would buy a month's worth of socks at Century 21 in lower Manhattan, take them to London, and then throw them away after wearing them because it was more expensive to wash them in Mayfair than buy them in New York. It said that something was fucking wrong, that it couldn't last, and at the end of the year he went short.

He thought the world was going to bust three or four times before it finally did. The credit market was such a confidence game that when it started to wobble, everyone got really scared, because they knew it was too big for them to get out. The first wobble came in February 2007, when there was a collateral dispute between Merrill Lynch and a Bear Stearns hedge fund. The market shat itself for a week—you didn't want to be the last guy in the swimming pool with a bunch of toasters. Kevin thought it was the beginning of the end and didn't cover his short, but the market came roaring back for five months—he got it completely wrong. If he'd gotten it right he'd be living in twenty thousand square feet.

In July, just after Kevin had sold a bunch of crappy Ukrainian bonds, a guy in his department came up to him and said, "You are the only person on this whole floor who is short. You are such a pussy."

"There are more than three hundred people on this floor," Kevin said. "Don't you think more than one guy ought to be short? Go ahead, here's the prices—you can have five million of everything you want up to a hundred million, I'll sell you everything." The guy said he'd get back to him, but Kevin never heard a thing—so who was the pussy?

That month brought the second wobble. The Bear Stearns hedge fund got another margin call, and this time the shit was so worthless that Bear had to step in and shut the fund down. Instead of eating the loss, the bank decided to assume the financing, which meant that Bear now had the virus and led directly to the third wobble, in March 2008, when Bear went down and Kevin's desk was one of the first to pull the wire.

Kevin spent the summer of 2008 traveling all the time, some for work, some for fun—Argentina, China, Ukraine. In mid-September, he landed in a former Soviet republic at 4:00 a.m., turned on his BlackBerry, and saw on his Bloomberg application that Lehman had filed for bankruptcy. Bear had just been a mortgage bucket shop; Lehman was a completely different animal, a global player in derivatives, and Kevin's bank had a ton of shit with them. It took him twenty-four hours to get back to London, then on to New York, where he had a good seat for the end of the world.

Within a few weeks he realized the scale of the destruction, the number of trades that had to be unwound, and it was a fascinating time to wake up and go in to work. It was the kind of seminal moment that few people got to experience. You found out what people were really like. The rank-and-file guys in the trenches next to him pretty much hung together, and his boss stayed loyal, but the ethical cream didn't rise to the top. Because of the bank's exposure to Lehman, someone from senior management came in one day looking for scapegoats and said, "Who the fuck did this?" Guys at the top were shoving one another out of the way to get in a lifeboat, all the while saying, "You'll be fine. Stay right here and help that book out of its risk and we'll have you with a fresh start next year." Kevin wasn't fooled: "Dude, I can feel the red dot on my forehead." He was a rook and the game was all about what the queens and kings decided. By the end of the year half the people in trading were gone, with good severance pay, including Kevin.

He was glad to be out of the industry, and he took a very detached view of the whole thing. Who was responsible? It was hard to say with anything that big. On one level, he always thought that finance was bullshit. He hadn't been doing God's work—it was a job, and he never ascribed any value to it. At the same time, a good financial system was beneficial to a lot of people. It kept borrowing costs low, it meant you could carry a plastic card in your pocket instead of gold coins. Without the juice of Wall Street behind it, something like Silicon Valley couldn't have exploded the way it did.

But when the private partnerships like Salomon started going public in the eighties, and boutique investment banks became huge trading houses, and dopey European banks like UBS got big into fixed income, and the repeal of Glass-Steagall erased the clear lines that had kept things in check, and the pay incentives were thrown out of whack, and the money got crazy—then people on Wall Street became greedy. Some of the worst were criminals, others were doing what they knew was just fucking wrong. Kevin didn't know if the answer was reregulation or a moral housecleaning. It was ridiculous for a hedge fund manager like John Paulson to make $3.8 billion in one year just for pushing paper around, but how could you stop it? It was too late to restore Glass-Steagall and go back to the 1950s. The financial sector had gotten way too big—those minds on the Street should have been finding the green energy cure or starting the next tech boom. That was the country's future, not banking.

Kevin spent a year traveling and seeing friends all over the world. He missed most of the recession at home, and anyway, New York came back pretty fast—there was a brief moment in the spring of 2009 when people wondered if they could still go out to restaurants. Wall Street came back, too, faster than anyone expected, and in 2010 Kevin got an offer from another European bank with a safe balance sheet. He hadn't made enough in his first ten years to stay out of the game, so he went back in. On Wall Street the financial crisis felt like a speed bump.

Nelini Stamp heard that a Canadian magazine had called for some kind of action around Wall Street at noon on Saturday, September 17, 2011—it was all over Facebook, plus she knew one of the organizers—but by the time she went downtown people had already left the Charging Bull statue in Bowling Green because it had been cordoned off by police. The word was that everyone had gone a few blocks north up Broadway to a park

under this big red thing. It was called Zuccotti Park—hardly anyone in
New York knew it existed—right across Trinity Place from Ground Zero,
where they were just finishing the 9/11 Memorial. Nelini got there in mid-
afternoon and found about three hundred people, including a few of her
friends, standing next to a giant sculpture of red steel beams rising like
outstretched arms three stories into the sky. She walked around the park
with her friends for a long time as the numbers grew. It was pretty cool.
Her friend who'd helped plan it said, "We're going to have a General
Assembly," and Nelini said, "Okay. I want to see that."

The General Assembly started at seven on the granite steps down
from the sidewalk along Broadway. Someone shouted *"Mic check!"* and
other people shouted back *"Mic check!"*

"What does that mean?" Nelini asked.

"We're going to use the people's mic," her friend said.

"What does *that* mean?"

Whatever the person speaking said, everyone around her repeated
as loud as they could, a few words at a time, then again in two or three
waves outward from the center, so that eventually everyone in the crowd
could hear without using amplification, because they didn't have a permit.
Nelini thought that was cool, too. It brought everyone together in a way a
normal microphone didn't. There were no leaders, just facilitators who'd
been trained in the technique of consensus. The GA wasn't about issuing
demands. People were in the park to express outrage at the banks and
corporations and the power they had over people's lives and democracy.

After the GA, they broke up into working groups and Nelini chose Outreach, because she was already thinking that they needed to get unions
on board and she knew a lot of people in the labor movement. There were
six or seven people in Outreach and they talked till almost midnight, and
suddenly someone arrived with boxes of pizza. Everyone was madly tweeting and the word had gotten out to some local pizza place, which donated
the pies. Nelini didn't do Twitter, didn't like the whole social networking
thing because people acted like it was real life and it wasn't. She was on
Facebook because it was the only way to communicate with some of her
friends. "What are you tweeting?" Nelini asked.

"Occupy Wall Street."

She would have to get on Twitter. It was kind of crazy, the whole thing
was crazy, but she decided not to go home that night. She didn't want to
give up the park, and she wanted to see what would happen in the morning.

Zuccotti was privately managed, and the organizers had researched it and found out that Brookfield Properties had to keep the park open to the public twenty-four hours a day. That night about sixty people slept there. It was freezing cold for September. Nelini laid a piece of cardboard on the hard granite ground by the planters along Cedar Street and cuddled with her friends and tried to get some sleep before the first full day of the occupation.

She was twenty-three, a Brooklyn girl, two credits short of a high school diploma. Her mom was Puerto Rican and worked in customer service for Time Warner Cable; her dad came from Belize, had four kids by four women, and wasn't part of her life. Nelini was short and hyper, with a wide mouth and caramel skin and hair that could be frizzy or straight, black or hennaed, depending on her mood. She liked to wear short skirts with tights, ankle boots, and sweaters over scoopneck tops. She smoked Camels and talked in a rapid run-on with a hoarse staccato laugh. At the beginning of 2011 she got a tattoo on her right forearm, the names of the five New York boroughs in Old Dutch, because she liked history, and also because she wanted to remember that things change.

When Nelini was a little girl, her mom came out as a lesbian, and Nelini's grandparents stopped talking to her for a while. Nelini thought it was weird that people didn't like gays as much as straights—her mom was her mom, and normal. Her mom's partner worked at Smith Barney, and the day in 1998 when the merger of Travelers/Salomon Smith Barney and Citicorp was announced—the biggest corporate merger in American history—was also Take Your Daughter to Work Day. Nelini, age ten, and the other kids were ushered into a large room where a press conference was just letting out. The new logo of Citigroup, the largest financial services company in the world, was projected onto a screen with the red umbrella, and Sandy Weill was all smiles (he had talked to Clinton and knew that the Glass-Steagall Act, the only legal obstacle to the deal, would be repealed). Nelini didn't know what a merger was, but at school the next day she had the jump on her friends: "Did you guys hear about Citigroup?"

Her mom's partner lost her job right before 9/11, and then they broke up, and Nelini and her mom ended up in a rental on Staten Island surrounded by Irish and Italian families. Nelini loved music, theater, and dance. As a kid she had a manager, acted in a couple of movies, and played cello on Divas Live 98 on VH1—then things got tight and she had to drop her private classes. The whole performing world was full of stress. You had to have the right body, the right hair, and make it big by your twenties, and what was success anyway? Signing with a major record label and putting out crappy music? But the other half of her personality, the realistic half, was drawn to stories of workers and struggle. At school she loved reading about the Great Depression and FDR—it all seemed so real. She liked looking at the iconic picture of workers eating lunch on the steel beam at Rockefeller Center way up over Manhattan, and she plowed through a huge biography of the labor martyr Joe Hill. She always thought her mom belonged to a union, and when she finally learned that that wasn't the case, she was crushed.

Ever since fifth grade Nelini had wanted to attend LaGuardia High School of Performing Arts, but in her senior year there she stopped being excited about her future. She had self-esteem issues and became depressed. The school was too big, and the educational system didn't care about her, so she stopped going to classes, and when the high school wouldn't let her walk at graduation because she still needed to attend summer school, she said "Aw, fuck it" and didn't bother with her diploma, which made her mother really mad. Nelini felt bad about being another person-of-color dropout, but the school only wanted her as a statistic for graduation rates. She spent the next year at home reading, and money was so tight that at one point Nelini answered the door and was served an eviction notice by a marshal.

She had to get a job, and she found one with the Working Families Party, a political organization with ties to the unions. They had cramped, cluttered offices in downtown Brooklyn. Nelini made thirty thousand a year canvassing door-to-door for progressive candidates in local elections and issues like campaign finance reform and paid sick days. She turned out to be a star canvasser. She could find the humanity in people even when they were closing the door in her face, and she didn't get discouraged. She hadn't given up on music and the arts, but she also wanted to organize, get down and dirty, be in the fight.

She was twenty when Obama emerged in the 2008 campaign. She thought it would be awesome to have a black man as president, but she wondered if he'd turn out to be as progressive as Hillary—he knew how to play to both sides. Then, suddenly, it began to feel like a popular movement was rising, for things like single-payer health care, and if Obama was the reason for that movement, she was going to be for him. When the

Wall Street crisis hit right before the election, she thought, "This is it, the financial system is coming to an end." She expected a return to the fifties and sixties, harsh regulations and a blue-collar economy, but without the bigotry (because the American dream in those days didn't make room for people like her and her mother). Then Obama got into office and it didn't happen. Instead, the banks were back in business, the corporations and the rich made more and more money while the rest of the country suffered. Nelini moved into a tiny bedroom in a group house with other activists in Bed-Stuy, two blocks from the Marcy Houses. Running campaigns for Working Families through the recession, she began to think that the democratic system was set up to protect capital, with lobbyists and everything else, and the only way anything was going to change would be by getting rid of capitalism.

But the struggle took so long, full of little battles that kept being refought, most of the time on the defensive, trying to get a Yonkers city councilman reelected or prevent cuts to the New York City budget. There was so much cynicism, and all the complaining about injustice that went on in all the living rooms and bars never sparked the bone-dry wood—until that Saturday just after the tenth anniversary of 9/11, when a small group of people lit a fire one block east of the site.

For two weeks Nelini woke up in the sleeping bag she'd brought to the park, rode the subway to work, hurried back downtown on her lunch break with stacks of flyers she'd copied at the office, returned to work, went home to Bed-Stuy for a shower and change of clothes, got back to the park for the evening GA, where other occupiers would tell her, "You look nice," and then spent another night sleeping outside. So much was happening and she was moving so fast that people who became her best friends in the movement later told her she'd been too crazed and distracted in those early days to hold a conversation.

Within a week there were two thousand people in Zuccotti Park. The occupiers renamed it Liberty Square, after Tahrir Square in Cairo. That second Saturday, they marched up Broadway to Union Square chanting *"All day, all week, Occupy Wall Street!"* and *"We—are—the ninety-nine percent!"* Nelini danced and jumped and led the chants, a dervish running on an emotional surge, and then things turned crazy, with marchers blocking traffic and cops making scores of arrests, and she had never seen anything like it before, friends of hers being hauled away, and suddenly she started crying. A white-shirted officer squirted four women in the face with pepper spray, and when Nelini and some others realized that the video was going viral over YouTube while they were still marching, they rushed back to the park and held a quick press conference. "We're here to be nonviolent," she told the assembled cameras, and that night her mom happened to watch it on New York 1 and called her.

"I saw you down there—what are you doing?"

"I've been here for a week, Mom."

The park, the video, and the brand fused and suddenly the media became obsessed with Occupy Wall Street, the name was all over the blogs and tweets. Singers, actors, and scholars started showing up at Zuccotti, and even though no one knew exactly what it was all about—since Occupy was proceeding along the "horizontal" lines of anarchist practice, and there were no demands, no structures, no leaders—visitors to the park couldn't miss the electricity in the air, the sense that something widely felt but long buried or dispersed had exploded spontaneously into the world and come together in this chaotic, thousand-headed form.

Nelini's boss at work, Bill, knew she was involved, and one day he asked her, "You've been down at Occupy, right? What is it?"

She told him: it was the coolest thing, it was a movement, it was really happening, more and more people were getting involved, all kinds of different people, not just activists.

"The unions want to do a march in solidarity," Bill said—but they were also wary of Occupy, of what it was or could turn into. "Is it okay to do that?"

Nelini agreed to help organize a solidarity march to Foley Square with thousands of union members and students. She became a liaison between the occupation and the outside groups. The word "leader" was pretty much banned, but she was becoming one. Her boss decided to let her work at Occupy full-time, and even after she stopped sleeping at the park she only got two or three hours a night at home, she was so frantic with adrenaline and a million things to do. Her visibility brought her to the attention of some right-wing websites, and they brandished Nelini's affiliation with the Working Families Party as proof that the whole thing was being secretly controlled by ACORN, the defunct community organization, which had helped to found the party.

Late on the night of Sunday, October 2, the day after she'd been arrested, along with seven hundred others, on the Brooklyn Bridge, Nelini got a call from Max, her new friend at Occupy. There was a conference in Washington first thing Monday morning, organized by the activist Van Jones's group Rebuild the Dream, a left-wing answer to the Tea Party. Max worked for the group, and Jones had asked him to pick someone from Occupy to come down and speak, but the original choice turned out to believe in global conspiracies and lizardmen, so he had to be dropped at the last minute. Could Nelini get on a train to D.C.? She reached Penn Station at 4:30 a.m., but her credit card didn't work, so she called Max, who was broke and woke up his boss at Rebuild the Dream, who bought Nelini a plane ticket since the train was going to get in too late. In Washington she ran from her cab into the conference and was out of breath when she took the stage and started speaking.

"I went down there and didn't realize it was going to change my life," she said, straining to reach the lectern microphone and put the unbelievable excitement of the past two and a half weeks into words. "I started sleeping on cardboard and pressuring labor and community organizations to come on down and check it out . . . A lot of people have asked about demands. We don't need demands. If we demand something from Wall Street, we're telling them that they have the power. And we have the power because we have strength in numbers."

Nelini had begun to think that Occupy Wall Street was the start of a revolution.

The park was a small rectangular block paved in granite, with fifty-five honey locust trees, in the shadow of skyscrapers. On the west end, facing the huge construction site at Ground Zero, a drum circle rolled out its wild, interminable beat, adrenaline for the occupiers and annoyance for the neighbors. The drummers' area was called "the ghetto," made up of hard-core anarchists and long-term homeless people, a world unto itself, where interlopers were made to feel unwelcome. Tents were forbidden by the police, so the overnight occupiers lay down on tarps over the unforgiving granite. The center of the park was crowded with various hubs dedicated to the occupation's self-organization: the kitchen tarp, where food prepared on the outside was served to anyone who lined up; the comfort station, where occupiers could obtain donated wet wipes, toiletries, and articles of clothing; the recycling site, where people composted food waste and took turns pedaling a stationary bike to generate battery power; the library, which grew to several thousand volumes stacked high on tables; the open-air studio, where computers and cameras streamed live footage of the occupation twenty-four hours a day.

On the east end, along the wide sidewalk next to Broadway, beneath the red steel sculpture called *Joie de Vivre*, the occupation and the public merged. Demonstrators stood in a row, displaying signs as if hawking wares, while workers on their lunch hour and tourists and passersby stopped to look, take pictures, talk, argue. An elderly woman sat in a chair and read aloud from Hart Crane's "The Bridge." Another woman stood silently while holding up a copy of *Confidence Men*, a book about the Obama presidency—day after day. An old man in a sport coat and golf cap held a sign: FOR: REGULATED CAPITALISM. AGAINST: OBSCENE INEQUALITY. NEEDED: MASSIVE JOBS PROGRAM. A union electrician in a hard hat: OCCUPY WALL STREET. DO IT FOR YOUR KIDS. A woman in a blue nurse's smock: THIS RN IS SICKENED BY WALL STREET GREED. TRUST HAS BEEN BROKEN. A young woman in jeans: WHERE DID MY FUTURE GO? GREED TOOK IT. There was WE'RE HERE. WE'RE UNCLEAR. GET USED TO IT, and also SOMETHING IS WRONG.

Everyone who wasn't holding a sign was taking pictures. The crowd was dense, the talk overlapping: ". . . part of the effort to destroy the middle class all over the world . . ." "The goal is to have everyone help decide what the goal is . . ." "When was Glass-Steagall enacted?"

Two friends were standing on the sidewalk, Shira Moss and Mazal Ben-Moshe, thirty and twenty-seven. Shira had a degree in midwifery but no job, Mazal was studying social work. Shira had gotten to the park at 5:30 in the morning—she had been waiting for this her whole life. Mazal had volunteered for Obama in 2008 and was thrilled when he was elected, but after that she disappeared, didn't even bother voting in 2010, and now she felt ashamed and wanted to step forward. A few guys in hard hats, on their lunch break from construction work on 4 World Trade Center, walked by and checked out the signs. One of them, Mike, saluted the protesters. "There's no work for us anymore—we're out of work a year at a time," he said. "It's because of them"—he waved toward the narrow canyons of the financial district. "The people who are holding us back. The banks, the government, anyone who controls the money."

Two middle-aged men stopped in front of Shira and began to argue with her in heavy Russian accents. "Cuba, North Korea, Venezuela is ultimate destination of what you're doing," the first Russian said.

"My wife is midwife—she has job," the second man said.

"Congratulations, that's great," Shira said.

"You can get job, too."

"I'd love one. Can't find one."

"This is waste of your time. Go look for job—put your time into that."

"Bottom line: go to North Korea," the first Russian said. "This is your final destination."

A fortyish man in a baseball cap who had been listening said to the first Russian, "There are oligarchs in Russia. Do you see any connection between that and what she's saying?"

"This is government problem, this is not banks' problem."

The second Russian began to complain about the people in Zuccotti. "They smoke in park! This is illegal. They think they are superior."

"True or false," Shira said: "things are absolutely fair for everyone in this country."

"True," the second Russian said.

A chorus of voices: "False!"

Ray Kachel lived all of his first fifty-three years within a couple of miles of his birthplace, in Seattle. He was a self-taught jack-of-all-trades in the computer industry. In 1984 he bought his first Mac, a 512K, dropped out of Seattle Central Community College, and was hired by a company that converted printed material into digital records. At night he was into the club scene, DJing at Tugs Belltown Tavern, spinning Eurobeat, Men Without Hats, Prince. On Monday nights he also played synthesizer and drum machine in a band called 5 Sides Collide, which broke up when the singer decided she was into women. Celebrities would go there for coke— Elton John was spotted at least once—and Ray used for several months, selling to support his habit, then decided he hated the way it felt and stopped doing drugs.

The scene fell apart in the mid- to late eighties, and Ray lost his day job, too. But for the next couple of decades he made a decent living on the margins of the Seattle technology world, keeping up with advances in audio and video production, picking up freelance work editing online content. Between tech jobs he worked in his parents' janitorial business. He spent his money on a few pleasures, like microbrewery beer and his vast DVD library. His favorite movie was *Stalker*, the 1979 sci-fi film by

Andrei Tarkovsky. "Three guys traipsing through the woods—it's visually and aurally very, very strange," Ray said. "Tarkovsky is famous for painfully long takes, creating an environment that's uncomfortable without it being clear why."

Ray lived alone in a one-bedroom apartment. He was an inconspicuous person—small of stature, with short-cropped hair, drab clothes, and a mild manner. After his parents died, he became something of a hermit, with few friends. On the other hand, a lot of tech workers were antisocial. The information economy employed millions of skilled, culturally literate, freelance oddballs. As long as the new economy made room for him, Ray lived the life he wanted.

When the recession hit, tech jobs in Seattle started drying up. After the death of the owner of his main client, a company that hired him to do DVD customization, Ray found that he no longer had contacts for other work. He cut back on expenses and quit drinking beer. At the end of 2010, he ordered from Amazon a green, apple-shaped USB stick containing the entire Beatles collection; just before it was due to ship, he canceled the order. "Around that time, I started realizing spending two hundred fifty dollars on something wasn't such a good idea," he said. "I'm glad I made that decision, because I wouldn't have enjoyed the stereo mix anyway."

In March 2011, Ray's mouth went dry. He felt sick with anxiety and could barely eat. He realized that he was coming to the end of his savings. He could survive as a barista or a delivery driver, but he didn't think he was capable of chatting with customers all day, and he had stopped driving years before. He applied for every tech opening he could find, but only one offer came, from Leapforce, a company that evaluated Web search results. Ray signed on as an "At Home independent agent," doing work on his iMac for thirteen dollars an hour, but almost immediately the hours dwindled to twenty or thirty minutes a day. That was his last job.

Over the summer, Ray went on eBay to sell off his computer equipment, like a drought-stricken farmer eating his seed corn: first his Mac-Book Air, then his iPad, then his iMac. He found buyers for his DVD collection, which had a thousand titles, after first ripping digitized copies of everything. The last thing Ray sold was his copy of Final Cut Pro, Apple's state-of-the-art editing suite. "I was hoping, by holding on to that, if I found another project, I could work on somebody else's machine. But it just wasn't happening." The sales brought in about twenty-five hundred dollars. In September, he fell behind on his rent. The only thing worse than being homeless, he thought, was being homeless in his hometown.

Ray had started tweeting in 2009, as a way to become more social. On Twitter, he met many people who were in similarly desperate circumstances, unemployed and facing destitution. And on Twitter he learned, in the last days of September, as he was getting ready to vacate the apartment, about a rash that had broken out in lower Manhattan.

The protesters at Occupy Wall Street were angry about things that Ray recognized from his own life: the injustice of a system in which the rich and the powerful sucked the life out of the middle class. He had long felt critical of the banks, the oil companies, the huge corporations that didn't pay taxes. Fracking was a particular concern of Ray's. He was also an obsessive follower of Rachel Maddow—he loved her wit, her agreeableness—and she was beginning to talk about Occupy Wall Street on her cable news program.

Ray had four hundred fifty dollars from the sale of his copy of Final Cut Pro. For two hundred fifty, you could travel anywhere in America on Greyhound. He had never been farther east than Dallas, but New York City was so dense and diverse, so full of ideas and ways to make money, that if he could learn to exist there he could surely find a *place* to exist. On the last night of September he went to bed telling himself, "Oh, this is just absolutely nuts, you can't do that." He woke up in the morning with a clear thought: "This is exactly what I'm going to do."

Ray didn't tell his few friends about the plan. But on the night of October 3, he wrote on his Wordpress blog, for anyone who might be reading: "About to board a bus to NYC. Not sure if I'll ever come back to Seattle . . . I have had some moments of panic, asking myself if I've completely lost my mind. That's entirely possible. But those moments pass quickly and my sense of adventure takes over and I'm ready to hit the road all the more." He had abandoned most of his remaining possessions; he was traveling with a small duffel and a daypack, and they contained not much more than a few changes of clothes, a portable hard drive with some of his movies, and a relatively stupid cell phone with enough memory to send and download tweets. The bus left at midnight. At five in the morning on October 6, Ray arrived at the Port Authority bus terminal in midtown Manhattan. By ten, he had made his way downtown to the occupation.

The leaves on the honey locust trees were still green. The park was swarming with clusters of sign holders, drummers, kitchen workers, groups holding meetings, barkers shouting about this or that issue. Sleep-deprived and hungry, Ray was beset by a feeling of déjà vu—everything around him seemed oddly familiar. He sat on the wall along Liberty Street and listened to a conversation among a few people nearby, and his head was going to explode—he seemed to have physically been in this space, talking to these people, knowing exactly what they were going to say. At one point, someone told him that a shower could be arranged if he went down to the comfort station in the middle of the park. In the déjà vu timeline, he had gotten the shower and his life continued in a normal, contented way, leading him back to his warm bed, for he had decided not to occupy Wall Street; but in reality, there was no shower to be had, and suddenly Ray was confronted with the fact of being homeless and broke in a strange city. He withdrew into himself, speaking to no one, curling up to sleep in his fleece and waterproof shell on the steps near the east side of the park.

One day, Ray overheard a group of young occupiers who were sitting on the steps just a few feet away talking about him as if he weren't there. "He's not going to make it here doing that," one of them said. "He isn't taking care of himself." They were right—his socks and shoes, drenched in a rain-storm, had been wet for several days. Ray saw that he couldn't survive here as his own independent, satellite self. He had to become part of the col-lective in an unreserved way—something that he'd never done in his life.

He volunteered for the newly formed Sanitation Working Group. To keep warm after dark, he spent part of each night scrubbing the paths and the sidewalks. Another occupier, seeing Ray working, gave him a sleep-ing bag and a tarp. He began making friends: Sean, an Irish immigrant from the Bronx who worked the graveyard shift spraying fire retardant on steel, then came downtown to spend his days at Zuccotti; a homeless sub-stitute teacher with a degree in physics; Chris, a drifter from Tarpon Springs, Florida, who had been so outraged by the pepper-spraying video on YouTube that he had ridden the rails to Manhattan in order to defend female honor.

Ray found a sign that said BAN FRACKING NOW, and, after working on his delivery, he spent a few days talking to strangers on the sidewalk along the south side of the park. It was a little like acting, and he discovered a voice inside himself that could speak out. He tweeted regularly, and his account, which had had a few dozen followers in Seattle, suddenly grew to well over a thousand.

October 8: There are elements of communal living. it's a really amazing experience tho totally out of my comfort level.

October 22: It surprises me i have a guardian angel. it doesn't surprise me he's a soft-spoken, hard working Irish guy from the bronx.

October 23: Dear mr. ferguson. i have lived in new york for over two weeks now. it does not smell of wee.

October 27: Keep seeing references to "horrendous police abuse" re: ows. i've been here 2+ weeks and have seen none and heard of little.

November 13: I lived in my old apartment in Seattle for nearly a decade and barely knew 2 other tenants . . . i've lived in liberty square for just over a month and regularly talk with many of my neighbors and have made many new friends.

So he didn't panic when, one rain-swept night, his duffel was stolen as he slept, and water entered the tarp in which he was rolled up, soaking his sleeping bag; and he stayed calm the next morning when his daypack—including the portable hard drive—was taken away by zealous members of the Sanitation Working Group who were clearing out waterlogged objects, leaving Ray with nothing but the clothes he had on. He turned to his new friends for help and was given a dry sleeping bag. By then, he belonged to the occupation. Liberty Square was his home.

On Wednesday, October 12, Mayor Bloomberg and the NYPD announced that the park would be cleared that Friday for cleaning. Neighbors were complaining about the nonstop drumming at the western end, the trashy look of the place, the reported incidents of public urinating and defecating. Nelini had been spending a lot of her time trying to get the drum circle to cool it. She attended meetings of the local community board, heard the complaints, and tried to work out an agreement under which the drumming would be limited to two hours a day. But when the city's announcement came, she and other occupiers took it as a disguised plan to shut them down.

They raised the alarm through social media, and around the city supporters bombarded elected officials with phone calls and Facebook posts. By Thursday night, thousands of people had descended on the park to prevent the police from clearing it. Zuccotti had never been so crowded—even people who had been skeptical of the occupation, who found the drum circle annoying and disliked the activists' clichés, were there in the belief that something important, something that belonged to all of them, was under threat.

No one from Occupy would talk to the mayor's office on principle (though the principle remained obscure). So Nelini's boss, Bill, was negotiating feverishly with the deputy mayor behind the scenes to keep the park open. Nelini went home late that night for an hour's sleep because Zuccotti was too crowded. When she came back at 5:00 a.m., the occupiers were already awake. Over the next hour Zuccotti filled up again, and by six, people were squeezed into every foot of granite from Broadway to Trinity Place. It was still dark when Nelini's phone rang.

"We won," her boss said.

"What?"

"We're not getting kicked out. Get to Becca right now."

Nelini's friend Becca was standing at the top of the Broadway steps. There was a message from Bill in her phone, and Nelini began reading it to the huge crowd.

"Late last night!" She waited as the human microphone carried her words from east to west in three receding waves. "We received notice from the owners of Zuccotti Park! Brookfield Properties! That they are postponing their cleaning!" The roar began before the first wave could carry the message across the park and continued for almost a full minute. Thousands of hands raised tens of thousands of fingers and wiggled them in the nonverbal anarchist language of approval. Nelini started again: "The reason why! Is because! They believe they could work out an arrangement with us! But also! Because we have a lot of people here!"

Afterward, she could hardly remember what happened during the single most dramatic moment of her life, it was so surreal. Her friend Max said, "This is going to make an excellent moment in the movie."

"You're ruining it," Nelini said.

"I wonder who's going to play you."

When Occupy started, Kevin Moore's colleagues at the bank were dismissive. One guy in the office said, "They should just take out the fucking billy clubs and get in there." But after ending his workday in midtown (most of Wall Street was no longer on Wall Street), Kevin made a point of going down to check it out, and then he kept going back. He liked the free flow of conversations on Broadway, the spectacle of the park. The scene in Zuccotti reminded him of the city back in the eighties, when he attended private school, listened to Run-D.M.C., and went down to Times Square to watch the games of three-card monte and the police raids— when New York was wilder and more ragged. The occupation of the park was a big strain on the police force and the neighborhood, and just sitting there was going to get old pretty fast. They'd have to figure out another way to keep the issues in focus. But he was glad that someone was calling attention to those issues. He knew some of them firsthand.

There were things Kevin didn't like about Occupy. The protesters needed a marketing director, and he thought they should be talking about the 0.1 percent, since he was part of the 1 percent and he had no control over politicians. He also didn't like the way some protesters demonized everyone who worked in finance, just the way his colleague at the bank demonized everyone in the park. It was like the Democrats and Republicans, talking past each other. Once, on a trip to London, Kevin saw some Occupy types storming what they thought was an investment house, but they had the wrong building—it was just a regular bank branch, and the snowballs were hitting back office workers. Kevin knew about the sins of Wall Street, but the level of the protesters' vitriol surprised him. If they wanted change, they'd have to appeal to the better angels of a banker's nature.

From lower Manhattan, the protean flame spread around the country and the world. Within weeks there were twenty-five, fifty, a hundred occupations. The movement's slogan, "We are the 99 percent," was simple and capacious enough to cover a multitude of discontents and desires. It became the name of a blog on Tumblr that collected a gallery of hundreds of faces in snapshots sent by readers, some obscured or half hidden by the anonymous autobiographical statement that each person wrote down on a piece of paper and held up for the camera. A face in darkness:

I did everything they told me to, in order to be successful.
I got straight A's and a scholarship.
I went to University and got a degree.
Now I'm sinking in student debt, unable to get a job.
I have an eviction notice on my door, and nowhere to go.
I have only $42 in the bank.
I AM THE 99%!

A woman's blurry features peering out from behind the sheet:

I am a 37 year old who makes $8.00 an hour in a management position. Our assistant and general managers make a decent 5 figures to do nothing but talk about employees/customers. I don't get 10 minute breaks, nor 30 minute meal periods.
After paying:
    Insurance
    Federal & State taxes
    Social Security
    Medicare
I am left working for the gas money to get to work.
I AM PISSED!

Read by the dozens, these compressed, homemade life stories amassed the moral force of documentary research from hard times, or a Steinbeck novel. And they explained why Occupy Wall Street became an instant brand name.

Uses of the phrase "income inequality" quintupled in the media, and President Obama gave a speech on the subject, talking about the 1 percent. Every celebrity and public figure had an opinion about Occupy. Colin Powell expressed guarded sympathy and recalled an earlier time when his parents in the South Bronx could always count on having a job. Robert Rubin talked about thirty years of falling median real wages (except for the late nineties): "They've identified issues that are really central to what's going to happen to our economy." Peter Thiel told an interviewer,

"In the history of the modern world, inequality has only been ended through communist revolution, war, or deflationary economic collapse. It's a disturbing question which of these three is going to happen today, or if there's a fourth way out." Elizabeth Warren, campaigning for the Senate, said, "I created much of the intellectual foundation for what they do." Newt Gingrich, campaigning for president, was heckled by Occupy protesters at Harvard, and afterward he told the audience at an Iowa family values forum, "All the Occupy movement starts with the premise that we all owe them everything. They take over a public park they didn't pay for, to go nearby to use bathrooms they didn't pay for, to beg for food from places they don't want to pay for, to obstruct those who are going to work to pay the taxes to sustain the bathrooms and to sustain the park, so they can self-righteously explain that they are the paragons of virtue to which we owe everything. Now, that is a pretty good symptom of how much the left has collapsed as a moral system in this country, and why you need to reassert something as simple as saying to them: 'Go get a job right after you take a bath.'" Asked for his opinion, Andrew Breitbart replied, "It depends if you're talking about the fecal angle, the public masturbation angle, the rape, or the grope angle of Occupy Wall Street. We're covering all of the circus." He narrated a film exposé called *Occupy Unmasked*, the last project he completed before his death, released posthumously. Jay-Z started selling an "Occupy All Streets" line of Rocawear T-shirts, but later on he defended entrepreneurs among the 1 percent from Occupy Wall Street's attacks. "This is free enterprise," Jay-Z said. "This is what America is built on."

Throughout October occupations sprang up everywhere. Occupy Youngstown drew some veterans of Save Our Valley, the movement to keep the steel mills open in the late seventies. On October 15, seven hundred people marched through downtown Greensboro, past the banks and the civil rights museum housed in the old Woolworth's building, to Festival Park. Dean Price was one of them. He had gone to the Occupy Greensboro planning meeting, and after the march he talked to the kids who pitched tents in the parking lot of the YWCA next to the park and were serving pasta to homeless men. They told Dean their stories of low-wage jobs, no health insurance, mountains of college debt, and it made him angry to think that anyone who got started around 1950 or 1960 had everything and didn't do fuck with it, just sat at the table and gorged themselves till they were full and then left the scraps for the next generation. Now young people were protesting on Wall Street because the whole thing was hog-tied, but Dean tried to make the occupiers see the change that was coming, right there in Greensboro.

In Tampa, Matt Weidner started blogging about Occupy just a few days after the protesters took the park, and didn't let up. He compared it to Shays' Rebellion just after the Revolutionary War, called it "the Tea Party with brains," and in a post titled "Mr. President—Tear Down This Wall (Street)," he wrote:

> The Occupy Wall Street movement is just the beginning. Admittedly small, but powerful and frankly quite dangerous. Both to the established order and to the way of life that this country is currently infected by. This current way of life is not sustainable. This country has become a lie. It has become a lie because our leaders, both elected and business, have become utterly corrupt. Truth and consequences no longer matter. Lies and greed drive all. Wall Street and Goldman Sachs have supplanted the ideals and principles embodied in our former national center, Washington, DC.

Occupy Tampa brought hundreds of marchers to a downtown park. Danny Hartzell wanted to be there, because he liked the message about corporate greed, but he didn't have time between Wal-Mart and the kids, plus there was the price of gas to think about. Sylvia Landis went down and saw retirees like herself, students carrying debt, families, unemployed people with underwater houses. Some of the younger protesters seemed aimless, and their anticapitalist rhetoric worried Sylvia. She didn't consider herself part of Occupy, but she brought them leftover mac and cheese that she'd made for a party, and she drove a group of them to a training session given by foreclosure defense attorneys in Sarasota. But after a few weeks, a few tropical squalls, and numerous trespassing arrests, downtown returned to its habitually depopulated character, and Occupy Tampa dwindled to eight or ten lonely protesters holding signs on the riverfront while an occasional passing car gave a honk, and eventually they agreed to move to an isolated park in West Tampa that was owned by the proprietor of a strip club called Mons Venus.

In late October, the rule against tents in Zuccotti Park was relaxed. Ray, who had inherited a zero-degree sleeping bag and a one-man tent when the substitute teacher landed a small share in a loft, claimed a patch of ground eighteen inches by six feet along the south side. Zuccotti quickly filled up with tents, so that it became hard to walk through, and Ray found that this closed the park off from the public, making it less lively and more squalid. He rose early every morning and walked a few blocks to watch the sun come up over the East River, then explored the Lower East Side and Chinatown before wending his way back to Zuccotti. The fish-bowl intensity of the park was starting to get to him—lyrics from the old XTC song "Senses Working Overtime" kept running through his head. The drum circle was starting to have the atmosphere of Fellini's *Satyri-con*. Ray missed having a TV to disappear into—he had left Seattle before the last two episodes of *Breaking Bad*, the most brilliant show since *The Wire*. His days were spent recharging his phone at Starbucks and taking care of other mundane business. He used his food stamp card to buy a few pieces of fruit and a bar of unsweetened 80-percent-cocoa chocolate at the Whole Foods north of Ground Zero. He ate so little that it didn't matter if he was down to just a few dollars, as long as the park's kitchen continued serving food. Around nine at night, Ray zipped himself up in his one-man tent, watched the Twitter feed for the Rachel Maddow show on his phone, then went to sleep early in order to get a few hours' rest before the noise of young people partying nearby woke him up. He never slept more than four or five hours. One night, the park filled with a sustained chorus of howling.

Ray found that it wasn't easy staying active in Occupy Wall Street. He got involved in an Occupy Central Park group, but it faded when the city refused to issue a permit. He rarely attended the nightly General Assembly by the red sculpture, where the human mic carried on for hours and nothing was ever resolved. The movement seemed to be losing its hold on the ordinary public. The same issue of its newspaper, the *Occupied Wall Street Journal*, was handed out for weeks. A loud lunatic element marred the conversations along Broadway. There were dozens of "working groups," and many of them held meetings a few blocks from the park, in the atrium of the Deutsche Bank building at 60 Wall Street. But a few activists seemed to dominate these groups, in an insular conversation about "the process" that kept returning to ideas for restructuring into smaller groups in order to refine the process and make it "more inclusive." A division was opening up between the activists talking in the atrium and the occupiers holding down the park. At one meeting of the Facilitation Working Group, a man asked Ray—an unfamiliar face—why he was there.

Ray knew why he was there. "As a symbol, the park needs to stay occupied," he said. "If they say, 'Okay, we'll listen to what you're saying— let's everybody chill out and go home and we'll continue the discussion,' the focus goes away, the TV trucks go away, and the people become complacent and get into their reality shows, and who knows what kind of bubbles get burst."

Around the time that Ray was growing disenchanted, Nelini was getting frustrated, too. In the euphoria of the early weeks, when seven hundred people attended a General Assembly, one person couldn't disrupt it. But as the meetings shrank to thirty or forty people in the atrium, two or three people from, like, the Direct Democracy Working Group could start an argument or block consensus and disrupt the whole thing, and sometimes they'd use race or gender as a pretext, so it was really hard for someone like Max, a white man, to call them on it. Nelini didn't know if they were provocateurs, but she wished someone would step up and tell them, "Actually, what you are saying has nothing to do with what they were addressing and this needs to be stopped."

Occupy was dominated by the kind of people who ran the Canadian magazine that had gotten the whole thing started, *Adbusters*—very educated postmodern anarchists. Nelini was self-conscious about never having finished high school—they'd read so many books she'd never heard of—and they also made her feel sometimes that she wasn't radical enough. She was an organizer, and she worried that Occupy was becoming too narrow, and she wanted to figure out how to turn it into a durable movement that could work on achieving practical goals, like getting people to close their accounts at the big banks and moving the homeless into foreclosed houses. She thought that at some point Occupy would need to come up with demands. She was even beginning to think that it might be better to move on from Zuccotti Park.

In November, as the leaves on the honey locusts turned yellow, the occupation started to fray. The park acquired a desperate edge—it felt more like a Hooverville than a sit-in. In Ray's neighborhood, the appearance of a ratty sofa became a source of considerable tension. Chris, the drifter from Florida who had been outraged by the video of women being pepper-sprayed, hauled the sofa off a Manhattan street. But it attracted revelers who had no interest in the movement, and it took up space that could go to two tents, and after much discussion the sofa was handed over to the drum circle. Then one night it was back. While Ray lay zipped up in his tent a few feet away, Chris, who had been drinking vodka, and another man got into an argument over the sofa that ended in Chris landing a punch and being led off under arrest. Within a few days, he was back.

Just after midnight on November 15, Nelini was in her room in Bed-Stuy when she got a call from her Occupy friend Yotam, wishing her a happy birthday—she had just turned twenty-four. While they were talking, she checked her Twitter feed. Questlove, the drummer for the Roots, one of her favorite hip-hop groups, had tweeted at 11:38: "Omg, drivin down south st near #ows. Somethin bout to go down yo, swear I counted 1000 riot gear cops bout to pull sneak attack #carefulyall."

Nelini told Yotam, "I think they're raiding the park."

Ray woke up to a clamor of voices. He soon made sense of what people were saying: the police were moving in. The park lights were shut off and a bank of klieg lights from the north end flooded the tents. Ray put his shoes on and stepped outside his tent to see a cop walking through the park, handing out leaflets that instructed occupiers to leave or be arrested. Loudspeakers were blaring the same announcement: Zuccotti Park was being closed because of fire and health concerns. Quickly, Ray broke down his tent. He packed his belongings into a plastic bin and carried it out of the park, along with his sleeping bag and pad. He began crossing Broadway as a wave of police swept into the park and tore down everything in their path.

Nelini's taxi got her to lower Manhattan around one in the morning. Cops in riot gear were everywhere and they had Broadway blocked off north of Liberty, police vans lined the side streets, corrections buses, garbage trucks, flatbeds loaded with metal barricades, and even a backhoe rumbled down Broadway, and helicopters clattering overhead shone searchlights into the financial district. A block away the red sculpture was bathed in floodlights and a loudspeaker was droning incomprehensibly. The streets were full of people who had heard the news and rushed downtown to rage at the police: "Fuck you! Get the fuck out of my country!" "Arrest the real criminals!" "You're making bin Laden proud, guys! Thanks for serving the Taliban! Make your brothers and sisters who died in Iraq and Afghanistan proud! Serve and protect the United States—who are you protecting?" A chant of *"We—are—the ninety-nine percent!"* started, and then *"This is what a police state looks like!"*

"I know what a police state looks like," a black cop said. "This is not it."

Nelini was close to people in the NYPD—both her aunts and a friend of her mom's were in the force. She used to blame the brutality on the administrators at the top, but after the Union Square arrests she thought, "Okay, all the white shirts are crazy," and finally she flipped it around— maybe there were some good individuals scattered through the lower ranks, but she had absolutely no respect for the institution.

She was in a group that was getting pushed up Broadway near Maiden Lane and she had her back turned to the cops with her hands up so they wouldn't have an excuse to grab her. She was on her phone when she turned around and felt the spray hit her face on the right side. Her contact lens popped out and her right eye burned as if it had been squirted with lemon juice. She ran into a store with others who'd been sprayed and bought milk and water to pour into her eye. A while later, she saw her friend Jeremy get arrested and she ran over, yelling, and when a cop grabbed her, people pulled her back and she got away. But at around 3:00 a.m. she was walking with friends farther up on Broadway when a police car pulled over—"That's her, that's her"—and three cops jumped out and tackled her to the ground as she yelled, "My hat!"

They put her in metal cuffs, drove her back to the park, and transferred her to a van, where she sat with four cops for what seemed like hours. She told one of the cops that she was having her period, and he expressed sympathy—he had teenage girls of his own. Finally they drove her to 1 Police Plaza for booking. On the way in she passed her friend Yotam, who had just been released. "Happy birthday, darling," he said. "See you later."

Nelini spent the first day and night of her twenty-fourth year in jail, singing songs of the revolution, thinking about the next stage, and trying to get some sleep.

As the financial district became a militarized zone, Ray's only thought was of escape. He decided to make his way along the route of his morning walks, now lugging his worldly possessions. He went past the Federal Reserve Bank of New York, past Chase Manhattan Bank (where he still had forty-two cents left in an account that he'd opened with Washington Mutual before it imploded during the financial crisis and was bought up by Chase), past the AIG building, then under the FDR Drive to the East River. He wanted to get away from all the tumult, and he found an isolated spot just south of the Brooklyn Bridge, where he sat on a bench and tweeted: "earlier than usual i'm at what has become a favorite morning spot. i fear i be no much of an occupier as i've left behind my comrades." Every now and then a police helicopter appeared overhead, but he was pretty well hidden.

Ray kept checking Twitter, but by four in the morning there was still no word about where the evicted occupiers were going to gather again. His phone battery was dying. He was alone: a homeless man in New York.

At dawn it began to rain. Zuccotti Park, surrounded by metal barricades, was empty except for the security guards in lime-green vests—once again a plain granite rectangle waiting for the first workers to begin their day on Wall Street.

2012

$2 BILLION PRICE TAG FOR PRESIDENTIAL ELECTION . . . But on Friday, the cavalry arrived: a $5 million check from Mr. Adelson to Winning Our Future, a "super PAC" that supports Mr. Gingrich. . . . "You graduated from college two years ago. We've been supporting you for two years and that's enough." "Do you know how crazy the economy is right now? I mean, all my friends get help from their parents." . . . With his hood up as the rain came down, Trayvon made his way to one gated community among many, the Retreat at Twin Lakes. Past a dozen storefronts, four of them vacant. Past signs and billboards shouting "Now Leasing!" and "Rent Specials!" His was a tour of a post-bust stretch of Sanford. . . . @BarackObama: "Same-sex couples should be able to get married."—President Obama . . . **TWO NFL PLAYERS GO HEAD TO HEAD ON GAY MARRIAGE** . . . Young people, selected by lottery, slaughter one another with kill-or-be-killed desperation in "The Hunger Games." The savagery is a yearly ritual mandated by the tyrannical regime of Panem, a broken nation built, after a terrible war . . . **WHY DO BILLIONAIRES FEEL VICTIMIZED BY OBAMA?** . . . The Kelleys were known for their lavish parties, with extravagant buffets, flowing Champagne, valet parking and cigars for guests from nearby MacDill Air Force Base, including David H. Petraeus and Gen. John R. Allen, who now commands troops . . . **WHAT BOTCHED THE FACEBOOK IPO?** . . . 47 percent of the people who will vote for the President no matter what. All right, there are 47 percent who are with him, who are dependent upon government, who believe that they are victims, who believe the government has a responsibility to care for them, who believe that they are entitled to health care, to food, to housing, to . . . On Nov. 5 "Start-Ups: Silicon Valley," a series that follows the lives of six entrepreneurs, premieres on the channel. "We were looking for a place that hadn't been saturated with a bunch of reality," Evan Prager, one of the executive producers, told . . . *We saw the lights of spiritual shining / Getting closer every minute* . . . **OBAMA'S NIGHT** . . . **"Something better awaits us"** . . . **AS ELECTORATE CHANGES, FRESH WORRY FOR G.O.P.** . . . *Then we skipped the rails, and we started to fail / And we folded up, and it's not enough / To think about how close we came / I wanna walk like a giant on the land*

SILICON VALLEY

The last time Peter Thiel went to the World Economic Forum was in January 2009. Davos was a highly visible status marker for the global elite, but inclusion that year seemed to designate you as part of the group of people who had messed up the world. Thiel went away resolved that for the next decade he would be short status, long substance. If a sort of unwinding was happening in America, status markers became weirdly problematic—in a screwed-up society, they could not be the correct, real things. Almost nothing that had high status was a good thing to invest in.

After the global financial crisis, Thiel developed a theory about the past and the future.

It went back to 1973—"the last year of the fifties." That was the year of the oil shock, the year when median wages in America began to stagnate. The seventies was the decade when things started going wrong. A lot of institutions stopped working. Science and technology stopped progressing, the growth model broke down, government no longer worked as well as in the past, middle-class life started to fray. Then came the eighties—when Thiel graduated from high school in 1985, things had seemed very optimistic, anything was possible. And the nineties—the Internet replaced heaven, fortunes were made, everyday life with a mouse pad seemed kind of miraculous. After the millennium and the dot-com crash, a down decade—Bush 43, violence and war, a weak economy, except on Wall Street, leading to the seismic events of 2008 and a new depression. Four decades—down, up, up, down. After forty years, you were flat.

That was harder to see during the middle years, when things seemed to be going up. It was even harder to see from Silicon Valley, where the years after the dot-com crash had still been pretty good ones—the Google IPO, Facebook, the rest of social media. But thirty miles east of the Valley, people were not doing well, especially after their only asset, their house, lost half its value. In effect, those middle decades were a kind of Indian summer following the seventies, and it lasted such a long time—about a quarter century, if you started with the end of the Reagan recession in 1982 and ended with the housing collapse in 2007—that it would be almost impossible to go back to where things stood before it all began and try to reset. Throughout the Indian summer, the same key institutions continued to erode, with a lot of recession years and financial panics along the way. One way to see the Indian summer was as a series of bubbles: the bond bubble, the tech bubble, the stock bubble, the emerging markets bubble, the housing bubble . . . One by one they had all burst, and their bursting showed that they had been temporary solutions to long-term problems, maybe evasions of those problems, distractions. With so many bubbles—so many people chasing such ephemera, all at the same time—it was clear that things were fundamentally not working.

In the spring of 2011, Mitt Romney came through Silicon Valley looking for supporters, and he stopped by Thiel's house in San Francisco for breakfast. Romney said that his campaign was going to focus on the economy, not social issues, and let the numbers make his argument. Thiel found him extremely polished and impressive, and he offered Romney a prediction: "I think the most pessimistic candidate is going to win, because if you are too optimistic it suggests you are out of touch." In other words, it would be a mistake for Romney just to argue that Obama was incompetent, and that things would automatically be much better with a different president. Reagan might have been able to make that argument against Carter in 1980, but in 1980 only 50 percent of the people thought that their children would be worse off than they were, while in 2011 it was closer to 80 percent. It would be smarter for Romney to say that things could be much better, but getting there would be very hard and would take more than changing presidents. But it was a point that Romney couldn't grasp. He assumed that the more optimistic candidate would always win. He assumed that things were still fundamentally working.

For example, what about the information age? Wasn't it working unbelievably well? Thiel, whom it had made rich, no longer thought so.

At Café Venetia in downtown Palo Alto—the spot where Thiel and Elon Musk had decided over coffee in 2001 to take PayPal public, five blocks up University Avenue from the original offices of PayPal, which were across the street from the original offices of Facebook and the current offices of Palantir, six miles from the Google campus in Mountain

View, less than a mile in one direction and half a block in the other direction from that secular temple of the new economy known as an Apple Store, in the heart of the heart of Silicon Valley, surrounded by tables full of trim, healthy, downwardly dressed people using Apple devices while discussing idea creation and angel investments—Thiel pulled an iPhone out of his jeans pocket and said, "I don't consider this to be a technological breakthrough."

Compared to the Apollo space program or the supersonic jet, a smartphone looked small. In the forty years leading up to 1973, there had been huge technological advances, and wages had increased sixfold. Since then, Americans beguiled by mere gadgetry had forgotten how expansive progress could be.

One of Thiel's favorite books was the French writer J. J. Servan-Schreiber's *The American Challenge*, published in 1967, the year of Thiel's birth. Servan-Schreiber argued that the dynamic forces of technology and education in the United States were leaving the rest of the world behind, and he foresaw a postindustrial utopia in America by the year 2000. Time and space would no longer be barriers to communication, income inequality would shrink, and computers would set people free: "There will be only four work days a week of seven hours per day. The year will be comprised of 39 work weeks and 13 weeks of vacation . . . All this within a single generation." The information age arrived on schedule, but without the utopia. Cars, trains, and planes were not much better than they had been in 1973. The rising price of oil and food showed a complete failure to develop energy and agriculture technology. Computers didn't create enough jobs to sustain the middle class, didn't produce revolutionary improvements in manufacturing and productivity, didn't raise living standards across classes. Thiel had come to think that the Internet was "a net plus, but not a big one." Apple was "mostly a design innovator." Twitter would give job security to five hundred people for the next decade, "but how much value does it create for the entire economy?" Facebook, which had made Thiel a billionaire, was "on balance positive," because it was radical enough to have been banned in China. But that was all he would say for the celebrated era of social media. All the companies he invested in probably employed fewer than fifteen thousand people. "You have dizzying change where there's no progress."

Information itself was a sign of the problem. The creation of virtual worlds had taken the place of advances in the physical world. "You can say the whole Internet has something very escapist to it," Thiel said. "You have all these Internet companies over the past decade, and the people who run them seem sort of autistic, these mild cases of Asperger's seem to be quite rampant, there's no need for sales, the companies themselves are weirdly nonsocial in nature. Google is sort of the archetype. But in a society where things are not great and a lot of stuff is fairly dysfunctional, that may actually be where you can add the most value. We have this messy real world where things are incredibly difficult and broken, and there are crazy politics, and it's hard to get good people elected, the system doesn't quite work. And then there's this alternate virtual world in which there's no stuff, it's all zeros and ones on a computer, you can reprogram it, you can make the computer do anything you want it to. Maybe that is the best way you can actually help things in this country."

The problem came down to this: Americans, who had invented the modern assembly line, the skyscraper, the airplane, and the integrated circuit, no longer believed in the future. The future had been in decline ever since 1973. Thiel called it a "tech slowdown."

Here was one example: the sci-fi novels of the fifties and sixties, the ones he'd grown up reading, with utopian visions of space travel and undersea cities, seemed like artifacts from a distant age. Sci-fi was now about technology that didn't work or worked in bad ways. "The anthology of the top twenty-five sci-fi stories in 1970 was, like, 'Me and my friend the robot went for a walk on the moon,'" Thiel said, "and in 2008 it was, like, 'The galaxy is run by a fundamentalist Islamic confederacy, and there are people who are hunting planets and killing them for fun.'" Together with Sean Parker and two other friends, Thiel had started an early-stage venture capital firm called Founders Fund. It published an online manifesto about the future that began with a complaint: "We wanted flying cars, instead we got 140 characters."

There was no single cause of the tech slowdown. Perhaps there were no more easy technological problems, those had all been solved a generation ago and the big problems left were really hard ones, like making artificial intelligence work. Perhaps science and engineering were losing their prestige along with their federal funding. The libertarian in him pointed to overregulation of things like energy, food, and drugs—it wasn't a coincidence that the fastest growth had come in one of the least regulated industries, computers—and the kind of narrow environmentalism that wanted all the solutions to look like nature, so that hundreds of new

nuclear reactors were not on the radar. Maybe (and this thought particularly disturbed Thiel, who had a deep aversion to violence) the loss of an
enemy in the Soviet Union had taken away the incentive to work on military innovations and the larger willingness to make sacrifices—maybe an
extended peace left people with less reason to work hard, and the decline
of the future had actually begun in 1975 with the joint Apollo-Soyuz
flight, which ended the space race. Maybe education, especially higher
education, was part of the problem. A younger friend of Thiel's described
his freshman orientation at Yale, where a dean had told the incoming
students, "Congratulations—you're set for life." People should never think
they're set for life.

Thiel was an elite among elites, but he directed his intellectual fire at
his own class, or people a couple of rungs down—professionals making
two or three hundred thousand a year. Elites had become complacent.
If they couldn't grasp the reality of a tech slowdown, it was because their
own success skewed them in an optimistic direction, and wealth inequality kept them from seeing what was happening in places like Ohio. "If you
were born in 1950 and were in the top ten percent, everything got better
for twenty years automatically. Then, after the late sixties, you went to a
good grad school, and you got a good job on Wall Street in the late seventies, and then you hit the boom. Your story has been one of incredible,
unrelenting progress for sixty years. Most people who are sixty years old
in the U.S.—not their story at all." The establishment had been coasting
for a long time and was out of answers. Its failure pointed to new directions, maybe Marxist, maybe libertarian, along a volatile trajectory that it
could no longer control.

Thiel's argument ran into resistance across the political spectrum.
On the right, market fundamentalism took the place of serious thinking
about innovation (that was why Romney hadn't understood Thiel's point
at their breakfast meeting). On the left, there was an official smugness
about innovation—just spend more money—while deep down lurked an
unspoken pessimism. President Obama probably believed that there wasn't
much to be done about decline except manage it, but he couldn't give
another "malaise" speech (after what happened to Jimmy Carter, no one
ever would again), so his picture of the future remained strangely empty.
Both Obama and Romney ended up in the wrong place: the former
thought American exceptionalism was no longer true and should be given
up, while the latter thought it was still true. Neither was willing to tell

Americans that they were no longer exceptional but should try to be again.

Thiel was no longer a hedge fund titan, but as he began to air his ideas, in published essays and at the kind of elite discussion/networking sessions that proliferated across America, he was becoming the intellectual provocateur he had dreamed of being at Stanford. In the summer of 2012 he was invited to the Fortune Brainstorm Tech conference in Aspen, Colorado, where he debated the chairman of Google, Eric Schmidt, on the future of technology. Schmidt, just the kind of sanguine liberal who brought out Thiel's cerebral malice, told the audience that transistors, fiber optics, and data analytics were making the world a better and better place, and that Moore's Law, which held that computing power would double every two years, still had at least another decade left.

"Eric, I think you do a fantastic job as Google's minister of propaganda," Thiel began.

The moderator broke in. "You said you were going to be nice."

"Well, he does a fantastic job." Thiel, his blue blazer buttoned at the middle and his white shirt open several buttons down, laid out his argument about the tech slowdown. As a libertarian, he placed most of the blame on regulation. "We've basically outlawed everything having to do with the world of stuff," he said, "and the only thing you're allowed to do is in the world of bits. And that's why we've had a lot of progress in computers and finance. Those were the two areas where there was enormous innovation in the last forty years. It looks like finance is in the process of getting outlawed, so the only thing left at this point will be computers, and if you're a computer that's good. And that's the perspective Google takes."

Schmidt was smiling to suppress his irritation. The moderator pointed at the Google chairman. "You're not accusing him of being a computer, are you?"

"You know, they like computers more than people in many cases," Thiel said. "That's why they missed the social networking revolution. But if you look at it from the perspective of forty years in the future, Moore's Law is good if you're a computer. But the question is, how good is it for human beings, and how does this translate into economic progress for humans?"

Thiel loved to scandalize respectable opinion. A passage from one of his essays, "The Education of a Libertarian," rocketed around the Web in 2009 and brought down the wrath of the bien-pensants: "The 1920s were the last decade in American history during which one could be genuinely optimistic about politics. Since 1920, the vast increase in welfare beneficiaries and the extension of the franchise to women—two constituencies notoriously tough for libertarians—have rendered the notion of 'capitalist democracy' into an oxymoron." Thiel tried to explain that he didn't want to take away women's right to vote—instead, he wanted to find a way around democracy, which was incompatible with freedom. He had a long record of donating to political causes. In 2009 he funded James O'Keefe, whose undercover videos subsequently took down ACORN. In 2011 and 2012 he gave $2.6 million to Ron Paul's Super PAC and another $1 million to the pro-free-market Club for Growth, while hosting a fundraiser for a gay conservative group, GOProud, in his Union Square loft, with Ann Coulter as the featured speaker. But more and more he wanted to get away from politics, a highly inefficient way to bring about change. He remained committed to the faith of his teenage years, but Americans would not vote for libertarians.

Technology, on the other hand, could change the world without other people's permission. In the same essay, he wrote:

> In our time, the great task for libertarians is to find an escape from politics in all its forms—from the totalitarian and fundamentalist catastrophes to the unthinking demos that guides so-called "social democracy" . . . We are in a deadly race between politics and technology . . . The fate of our world may depend on the effort of a single person who builds or propagates the machinery of freedom that makes the world safe for capitalism.

Thiel set out to become that person.

On a rainy spring morning in Silicon Valley, Thiel, in windbreaker and jeans, was at the wheel of his dark blue Mercedes SL500, trying to find an address in an industrial park between Highway 101 and the bay. The address was for a company called Halcyon Molecular, which wanted to cure aging. Thiel, who was the company's biggest investor and sat on its board, was driving with his seatbelt off. He oscillated on the seatbelt question—the pro-seatbelt argument was that it was safer, and the anti-seatbelt argument was that if you knew that you were not as safe, you would be a more careful driver. Empirically, it would be safest if you wore a seatbelt and were careful at the same time. He made a left turn and fastened his seatbelt.

In spite of oscillating on the seatbelt question, Thiel had never lost the three-year-old's primordial dismay at the news of death. He refused to submit to what he called "the ideology of the inevitability of the death of every individual." He saw it as a problem to be solved, and the sooner the better. With the current state of medical research, he expected to live to be 120—a sorry compromise, given the grand possibilities of life extension. But 150 was becoming thinkable, and immortality wasn't out of the question. In his last years, Steve Jobs had given speeches about how motivated he was by the prospect of death, but Thiel didn't agree. Death was very demotivating. It ended up having a depressing effect, it gave a desperate tone to things and imposed constraints on what people tried to achieve. It would be healthier to live every day as though life were going to go on forever. Immortality would make people treat one another better, if they thought they were going to see one another over and over forever. There was a line from the old song "American Pie": "with no time left to start again." The idea of your own decline was like the idea of America's— you wanted to be in a place where it was never too late to start again.

In 2010, Luke Nosek, Thiel's friend and partner at Founders Fund, told him about a biotech start-up that was developing a way to read the entire DNA sequence of the human genome through an electron microscope, potentially allowing doctors to learn everything about their patients' genetic makeup quickly, for around a thousand dollars. Halcyon Molecular's work held the promise of radical improvements in detecting and reversing genetic disorders, and Thiel decided to make Founders Fund the first outside investor. He knew little about electron microscopy DNA sequencing, but then the young scientists at Halcyon hadn't yet mastered it, either—no one had, which was why it excited Thiel. He took note of their talent and passion, and when they asked for fifty thousand dollars he gave them a first round of five hundred thousand.

Thiel finally found Halcyon's offices, parked, and hurried inside. In the hallway, a row of posters asked WHAT IF WE HAD MORE TIME? A photo of a futuristic library, a giant cage of metal bookshelves, was captioned "129,864,880 known books. How many have you read?" In the conference room, an all-hands meeting was going on: forty or so people, almost all in their twenties and thirties. They took turns giving slide presentations on their team's progress while Halcyon's founder, William Andregg, asked the occasional question. Andregg, a lanky twenty-eight-year-old, was wearing cargo pants and a rumpled, untucked pink button-down shirt. One day, as an undergrad studying biochemistry at the University of Arizona, he had made a list of all the things he wanted to do in life, which included traveling to other solar systems. Suddenly he knew that he would never live long enough to do even a fraction of them. He plunged into gloom for a few weeks, before deciding to put "cure aging" at the top of the list. At first he was guarded about using the phrase, but Thiel urged him to make it the company's message: some people might think it was crazy, but others would be attracted.

At the meeting, Thiel listened with his lips pursed in a frown of concentration and took notes on a yellow legal pad. "I realize this is a dangerous question to ask, but what's your over/under for prototype A?"

"Fifty percent by the beginning of summer," said the scientist at the screen, laser pointer in hand. His hair and beard appeared to have been cut by a macaque. "Eighty percent by the end of summer."

"Very cool."

As part of the weekly meeting, several staff members gave presentations about themselves. Michael Andregg, William's brother and Halcyon's chief technology officer, showed a slide that listed his hobbies and interests:

cryonics, in case all else fails
dodgeball
self-improvement
personal digital archivization
super intelligence through AI or Uploading

On his way out, Thiel dispensed some business advice: by the following Monday, everyone in the company should come up with the names of the three smartest people they knew. "We should try to build things through existing networks as much as possible," he told the assembly. It was what he had done at PayPal. "We have to be building this company as if it's going to be an incredibly successful company. Once you hit that inflection point, you're under incredible pressure to hire people yesterday."

Biology joined with computation to extend life: that was the kind of radical future where Thiel was placing his effort and money. In the deadly race between politics and technology, he was investing in robotics (robot-driven cars would put an end to congestion, and not one more road would have to be built in America). After the sale of PayPal, Thiel's old colleague Elon Musk had gone on to found a company called SpaceX, to make commercial space exploration affordable, and Founders Fund became the first outside investor, with $20 million. Through his foundation, Thiel funded research in nanotechnology. He gave $3.5 million to the Methuselah Foundation, whose goal was to reverse human aging, and he supported a nonprofit called Humanity Plus, dedicated to transhumanism—the transformation of the human condition through technology. When a friend told Thiel about a reality TV show in which ugly women's lives were changed by extreme makeovers such as plastic surgery, liposuction, and tooth whitening, he became excited and wondered what other technologies were available to transform the human body.

He was the largest patron and a board member of the Seasteading Institute, a libertarian nonprofit group founded by Patri Friedman, a former Google engineer and Milton Friedman's grandson. "Seasteading" referred to the founding of new city-states on floating platforms in international waters—communities beyond the reach of laws and regulations. The goal was to create more minimalist forms of government that would force existing regimes to innovate under competitive pressure. (Thiel had come to believe that the U.S. Constitution was unworkable and had to be scrapped.)

If there was one breakthrough technology, it was likely to be artificial intelligence. As computers became capable of improving themselves, they would eventually outsmart human beings, with unpredictable results—a scenario known as the singularity. Whether it would be for better or worse, it would be extremely important. Founders Fund invested in a British AI company called DeepMind Technologies, and the Thiel Foundation gave a quarter million dollars a year to the Singularity Institute, a think tank in Silicon Valley. AI could solve problems that human beings couldn't even imagine solving. The singularity was so weird and hard to visualize that it was under the radar, completely unregulated, and that was where Thiel liked to focus.

On the other hand, he shied away from investing in the area that would provide the most immediate help to struggling Americans—food and energy. Those were too regulated, too political. If there was something inegalitarian about his investments, every technological advance had an unequal component—you were doing the new thing, and the new thing could seldom be instantaneously transmitted to everybody. The starkest example was life extension: the most extreme form of inequality was between people who were alive and people who were dead. It was hard to get more unequal than that. The first people to live to be 150 would probably be rich—but Thiel believed that every technological breakthrough eventually improved the lives of most people, and anyway, none of it would happen if it were left to a popular vote.

The scientists at Halcyon Molecular were refugees from research universities, disenchanted with academic science, convinced that the best way to change the world was to start a company—ideal finds for Thiel, who believed that the latest bubble in the U.S. economy was education. He compared university administrators to subprime mortgage brokers and called debt-saddled graduates the last indentured workers in the developed world, unable to get free even through bankruptcy. Nowhere was the complacency of the establishment, with its blind faith in progress, more evident than in its attitude toward an elite degree: as long as my child goes to the right schools, upward mobility will continue. A university education had become the equivalent of a very expensive insurance policy, like owning a gun. "The future is so-so, but you can sort of navigate through it if you have a house with a gun and an electric fence and a college degree. And if you don't, you're just screwed. What's gone wrong? Why is that? If all the debates are about how do we get everybody to have a gun, that might be ignoring the crime problem." In the midst of economic stagnation, education had become a status game, "purely positional and extremely decoupled" from the question of its benefit to the individual and society.

In Silicon Valley you didn't have to look far for evidence. The public schools that had once been the pride of California belonged to a statewide system ranked forty-eighth in the country, chronically underfunded and in crisis. Private schools had become the option for more and more families, but so had something novel in American history: a privatized public education. Schools in the prosperous towns of Silicon Valley had come to depend on massive fundraising to stay at the top. The elementary school in Woodside, with four hundred seventy kids, was supported by a foundation—begun five years after Proposition 13, in 1983, to save the job of a special ed teacher from budget cuts—that pulled in two million dollars a year. At least half a million came in its annual evening grand auction at the school. The theme in 2011 was "Rockstar." Parents dressed in leopard print shirts, skintight minidresses, and Spinal Tap or Tina Turner wigs, ate "Jumpin' Jack Flash" hanger steaks, danced to an eighties band called Notorious, and were goaded by the auctioneer to bid skyward on Pimp My Hog! and Rockin' Goddess Retreat. A tour of the famous Japanese garden of Larry Ellison—CEO of Oracle, the third-wealthiest American, and the highest-paid executive of the decade—went for twenty thousand dollars; a *Mad Men*–themed dinner for sixteen at a private home ("Amid the libations and smokes, inhibitions are shed and your behavior is worthy only of regret") was pumped up to forty-three thousand dollars by a real estate investor and his wife.

A few miles away, in East Palo Alto, elementary schools had no foundations and chronically lacked textbooks and classroom supplies. In California's public schools there was a long way to fall.

The same held true for universities. The University of California's world-class system saw its budget cut by nearly a billion dollars, more than 25 percent, in four years, and by 2012, facing billions more in cuts, was on the verge of collapse. That year, Stanford announced that it had raised $6.2 billion in a five-year capital campaign, during a financial crisis and recession—the largest amount in the history of higher education. While Silicon Valley was booming, Stanford built a new medical school, business school, engineering center, institute of design, interdisciplinary law building, environment and energy building, center for nanoscale research and technology, cognitive and neurobiological imaging building, bioengineering center, automotive innovation facility, and concert hall. The university gave birth to more than five thousand companies and licensed eight thousand inventions that brought in $1.3 billion in royalties. Areas of the campus that in the seventies had been empty fields now looked like a gleaming vision of Oz.

In Thiel's eyes, this frantic education chase in a stratified society was another sign of things not working. He thought highly of Stanford, had studied there for seven years, now taught the occasional course. But the university seemed strangely separate from Silicon Valley—the new companies were started by students, not professors, who were more and more specialized in esoteric fields. He disliked the whole idea of using college to find an intellectual focus. Majoring in the humanities struck him as particularly unwise, since it so often led to the default choice of law school. The academic sciences were nearly as dubious—timid and narrow, driven by turf battles rather than the quest for breakthroughs. Above all, a college education taught nothing about entrepreneurship.

Thiel thought about starting his own university, but he concluded that it would be too difficult to wean parents off the prestige of Stanford and the Ivies. Then, on a flight from New York back to San Francisco, he and Luke Nosek came up with the idea of giving fellowships to brilliant young people so that they would leave college and start their own technology businesses. Thiel liked to move fast and make a splash (he did it on a regular basis). The next day, at Tech Crunch, an annual conference in San Francisco, he announced the Thiel Fellowships—twenty two-year grants of a hundred thousand dollars each to young people under the age of twenty who had an entrepreneurial idea that would make the world a better place. Critics accused him of corrupting youth into chasing riches while short-circuiting their educations. He pointed out that the winners could return to school at the end of the fellowship, but no small part of his goal was to poke a stick in the eye of top universities and steal away some of their best.

After Thiel's visit to the biotech start-up, he drove up the peninsula to Clarium's offices in San Francisco. He had a round of interviews scheduled with a few fellowship applicants from the group of fifty that had made the final cut out of an original six hundred. The first candidate to sit down at the dark-stained conference table was a Chinese American grad student from outside Seattle named Andrew Hsu. A nineteen-year-old prodigy, he still had braces on his teeth. At five he had been solving simple algebra problems; at eleven he and his brother cofounded a nonprofit group, the World Children's Organization, that provided schoolbooks and vaccinations for kids in Asian countries; at twelve he entered the University of Washington; at nineteen, as a fourth-year Ph.D. candidate in neurosciences at Stanford, he decided to leave his education behind to start a company that made educational video games based on the latest neuroscientific research. "My core goal is to disrupt both the education and the game sectors," he said, sounding like Peter Thiel.

Thiel expressed concern that the company would attract people with a nonprofit attitude, who felt that "it's not about making money, we're doing something good, so we don't have to work as hard. And I think this has been an endemic problem, parenthetically, in the clean-tech space, which has attracted a lot of very talented people who believe they're making the world a better place."

"They don't work as hard?" Hsu asked.

"Have you thought about how to mitigate that problem?"

"So you're saying that might be a problem just because the company has an educational slant?"

"Yes," Thiel said. "Our main bias against investing in these sorts of companies is that you end up attracting people who just don't want to work that hard. And that, sort of, is my deep theory on why they haven't worked."

Hsu caught Thiel's drift. "Yeah, well, this is a game company. I wouldn't call it an educational start-up. I would say it's a game start-up. The types of people that I want to bring in are hard-core game engineers. So I don't think these are the types of people that would slack off."

Hsu would get a Thiel Fellowship. So would the Stanford sophomore from Minnesota who had been obsessed with energy and water scarcity since age nine, when he tried to build the first-ever perpetual motion machine. "After two years of being unsuccessful, I realized that even if we solved perpetual motion we wouldn't use it if it was too expensive," he told Thiel. "The sun is a source of perpetual energy, yet we're not harnessing that. So I became obsessed with cost reductions."

At seventeen he had learned about photovoltaic heliostats, or solar trackers—"dual-access tracking mirrors that direct sunlight to one point." If he could invent a cheap enough way to produce heat using heliostats, solar energy could become financially competitive with coal. At Stanford he started a company to work on the problem, but the university refused to count his hours on the project as academic units. So he went on leave and applied for a Thiel Fellowship.

"I think I'm getting the best possible things out of Stanford," he said. "I'm staying in this entrepreneurial house called Black Box. It's about twelve minutes off campus. And so that'll be really fun, because it's really close to our office, and they have a hot tub and pool, and then just go to Stanford to see my friends on the weekends. You get all the best of the social but get to fundamentally work on what you love."

A pair of Stanford freshmen—an entrepreneur named Stanley Tang and a programmer named Thomas Schmidt—came in next, with an idea for a mobile phone application called QuadMob, which would allow you to locate your closest friends on a map in real time. "It's about taking your phone out and knowing where your friends are right now, whether they're at the library or at the gym," Tang, who came from Hong Kong, said. He had already published a book called *eMillions: Behind-the-Scenes Stories of 14 Successful Internet Millionaires.* "On Friday night, every single week, I go to a party, and somehow you just lose your friends—people roll out to different parties. And I always have to text people, 'Where are you, what are you doing, which party are you at?' and I have to do that for like ten friends, and that's just like a huge pain point and it's just really annoying, and I think this is the reason why we're solving a pain point that we personally have experienced and probably most college students."

Schmidt, another Minnesotan, explained the name of the app. "Back in the eighties, in the seventies, before Facebook, before the Internet, the Quad Center was the place to hang out—like, people would just chill there, talk to their friends, and now the Quad is totally deserted except for tourists and people biking through it, and so we feel like it's kind of silly, it's wrecking social interaction. There are so many cool people here and you really don't get to meet that many people."

Tang was asked how QuadMob would change the world. "We're redefining college life, we're connecting people," he said. "And once this expands outside of college life, we're really defining social life. We'd like to think of ourselves as bridging the gap between the digital and the physical world."

Thiel was skeptical. It sounded like too many other venture start-ups looking to find a narrow opening between Facebook and Foursquare. It certainly wasn't going to propel America out of the tech slowdown. The QuadMob candidates would not get a Thiel Fellowship.

That night, Thiel hosted a small dinner party at his mansion in the Marina. A chessboard and a bookcase full of sci-fi and philosophy titles were the only indicators of who lived there. The elegant blond assistants in black refilled wineglasses and called the guests to dinner. A menu at each place around the table announced a three-course meal, with a choice of poached wild salmon with grilled asparagus, spring onions, forbidden rice, and a Meyer-lemon-scented ravigote sauce, or pan-roasted sweet pepper polenta with sautéed winter mushrooms, braised dino kale, cara-melized cippolini, and niçoise olive puree.

Thiel's guests seemed as out of place in this candlelit formality as their host. There was David Sacks, Thiel's friend from Stanford and Pay-Pal, coauthor of *The Diversity Myth*, and the founder of Yammer, a social network within organizations. There was Luke Nosek, another PayPal mafioso and the biotech specialist at Founders Fund—he was a member of the Alcor Life Extension Foundation, a nonprofit devoted to cryonics, and had signed up to have his body filled with liquid nitrogen upon his official death so that it could be restored to full health upon the invention of new technology. There was Eliezer Yudkowsky, an artificial-intelligence researcher who had cofounded the Singularity Institute—an autodidact who never went past eighth grade, he was the author of a thousand-page online fanfic called *Harry Potter and the Methods of Rationality*, which recast the original story in an attempt to explain Harry's wizardry through the scientific method. And there was Patri Friedman, the founder of the Seasteading Institute. An elfin man with cropped black hair and a thin line of beard, he was dressed in the eccentrically antic manner of Raskol-nikov. He lived in Mountain View in an "intentional community" as a free-love libertarian, about which he regularly blogged and tweeted: "Polyamory/competitive govt parallel: more choice/competition yields more challenge, change, growth. Whatever lasts is tougher."

Over dinner, Nosek argued that the best entrepreneurs in the world were seized with a single idea to which they would devote their lives. Founders Fund backed these visionaries and kept them in charge of their own companies, protecting them from the meddling of other venture capitalists, who were prone to replacing them with plodding executives.

Thiel picked up the theme. There were four places in America where ambitious young people went, he said: New York, Washington, Los Ange-les, and Silicon Valley. The first three were tired, used up. Wall Street lost its allure after the financial crisis; the D.C. excitement of the Obama presidency was over; Hollywood hadn't been a cultural mecca for years. Only Silicon Valley still attracted young people with big dreams.

Nosek recalled that he had failed a high school English class in Illi-nois because the teacher said that he couldn't write. If something like the Thiel Fellowships had existed, he and others like him could have been spared a lot of pain. Too many gifted people passed through college and grad school with no plan for the future. The Thiel Fellowships would find these talents and allow them to become entrepreneurs before they had a chance to lose their way or be snuffed out by the establishment.

Education, Thiel said, was like a "tournament," with successively difficult stages of competition. "You keep trying to be number one. The problem with the university is what it does to your confidence when you find you're no longer number one."

There was wine on the table, but the guests did less drinking than talking. Throughout the meal the two subjects remained the same: the superiority of entrepreneurs and the worthlessness of higher education. At 9:45, Thiel suddenly pushed back his chair.

"Most dinners go on too long or not long enough," he said.

His guests went out into the cool San Francisco night. The Palace of Fine Arts was brilliantly lit, its rotunda reflected in the pond. Thirty miles south, the labs of Silicon Valley were burning with fluorescent light. Thirty miles east, people weren't doing well. Thiel retreated upstairs to answer e-mail alone.

JEFF CONNAUGHTON

Connaughton moved to Savannah. He wanted to live in the South again, near the ocean, so he bought a turreted three-story late-nineteenth-century Victorian—twice the size of his Georgetown house for half the money—near the pretty squares lined with live oak and Spanish moss.

Beneath its quaint stylishness, Savannah was just another city hit hard by the crisis. In his neighborhood there was a sign for a ten-thousand-square-foot house that was marked down from $3.5 to $1.5 million. The guy who gave tours of historic Savannah was an unemployed mortgage banker. Soon after Connaughton's arrival, his neighbors invited him to a monthly potluck gathering, where the host that month was a prosperous-looking man in his sixties with holdings in real estate. A week later, he heard that the man had killed himself—the rumor was that he'd gotten overextended.

Connaughton volunteered once a week at the local legal services office. He acquired a shelter dog, part chow and part golden retriever, and named her Nellie. She was a stressed-out creature with a rough past and a bad case of heartworm. After a round of shots he brought her home and put her on antibiotics. One night, Nellie's breathing sped up to three or four times a second, and he spent the whole night by her crate, keeping her calm. After ten days of convalescence in the house, he took her out for a walk to a nearby park. Within a few weeks, Nellie settled down as his constant companion.

In Washington, Connaughton used to spend every Sunday morning flipping between the TV talk shows, like everyone else in town, while reading the *Times* and the *Post* during commercials. The ritual exchange between high-profile hosts and guests became essential conversation fodder for the D.C. week. In Savannah, it seemed completely absurd. All but his closest Washington friends dropped away, as if he'd moved to the other side of the earth. As long as he had money it would be easy to insulate himself from the country's problems—to give up on changing Washington and enjoy his life far from the morass, while America went about its long-term decline. He could feel that temptation, and the other one, too—the itch of public service, the Biden itch. It was still there. Every now and then someone sent a feeler his way, an opening at the White House, a good nonprofit job. Each time he said no.

He wanted to burn his ship so that he would never be able to succumb and sail back to his former life. With Nellie lying at his feet, he spent each morning writing a book about what had happened to Washington in his years there. It would be called *The Payoff: Why Wall Street Always Wins*. It would say everything.

TAMPA

The Republicans converged on Tampa at the end of August simultaneously with Hurricane Isaac, which canceled the first day of the convention. At the last hour the storm veered west over the Gulf of Mexico, leaving the city soaked but unscathed. Meanwhile, fifty thousand Republicans, media members, protesters, security officers, and thrill seekers made landfall directly in downtown Tampa. The welcoming committee got the city ready by limiting access to the new Riverwalk, rerouting traffic away from the convention hall, and cutting up the downtown grid with black chain-link fencing, concrete barriers, and Hillsborough County dump trucks. Local people left town or stayed away, and on the canceled Monday the office buildings and surface parking lots downtown were nearly empty. In spite of the diminished car traffic, the city looked less like Jane Jacobs's heaven than ever, the sidewalks even more deserted than usual, the only eyes on the street those of security officers clustered at every intersection—Tampa police mounted on black bikes, sheriff's deputies from counties all over Florida, state troopers, national guardsmen in military fatigues, private rent-a-cops, black temporary hires wearing size XXL white T-shirts that said, without further explanation, STAFF. Armed skiffs patrolled the Hillsborough River, helicopters continuously clattered a few hundred feet overhead. All the public trash barrels were gone. Tampa was never safer, or more dead.

After the violence at the 2008 Republican convention in Minneapolis, the phenomenon of Occupy Wall Street and its aftershocks and portents, the predictions that Tampa 2012 was going to give Chicago 1968 a run, the city prepared for a riot. In the days before the convention, Matt Weidner's blog scaled new rhetorical mountaintops:

> . . . you really cannot be prepared for your city turning into a heavily fortified warzone until you're sitting in the middle of it. And

driving to work, I realized, I'm sitting at Ground Zero for the Republican National Convention here in Tampa / St. Petersburg . . . So this is what this failed democracy has come to? The St. Pete Police Department building, located just a few steps from my office, is being turned into a bunker, but the row after row, tens of miles of concrete barriers and fencing are what really catches your eye and makes my heart turn cold. It truly is a disturbing commentary on our national politics that so much effort must be made to barricade the ruling class from the peasants and the proletariat.

Weidner's radicalism had no natural home in American politics. Despite his belief in massive worldwide debt repudiation, he was enough of a libertarian to become an avid Ron Paul supporter. When Paul's delegates were forbidden to bring their own signs onto the convention floor in Tampa, and twenty of his Maine delegates were stripped of their credentials, and Paul wasn't allowed to speak because he hadn't endorsed the Nominee, Weidner announced that he was ending his lifelong membership in the Republican Party. He wouldn't become a Democrat, though— the party of Obama, the "statist in chief"—"so I'm electing to change my registration to NO PARTY AFFILIATION!" He urged his readers to do the same. Then Weidner drove with his new wife and their four-week-old baby out of the warzone to rural Florida, where he waited out "the whole undeniably engrossing spectacle."

Mike Van Sickler was covering the convention for the *St. Petersburg Times*, which, as of the first of the year, had become the *Tampa Bay Times*. His assignment was the Florida delegation. The Florida Republican party was being punished by the national party for jumping the gun on the primary schedule, and part of the punishment was for the Florida delegates to be exiled to the Innisbrook Golf and Spa Resort in Palm Harbor, an hour's drive from the convention hall. One night, due to bus congestion and transit malfunctions, the delegates got back to their rooms at three in the morning, and Van Sickler wrote a wry piece imagining how things might have been different if Tampa Bay had commuter rail, like Charlotte, where the Democratic convention was to be held the following week.

After the conventions, Van Sickler was going to join the paper's Tallahassee bureau, where his beat would include Governor Rick Scott. He had spent his career covering city halls and county commissions, running title searches and mapping foreclosures, beats where there were no communications strategists and press flaks, only the buried facts of folly and corruption, which he knew how to dig up as well as any reporter around. He had never covered real politics before, and he was nervous as hell, loving the action, going on adrenaline and fear, trying to figure out what questions to ask.

For example, what should he ask Governor Scott's mother? There she was on the second night of the convention, in a big black skirt and floral top, sitting with the Florida delegates directly in front of the podium, listening to Janine Turner from *Northern Exposure* (dyed blond, like most of the women present), and waiting for the Nominee's wife to speak. Should he ask Mrs. Scott a gotcha question? What would be the point? The chances of getting any news were small. She probably wouldn't even answer him. He decided to let her listen to the speeches.

Van Sickler worried that he didn't have the speed and fluency for the big leagues. He knew that he would have to play ball with Rick Scott, pay attention to nuances, be a drama critic after a State of the State address, make trades with his handlers to stay in the game and get his calls returned. That was how politics was covered at the highest levels, and it didn't come naturally to him. He was much better operating out in the open—making them talk to him because he had dug up facts. Facts were Van Sickler's strength, and he decided to stick with them as much as possible in this new phase of his career.

The convention was in Tampa, but inside the hall it was rare to hear anyone mention the foreclosure crisis, ghost subdivisions, robo-signing, mortgage fraud, bankruptcy, or homelessness. No speaker told the story of how Wall Street and lenders and developers and local officials had created the conditions for a catastrophe that still had not receded from Tampa Bay. No one spoke for Usha Patel, or Mike Ross, or the late Jack Hamersma, or the Hartzells. Instead, leading Republicans took the podium one after another to sing the praises of the successful business owner and the risk-taking investor.

The Republicans felt nothing for their Nominee. They had chosen him, as the Democrats once chose John Kerry, in the hope that others would like him better than they did. There was no relief at the top of the ticket for their fever, no love to ennoble the scalding hatred of the president and his America that had energized the resurgence in the Republican grassroots since 2009. The beating heart of the party was not to be found in the loveless convention hall, where only loyal delegates and visitors with the right credentials could enter, bused in on a single clogged access road, funneled on foot through a single checkpoint, stepping in bright red dresses and high heels between concrete barriers, sweating into the armpits of sport coats as they walked in darkness under the Crosstown Expressway and looked around for a store that sold bottled water.

Four decades after his first try for Congress, Newt Gingrich was in Tampa, posing for pictures with Callista, his buttoned suit jacket emphasizing his width, speaking at his mobile "Newt University" for two hours a day, every day, including the canceled day, holding forth in the Royal Palm Ballroom at the Wyndham Tampa Westshore on the subject of America's energy future to whoever would listen. Morning Joe listened for a few minutes, then did a stand-up with Gingrich out in the corridor. Everyone knew that Gingrich and the Nominee despised each other. Why, Morning Joe asked, was Newt here in Tampa to lend his support? "How do you avoid making it personal?"

"We have an overarching agreement that in the end we're all Americans," Gingrich said. "This is what makes us so powerful, because we can come together in a way that Adolf Hitler or Tojo or Khrushchev never could." Warming to his theme of civic unity higher than politics, he smiled, and smiling made him look like a boy who's thought of a clever answer. "I think it was a remarkable thing that I was allowed to run. It's a remarkable thing that I'm allowed to be on your show. I so much love being a citizen."

Morning Joe cracked a few jokes with Gingrich, thanked him, and hurried out of the hotel. Gingrich turned toward a French TV camera and was asked for reasons to vote for the Nominee. Gingrich stopped smiling, his face dropped, the corners of his mouth turned down in deep grooves, and under the white helmet of hair his eyes narrowed in a hard humorless stare. "Obama stands for fundamentally radical values that will transform America," Gingrich said, quickly and automatically, for the ten thousandth time, far too many times to know if he really meant it, any more than if he meant that in the end we were all Americans, or if he was even subliminally aware of the contradiction, but it didn't matter anyway because he was already on his way back inside the Royal Palm Ballroom, where there was more talking to be done, always more talking, for not to talk would be to die.

Gingrich was one of Karen Jaroch's personal heroes. Karen had supported him in the Florida primary after her first choice, Herman Cain (for whom she had served as county chairwoman), dropped out. One night during convention week, she attended the Faith and Freedom Rally at the Tampa Theater and heard Gingrich speak, along with other heroes of hers, including Phyllis Schlafly, who was eighty-eight years old but still looked like the firebrand housewife (the same as Karen Jaroch) from the 1964 Goldwater campaign. Karen had made her peace with the party's Nominee for 2012—"anybody but Obama"—but she didn't care much for the convention itself, the kind of insider establishment event that had kept her away from politics most of her life. In a way, Karen didn't need to be there, because in Tampa the fringe had made it to the floor, the podium, and the platform. There was even a plank condemning Agenda 21, the twenty-year-old UN resolution that obsessed opponents of rail.

Karen was working full-time in a new job. At the start of the year, she had become the Hillsborough County field director for Americans for Prosperity, the pro-free-enterprise group funded by the billionaire Koch brothers. The week before the convention she opened the field office in a small strip mall in North Tampa, next to a Serbian massage therapy parlor and downstairs from a realty company. Karen was making thousands of "issue" calls, trying to identify potential supporters and direct them to the group's website. Around the office were empty desks waiting for phones, computers, and volunteers. One night, a group had come to watch a screening of *Who Is John Galt?*, the second part of a film version of Ayn Rand's *Atlas Shrugged*. Jaroch hadn't read the novel—she wasn't a big reader of books—but agreed completely with its principles. She had found her purpose, now joined to a national organization with bottomless amounts of money, and she applied herself with the unflagging energy of an adherent whose worldview couldn't be disturbed by any argument or fact. Beneath her politics was a basic feeling that she and her husband had always played by the rules without ever cutting corners or asking for help.

The job was Karen's first in years, and although she had vowed not to make a career of politics when she first started the Tampa 9/12 Project, her family needed the paycheck. But she would do it even without one. "This is where my heart is."

The Hartzells spent a little time watching the convention, but not as much as they spent watching "Sexy and I Know It," a music video by LMFAO—Laughing My Fucking Ass Off, an electropop duo—with Brent and Danielle dancing in the living room. Not as much time as Ronale spent on the rental laptop entering Disney World contests and cash sweepstakes. Not close to as much time as Danny spent online playing League of Legends rank matches at Level 30.

It wasn't that Danny and Ronale weren't interested in politics. They thought and talked about politics more than they used to. Working at Wal-Mart pushed it in your face. Danny was making $8.50 an hour—Dennis was making $8.60, after two years—and he hated the job. He hated the superior attitude of the managers, the way they just pushed the old potatoes and onions to the back of the bin, the customers who interrupted him while he was shelving stock to ask where the frigging bananas were, the fact that he was an "associate" instead of an old-school "employee," the phony Tampa police car that the store rented for thirty thousand a month and parked out front as a deterrent to shoplifting. On his break Danny went out into the parking lot and stood there in his uniform khakis and blue shirt and smoked 305s—he had picked up the habit working at Wal-Mart—and thought about his old welding job. He liked dirty jobs, where you made something and had a feeling of accomplishment. He was blue-collar, and if somehow he could get a loan and open his own welding business he would feel like a king, but that wasn't going to happen. He had read that 47 percent of Americans were now too poor to pay income taxes. Forty-seven percent! How did that happen? Greed. Just corporate greed. Sometimes he thought it would be better to get rid of money and go back to the barter system, wheat in exchange for milk and eggs. Here was Danny, the little guy doing the heavy lifting and helping the customers—the backbone of the workforce—making ten grand a year, while the guy who sat behind a desk doing nothing but watching the little guy work made eight or nine million. Why was that fair? The rich got richer, the poor got poorer. You couldn't ever get ahead. You just got used to it—that was life. At this point he was doing it for his children, hoping they'd be better off.

The only rich person Danny respected was Bill Gates, because he made his money honestly and then spent it saving third world countries. Sam Walton had seemed like a pretty decent man, but after he passed on, his kids got greedy. Ronale wanted to shake the hand of Warren Buffett, and also Oprah, and Michelle Obama because of how sincere she was, jumping rope with kids and getting them to eat healthy. Ronale liked watching *Secret Millionaire* because every week a rich person had to live just like poor people, and at the end of the show he had a change of heart and gave hundreds of thousands of dollars to a charity. But she also had a disturbing vision of the greed that lay behind everything else: "In the background there is this horrible nightmare that stands behind the good, getting bigger and bigger, and it's like a black cloud and it's consuming everything and actually taking life away from people."

All the same, Ronale bought everything at Wal-Mart, because you couldn't beat their prices. Except for meat, because Danny and Dennis told her how they left food racks outside the cooler for hours. But everything else. You just had to give in. Danny was beginning to think that Wal-Mart and big oil ran the whole world, and when the family went shopping he stayed in the car.

Then, one morning not long before the convention, he told some co-workers on break how much he hated his job, and the word got back to his manager, and the manager confronted Danny right in the produce section and humiliated him in front of customers. The next day Danny woke up with the manager's words burning in his ears and he couldn't take it, his impotent pride raged, and he didn't go in to work. So they were back where they started.

On the last day of the convention, Danny, Ronale, Dennis, Brent, and Danielle sat in their living room. HGTV was on. Brent's hair was cut short—he was in ninth grade and had joined Junior ROTC. Danielle was at the computer doing her classwork. The Hartzells had been unable to get her into a decent middle school, so she was enrolled in the Hillsborough Virtual School for sixth grade (which worked okay until they could no longer pay for Internet and lost their service). Danny was sipping a Diet Pepsi and helping Danielle with her work. He already regretted the hotheadedness that had cost him his job.

Ronale was still seething about the speech of the Nominee's wife. "She was pouring the sugar out and everything, and I don't get how they would not notice the fake. 'I had breast cancer, I had MS'—but they want to take Planned Parenthood away. It's assistance for women that could not afford mammograms, pap smears, preventive cancer. If a woman's diagnosed with breast cancer, what's she going to do if she ain't got the money?"

Danny said, "My view on everything—if you want to change this country, you have to put a person in office who has never done it for a day. Put a regular old guy like me, someone who's lived it and never done nothing else but live it." He sipped his Diet Pepsi. "We're struggling, but we're not starving. There's no life, but there's a roof over your head."

"It's the price of freedom," Dennis said. "I can come home, I have a bed to sleep on, I have food, a soda to drink, or tea—I'm fine. I wish I could have more, like everybody, but it's never going to be perfect as long as the world runs the way it runs and people make the decisions they make."

It was the second-to-last day of August. While the Republicans concluded their $123 million convention fifteen minutes away, the Hartzells, having paid all their bills, had five dollars left till the first of September.

TAMMY THOMAS

One day in the spring of 2012, Tammy left her purse in the Pontiac and walked up to the broad front door of the brick house on Tod Lane. She couldn't find a street address, and she wondered what had happened to the rose garden under the front windows, but this was the house—there was the curved patio off on the right side, there was the tree she got spanked for climbing. Dogs were already barking before she could summon the nerve to knock. The door swung open and a tiny white-haired white woman appeared.

"Yes?" The woman stood bowlegged in sweatpants and a sweatshirt that said BODYWORKS.

"Hi!" Tammy stayed on the circular drive that ran along the front steps. "I know you're probably wondering why is this lady standing in my driveway."

The woman withdrew to put the barking dogs away, then returned to the door.

Tammy said, "Can I come up and shake your hand?"

"Mm-hmm."

Tammy approached, and the woman accepted her hand warily. "My name is Tammy Thomas, and I want to tell you that the lady that used to live in this house—"

"Purnell?"

"Miss Purnell. My great-grandmother used to work for her, and when Miss Purnell—I remember her very vaguely—when she passed, we actually stayed here for a little while."

"Yeah. Mm-hmm."

"And I have so many vivid memories of this house," Tammy's voice was getting thick, "and I've been wondering if they are all of them just memories, or is it for real." She mentioned the rose garden and the curved patio, the ballroom upstairs, the grand staircase, and Miss Lena's long bathroom, with the gold-colored tiles and the stand-up shower. "I started kindergarten here," Tammy said, "and I don't even know what else to say."

The woman confirmed that all the memories were real, but it was the emotion in Tammy's eyes and voice that made her say, "You can come in and look at it. I'm in the process of redoing it."

Tammy stepped inside. The grand staircase was straight ahead—just a flight of stairs with a threadbare runner. The foyer and living room, where she had learned to ride a bike, looked much smaller than she remembered. The hardwood of the floors had the same pattern, but the shine was worn off and they were all scratched up. The buzzer was gone from the dining room floor.

The woman's name was Mrs. Tupper. The house had cost two hundred thousand dollars in 1976 but now it was worth less than that. Her husband had been an executive at Packard Electric, but he was long dead, her children moved out, and she talked on, explaining the shabby state of things, in the way of someone living alone and completely absorbed in a task. "Like I said, I'm not going to be around much longer, and the original carpet—I haven't changed the carpet because of the dogs. All carpet today has a rough backing and it would destroy the floors. It would destroy everything. You have to have a soft backing. Even if you have padding down it still doesn't help."

Mrs. Tupper had just come from her ballet lesson. She still did ballet at her age but your knees started going as you got older and she no longer did tap. Tammy followed her from room to room, gazing at walls and ceilings, losing herself in a memory (was that chandelier original?), then coming back to the present and this woman, finding her where she was—in a house that she was slowly and painfully renovating herself, with the thought of selling it before she died—instinctively knowing how to make a connection with an old woman.

When they were out on the curved patio facing the garden, Mrs. Tupper suddenly looked at Tammy as if for the first time. "I do know what it feels like to go back and see things."

She and her sister had been born in Ohio, taken to Washington by their rich parents, and then abandoned, put in a children's home, and she had recently gone back to Washington to see it. "I grew up back when we had reform school. Mothers, if you don't take care of your child, your child goes to a reform school if he's bad, and if you don't want to take care of him, you put him in a children's home. Not a thing wrong. Perfect. I was given more than I could ever give my children."

Mrs. Tupper's backyard looked across the street at the empty fields where Rayen High School had once stood. Rayen was where Barry, Tammy's ex-husband, her first child's father, had gone, and also Geneva, her best friend, who had been thrown to the street and shot in the head. Built in 1922, torn down after it closed in 2007. Mrs. Tupper was glad to see it gone. The house between hers and the school had been a drug house, and the Crips and Bloods used to fight there. Once, two boys with guns were chasing and shooting at a third, who broke down her fence and ran right up onto her porch into her house. Mrs. Tupper made him sit down and asked him a bunch of questions, but all he would say was that he was with the gang, he was a Crip and they were Bloods, and they were after him and he was saving his life. A few days later he went back to the drug house with a gun, because he'd had enough. From the third floor Mrs. Tupper heard a boy cry out for his mother just before the gun went off. One boy walked to the schoolyard and died there, the other lay on the driveway until the ambulance Mrs. Tupper called came, but he was already dead.

"This was in the late eighties, early nineties?" Tammy asked.

"Something like that."

"Do you remember their names?"

"No. It never showed up in the newspaper. The only things they could have been after him for—he wouldn't say—was either drugs or a woman."

"It was probably drugs," Tammy said.

"Right. I didn't realize it because he looked so young. It was really sad."

"Sure, yeah."

"When they're thirteen or fourteen years, I believe in putting them in the reform school, and when I say reform, what does reform mean? They can reform you to want to be a good citizen, and then from there you go into the service. Mom and Dad don't care about you anyway, so the reform school can take you. You understand? And it's going to give you something to hold on to in life. Make sure you have a good education, and you'll have fun in there, you'll go to the circus. I did all of these things. It's getting cold."

"My eyes are watering," Tammy said.

She stayed for over an hour. It felt like she could have stayed all day because once Mrs. Tupper started talking she wouldn't stop, but Tammy had to get back to work. Before leaving, Tammy asked if she could come back and have tea, or bring lunch.

"I'd love to have you," Mrs. Tupper said.

Tammy got in her Pontiac and drove away, past Crandall Park, where she had once fed the swans. The house was a lot smaller than she remembered, and less glamorous. It hadn't been kept up well, and a bad neighborhood was closing in. But as Tammy stood in the foyer, her mother was hurrying down the stairs, saying she didn't like staying there because the house was haunted, and as Tammy stood in the kitchen, her granny was calling for her to come help with the laundry, and in those moments she felt close to them again.

The Front Porch Café was on the ground floor of a brick building with a burned-out second floor, next to the interstate near downtown Akron. Inside, fifty people were sitting at tables, a few black and white women and a lot of black men, many of them former convicts. Miss Hattie was there, with a big picture of Obama on her T-shirt. Tammy was standing in front of a screen, wearing jeans and a long loose synthetic shirt with purple and white swirls. Her hair was cut short and hennaed on top.

A couple of days before, she had been at a community center in Cleveland, talking about Social Security and Medicare to a room full of old people, the women listening, the men playing dominoes. She'd had one of her leaders with her in Cleveland, Miss Gloria, who was seventy-one, and Miss Gloria was supposed to talk about living on retirement benefits and how they were under threat, but they couldn't hear Miss Gloria very well so Tammy had to do most of the talking while she set up the projector she was lugging around in order to show them a video about the Koch brothers, Charles and David, who were shown in a cartoon as two heads growing out of an octopus, and after the video, one of the women, Linda, had asked, "Where did these two Koch brothers come from? Why haven't we heard of them before?" and another woman, Mabel, had said, "Koch brothers going to make the Negroes pay the bill." After Cleveland, Tammy had a Food Policy Council meeting in Youngstown, then she had to prepare a presentation for a minority health conference. In the middle of it all she was getting ready for her wedding on the beach near Tampa to a roofer named Mark, a guy she'd known when they were at East High

School, and suddenly Mark's uncle from East Cleveland had shown up with financial problems, and so the uncle was now living with them in her house in Liberty.

She was tired.

"I grew up in a place where you could sit on my front porch and you could smell the sulfur in the air," Tammy was telling the group at the Front Porch Café. "And everybody in that community was working. We were at a hundred fifty thousand people at that time. And guess what? One day, the jobs left. September of '77, the mills stopped working. We lost over fifty thousand jobs within a ten-year time frame. I was fortunate enough as an adult that I was able to get a job at Packard. Eleven thousand jobs in its heyday, down to three thousand jobs, and when we all left it had less than six hundred jobs. I just want to let you know, that story of Youngstown is the epitome of any older industrial city across the United States."

MVOC's survey map of Youngstown was projected onto the screen, with the east side a sea of green. "The house that my grandmother worked very hard, cleaning people's floors, washing their clothes, cooking their food, so that we could have a home—that home now sits on a street with four houses on it. Two of them are vacant, and one of them is ours. The majority of our community lives like that."

Tammy was going on notes that she'd written up the day before—turning her life story into a speech, in order to teach the people in the group how to tell their own stories and tie them to a campaign during the presidential election for better jobs in Ohio.

"When we look at our children and the blight that has come to our communities, how can you continuously attack good-paying union jobs, like the jobs we lost at Packard Electric? No one ever could have told me I would not have retired from that job. We need jobs in Ohio. We need jobs that pay a living wage in Ohio. Jobs are the connective tissue to everything surrounding us."

In 2012, jobs were slowly coming back to Ohio, some of them in the area around Youngstown: jobs in natural gas exploration of the Utica shale, which ran right under the Mahoning Valley; new shifts at the GM plant northwest of town; manufacturing work in auto parts factories; even a few jobs in steel mills. So far, though, the new opportunities had hardly reached the people who needed them most, such as the poor and chronically unemployed men and women who still lived in Youngstown, especially those—like so many at the Front Porch Café—who had done time in prison. MVOC did not have an economic development strategy. Its jobs campaign simply called for private employers to hire local people first and give felons a chance, and for government to be the employer of last resort.

"When I got pregnant, it broke my grandmother's heart," Tammy said, winding up her speech. "I wanted to make sure I graduated from high school because I knew that was the only way I could give my daughter a better life. I have three adult children that I raised in our community, and they all moved away. Youngstown could be a wonderful place to live again—it should be."

Tammy was so busy with her organizing work that she hardly had time to canvass for the election. But on November 5, she spent two hours going door-to-door with Kirk Noden around Lincoln Park on the east side, the part of the city where she had grown up. There was a rumor that a misleading piece of paper was circulating in the neighborhood, telling people that they could sign it as a substitute for voting. So Tammy asked everyone she met whether they had already voted, or intended to vote the next day, or needed a ride to the polls. To her surprise, the enthusiasm for Obama was even higher than in 2008, with none of the concerns about whether the country was ready and a black president would survive.

And when he was reelected the next night, Tammy found herself even more emotional than the first time. She had gotten caught up in the daily mechanics of the race, the close polls in Ohio, the fear that Obama might lose. She had been thinking about the election negatively: if he lost, the people she had helped to recruit and train, people like Miss Hattie and Miss Gloria and the men at the Front Porch Café, might feel that the work was in vain, and a few years of her life might have been lost. Tammy hadn't allowed herself to think about what it would mean if he won. And when it was over, she thought: "My God, it means we've got a chance to do something for real."

DEAN PRICE

One day in the spring of 2011, around the time he stopped going up to Red Birch, Dean was sitting in the Rockingham County economic development office, looking through the literature on display there, when he found a study by a professor at Appalachian State University, in Boone, on waste cooking oil in North Carolina. A chart showed the population of each of the state's one hundred counties, the number of restaurants in each county, and the gallons of cooking oil that those restaurants got rid of. It turned out that in each county, even the smallest and poorest ones, the amount of oil for every man, woman, and child was about three or four gallons a year. There was a direct correlation between the amount of waste cooking oil a county created in a year and the amount of fuel a county's school buses would use in a year.

Dean stood up at his chair. Just like when he first read about peak oil, his knees went weak and he stumbled back. Ever since leaving Red Birch and going off on his own, he had been looking for alternatives to canola oil, which was unprofitable as long as gas stayed below five dollars a gallon. That was why Red Birch had a failed business model—Dean said it to anyone who would listen. On the other hand, waste cooking oil was cheap: some restaurants charged fifty cents a gallon to pump it out of the barrels in back and take it away, some gave it away for free, and some even paid to have it removed. Fried chicken, livers and gizzards, pulled pork, fish, corn fritters, fried okra, french fries—just about everything eaten at restaurants in North Carolina was cooked in shiny reddish-brown vegetable oil that sat bubbling in deep metal fryers. And all that oil had to be thrown out.

The companies that hauled the oil away were called renderers. Besides restaurant oil, renderers also collected animal carcasses—pigs and sheep and cows from slaughterhouses, offal thrown out by butcher shops and restaurants, euthanized cats and dogs from the pound, dead pets from veterinary clinics, deceased zoo animals, roadkill. Mounds of animals were trucked to the rendering plant and bulldozed into large pots for grinding and shredding; then the raw meat product was dumped into pressure cookers, where fat separated from meat and bones at high heat. The meat and bones were pulverized into protein meal for canned pet food. The animal fat became yellow grease, which was recycled for lipstick, soap, chemicals, and livestock feed. So cows ate cow, pigs ate pig, dogs ate dog, cats ate cat, and human beings ate the meat fed on dead meat, or smeared it over their faces and hands. Rendering was one of the oldest industries in the country, going back to the age of tallow, lard, and candlelight, and one of the most secretive. A book on the subject was titled *Rendering: The Invisible Industry*. It was the kind of disgusting but essential service, like sewers, that no one wanted to think about. The companies pretty much regulated themselves, and the plants were built far from human habitation, and outsiders were almost never allowed into one, or even knew it existed unless the wind blew the wrong way.

Renderers turned the waste cooking oil they collected into yellow grease, but it had a different use than animal fat, one that the companies were only just starting to figure out: because it jelled at lower temperatures than animal fat and burned clean, the oil was ideal for making fuel.

When he read the study from Appalachian State, and saw the chart showing county-by-county population and gallons of waste cooking oil, Dean suddenly put it together. Every little corner of North Carolina had the seedlings of a biodiesel industry. And if it was true in North Carolina, it was true in Tennessee, and Colorado.

"This goes back to Gandhi," Dean said. He had bought a book called *The Essential Gandhi* and read about *swadeshi*, which meant self-sufficiency and independence. "Gandhi said it was a sin to buy from your farthest neighbor at the neglect of your nearest neighbor. It's not about mass production, it's about production by the masses. Every community college I talk to wants to start a biofuels project but can't because they don't have the feedstock—every stage is hog-tied by major corporations. It's going to take disruptive technology in the weakest link of the chain as the point of attack. Waste cooking oil is the weakest link. It's an archaic, antiquated industry, a hundred thirty years old, modern-day buggy whip makers. They know the shelf life on their old business plan is coming to an end— because they've got the only source of energy in every community for biofuels."

On his bookshelf there was a volume called *The Prosperity Bible*, an anthology of classic writings on the secrets of wealth. Dean's second favorite after *Think and Grow Rich* was *Acres of Diamonds*, a lecture that a Baptist minister named Russell Conwell first published in 1890 and that he gave at least six thousand times before his death in 1925. Conwell had been a captain in the Union army, dismissed for deserting his post in North Carolina in 1864. He went on to write campaign biographies of Grant, Hayes, and Garfield, and later became a minister in Philadelphia. The lecture that made him famous and rich—rich enough to establish Temple University and become its first president—was based on a story Conwell claimed to have been told by an Arab guide he hired in Baghdad in 1870 to take him around the antiquities of Nineveh and Babylon. In the story, a Persian farmer named Al Hafed received a visit from a Buddhist priest, who told Al Hafed that diamonds were made by God out of congealed drops of sunlight, and that he would always find them in "a river that runs over white sand between high mountains." So Al Hafed sold his farm and went off in search of diamonds, and his search took him all the way to Spain, but he never found any diamonds. Finally, despairing and in rags, he threw himself into the sea off the coast of Barcelona. Meanwhile, the new owner of Al Hafed's farm took his camel out for water one morning and saw in the white sands of a shallow stream a flashing stone. It turned out that the farm was sitting on diamonds—acres of them—the mine of Golconda, the greatest diamond deposit in the ancient world.

There were two morals in Conwell's lecture. The first was provided by the Arab guide: instead of seeking for wealth elsewhere, dig in your own garden and you will find it all around you. The second was added by Conwell: if you are rich, it is because you deserve to be; if you are poor, it is because you deserve to be. The answers lie in your mind. This was also the thinking of Napoleon Hill, the belief that there was divinity in the human self, that sickness came from the mind and could be healed by right thinking. It was called New Thought, a philosophy of the Gilded Age of Carnegie and Rockefeller, an age of extremes in wealth just like the age Dean lived in. William James called this philosophy "the Mind-cure movement." It appealed deeply to Dean.

After traveling in search of wealth, Dean had returned to his farm—unlike the ancient Persian—and dug for his fortune there. Acres of diamonds! They had to be all around him, right under foot—behind the counter of the P&M diner on Route 220 where he stopped for breakfast, and in the kitchen of Fuzzy's Bar-B-Que in Madison, and in the fryers at the Bojangles' right next to his house, the one that he had built and then come to hate.

Acres of diamonds!

Dean began to think about how he could separate those archaic and secretive rendering companies from their waste cooking oil. A lot of the bigger restaurants and chains around North Carolina and Virginia had longstanding contracts that paid one giant company, Valley Proteins, to take their oil. Others just gave it to whatever local renderer would remove it. Dean would have to find a way to make all those restaurants give it to *him*.

When Katrina had hit the Gulf Coast, the public schools in North Carolina came within a couple of days of shutting down for lack of diesel in the school buses. Every county in the state relied on a fleet of buses, and every one of those buses ran on diesel. At the start of the new century it had cost fifty cents a gallon; by the spring of 2011 it was over four dollars. Was that sustainable? Millions of dollars burned up in fuel costs for schools that were suffering the worst budget crisis in decades, laying off teachers and teacher's assistants in the middle of the recession? Dean read an article about a nine-year-old girl who lived with her mom down a country road in Warren County and who had to walk a mile to catch the school bus after it could no longer afford to drive down that road and pick her up.

Public schools were often the biggest employer in the county. They offered the gateway to the American dream. They were the country's entire future. Dean came to see that if he could get the schools on his side, he could lay his hands on all that waste cooking oil. And he thought up a way to do it.

What if every county in North Carolina made its own biodiesel for its school buses? Think how much taxpayer money could be saved, how many teachers could stay in classrooms, how much healthier the kids would be, how much cleaner the environment. All it would take was a reliable feedstock and a relatively inexpensive refinery. What if Dean went from county to county and offered to collect the local restaurant oil and process it into fuel for school buses at a facility that the county would build? Eventually, with the right equipment, he could crush canola seeds into food-grade oil, sell that to the restaurants for frying, collect the waste oil, and convert it into fuel—thereby bringing local farmers into the loop and putting the oil to use twice.

It would be like handing buckets of money over to the schools. The restaurants would all want to sign on and get credit for helping out kids. One day Dean came up with the perfect metaphor for his project. He would call it "the ultimate school fundraiser."

He started close to home. It wasn't easy getting hold of the Rockingham County commissioners—the people under them were there to keep you away—but with persistence, on the hundred and first blow of the hammer, he was able to set up a date for his presentation. The commissioners were enthusiastic, and a little item about it ran in the Greensboro paper, but afterward Dean didn't hear anything and figured they hadn't bought into it. A few weeks later, he ran into the chairman of the commission at the P&M diner on 220. The chairman told Dean, "I got a bunch of e-mails from local businessmen telling me now isn't the time for us to do this."

"Who are the businesses?" Dean asked.

"You know I can't tell you that."

"Why can't you tell me?"

It had to have been his nemesis, Reid Teague, the local oilman who had cut off his fuel up at the Bassett truck stop, driven him out of business, then come after his house. Teague probably saw the article in the paper and got on the phone to the commissioner. Dean didn't know this for sure, but he believed it. A prophet was always an outcast in his own land. Thank God there were ninety-nine other counties in North Carolina.

Dean paid thirty-five hundred dollars at a local used car lot for a 1997 Honda Civic with 196,000 miles and a broken air conditioner, and he began taking his idea around the state, seeking acres of diamonds from the Appalachians to the coastal plain.

Dean had an apartment in his basement that he rented for $225 a month to a twenty-five-year-old named Matt Orr. Matt had grown up in the area, done more than his share of drinking and smoking and partying, then joined the army for the discipline and served a tour in Iraq in 2006–2007. America looked beautiful after Tikrit—on the drive into Stokes County from the Greensboro airport with his dad, Matt saw trees, hills, and green grass, and he felt he was waking up from a bad dream. But he came home with a thousand-mile stare and no prospects of gainful employment. He was hired by an auto parts store—he'd been a mechanic with the 25th Infantry Division—but they never raised him above $7.75 an hour. He quit and worked briefly at a copper tubing factory, the same one where Dean had a job after high school, but Matt was paid eight dollars an hour—less than Dean had made in 1981. After quitting that, Matt got a job at the Kmart in Madison as a "loss prevention manager," which meant that he spent ten hours a day looking for shoplifters and placing the ones he caught in nonviolent restraint, including a forty-year-old jobless man who was trying to steal a tent because his mother had kicked him out of her house. This was not what Matt had wanted to come back to—he had hoped to make more of a difference—but he couldn't turn down ten dollars an hour. Then Kmart knocked him back to $8.50.

What really depressed Matt was how monetary everything had become in America, how it was just the biggest profit at the lowest cost. It was all about me, me, me, and no one wanted to help anyone else. The lobbyists, the politicians—they were all corrupt, taking everything from those who had the least. His favorite thing to do when he was alone in Dean's basement relaxing with a beer was to watch old episodes of *The Andy Griffith Show*. It was a better America back then. If he could have grown up at any time it would have been in the fifties, which was the last great time in America. He hated to say it but it was true.

Dean tried to do anything he could for Matt, but after Matt went five months without being able to pay his rent, Dean had to ask him to move out.

The Andy Griffith Show was still popular in the region (even after Andy made an ad for Obamacare), with reruns every afternoon, because the original for Mayberry RFD was the town of Mount Airy, up at the Virginia border—now just another hard-hit textile town trying its best keep up a quaint appearance on Main Street for the sake of the tourists, shop windows displaying posters and photos and memorabilia with those goofy, reassuring, all-white faces from the show. At the end of July, a few days after his bankruptcy hearing in Greensboro, Dean made the hour's drive to Mount Airy to see a woman on the city commission. He had been trying for four months to get a county to sign on to his proposal, driving all over the state, talking to officials in at least thirty counties, without success. They were like lemmings, just waiting for the first one to jump, but something held them back.

Dean hadn't spoken to Gary in months. He didn't want Gary to find out about this new idea, because in Dean's mind Gary was a pirate, a modern-day pirate. Any idea Dean ever gave him, Gary would steal and claim as his own. It went back to what Napoleon Hill wrote about the "Mastermind alliance"—he and Gary never had it. Gary didn't believe in what Dean told him about the third mind. And Gary was a Tea Party Republican. Once, when Dean was having beers with a tobacco farmer, the subject of partnerships came up. "Partnerships are good for two things," the farmer said. "Dancing and fucking." For now, Dean was on his own.

The woman in Mount Airy was named Teresa Lewis. They met at her office in a shopping mall outside the center of town, where Teresa ran a temp service. She was in her early fifties, dyed blond, wearing a blue suit and pearls. There was a poster of Elvis on the wall, and pictures of John McCain and the state's Republican senator. Dean put his jars of canola seed and oil on Teresa's desk and explained his concept.

"It's really a grassroots community effort," he said, "where not only are the farmers involved, but the restaurant owners, the school system, and the government."

"Well, Dean," Teresa said, in a breathy drawl, "what would stop somebody from doing this? It doesn't sound like there's a downside."

"There is none."

"We're a big agricultural community. Tobacco built every building in this city." Teresa smiled. "Now, you used two words, Dean—'sustainability' and 'green.' People here don't like those words."

Teresa gave Dean a lesson in local politics. She was a Republican, of course, but a Chamber of Commerce, United Fund, civic improvement Republican—not a Tea Party Republican. In 2010 she had lost the race for mayor of Mount Airy to a very conservative woman—a former textile worker and Glenn Beck fan—and the Tea Party had taken over the Surry County board of commissioners. On the city commission, a proposal to institute curbside recycling had inflamed passions on both sides, with some opponents describing it as a liberal, green, big government effort to impose a burden on the taxpayers of Mount Airy, and Teresa had cast the deciding vote in favor. She still seemed bruised by the year's battles.

"People here like 'savings,' they like 'farming,' they like 'receiving income back,'" Teresa said. "And they like 'alternative sources.' 'Alternative' will not get the same reaction as 'sustainability.'"

"Yes, ma'am."

"You're running into five very conservative county commissioners from the last election," she said. "I like you—I just want to warn you, these words are not popular."

Teresa said she would help Dean get his idea to the Surry County Commission, but weeks went by and he never heard anything definite.

•

Dean put fifty thousand miles on the used Honda. He drove the length and breadth of the state with his jars, wearing his red Coca-Cola baseball cap that was faded to pink. He talked to anyone who would listen. He talked to the hippies at Piedmont Biofuels, which was a worker-owned co-op near Chapel Hill—prosperous and progressive North Carolina, where people moved from out of state—and he talked to a school board member in Greensboro who was so right-wing that he wasn't sure there should even be public schools.

He talked to Eva Clayton, a retired black congresswoman from War-ren County. They sat in her office in Raleigh and Dean said, "The way I look at it, this economy is demonstrating that it cannot provide the amount of jobs necessary for the current population. So therefore we have to start thinking differently, and I think that this new green economy is really a different mind-set, and I can't see this economy starting any other way than with an energy source," and Eva Clayton, who was tiny and elegant and unsmiling, said, "Mm-hmm. What is the ask?" and Dean said, "We ask the restaurant owners to be part of this movement, where they either donate or we get the oil at a discount. Second thing is to work with these school boards where they get these bus garage guys to intro-duce this new fuel to the school buses. That's the seed, the starting point. From there we go to canola," and Eva Clayton said, "We're asking farmers to grow?" and Dean said, "To grow canola. We're going to build a small-scale crushing facility to get oil from that seed," and Eva Clayton, taking Dean's jars and sliding them on top of her conference table, said, "You're going to get farmers to grow this," and Dean said, "Yes, ma'am. In order to get them to grow this it's all about money," and Eva Clayton said, "I see a gentleman who has an idea that may help these distressed people, but the distress is right now—'I need food now, I need to pay bills now'—and this idea is a year or two away." Eva Clayton finally smiled. "But hope comes from these ideas, with people saying we can do better."

He talked at a green-jobs fair in a refurbished armory in Warrenton, before a crowd of three hundred people looking for work, 80 percent of them black. He had done some research before going to Warrenton, and he had read about Soul City, which was just five miles outside town. Soul City was started in the seventies by a black activist named Floyd McKissick, with help from Eva Clayton and her husband, on five thousand acres of dirt-poor tobacco fields. It was intended to be a self-sufficient, multiracial community, with housing planned for eighteen thousand people, and the Nixon administration gave a federal grant under the Model Cities program after McKissick joined the Republican Party—which infuriated Dean's father, who hated the whole idea of Soul City—but the population never grew beyond a couple of hundred, and no businesses were established. Instead, Soul City died a slow death, and by 2011 there was just a vandalized health clinic and a few two-bedroom houses on streets named Liberation and Revolution, next to the red clay cornfields.

Dean read about all this, and it blew his mind, and he stood up at the green-jobs fair and said, "My name is Dean Price but I want you to call me Green Dean. In my opinion one of the greatest men ever to live was Martin Luther King." If his father could have heard that! When Congress was debating whether to make King's birthday a national holiday, his father had said, "If they killed four more you could give 'em a whole week." Dean had always thought that King was a black leader at best, not a leader of all men, but his views had changed in recent years, and now, before this mainly black crowd, who couldn't often have heard a white man with a southern country accent say such things, he went on, "Martin Luther King once said, 'We all came here on different ships but we're in the same boat now,'" and he heard a gasp from the crowd. "There's another man who came to Warren County forty years ago by the name of Floyd McKissick." Another gasp, from the older people in the crowd. "Floyd McKissick had a dream, too, and that was to build a city for all men—white, yellow, black, brown, green—so they could work together with equal opportunity for all. And I'm here to tell you that dream is still alive! Floyd McKissick was a visionary. He was swimming upstream, but the tide has turned and we're swimming with the stream because cheap energy is leaving here. Cheap energy allowed globalization to take place, and what will allow the reverse of globalization will be high energy costs, and it goes back to Gandhi. Gandhi said it was a sin to buy from your farthest neighbor at the neglect of your nearest neighbor." And he told them how they could make their own energy right here in one of the poorest counties in North Carolina.

They ate it up with a spoon. Afterward, people called out to him, "Green Dean! Green Dean!" An old black man with blue eyes told him, "If I had a million dollars I'd put it in your idea." Acres of diamonds in Warren County. But the board of commissioners didn't have the right sense of urgency, they spent months kicking the tires without making the sale, and nothing came of Dean's speech.

He talked to Kathy Proctor, a fifty-five-year-old white single mother of two down near High Point, who had lost her job at the furniture factory during the bank bailouts. With her unemployment benefits she had gone back to study biotechnology at the community college in Winston-Salem—not just to find a new career, but to set an example for her daughters. One day, President Obama visited the college to talk up retraining and manufacturing, and when he came through Kathy's lab and asked if anyone had a story, Kathy told him hers. The next thing Kathy knew, she was Michelle Obama's guest at the 2011 State of the Union address (and she hadn't even voted for Mrs. Obama's husband in 2008, though she might well the next time around). When the president mentioned Kathy Proctor's name in his speech, she was so surprised that the cameras caught a stout woman with lank dark hair turning to the people seated beside her in the First Lady's box and saying, "That's me."

By the time Dean went down to see Kathy Proctor, and they sat together in the cramped living room, which was furnished with dark-stained pieces made in the defunct local factories where she had worked all her life, Kathy had been hired to do quality control at an online twenty-four-hour vitamin distribution center. She was making thirty thousand a year—less than at the furniture factory, not the lab job she'd hoped for with her associate's degree, but it was better than minimum wage, better than living on the streets, it paid her bills.

Dean described how he had met Obama, too, and then he told her about his project.

"I didn't know about this biofuels," Kathy, a lively and curious woman, said.

"Let's start a new industry," Dean laughed.

"We might. I'm interested in this. It's fixin' to take off. How long you been working on this, Dean?"

"Since 2005—and it has been a struggle."

The White House had invited Kathy to hear Obama speak at a community college in Greensboro the next day. "If I get a chance to talk to the president tomorrow," she told Dean, "I'll mention it to him."

Dean and Kathy exchanged a high five. But he no longer expected much from the president. Up at Red Birch, he had thought that change would come from Obama getting elected, or Tom Perriello helping make it happen. As polarized as the country was, Obama had his best chance with a majority in Congress, but he couldn't muster the support to pass cap and trade. Obama had failed, and Perriello was gone—working for a Washington think tank. Change wasn't going to come from new laws. It wasn't going to come from Washington, or Raleigh. It might come from Stokesdale. The country was stuck and no politician could fix that. It was going to take an entrepreneur. "It's like a dam that develops a crack, and the water starts seeping through, and it's not long before the whole dam comes down, and I think it's that way with this economy. And that crack is the relationship between the rendering company and the restaurant owner."

That was Dean's belief, his faith. Forty-eight years old, with no job, no partner, hardly any money, driving from county to county and talking to hundreds of people, some nibbles but no solid bites—these months were the strongest test of his faith. Maybe he didn't know how to talk to county bureaucrats. They were even more cautious than farmers, knowing they needed help but afraid to take the first step into something they couldn't see—which was the actual definition of faith. Sometimes, while Dean was describing his vision, he would get too far out ahead of himself and start to lose them. One of his brochures said, "Our hard earned tax dollars go to support terrorists and jihadists, the very people we are at war with. Enriching their lives, while we struggle to maintain our basic infrastructure," and that freaked out a few school administrators.

Once, when he was driving in Franklin County, his son Ryan called him from school. A sheriff's deputy was looking for Dean—while trying to serve a civil summons, he'd found the house door ajar and was concerned about a break-in. The summons was from a food company that hadn't gotten the word about Red Birch of Martinsville's bankruptcy. Dean's mother couldn't hide her worry. Wasn't this a little crazy? When was he going to make some money? Was it time to give up and get a secular job?

And all around him was brokenness.

One day in October, Dean was driving through Forsyth County and he stopped in a little place called Rural Hall, where they still held tobacco auctions at the Old Belt Farmers Co-Op—some of the last anywhere in the state, if not the country. It was the end of the season, and the cavernous warehouse with the sharp strong smell of tobacco hanging in the air was almost empty, and six or eight men in golf shirts were walking up and down rows of four-foot-high tobacco bales. As they moved from bale to bale the buyers grabbed fistfuls of golden brown leaves and the auctioneer called out a price per pound, "Dollar fifteen dollar ten ten dollar ten ten ten dollar ten ten dollar five five dollar five," and one of the buyers, a man from Bailey's Cigarettes in Virginia, said "Eighty," and the auctioneer said, "Eighty. Bailey," and the clerk wrote it down on a scrap of paper and slapped it on top of the bale. The other buyer was from Kentucky. "'Bacca pays bills," he was saying. "I was told that when I was a little boy and the rest is bull." A few of the men had just come to watch, like Dean, retired farmers and warehousemen who couldn't get it out of their system.

The young farmer who was selling the tobacco leaned on a bale at a distance and watched the older men in golf shirts. They were auctioning the part of his crop that the big company in Danville where he had a contract, Japan Tobacco International, wouldn't take. The farmer's name was Anthony Pyrtle, and he said that with the price of diesel this year he would be lucky to make a profit. His childhood buddy Kent Smith had come along to help unload the bales. Smith worked in a copper factory making $14.50 an hour. "I used to think how lucky he was he didn't have to work in the factory," Smith said. "Now I think I'm better off than he is."

Pyrtle had heard about Dean and Red Birch. Dean told him, "This country should pay you six dollars a gallon for biodiesel, instead of sending three dollars to Saudi Arabia."

"I'd change in a minute," Pyrtle said, "and raise corn or whatever fuel crop I could find."

Dean walked out of the Old Belt Farmers Co-Op and got into his Honda. When he was a boy, the auctions had been a regional celebration—the excitement, the cash in hand, the Christmas shopping. The tobacco warehouses hummed with people who came to socialize and talk politics. But the auction today was something quick and dirty, done in private with a few onlookers, and Anthony Pyrtle was just hoping to break even.

Maybe to suit his mood, Dean drove home through the back roads of Stokes County. The county manager had told him that 30 percent of the people in Stokes couldn't afford to put food on the table, and the suicide rate was twice the national average. Dean's accountant lived in Stokes, and his stepson had lost eight friends since high school, three from suicide. Dean drove through the town of Walnut Cove and parked at the East Stokes Outreach Ministry. There was a food pantry in front, with canned goods and bags of pet food on plywood shelves, and in the fridge there was ground deer meat donated by local hunters. The lady who ran the place told him that a police officer who was shot in the line of duty and was getting workmen's compensation, but didn't want to go on disability, had come in a week ago asking for food. So had a court stenographer with a broken hand. A sign in the office said "Due to lack of funds there will be NO fuel or kerosene assistance this year. We are doing all we can to keep our pantry full. Please make other arrangements for heating assistance ASAP." An obese woman with oxygen tubes in her nostrils and a clothing voucher in her hand was waiting for a double-large shirt. She said, "We're a family of nine and we're doing fine." The lady in charge told Dean, "You realize that we live in the economy where one flat tire or one month without a paycheck could alter most anybody's world."

On his way out Dean felt a shudder. There but for the grace of God. Once it happened to you, it was almost impossible to get out. And to think how many times he believed he'd been about to break through, only to have it pulled back at the last minute and find he was farther away than ever. On the drive home an old church hymn got stuck in his head.

> How tedious and tasteless the hours
> When Jesus no longer I see!
> Sweet prospects, sweet birds and sweet flowers
> Have all lost their sweetness to me.

Tedious and tasteless. He went cold and started to cry. Then a voice like the voice in his dream about the old wagon road spoke to him and said, "This is the *only* way it will work."

And then the breakthrough came.

One night in October, Dean was reading *The Prosperity Bible* when he came across a sentence by Ralph Waldo Trine, a nineteenth-century author. It said, "Never go to the second thing first."

It suddenly hit him why he was having so much trouble with the schools. He was going to the second thing first—telling them they could make their own fuel for the buses if the county built a four-hundred-fifty-thousand-dollar reactor. But the counties didn't have the money, and anyway the project was too risky and too complicated for them to understand, especially when he started into the next phase with canola crops and food-grade oil. He'd had to explain it to Eva Clayton three times, and even then he wasn't sure she got it. He had everything ass-backwards. The first thing was to get the dadgum oil! Otherwise, how would you know how big a refinery a county should build? He ought to just tell the schools that he would collect restaurant cooking oil in their name, sell it to an existing biodiesel company, and give them half the profits. The money could be used to keep teachers in classrooms, or anything else they wanted. Just a simple cash donation, a school fundraiser—that was a metaphor they could understand. And the local restaurant owners would understand, too, which was why they'd sell their oil to Dean. Building a refinery, making the fuel, getting farmers to grow canola—all that could come later.

Around the time he had this revelation, Dean met a man named Stephan Caldwell. Stephan was thirty-two years old, from a small town in Ohio, the son of an oral surgeon and gentleman apple farmer. He had started a career in advertising in Raleigh, but the industry had been battered by the financial crisis, so he decided to get out of advertising and into what he had always loved—machinery and farming. His interest led him to biodiesel, and he set up a little waste oil recycling company called Green Circle, renting a shop from a retired welder named Barefoot a mile from a hog slaughterhouse on lonely farmland in Johnston County. When Dean went out to see Green Circle, he thought Stephan's plant looked like Red Birch, just in a new place—smelled like it, too.

Everyone doing biodiesel in the Piedmont knew about Red Birch. The word that had reached Stephan's ears wasn't good—Red Birch didn't pay farmers, and it sold bad fuel. But he liked Dean Price's passion and didn't want to blame Dean for what he took to be the sins of others. Quiet and hardworking, Stephan was barely surviving on contracts with just a handful of restaurants around Raleigh, and the long hours pumping waste oil were putting a strain on his marriage.

Dean came with an idea that promised much more than Stephan could hope to make on his own. And Stephan came with the infrastructure—plant, equipment, truck—that Dean lacked. He also had a degree in graphic design, and when Dean told him about his revelation, Stephan spent the weekend drawing up a vivid brochure in green and yellow, called "Biodiesel 4 Schools," that explained the new concept with simplicity and clarity, so that any fool of a bureaucrat could see this was the right thing to do.

Over Thanksgiving, Dean and Stephan decided to turn Green Circle into a partnership. Dean thought it should divide 70–30 in his favor, since Stephan's business model was failing, but Stephan convinced him that at

55–45 they would be more like real partners. Armed with the brochure, Dean went back to some of the officials that he'd met with earlier in the year, in some cases eight or nine times. Right before Christmas, he called an agriculture expert on the board of education in Pitt County, whom he'd seen in April and then never heard a word. "I had it wrong," Dean told him. "I went back and learned from my mistakes. Now I got it right. Let me come back and give my presentation."

Pitt County was in eastern North Carolina. Unlike the Piedmont it was flat, and you knew the coast was nearby because of the bright silver light, but like the Piedmont it had seen tobacco fade away, and it had three things Dean considered vital for the success of his idea: fallow farmland, long driving distances, and a whole lot of restaurants in the county seat of Greenville. Between Christmas and New Year's he was given a meeting with the chief financial officer of the Pitt County schools, who listened carefully before exclaiming, "It's ingenious!"

Those words were balm to Dean's heart. He still had to sell it to a dozen other officials, and they tried to poke any hole in it they could, wanting to be sure the schools weren't signing on with some fly-by-night operator or uncontrollable maverick. But on March 5, 2012, the Pitt County school board voted unanimously to enter a deal with Green Circle, splitting the profits from the sale of the oil after the company covered its costs. It had taken Dean a full year to get his first win.

He was reading a biography of Steve Jobs that talked about the rarefied air you breathe when you have an idea that you know is going to change the world and nobody knows it yet. He believed that was where he was. Pitt County and North Carolina could be the Silicon Valley of the bio-fuels industry. Just sitting on an economic boom. Acres of diamonds in Greenville.

It was strange how small the idea had to get before anyone would give it a chance. A school fundraiser—as if Dean was a chocolate chip cookie dough salesman. But that's what he had to become. The work could not have been less auspicious, less like the making of the Apple II. Dean went from restaurant to restaurant. He stood at the counter with the Denny's manager and said, "We would pick it up for free and you get all the PR that goes with it, let all the parents know that Denny's is supporting the schools." In the kitchen of a Thai restaurant the owner asked, "Are you a teacher?" and Dean said, "With the schools, and we're promoting this program and trying to save the schools money, and we're also trying to start a new industry in Pitt County." He spent two hours with the mother of the owner of Greenville's biggest barbecue restaurant, getting nowhere. Chinese restaurants were the easiest to sign up because the owners were eager to be part of the community. By June 2012 he had ninety-three restaurants. By August, Green Circle was pumping two thousand gallons a week.

One night, the two partners drove around after dark in Stephan's pickup. They pulled in to a mall and parked in the space in back of a barbecue joint. Stephan walked through the kitchen past the bubbling fryers to the little office of Freddy the manager, where a sign said I'M REDNECK PROUD, was given the keys, and went out again to unlock the cinder block shed where the restaurant kept its seven metal barrels full of waste oil. He and Dean ran a hose from the tank on the bed of the truck into the shed and stuck the sucking end into the first of the barrels and started up the pump. The oil was black-brown, flecked with bits of animal fat, the shine of grease at the top of the barrel swirling like galaxies in a night sky. On the other side of the shed were barrels full of pig parts—backbones, shoulders, feet—that would be hauled away by a big rendering company. The air had the burnt smell of good meat just starting to rot. Everything was sticky with dried oil—the barrels, the hose, the bed of the truck, their hands. The stickiness reminded Dean of the tar that came off on his hands when he was priming tobacco leaves as a boy. After so many months of thinking and talking, he was happy to be doing physical work.

An air leak in Stephan's pump stretched out twenty minutes' work to an hour and a half, but they drove away with 240 gallons of waste cooking oil, for which they paid the barbecue joint $108, and which would earn them $2.50 a gallon, six hundred dollars, from a biodiesel company. The plan was eventually to get to where they could manufacture the oil into fuel themselves.

They drove around with a tank full of waste cooking oil in back and Dean looked out the passenger window at all the restaurants. There must have been three or four in every strip mall. And if you thought about the hospital, the university, the football stadium—Lord have mercy.

"Dadgummit, they're everywhere," he said. "Look at all that oil. We'll get it, man. We'll get it."

"Humble beginnings," Stephan said. "We'll appreciate it someday."

"This is how you're going to make your fortune, hoss!"

Dean knew exactly what he was going to do with his fortune, once he made it. He had known for years, though he had told only a couple of people, always saving it up as his last thought at night before falling asleep. First, he would build a great big house, a mansion, just like the one Moses Cone, the nineteenth-century denim baron of Greensboro, built looking out over the Blue Ridge Mountains, with gables and dormers and huge front porches all painted white. Dean's would be off the grid, with geo-thermal heat and air-conditioning, and solar panels on the roof.

Then he would fill this sprawling house with abandoned children. The house would sit on a farm, a working farm, so that he could teach these children whom no one else wanted the skills and the ethic of that life—teach them to be Jefferson's cultivators of the earth, the most valuable citizens, the most vigorous, the most independent, the most virtuous.

And he knew where the house would be: on the Price tobacco farm, right there on the hill near the graveyard where four generations of Prices lay buried, the last his father, "Just a sinner saved by grace." Dean would be buried there, too, one day. He had misgivings about putting the house on that land. His poverty thinking came from there, from that family. He had tried to pull the weeds and water the seeds, but when he got around those graves they brought the thinking back. But wasn't that the very rea-son to build the house there? Wasn't it where he would finally get his freedom? And even though he was going to lose his piece of the family farm to a foreclosure sale, because his bankruptcy case had been re-opened, and his nemesis, the oil man, was going after the only asset Dean had left, which was the land—none of that mattered. He still had a dream of building a big white house and filling it with children. He would get the land back.

A NOTE ON SOURCES

This book is based on hundreds of hours of interviews with the people whose stories it tells, and with others who shared information and insight, supplemented by written sources, the most significant of which are listed below. The biographical sketches of famous people are drawn entirely from secondary sources, most usefully those listed below; the sketches sometimes paraphrase or quote the subjects' own words as found in books, articles, and songs. The collages of individual years draw on a variety of sources—newspapers, magazines, books, speeches, songs, advertisements, poems, movies, television programs—all of which were written, published, recorded, or shown in the given year. (A list can be found at www.fsgbooks.com/theunwinding.) Though this book is a work of nonfiction throughout, it owes a literary debt to the novels of John Dos Passos's great *U.S.A.* trilogy, published in the 1930s and overdue for a revival.

NARRATIVES
DEAN PRICE AND THE PIEDMONT
Allen Tullos, *Habits of Industry: White Culture and the Transformation of the Carolina Piedmont* (Chapel Hill: University of North Carolina Press, 1989).

JEFF CONNAUGHTON AND WASHINGTON, D.C.
Joe Biden, *Promises to Keep* (New York: Random House, 2008).
Jeff Connaughton, *The Payoff: Why Wall Street Always Wins* (Prospecta Press, 2012). The author generously shared an early draft.
Robert G. Kaiser, *So Damn Much Money: The Triumph of Lobbying and the Corrosion of American Government* (New York: Vintage Books, 2010).

TAMMY THOMAS AND YOUNGSTOWN
Barry Bluestone and Bennett Harrison, *The Deindustrialization of America: Plant Closings, Community Abandonment, and the Dismantling of Basic Industry* (New York: Basic Books, 1982).
Terry F. Buss and F. Stevens Redburn, *Shutdown at Youngstown: Public Policy for Mass Unemployment* (Albany: SUNY Press, 1983).
Stephen F. Diamond, "The Delphi 'Bankruptcy': The Continuation of Class War by Other Means," *Dissent* (Spring 2006).
David M. Kennedy, *Freedom from Fear: The American People in Depression and War, 1929–1945* (New York: Oxford University Press, 1999).

Sherry Lee Linkon and John Russo, *Steeltown U.S.A.: Work and Memory in Youngstown* (Lawrence: University Press of Kansas, 2002).

John Russo, "Integrated Production or Systematic Disinvestment: The Restructuring of Packard Electric" (unpublished paper, 1994).

Sean Safford, *Why the Garden Club Couldn't Save Youngstown: The Transformation of the Rust Belt* (Cambridge, MA: Harvard University Press, 2009).

PETER THIEL AND SILICON VALLEY

Sonia Arrison, *100 Plus: How the Coming Age of Longevity Will Change Everything, from Careers and Relationships to Family and Faith*, with a foreword by Peter Thiel (New York: Basic Books, 2011).

Eric M. Jackson, *The PayPal Wars: Battles with eBay, the Media, the Mafia and the Rest of Planet Earth* (Los Angeles: World Ahead Publishing, 2010).

David Kirkpatrick, *The Facebook Effect: The Inside Story of the Company That Is Connecting the World* (New York: Simon & Schuster, 2011).

Jessica Livingston, "Max Levchin," in *Founders at Work: Stories of Startups' Early Days* (New York: Apress, 2008).

Ben Mezrich, *The Accidental Billionaires: The Founding of Facebook* (New York: Anchor, 2010).

David O. Sacks and Peter A. Thiel, *The Diversity Myth: Multiculturalism and Political Intolerance on Campus* (Oakland, CA: The Independent Institute, 1998).

TAMPA

Richard Florida, *The Great Reset: How New Ways of Living and Working Drive Post-Crash Prosperity* (New York: HarperCollins, 2010).

Alyssa Katz, *Our Lot: How Real Estate Came to Own Us* (New York: Bloomsbury, 2010).

Robert J. Kerstein, *Politics and Growth in Twentieth-Century Tampa* (Gainesville: University Press of Florida, 2001).

Paul Reyes, *Exiles in Eden: Life Among the Ruins of Florida's Great Recession* (New York: Henry Holt, 2010).

BIOGRAPHICAL SKETCHES
NEWT GINGRICH

Adam Clymer, "The Teacher of the 'Rules of Civilization' Gets a Scolding," *New York Times* (January 26, 1997).

Steven M. Gillon, *The Pact: Bill Clinton, Newt Gingrich, and the Rivalry That Defined a Generation* (New York: Oxford University Press, 2008).

Newt Gingrich, *Lessons Learned the Hard Way* (New York: HarperCollins, 1998).

Newt Gingrich, *To Renew America* (New York: HarperCollins, 1999).

Newt Gingrich with David Drake and Marianne Gingrich, *Window of Opportunity: A Blueprint for the Future* (New York: Tor Books, 1984).

John H. Richardson, "Newt Gingrich: The Indispensable Republican," *Esquire* (September 2010).

Gail Sheehy, "The Inner Quest of Newt Gingrich," *Vanity Fair* (September 1995).

OPRAH WINFREY

Barbara Grizzuti Harrison, "The Importance of Being Oprah," *New York Times Magazine* (June 11, 1989).

Kitty Kelley, *Oprah: A Biography* (New York: Three Rivers Press, 2011).

Ken Lawrence, *The World According to Oprah: An Unauthorized Portrait in Her Own Words* (Kansas City, MO: Andrews McMeel, 2005).

RAYMOND CARVER

Raymond Carver, *Fires: Essays, Poems, Stories* (New York: Vintage Books, 1984).

Raymond Carver, *What We Talk About When We Talk About Love: Stories* (New York: Vintage Books, 1989).

Raymond Carver, *Where I'm Calling From: Stories* (New York: Vintage Contemporaries, 1989).

Conversations with Raymond Carver, Marshall Bruce Gentry and William L. Stull, eds. (Jackson: University Press of Mississippi, 1990).

Carol Sklenicka, *Raymond Carver: A Writer's Life* (New York: Scribner, 2010).

SAM WALTON

Bob Ortega, *In Sam We Trust: The Untold Story of Sam Walton and How Wal-Mart Is Devouring America* (New York: Crown Business, 1998).

Sam Walton with John Huey, *Sam Walton, Made in America: My Story* (New York: Doubleday, 1992).

COLIN POWELL

Karen DeYoung, *Soldier: The Life of Colin Powell* (New York: Knopf, 2006).

John B. Judis, *The Paradox of American Democracy: Elites, Special Interests, and the Betrayal of Public Trust* (New York: Routledge, 2001).

Colin L. Powell with Joseph E. Persico, *My American Journey* (New York: Ballantine, 1996).

ALICE WATERS

Thomas McNamee, *Alice Waters and Chez Panisse: The Romantic, Impractical, Often Eccentric, Ultimately Brilliant Making of a Food Revolution* (New York: Penguin, 2008).

Alice Waters with Daniel Duane, *Edible Schoolyard: A Universal Idea* (San Francisco: Chronicle Books, 2008).

ROBERT RUBIN

William D. Cohan, *Money and Power: How Goldman Sachs Came to Rule the World* (New York: Doubleday, 2011).

William D. Cohan, "Rethinking Robert Rubin," *Bloomberg Businessweek* (September 30, 2012).

Jacob S. Hacker and Paul Pierson, *Winner-Take-All Politics: How Washington Made the Rich Richer—And Turned Its Back on the Middle Class* (New York: Simon & Schuster, 2010).

Bethany McLean and Joe Nocera, *All the Devils Are Here: The Hidden History of the Financial Crisis* (New York: Portfolio/Penguin, 2010).

Robert B. Reich, *Locked in the Cabinet* (New York: Vintage Books, 1998).

Robert E. Rubin and Jacob Weisberg, *In an Uncertain World: Tough Choices from Wall Street to Washington* (New York: Random House Trade Paperbacks, 2004).

JAY-Z

Zack O'Malley Greenburg, *Empire State of Mind: How Jay-Z Went from Street Corner to Corner Office* (New York: Portfolio/Penguin, 2011).

Jay-Z, *Decoded* (New York: Spiegel & Grau, 2011).

Jay-Z, "December 4th," *The Black Album* (Roc-A-Fella/Def Jam, 2003).

Jay-Z, "Empire State of Mind," *The Blueprint* 3 (Roc Nation, 2009).

Jay-Z, "Rap Game/Crack Game," "Streets Is Watching," "You Must Love Me," *In My Lifetime Vol. 1* (Roc-A-Fella/Def Jam, 1997).

Jay-Z, "Can I Live," "Dead Presidents II," "D'Evils," "Regrets," "22 Two's," *Reasonable Doubt* (Roc-A-Fella, 1996).

Jay-Z, "Brooklyn Go Hard" (Roc-A-Fella/Def Jam, 2008), "Glory" (Roc Nation, 2012).

Kelefa Sanneh, "Gettin' Paid," *New Yorker* (August 20, 2001).

Touré, "The Book of Jay," *Rolling Stone* (December 15, 2005).

Kanye West, "Diamonds from Sierra Leone," *Late Registration* (Roc-A-Fella/Def Jam, 2005).

ANDREW BREITBART

Christopher Beam, "Media Is Everything. It's Everything," *Slate* (March 15, 2010).

Andrew Breitbart, *Righteous Indignation: Excuse Me While I Save the World!* (New York: Grand Central Publishing, 2011).

Chris K. Daley, *Becoming Breitbart* (Claremont, CA: Chris Daley Publishing, 2012).

Rebecca Mead, "Rage Machine," *New Yorker* (May 24, 2010).

ELIZABETH WARREN

Suzanna Andrews, "The Woman Who Knew Too Much," *Vanity Fair* (November 2011).

Noah Bierman, "A Girl Who Soared, but Longed to Belong," *Boston Globe* (February 12, 2012).

Harry Kreisler, *Political Awakenings: Conversations with History* (New York: The New Press, 2010).

Teresa A. Sullivan, Elizabeth Warren, and Jay Lawrence Westbrook, *As We Forgive Our Debtors: Bankruptcy and Consumer Credit in America* (New York: Oxford University Press, 1989).

Teresa A. Sullivan, Elizabeth Warren, and Jay Lawrence Westbrook, *The Fragile Middle Class: Americans in Debt* (New Haven, CT: Yale University Press, 2000).

Jeffrey Toobin, "The Professor," *New Yorker* (September 17, 2012).

Elizabeth Warren, interview by Jon Stewart, *The Daily Show with Jon Stewart*, Comedy Central, April 15, 2009, and January 26, 2010.

Elizabeth Warren and Amelia Warren Tyagi, *The Two-Income Trap: Why Middle-Class Mothers and Fathers Are Going Broke* (New York: Basic Books, 2003).

ACKNOWLEDGMENTS

I am grateful to the people whose lives compose the heart of this book.

For assistance on the road, I thank George and Page Gilliam of Charlottesville; Sherry Lee Linkon and John Russo of Youngstown; Barbara Price of Stokesdale, North Carolina; the reporters and editors of the *Tampa Bay Times*; and especially Pancho Sanchez of Tampa and his family. Thanks also to Gary Smith and the American Academy in Berlin for a 2009 Holtzbrinck Fellowship, and to Jean Strouse and the Cullman Center at the New York Public Library for their invitation to give the 2011 Joanna Jackson Goldman Memorial Lectures in American Civilization and Government.

For expert help of different kinds, I thank Nancy Aaron, Kathleen Anderson, Neil Belton, Julia Botero, Lila Byock, Peter Canby, Ray Chipault, Rodrigo Corral, Tom Ehrlich, Jiayang Fan, Tim Farrell, Amy Hanauer, Stephen Heintz, Henry Kaufman, Alissa Levin, Jonathan Lippincott, Rebecca Mead, Ellie Perkins, Chris Peterson, Chris Richards, Nandi Rodrigo, Ridge Schuyler, Jeff Seroy, Michael Spies, Scott Staton, Julie Tate, Matthew Taylor, Sarita Varma, Jacob Weisberg, Dorothy Wickenden, Laura Young, and Avi Zenilman. I am especially grateful to Sarah Chalfant, Jonathan Galassi, David Remnick, Alex Star, and Daniel Zalewski—there are none better.

I can never repay my debt to those friends and family members whose insight and enthusiasm sustained me through the years of work—Daniel Bergner, Tom Casciato, Bill Finnegan, Kathy Hughes, Carol Jack, Michael Janeway, Ann Packer, Nancy Packer, Eyal Press, Becky Saletan, Bob Secor, Marie Secor, and especially Dexter Filkins; and most of all to Laura Secor, who makes everything possible.

A NOTE ABOUT THE AUTHOR

George Packer is a staff writer for *The New Yorker* and the author of *The Assassins' Gate: America in Iraq*, which received several prizes and was named one of the ten best books of 2005 by *The New York Times Book Review*. He is also the author of two novels, *The Half Man* and *Central Square*, and two other works of nonfiction, *Blood of the Liberals*, which won the 2001 Robert F. Kennedy Book Award, and *The Village of Waiting*. His play, *Betrayed*, ran off-Broadway for five months in 2008 and won the Lucille Lortel Award for Outstanding Play. His most recent book is *Interesting Times: Writings from a Turbulent Decade*. He lives in Brooklyn.